Mobilizing for Elections

Politicians in Southeast Asia, as in many other regions, win elections by distributing cash, goods, jobs, projects, and other benefits to supporters, but the ways in which they do this vary tremendously, both across and within countries. *Mobilizing for Elections* presents a new framework for analyzing variation in patronage democracies, focusing on distinct forms of patronage and different networks through which it is distributed. The book draws on an extensive, multi-country, multi-year research effort involving interactions with hundreds of politicians and vote brokers, as well as surveys of voters and political campaigners across the region. Chapters explore how local machines in the Philippines, ad hoc election teams in Indonesia, and political parties in Malaysia pursue distinctive clusters of strategies of patronage distribution – what the authors term *electoral mobilization regimes*. In doing so, the book shows how and why patronage politics varies, and how it works on the ground.

Edward Aspinall is Professor of Political Science and Social Change at the Australian National University. He is the author of *Opposing Suharto: Compromise, Resistance and Regime Change in Indonesia* (2005), *Islam and Nation: Separatist Rebellion in Aceh, Indonesia* (2009) and *Democracy for Sale: Elections, Clientelism and the State in Indonesia* (2019, with Ward Berenschot).

Meredith L. Weiss is Professor of Political Science at the University at Albany, SUNY. She is the author of *Protest and Possibilities: Civil Society and Coalitions for Political Change in Malaysia* (2006), *Student Activism in Malaysia: Crucible, Mirror, Sideshow* (2011), and *The Roots of Resilience: Party Machines and Grassroots Politics in Southeast Asia* (2020).

Allen Hicken is Professor of Political Science at the University of Michigan. He is the author, editor, or co-editor of *Building Party Systems in Developing Democracies* (2009), *Politics of Modern Southeast Asia* (2010), *Party and Party System Institutionalization in Asia* (2014), and *Electoral Dynamics in the Philippines* (2019).

Paul D. Hutchcroft is Professor of Political Science and Social Change at the Australian National University. He is the author of *Booty Capitalism: The Politics of Banking in the Philippines* (1998) and editor of *Mindanao: The Long Journey to Peace and Prosperity* (2016) and *Strong Patronage, Weak Parties: The Case for Electoral System Redesign in the Philippines* (2019).

Mobilizing for Elections

Patronage and Political Machines in Southeast Asia

EDWARD ASPINALL
Australian National University

MEREDITH L. WEISS
University at Albany, State University of New York

ALLEN HICKEN
University of Michigan

PAUL D. HUTCHCROFT
Australian National University

CAMBRIDGE
UNIVERSITY PRESS

Shaftesbury Road, Cambridge CB2 8EA, United Kingdom

One Liberty Plaza, 20th Floor, New York, NY 10006, USA

477 Williamstown Road, Port Melbourne, VIC 3207, Australia

314–321, 3rd Floor, Plot 3, Splendor Forum, Jasola District Centre, New Delhi – 110025, India

103 Penang Road, #05–06/07, Visioncrest Commercial, Singapore 238467

Cambridge University Press is part of Cambridge University Press & Assessment, a department of the University of Cambridge.

We share the University's mission to contribute to society through the pursuit of education, learning and research at the highest international levels of excellence.

www.cambridge.org
Information on this title: www.cambridge.org/9781009074827

DOI: 10.1017/9781009075015

First published 2022
First paperback edition 2024

A catalogue record for this publication is available from the British Library

Library of Congress Cataloging-in-Publication data
NAMES: Aspinall, Edward, author. | Weiss, Meredith L. (Meredith Leigh), 1972- author. | Hicken, Allen, 1969- author. | Hutchcroft, Paul D. (Paul David), author.
TITLE: Mobilizing for elections : patronage and political machines in Southeast Asia / Edward Aspinall, Meredith L. Weiss, Allen Hicken, Paul D. Hutchcroft.
DESCRIPTION: Cambridge ; New York, NY : Cambridge University Press, 2022. | Includes bibliographical references and index.
IDENTIFIERS: LCCN 2021063115 (print) | LCCN 2021063116 (ebook) | ISBN 9781316513804 (hardback) | ISBN 9781009074827 (paperback) | ISBN 9781009075015 (epub)
SUBJECTS: LCSH: Politics, Practical–Southeast Asia–Case studies. | Patron and client–Southeast Asia–Case studies. | Southeast Asia–Politics and government–1945—Case studies. | BISAC: POLITICAL SCIENCE / World / General
CLASSIFICATION: LCC JQ750.A91 A78 2022 (print) | LCC JQ750.A91 (ebook) | DDC 320.959–dc23/eng/20220304
LC record available at https://lccn.loc.gov/2021063115
LC ebook record available at https://lccn.loc.gov/2021063116

ISBN   978-1-316-51380-4   Hardback
ISBN   978-1-009-07482-7   Paperback

Contents

Figures

Tables

Acknowledgments

This book[1] is the culmination of a multiyear and multistranded research effort, and our eighth major publication to date from a study of money politics in Southeast Asia that we began in 2012.[2] In the succeeding years, we collaborated with large teams of local researchers to observe on-the-ground dynamics in the Malaysian national elections in 2013, Indonesian national elections in 2014, and Philippine national elections in 2016. Our original plan was to undertake a similarly detailed examination of the Thai national elections, supposed to have been held sometime around late 2014 or 2015, but the military coup of May 2014 put those plans indefinitely on hold. We have, however, had the opportunity to observe a range of other elections in the region, including the 2013 and 2019 midterm elections in the Philippines, the 2016 state elections in Malaysia's Sarawak, and numerous polls in Indonesia: village-head elections, the 2019 legislative and presidential elections, and a range of *pilkada* (from *pemilihan kepala daerah*, or elections of regional heads) – most especially the large, simultaneous *pilkada* exercise held in seven different locations across the archipelago in February 2017. We also conducted similar research, though at a smaller scale, in Timor-Leste, Singapore, and Thailand. These discrete strands of research fed into the publications preceding this one, including several edited volumes on particular countries, featuring cases studies of "money politics" across locales, mostly written by our

[1] Author order for this book was determined randomly.

[2] These publications include Weiss 2014; Aspinall and Sukmajati 2015, 2016; Weiss and Puyok 2017; Aspinall and Berenschot 2019; Hicken, Aspinall, and Weiss 2019; Muhtadi 2019; Weiss 2020c; Teehankee and Calimbahin 2022. In addition, a contribution to debates on constitutional revision in the Philippines drew major inspiration from this project; see Hutchcroft 2019b. The project's findings have further generated a wide range of articles (too numerous to list here) and contributed to several dissertations on related topics.

Southeast Asian research partners. The objective of this book is to synthesize and build from our earlier studies, and to present our key findings and identify critical patterns across all our country cases – with a particular focus on national-level characteristics and subnational variation in Indonesia, Malaysia, and the Philippines.

Involving more than 200 researchers across 6 countries, our project has benefited enormously from collaboration with leading universities and public-opinion survey firms. We express our deep thanks to those local research partners and institutions, without whose insights, guidance, and collaboration we would not have been able to conduct such an ambitious study nor bring together such a rich array of observations. Our partners included Universitas Gajah Madah (especially Mada Sukmajati, Amalinda Savirani, Wawan Mas'udi, the late Cornelis Lay, and the other members of the PolGov research center) and Lembaga Survei Indonesia (especially Burhanuddin Muhtadi) in Indonesia; University of Malaya (especially E. Terence Gomez and Surin Kaur), Universiti Malaysia Sarawak (especially Arnold Puyok), and the Merdeka Center for Opinion Research in Malaysia; and De La Salle University (especially Julio Teehankee) and Pulse Asia Research (especially Ronnie Holmes) in the Philippines. We learned a great deal from all these individuals and their organizations, shared many memorable experiences with them, and owe them an enormous debt of gratitude.

We worked closely with scores of researchers in each country. Though they are too numerous to name individually, we wish particularly to thank, in Indonesia, Burhanuddin Muhtadi, Noor Rohman, Zusiana Elly Triantini, David Efendi, Muhammad Mahsun, Rudi Rohi, and Muhammad Uhaib As'ad; in Thailand, Noppadon Kannika, Viengrat Nethipo, and Prajak Kongkirati; in Malaysia, Andrew Aeria, Chiok Phaik Fern, Faisal Hazis, Regina Lim, Ngu Ik Tien, and Tony Paridi Bagang; and in the Philippines, Tetchie Aquino, Cleo Calimbahin, Grace Labalan, Regina Macalandag, Neil Pancho, Ditas Ravanilla, Allen Surla, and Glenn Teh. Joel Rocamora provided particularly valuable insights from his national- and local-level perspectives. We thank Dotan Haim and Michael Davidson for research assistance and coordination and Nico Ravanilla for his collaboration with the broker-survey work in the Philippines. In Timor-Leste, we benefited hugely from our close research collaboration with the late James Scambary, a scholar whose generosity of spirit and commitment is greatly missed. In the course of conducting research for this volume, Edward Aspinall was working on a related book (on Indonesia) with Ward Berenschot; Aspinall's contribution to the current volume owes a large intellectual debt to this collaboration. Meredith Weiss was likewise working on a related book on Singapore and Malaysia; she thanks especially Eileena Lee and Loke Hoe Yeong in Singapore and Anna Har in Malaysia, beyond those listed above, for their insights and help. Paul Hutchcroft's four-year stint as Lead Governance Specialist for the Australian aid program in the Philippines pulled him away from most election-observation opportunities, but by late 2017 he resumed his role in the project.

Working with such a diverse group of researchers not only enriched our study, but it was also personally enriching, making our experiences in the field for this project among the most memorable – and eye-opening – of our research careers to date. Accordingly, we also express our gratitude to the hundreds of candidates, campaign staff, experts, and ordinary citizens who sat down for interviews as part of this project, or who participated in focus groups and surveys. We owe a great deal to the openness, patience, and generosity of a great many people.

Our primary financial debt is to the Australian Research Council, from which a Discovery Grant (DP140103114) funded the bulk of our research (we also drew on research funded through grants DP120103181 and FT120100742). We benefited from supplemental research grants, too. The Centre for Democratic Institutions at the Australian National University funded initial project workshops where our research framework and planning came together. The Australian Department of Foreign Affairs and Trade (DFAT) funded major research efforts on elections in Indonesia, Timor-Leste, and the Philippines. The University of Malaya did the same for Malaysia. We thank our own universities, as well – the Australian National University, the University at Albany of the State University of New York, and the University of Michigan – for their financial and in-kind support. We also thank our hosts for writing workshops as we completed this book: the Center for Southeast Asian Studies at Kyoto University (especially Carol Hau), the Penang Institute (especially Ooi Kee Beng and Ong Siou Woon), and Chiang Mai University (especially Malinee Khumsupa and Tanet Charoenmuang).

Finally, we thank our partners and families for their love and support.

Terms and Acronyms

1MDB	1Malaysia Development Berhad
Barangay	village or urban ward (Philippines)
Barisan Nasional	National Front, BN (Malaysia)
BARMM	Bangsamoro Autonomous Region in Muslim Mindanao
Bersatu	Parti Pribumi Bersatu Malaysia, Malaysian United Indigenous Party
BR1M	Bantuan Rakyat 1Malaysia, 1Malaysia People's Aid
Bumiputera	Indigenous (lit., "sons of the soil"; Malaysia)
Bupati	Regent (Indonesia)
DAP	Democratic Action Party (Malaysia)
DPR	Dewan Perwakilan Rakyat, People's Representative Council, national parliament (Indonesia)
DPRD–K	Dewan Perwakilan Rakyat Daerah–Kabupaten/Kota, rural district/city legislative council (Indonesia)
DPRD–P	Dewan Perwakilan Rakyat Daerah–Provinsi, provincial legislative council (Indonesia)
Gerindra	Partai Gerindra, Greater Indonesia Movement Party
Kabupaten	rural district (Indonesia)
KBL	Kilusang Bagong Lipunan, New Society Movement; or *kasal, binyag, libing*, weddings, baptisms, funerals (Philippines)
Kelurahan	urban ward or precinct (Indonesia)
Kepala desa	rural village head (Indonesia)
Kota	city (Indonesia)
Kyai	religious scholar (Indonesia)
Lider	vote broker (Philippines)
LP	Liberal Party (Philippines)
MCA	Malaysian Chinese Association

MCP	Malayan Communist Party
MIC	Malaysian Indian Congress
NU	Nahdlatul Ulama, "traditionalist" Islamic organization (Indonesia)
NP	Nacionalista Party (Philippines)
PAP	People's Action Party (Singapore)
PAS	Parti Islam seMalaysia, Pan-Malaysian Islamic Party
PDI	Partai Demokrasi Indonesia, Indonesian Democracy Party
PDI–P	Partai Demokrasi Indonesia–Perjuangan, Indonesian Democracy Party–Struggle
PDP–LABAN	Partido Demokratiko Pilipino–Lakas ng Bayan, Philippine Democratic Party–Strength of the Nation
Pesantren	Islamic boarding schools (Indonesia)
PH	Pakatan Harapan, Alliance of Hope (Malaysia)
Pilkada	*Pemilihan kepala daerah*, regional head elections (Indonesia)
PKB	Partai Kebangkitan Bangsa, National Awakening Party (Indonesia)
PKI	Partai Komunis Indonesia, Indonesian Communist Party
PKK	Pemberdayaan Kesejahteraan Keluarga, Family Welfare Movement (Indonesia)
PKR	Parti Keadilan Rakyat, People's Justice Party (Malaysia)
PNI	Partai Nasional Indonesia, Indonesian National Party
PPP	Partai Persatuan Pembangunan, Development Unity Party (Indonesia)
Preman	gangsters (Indonesia)
Purok	neighborhood (Philippines)
Tim sukses	success team (Indonesia)
Ulama	religious scholar (Indonesia, Malaysia)
UMNO	United Malays National Organisation (Malaysia)
Wanita UMNO	women's wing of UMNO (Malaysia)

Patronage and Political Machines in Southeast Asia

The day before the May 2016 elections in the Philippines, following a whirl-wind week of interviews across the central and southern regions of the country, we found ourselves gathered in the front yard of a house owned by a campaign operative – we'll call him Obet – in a small town in southeastern Luzon. Sitting under a mango tree at a table roughly hewn from bamboo slats, and taking a break from the final stages of his work coordinating a mayoral campaign, Obet was about to extend our education into the finer points of Philippine-style electioneering.[1]

The first lesson was about money. Obet explained that any serious candidate must amass a substantial campaign war chest ahead of the elections. Campaigns are expensive, and without substantial resources one cannot hope to get into the game. "When I entered politics," he told us, "I soon realized that if you have no money, if you don't resort to vote buying, then you will never win." Over time, in fact, he began to think that perhaps the proper term should be "vote selling" rather than "vote buying." This is because, when he was a newly elected councilor more than a decade earlier, Obet was regularly approached by voters keen to offer "their family's support [i.e., votes] in exchange for some monetary compensation."

Now, Obet instructed his team of local vote-brokers (termed "*liders*," from the English word "leader") to distribute money house to house, two to three days ahead of the election. The usual understanding – difficult to enforce – is that persons receiving the money will vote for Obet's mayoral and councilor candidates. Occasionally, in an arrangement that is easier to be sure of, supporters of the opposing candidate will receive money in exchange for not voting

---

[1] All quotes from Obet come from our interview on May 8, 2016.

at all, a slight variation of which is to sponsor a day trip to a local resort – thus ensuring that such voters won't be able to reach the polling place.

The distribution of money, Obet explained, is "a signal to voters that you are a serious candidate." This helps explain why the primary targets of money distribution are loyal, core supporters, with undecided voters a secondary concern. As other candidates and campaigners in the Philippines likewise told us, the standard game plan is to provide funds in the first round of distribution and then to gauge the opposing candidate's money-distribution strategy. Doing so serves the dual goals of estimating both the rival's remaining resources and his or her willingness to expend them: in Philippine parlance, both the depth of their pockets and the length of their arms. Whenever possible, the last distribution of funds to voters – particularly to those whose support is considered most shaky – should be made by one's own campaign. Obet's campaign had set aside 8–10 million Philippine pesos (roughly USD165,000–207,000) for vote buying, with the goal of providing 10,000 voters with 1,000 Philippine pesos (around USD21) each – roughly four times the daily minimum wage in this part of the Philippines – as an inducement to support the entire slate of mayor, vice-mayor, and town councilors.[2]

In fact, as Obet explained, electoral success also depends on a politician's prior involvement in the everyday life of the community. This may start in the church, where candidates strategically present themselves as "sponsors" or *compadre/comadre* (godfather/godmother)[3] at *kasal* (weddings) and *binyag* (baptisms) and as mourners at their constituents' *libing* (funerals and wakes) – a trio of activities that has come to be known as KBL.[4] Each activity generally involves financial contributions, whether to the newlyweds, new parents, or grieving relatives. Forging this bond of fictive kinship often leads to additional requests for assistance at later points, for everything from legal aid to help in coping with family emergencies. Obet was himself a cousin of the mayoral candidate and a godson of the congressperson, with whom his father – a businessman and politician – had long been a close friend.

To construct the campaign team, Obet relied primarily on a combination of his own relatives; the ties of fictive kinship forged in baptisms, weddings, and funerals; his father's political-business networks; and his own networks from a stint on the town council. As much as possible, the liders he recruits at the community level should be loyal to the candidate. Even so, he explained, "you can't really avoid cases where some of your liders will betray you. It's part of

---

[2] Every election season, the Philippines experiences a shortage of small bills as campaigns withdraw them in massive quantities. Conveniently for Obet, his wife worked at a local bank and was able to set aside stacks of pesos for the final push ahead of the elections.

[3] Fictive kinship, in a larger system known as *compadrazgo* or co-parenthood.

[4] The term "KBL" is meant to allude humorously – but with no direct connection – to the New Society Movement or Kilusang Bagong Lipunan (KBL) ruling party of former dictator Ferdinand Marcos, whose martial law regime extended from 1972 to 1986.

the game." Early in his political career, when he was "lenient" with his liders, "some of them pocketed the money meant to buy votes." This led him to take a tougher stance, showing them "who is the boss" by making threats, destroying their reputations, and even sometimes resorting to physical assaults.

The members of Obet's local political machine worked closely together – including by sharing in the costs of and cooperating in the organization of liders. Of decidedly secondary importance was the machine's affiliation with a national political party. As the election approached, Obet's team adopted the brand of the Liberal Party (LP) of then-president Benigno Aquino. This was also the party affiliation of the congressperson, who generously covered many expenses of the local machine. In the crunch of the campaign effort, however, the focus was solidly on the local race. Straight-party voting is rare, and Obet was frank in explaining the gist of the message he told his liders to convey:

We tell the voters to focus on the mayor and the city councilors. If they still have the energy to go to the governor, please vote for the governor, if you still have the energy to vote for Congress, please vote for the congressman, then if you still have the energy to vote for the president, please do so. But focus first on the mayor and the councilors, that's the marching order.

With national surveys ahead of the 2016 presidential election strongly predicting the victory of Rodrigo Duterte, Obet readily acknowledged that the local machine would shift its affiliation to Duterte's party (PDP–LABAN) should the Davao mayor be elevated to the country's top post – as in fact happened the very next day. Obet's key concern was to maintain the vigor of his local machine, whatever its connections with tiers above.

UNDERSTANDING PATRONAGE POLITICS: OUR
CORE QUESTIONS

Obet's experience provides insight into a form of politics found around the world: the distribution of patronage. Patronage – which we define in brief as *a material resource distributed for particularistic benefit in order to advance political goals* – is central to political competition and mobilization in many countries. Cash payments to individuals – a major focus of Obet's strategizing – often attract media and scholarly attention, but patronage can consist of a virtually endless variety of gifts, jobs, projects, favors, and other benefits distributed to both individuals and groups. Recipients can be voters, as in Obet's scheme, but they can also be campaign workers, community leaders, lower-level politicians, and party cadres, or, in a more collective vein, women's groups, local sports clubs, or religious organizations.

The practice of patronage politics poses formidable organizational and strategic challenges, many of them implicit in Obet's description. How do patronage wielders identify recipients and distribute benefits in ways that increase the odds voters will repay their largesse with votes? Where do candidates gain funds and other resources to distribute? How do they maximize the political benefits from patronage while minimizing leakage? How do they recruit and reward effective and loyal brokers? How can they convince voters their promises of largesse are credible? All politicians dispensing patronage confront these challenges, but they do so in widely differing social and political contexts, and with different institutional tools at hand. Accordingly, patronage politics itself varies widely.

Much existing literature simplifies the study of patronage politics by focusing only on certain forms of the phenomenon (e.g. pork-barrel spending, vote buying, or patronage jobs) or by merging varied practices under one catch-all category (most commonly, "clientelism"). We address instead the variation in the ways that politicians across Southeast Asia respond to the challenges of patronage politics, seeking to explain those differences. In Indonesia, many candidates we encountered – like Obet's mayoral candidate in the Philippines – distributed cash gifts to large numbers of individual voters. To do so, they also recruited brokers and organized them into teams with similar structures to those used in the Philippines. Indonesian candidates also fretted about the "loyalty" of both the voters they provided with cash and the brokers they used to distribute it. And, like their counterparts in the Philippines, Indonesian candidates complemented their handouts to individuals with patronage targeted toward groups, for example, providing funds or materials to help local communities build or repair houses of worship, meeting halls, or roads and bridges. In other ways, however, the Indonesian pattern was distinctive. Unlike Obet's mayoral candidate, Indonesian candidates relatively rarely collaborate closely with other candidates in designing campaign strategies, building brokerage networks, or distributing patronage. Relatively few of them rely to the same extent as Obet on long-term ties of dependence and reciprocity built up with voters between elections, instead constructing campaign teams premised on much more ephemeral and insecure ties with brokers.

In Malaysia, by contrast, politicians far less frequently distribute cash or other gifts to individual voters (though doing so is certainly not unknown, especially in some parts of the country). Relative to their counterparts in either Indonesia or the Philippines, they are also less likely to rely on their own personal funds to underwrite their patronage strategies. Patronage politics is still widespread; it is just that most of the benefits that tie voters to parties are government or party handouts rather than private or personal gifts. Moreover, in Malaysia, strong national parties, rather than individual politicians and their personal machines, are the key actors in patronage politics – however much individual candidates also rally personal support, with the help of trusted loyalists. Major discrepancies in the patronage resources available to politicians affiliated with government parties and those from the opposition also greatly affect their strategies.

In this book, we probe not just any one of these practices but instead focus on what explains the mix and proportion in which they appear across electoral settings. To make sense of such variety, we introduce the concept of *electoral mobilization regimes*, through which we seek to capture how networks and resources combine. Doing so allows us to integrate, recenter, critique, and widen insights in the literature on patronage politics.

The concept of electoral mobilization regimes is the product of our efforts to answer a set of five primary questions, conceived at the beginning of our project and refined over the course of our fieldwork in Southeast Asia. *First*, and most fundamentally: what distinguishes the forms of patronage that candidates, parties, and campaigners deliver to voters and other supporters across and within our country cases? *Second*, through what sort of political networks do they distribute that patronage? *Third*, to what extent do specific types of political networks tend to be associated with particular forms of patronage? *Fourth*, how do these distinctive patterns of patronage politics actually work; i.e. how, and to what extent, do they influence voters? These first four questions are broadly descriptive, as we identify general patterns and explain how they operate. This descriptive work is a major contribution of this book and necessary for the comparative analysis that we (and others) seek to undertake. Our *fifth* and final question focuses attention on analysis and causation: what *explains* the patterns we observe both across and within countries? In answering this question, we explore both why certain types of networks and patronage tend to align and why some forms of patronage politics and networks occur in some countries or regions but not in others.

We will later summarize our answers to each of these questions but first jump briefly to our fifth question. We argue that these patterns of networks and patronage – which, again, we refer to as electoral mobilization regimes – are largely shaped by historical-institutional factors, in particular the character of states, parties, and electoral systems. Long-term institutional development privileges certain types of networks, particularly the relative strength and penetration of national political parties or local machines, with differing levels of capacity and opportunity to capture and coordinate state resources. Each network structure, in turn, commonly aligns with a particular mix of patronage types. These patterns of networks and patronage tend to dominate electoral campaigning, subsuming other bases for mobilization. However, while we can identify national-level electoral mobilization regimes, subnational variation remains salient, as well. We offer a set of three electoral mobilization regimes, each characterizing one of our three core cases – Indonesia, Malaysia, and the Philippines – and further investigate why certain regional pockets diverge from the national norm. These regimes are not unique to these states, nor is this set exhaustive. Rather, the approach and framework we model here will allow scholars of other polities to examine patronage politics through a new lens, building on the taxonomy we have started.

In order to begin answering our guiding questions more comprehensively, we next introduce the conceptual foundations of our study by elaborating upon our definition of patronage and by introducing a schema to understand its variation. We draw upon that conceptual framework to sketch our core arguments, briefly explaining the broad patterns of patronage politics we encountered in Southeast Asia. We then situate our study within the context of previous work on patronage politics in the region, explain our case selection, elaborate on our methods, and survey the structure of the remainder of the book.

CONCEPTUAL FOUNDATIONS: UNTANGLING PATRONAGE AND CLIENTELISM

We contend that the conceptual language scholars commonly utilize has unnecessarily straitjacketed previous attempts to understand how and why politicians use patronage strategies. In particular, over recent decades, the concept of *clientelism* has provided the dominant framework for comprehending such phenomena. The concept has its origins in studies of patron-client relations in traditional agrarian societies but has expanded in meaning to encompass vote buying and similar forms of targeted material distribution during elections. The key challenge is the lack of differentiation between two closely related but distinctive terms: "patronage" and "clientelism." While some scholars treat the two terms as synonymous (e.g., Kitschelt and Wilkinson 2007), here we use distinct definitions intended to overcome long-standing conceptual confusion (building on Hutchcroft 2014b).

To expand on the brief definition provided earlier, patronage is a *material resource, disbursed for particularistic benefit for political purposes and generally (but not always) derived from public sources.* Our definition refines previous attempts to conceptualize patronage, including Shefter's (1994, 283) definition: "Patronage ... involves the exchange of public benefits for political support or party advantage," and politicians distribute it to "individual voters, campaign workers, or contributors." Our modifications of this definition are three-fold and follow from our earlier discussion. First, patronage is usually but not always secured from public sources. It can also have private components, as when politicians dip into their own resources, tap into funds from illicit activities, or (most commonly) accept donations from businesspersons and companies to fund their largesse. Most obviously, when politicians distribute personal cash payments or other gifts to voters, they generally present these as private gifts, even if the ultimate source of such gifts is money corruptly attained from government office. Second, as we elaborate later, politicians and their machines or parties often distribute patronage not just to individuals but also to groups of various sorts. Third, we emphasize that patronage extends well beyond candidate–voter ties at election time. Patronage is commonly also dispensed across tiers of government (from national to subnational) and throughout the electoral cycle (that is, throughout the entire period from the conclusion of one election to the holding of the subsequent election).

Clientelism, on the other hand, describes a *personalistic relationship of power*. In its classic definition, persons of higher social status (patrons) are linked to those of lower social status (clients) in face-to-face and enduring ties of reciprocity that can vary in content, purpose, and direction across time. As James Scott (1972, 93) explains, "There is an imbalance in exchange between the two partners which expresses and reflects the disparity in their relative wealth, power, and status." Clientelist relationships are thus typically hierarchical and involve ongoing, iterated personal interactions in which the behavior of each party is contingent on the behavior of the other (Hicken 2011).

Using these definitions, patronage, as an adjective, modifies resources and flows, and clientelistic, as an adjective, modifies relationships, linkages, and ties. Untangling the definitions of patronage and clientelism allows for greater analytical precision. Not all patronage involves clientelism, as some patronage flows are impersonal and others are personal. And not all clientelism involves patronage, as the exchange of goods and services (as Scott describes) may or may not involve the quest for "political support or party advantage" (per Shefter). Indeed, the classic clientelistic tie, between landlords and tenants, exists largely outside the state.

With patronage and clientelism thus disentangled, we can proceed to differentiate among three major types of patronage (again taking off from Hutchcroft 2014b). The first, *micro-particularism*, involves the disbursement of benefits to individuals and households. Examples include vote buying or the distribution of public-sector jobs for political advantage, including low-skilled positions that offer partisan benefits (Brierley 2021). At a higher level, micro-particularism can involve extra dollops of constituency development funds to individual legislators based on special ties they enjoy with party or government leaders. We can also refer to this type of particularism as personalistic patronage, as it often involves quite direct ties between those who dispense and those who receive.

Second, the beneficiaries of *meso-particularism* are larger collectivities, whether geographic (e.g., a village or congressional district), associational (e.g., a local religious group), or sectoral (e.g., a labor union or occupational organization). Examples of material benefits include everything from small- to medium-sized infrastructure projects to equipment for clubs or associations. Meso-particularism does not necessarily involve personalistic ties between donor and recipient. This category broadly corresponds to "club goods," or "local public goods," terms commonly used in the economics literature that we are happy to appropriate;[5] our alternative characterization, however, puts greater focus on the unit of aggregation and political rather than

---

[5] The conventional view understands club goods as being excludable (only a limited class of persons can access them) but non-rivalrous (one consumer's use does not exhaust the good or prevent others from using it). As we elaborate in Chapter 5, more salient to us is that these are collective rather than individual goods rather than who, precisely, may use them.

market-oriented characteristics. Club goods are excludable to those outside the group's boundaries but not to those within those boundaries. Examples include local roads, improved schools, and other local infrastructure that target particular groups or communities but not others (Magaloni 2006; Kitschelt and Wilkinson 2007; Diaz-Cayeros et al., 2016).[6]

The third major type is *macro-particularism*, involving national-level or regional-level programs that parties or politicians "hijack." In these cases, the targeting of beneficiaries ostensibly follows programmatic and universalistic criteria – cash benefits to indigent families, pensions to persons over a particular age, scholarships to students who perform well in a university entrance exam, and so on – but politicians, in appearance or reality, intervene to direct the benefits to political supporters.

We further disaggregate macro-particularism across three sub-categories. *Credit-claiming* involves efforts to convince voters that parties or politicians are responsible for recipients' access to national or regional programs, even if these programs do not, in fact, involve the exercise of discretion outside the bureaucracy.[7] *Facilitation* refers to helping constituents access programs for which they are formally qualified. Facilitation is often an entirely above-board form of constituency service, as when a national legislator helps a local council lodge an application to a government agency (e.g., for a local transportation, health, or environmental initiative), but it can also involve bureaucratic string-pulling and calling in favors (as when a politician phones the head of a local hospital in order to help a constituent gain admittance as an inpatient). *Morselization* occurs when legislators cut a national or provincial program into discrete chunks and then use their discretion to disburse them for political or electoral benefit, as when a politician gets access to a quantity of health insurance cards or scholarships and hands them out to party workers, or when she intervenes in a budgetary process to direct a packet of school rehabilitation grants to her own electoral district. In effect, this can involve politicians turning pieces of national or regional programs into either micro- or meso-particularistic patronage. However, because their ultimate source is a broad program at least ostensibly allocated according to nonpolitical criteria – that is, because the policies or benefits in question *are* usually at root programmatic, with discretion, generally, only at the margins – we refer to all as macro-particularism.

---

[6] Club goods and local public goods contrast with public goods, which are fully non-excludable as well as non-rivalrous.

[7] An illustration from outside the region serves to clarify: the US Congress passed a series of COVID-19 relief measures in 2020. As president, Donald Trump exercised no discretion over distribution of these benefits. Yet he cultivated political advantage by signing his name to relief checks the Internal Revenue Service distributed to all taxpayers below a specified income ceiling. This step drew flak for exceeding the credit-claiming norm in the US (Costa and Rucker 2020).

We present these three overarching categories of particularism for their heuristic value; they serve as the foundation for our subsequent analysis. At the same time, we readily acknowledge that the boundaries among them can blur in practice. These types are best understood as existing on a continuum, running from fully particularistic (involving unfettered discretion) to fully programmatic (no discretion), with micro-, meso-, and macro- specifying the scale at which particularistic distribution occurs. This fuzzy demarcation is apparent, at the most basic level, in characterizing policies. As Gregory Noble (2010) explains in an analysis of particularism in Japanese politics, education can be viewed as a programmatic good, in that it is widely distributed and brings benefits both to school children and to society in general. It can, however, simultaneously involve an element of particularism based, for instance, on who obtains a contract to build a school. The same could be said for contracts to build a hospital, or decisions on the placement of a train line (on the latter, see Johnson 1986, 9). Public education, health care, and mass transit are programmatic goods, but their implementation can nonetheless yield lucrative particularistic benefits.

As we highlight in the subsequent chapters, this inherent blurriness, extending also to the scale of particularistic benefits (micro, meso, and macro), is all the more apparent in terms of electoral impact. A scholarship under a national education scheme that a politician gives in the middle of the electoral cycle to the child of a long-time supporter of her family's local machine is, in our categorization, macro-particularism. It is a national program that has been morselized and turned into a targeted benefit over which the politician has some discretion. However, in its micro-targeting, it could have similar political impact to a cash handout provided at election time or a town-hall job provided in the wake of an election (both of which we categorize as micro-particularism). Regardless of how it is categorized, ultimately, the desired political impact is to influence a particular voter (or household of voters) to provide electoral support. These examples are qualitatively different from what we would anticipate from meso-particularism, such as a small infrastructure project that a politician builds for the benefit of an entire village.

Of course, these strategies are not mutually exclusive: they can be, and typically are, mixed. But the mix of these strategies differs considerably among patronage-oriented polities. Such variation results not merely from differentiation in the *degree* of patronage vs. programmatic appeals – the primary focus of much preceding research – but also in terms of the *forms* of patronage dispensed. We find all three forms of particularism in each of the three cases that make up the core of this book, but they occur in different combinations.

Before we proceed, it is important to clarify one further dimension of variation in patronage politics: the level of government involved. Across the world, including in the countries we study here, election-related patronage tends to become progressively less intensive as one moves up from local- through provincial- to national-level politics. In part, this is because the smaller scale of local-level politics facilitates face-to-face contact between dispensers and recipients of patronage, but it is also simply a matter of practicality: running a vote-buying operation in a national constituency with millions of voters poses much greater organizational challenges and is far more expensive than running one in a district constituency with a few thousand voters. It is generally more efficient to rely on programmatic, partisan, or charismatic appeals at greater scale, even if local political operatives associated with a national campaign still have incentives to hijack national programs for their own purposes. Thus, in both the Philippines and Indonesia, practitioners sometimes contrast the "ground wars" of local races, which involve extensive vote buying and gifting, with the "air wars" of presidential elections, which depend more on media campaigning and advertising.

SKETCHING OUT EMPIRICAL PATTERNS: ELECTORAL MOBILIZATION REGIMES IN SOUTHEAST ASIA

We are now in a position to sketch our core arguments in response to the questions that guide our research. The first four questions invite us to identify and analyze the patterns of patronage and types of networks we observe across our three countries, combining to form what we term "electoral mobilization regimes"; the fifth digs deeper into the *why* behind those patterns. Recall that the *first* question concerns the mix of patronage strategies used. We find, of course, a wide range of types of appeals from one country to another – as well as across locales and levels of government within countries. Even so, distinctive patterns emerge. In the Philippines – as should be obvious from Obet's story that opened our book – micro-particularism predominates, as well as substantial meso-particularism in the form of pork-barrel projects of many creative varieties (Holmes 2019), alongside ample opportunities to claim credit for, and morselize, national government programs. In contrast, in Malaysia patronage politics is characterized fundamentally by "hijacking" of macro-level public programs. For decades, the Barisan Nasional (National Front)-led government sustained itself in power by rolling out national programs that conferred various benefits, especially to its core Malay supporters, drilling into the recipients that they would continue to receive these benefits only if they supported the Barisan Nasional politically. While such credit-claiming and facilitation are not absent in Indonesia, the most prominent pattern there is a mixture of private micro- and meso-level patronage. In Indonesia, candidates for political office are especially likely to invest personal funds in distributing small-scale infrastructure projects and other benefits to villages, neighborhoods, and community groups, and in distributing gifts to individual voters.

We observe differences, too, in temporal patterns. Some Indonesian politicians – especially regional government heads and, to a lesser degree, incumbent legislators – are able to access state resources to support their patronage strategies; such elected officials have tried hard to acquire greater discretionary authority over the allocation of state funds since the transition to democracy twenty years ago. However, some Indonesian politicians experience difficulties in accessing state resources. (As we explain later and in more detail in Chapter 2, this is because much control remains in the hands of unelected bureaucrats, and because politicians' parties provide them with little assistance in this regard.) As a result, many politicians have little alternative to investing private resources in their patronage strategies, which, in turn, means they frequently limit their disbursement to election times. In contrast, both Malaysian and Philippine politicians are better able to access and distribute state resources across the entire electoral cycle – the former by virtue of their connections to national parties and government programs; the latter by capturing local office, from whence they can not only access resources from the national level but also exercise high degrees of discretionary authority over the distribution of funds.

Again, we must stress that none of these distinctions is sharp-edged: each form of patronage, and each temporal pattern, is present in each country, but to differing degrees.

Our *second* question concerns the types of networks that politicians use to organize and distribute patronage. Here the patterns are even more distinctive. The primary locus of activity in the Philippines is the *local* – and generally familial – *political machine*, which has often tenuous (and promiscuous) links to national political parties. This type of network can be very stable and enduring over time, even if a local machine's connection with higher levels of the political system is quite fickle from one election to the next. Malaysia offers a striking contrast, as its core networks are centered very firmly on *national political parties and coalitions*. Political actors' loyalties to parties are often very strong and enduring, and those who hitch their wagon to a winning party organization can anticipate being rewarded with a range of benefits, from financial assistance in times of need to positions in the government. This type of political network displays a strong degree of institutionalization, with significant consistency in power relationships throughout the electoral cycle and across levels of government. A third distinct pattern is evident in Indonesia, where the prevailing network is generally *ad hoc personal campaign teams* (often known as *tim sukses* or "success teams"). Local campaign organizations are therefore much less coherent than in the Philippines, but Indonesian candidates' linkages to national political parties are generally stronger than for their Philippine counterparts – indeed, Indonesian electoral rules (largely) proscribe local parties and mandate national party linkages. The Indonesian ad hoc team is the least stable of the three types of political network in terms of its structure at the base: while incumbent politicians are often able to draw on the support of loyal clients in repeat election cycles, most candidates more or less build their teams from scratch each election.

Our *third* question invites us to put these pieces together, to examine how patterns of patronage and network types interact. As each of these types of network is broadly associated with a particular mix of forms of patronage (see also Aspinall and Berenschot 2019), we combine the two elements into the concept of electoral mobilization regimes. Characterizing each electoral mobilization regime is a mutually constitutive mix of networks and patronage strategies (see Table 1.1; we explore this table in more detail in Chapter 3).

The party-based machines that define Malaysian politics go hand-in-hand with mobilization strategies that combine an abundance of macro-particularism, meso-particularism, and programmatic policies, with most distribution occurring outside of the electoral season. Politicians seldom target individuals or households directly, corresponding to quite low levels of micro-particularism outside certain anomalous regions (as we discuss in Chapter 8), and most patronage resources come from public sources and government programs. This stands in stark contrast to the Philippines, with its local

TABLE 1.1. *Mobilization networks and patronage patterns in Southeast Asia*

	Party machines (Malaysia)	Local machines (Philippines)	Ad hoc teams (Indonesia)
Micro-particularism (Chapter 4)			
Ubiquity	limited	extensive	extensive
Main timing of distribution	–	between and during elections	during elections
Meso-particularism (Chapter 5)			
Ubiquity	moderate	extensive	moderate
Main timing of distribution	between elections	between and during elections	some between, mostly during elections
Macro-particularism/Hijacking (Chapter 6)			
Ubiquity of credit-claiming	extensive	extensive	moderate
Ubiquity of facilitation	extensive	moderate	limited
Ubiquity of morselization	limited	extensive	moderate[a]
Main timing of distribution	between elections	between and during elections	between and during elections
National public goods			
Ubiquity	moderate	limited	limited
Primary sources of patronage			
Public vs. private resources	public	public and private	private

[a] Limited for legislators; extensive for regional executives.

machines, and Indonesia, with its ad hoc teams. The targeting of individuals and households is rampant in both of these cases, but in the Philippines, micro-particularism is commonly mixed with both meso- and macro-particularism, and is funded by both public and private sources. Patronage distribution occurs across the entire electoral calendar, with micro-particularism particularly predominant during election campaigning. By comparison, distribution of micro- and meso-particularism in Indonesia is concentrated around elections (with less in the way of macro-particularism) and is much more likely to be funded through private resources than is the case in the Philippines. These combinations have an internal logic; they are not merely coincidental, as we will discuss in more detail in the following section.

Our *fourth* question moves into the realm of mechanics, asking how these different forms of patronage operate. When politicians distribute material benefits to supporters, who exactly do they target, to what extent do they expect recipients to reciprocate, and what steps do they take to make sure recipients do so? In other words: how does patronage actually work so as to help deliver electoral victories? Here we argue that much of the literature on clientelism has placed too high a premium on the element of *contingency* – that is, the operation of a clear quid pro quo in which politicians ensure that they offer patronage only in exchange for political support (building on Hicken and Nathan 2020). We argue that true contingency only occurs when dispensers of patronage make concrete efforts to ensure that recipients of their largesse reciprocate as expected, notably through a combination of (a) monitoring the behavior of recipients (to increase the chances that they truly deliver on their promised votes) and (b) attempting to enforce the desired outcome (e.g., by threatening consequences if voters fail to deliver). We show that such efforts are rare across Southeast Asia, indicating that when political candidates distribute patronage, they are often, in fact, performing other functions, including *credibility buying* (advertising themselves as serious and capable candidates), *turf protection* (defending clientele they have long cultivated from poaching by rivals), or *brand building* (increasing their name-recognition). These strategic objectives, in different mixes, motivate the forms of patronage that characterize our three regimes.

OUR EXPLANATORY FRAMEWORK: ACCOUNTING FOR PATTERNS AND VARIATION

Our *fifth* and final line of inquiry entails explaining the variation we observe: why do we see these dominant patterns at the national level, as well as divergences from them subnationally? Picking up from the synopsis provided earlier, we focus on two different sets of explanations. First, we explore the links between the combinations of mobilization networks and mobilization strategies we observe across our cases. In other words, we examine how the types of patronage strategies candidates employ reflect the opportunities and limitations of the mobilization networks that predominate, and then explain why certain characteristics tend to hang together within our three types of mobilization regimes. Second, we investigate the historical and institutional determinants of these various mobilization regimes. Why do distinctive networks, with their particular mixes of patronage types, come to dominate in particular countries? What accounts for the subnational variation that further complicates broad cross-country comparisons? The following discussion briefly introduces our more extended analysis in Chapters 2, 3, and 8.

Understanding the Patterns within Mobilization Regimes

In the previous section, we identified three types of mobilization regimes – three distinct combinations of patronage patterns and mobilization networks across our cases. We argue that these configurations are not random. Patterns of patronage distribution reflect, in part, the mobilization networks through which they flow.

Strong party-based machines, especially those that exercise national dominance not just for years but for decades, as in Malaysia, enjoy a high degree of privileged access to state resources and programs. Capture of the state explains the primacy of macro-particularism: ruling-party politicians are able to particularize state programs with relatively little impediment. Indeed, alongside the patronage component, such a polity displays an important element of programmatic political appeals. Both credit-claiming and facilitation are prevalent, as local politicians engage in practices designed both to further their personal electoral goals and to promote the interests of the national party. Micro-particularism is relatively rare because political candidates are either running under government parties and can claim credit for or facilitate access to government programs – and therefore do not need to distribute resources to voters individually to win elections – or are running for opposition parties and so lack resources to distribute as patronage (though they rapidly adapt to prevalent patterns once they win office).

Where the other two types of networks, namely local machines and ad hoc teams, prevail, local-level politicians coordinate weakly, at best, with the national level. Effective local politicians can certainly negotiate and access patronage resources by allying with national leaders, but there is nothing to match the regular, ordered, and consistent delivery of national programs that comes through a strongly institutionalized governing national party or coalition as in Malaysia. Consequently, these polities have a much weaker orientation to programmatic appeals, and local politicians rely much more on distributing patronage.

But there remain important contrasts in how local machines and ad hoc teams deploy patronage. In the Philippine case, the fact that local-level machines – often based around a single family – are able to control the local organs of the state, sometimes for decades, entrenches them in local power structures. This entrenchment gives them considerable opportunity to access government programs distributed from the center, enabling them to build sustained relationships with brokers and voters alike, including by distributing benefits between elections. In the Indonesian case, personal brokerage teams are generally based on fleeting relationships. As a result, much of the patronage distribution to voters that occurs is equally ephemeral, being concentrated around election times. Thus, for example, while there is often a frenzy of meso-particularism in Indonesia during a campaign – with candidates distributing all sorts of small-scale projects and goods to villages, neighborhoods, religious groups, and other collectivities – the overall quantum of such gifting is no match for the steady stream of pork-barrel projects that local machines organize across the election cycle in the Philippines. Indonesian politicians at the local level dream of attaining access to such enduring resource streams; though they have made some progress on this score, their achievements still fall short of those of their Philippine counterparts.

Explaining Cross-case and Within-case Variation

In this book, we seek to analyze the patterns we observe across our cases – why certain types of networks and patronage mixes are mutually constitutive. Entangled with this puzzle are questions of why distinctive networks, with their particular mixes of patronage types, come to dominate in particular countries, and what accounts for the subnational variation that further complicates broad cross-country comparisons.

We argue that to answer such questions, it is necessary to draw back from the day-to-day operation of patronage politics and focus on historical and institutional development over the long term. Our approach is not necessarily at odds with recent scholarship – though our cases do suggest important limits to prevailing assumptions, for instance, regarding clientelism as contingent. But we shift the frame to allow a perspective that is systemic and foundational rather than mechanical, and comparative and dynamic rather than a static snapshot. Much of the relevant literature in recent times has focused on explaining the microfoundations and internal logic of clientelist exchange (e.g., Stokes 2005; Nichter 2008; Stokes et al. 2013). To the extent that scholars see slow-moving processes of social change as important, their focus is often on long-term economic development and the gradual growth of a middle-class constituency for programmatic politics that provides disincentives for patronage politics (e.g., Kitschelt 2007; Nathan 2019; Stokes et al. 2013; Weitz-Shapiro 2014; Wilkinson 2014).

The new emphasis on microfoundations has greatly expanded our understanding of how patronage politics works. However, we contend that comprehending the variety found in patronage systems requires that we understand them first and foremost as historical and institutional products. Specifically, we focus on the characteristics of, and historical development of, the state and political parties, alongside the emergence of distinct "constituencies for patronage" and the choice of (as well as reforms of) electoral systems. In making our argument, we build upon another strand in the literature that sees patronage politics as a product of long-term processes of state- and party-building (see especially Shefter 1994).

Our next two chapters delve into our historical and institutional arguments, allowing us to be brief here. First, taking a top-down perspective, sequencing is critical. If, at an early stage of the development of a modern state, a single party is able to capture the central government, monopolize its resources, and use its own networks to mobilize voters, it will be able to rely largely on macro-particularistic credit-claiming to mobilize support. This is the pattern that occurred in Malaysia, where a single party – technically a coalition of parties but registered conjointly[8] – was able to capture governmental authority early on during the transition to independence. With a centralized patronage party dominating access to government resources, political candidates later either had few incentives (if from the governing coalition) or opportunities (if in opposition parties) to invest in private forms of patronage.

In both the Philippines and Indonesia, by contrast, historical and institutional factors conspired to nurture very different patterns of patronage distribution. In the Philippines, strong local machines established their dominance early in the twentieth century, when US colonial administrators concentrated their attention not on developing a robust national bureaucracy but rather on the creation of local-level elective posts – followed soon thereafter by a fully elected national assembly and, eventually, Senate (Hutchcroft 2000). Restrictions on the suffrage and resource advantages allowed powerful local landed elites to acquire political power; they soon enjoyed substantial sway over bureaucratic appointments, pork-barrel resources, loans from state-owned banks, and more. Provincial machines headed by locally powerful families became the major building blocks of politics, linked upward to national legislative posts dominated by politicians from these same families. Even as suffrage expanded in later decades, these machines remained the most important networks for distributing patronage to voters, discouraging the development of strongly programmatic national political parties. Again, sequencing was key, as the opening up of elective offices preceded the development of a strong centralized bureaucracy.

In Indonesia, despite strong traditions of party politics early in the country's postindependence history, the legacy of a long period of authoritarian rule between 1966 and 1998 means that parties as collective actors have been unable to monopolize distribution of public resources. This is largely because Suharto's authoritarian New Order regime built up the bureaucracy as its

---

[8] The United Malays National Organisation (UMNO), Malayan Chinese Association, and Malayan Indian Congress formed the Alliance in the 1950s, then (with additional partners) the Barisan Nasional (National Front) in the 1970s. UMNO has dominated the coalition throughout, though less starkly initially.

principal vehicle of rule – including in the distribution of patronage. Even after the reintroduction of democratic elections following the fall of Suharto, the bureaucracy has retained much authority and control over resources (see Aspinall and Berenschot 2019, 41–65). With considerable control over how programs are distributed being vested in the bureaucracy – or among elected local officials such as district heads and governors, as individuals rather than as party representatives – parties have largely been unable to capture sufficient funds to assist candidates in their patronage strategies. On the contrary, higher-level party leaders often charge candidates fees for the privilege of being nominated to compete in an election (Mietzner 2010; Hendrawan et al. 2021). Further undermining the cohesion of parties and machines, even at the local level, has been the introduction of electoral rules that favor personal campaigns and inhibit cooperation among candidates, encouraging the development of personalized election machinery and individualized, one-shot micro-patronage.

Looking now from a bottom-up perspective: the density and relative autonomy of social networks and of the identities that sustain them also matter for the nature and mix of patronage strategies, but these too are shaped by the historical evolution of states and parties. Where social networks retain significant autonomy, internal cohesion, and hierarchy, their leaders can bargain with candidates and parties to deliver collective benefits that further the interests of members of the network. Weak or coopted social networks lack such leverage.

Historically, the Philippines lacks the array of large-scale vertical social organizations that emerged in Indonesia in the latter decades of Dutch colonial rule. This is seemingly related to two factors: the social dominance of the Catholic Church throughout most of the lowland Philippines, and the process by which family dynasties captured provincial political power in the early twentieth century Philippines and then constructed local machines based on patron-client ties.[9] Philippine political machines developed independent bases of power but nonetheless maintained shifting ties with national political parties based on a mutually beneficial exchange (in essence, delivering votes in exchange for patronage resources). In particular, the emergence of a national oligarchy generally discouraged political mobilization on the basis of regional, religious, and ethnic networks. To this day, with the notable exception of Muslim Mindanao and (to a much lesser extent) the upland Cordillera region in northern Luzon, ethnic cleavages are not major foundations for political mobilization. They may at times influence patronage distribution, as when the Marcos dictatorship took special care of the First Couple's home regions,

---

[9] The same cannot be said of horizontal or class-based political mobilization in the Philippines: a long history of peasant rebellion serves as the backdrop to a communist movement that remains strong in many (particularly rural) areas. We do not focus on that movement given its generally marginal integration into electoral patronage networks.

but even in that case, the regime allocated pork very broadly with the goal of building alliances throughout the archipelago.

By contrast, in both Malaysia and Indonesia, mass organizations, parties, and the underlying solidarities that sustain them evolved prior to the establishment of full electoral politics, and even of independence. Islamic politics was especially important in both countries. But the way these political networks and associated social identities developed over time diverged. In Malaysia, social networks associated with ethnicity and religion largely transformed into or attached themselves to political parties, whether governing or opposition, such that large-scale identity politics became an important foundation of the national party and political system, providing the party system in particular with much of its coherence and resilience. Indonesia was evolving in a similar direction in the early postindependence period, but three decades of measures to disarticulate social-movement politics under the New Order produced a social-network map that is both more fragmented and more autonomous of formal politics. There, a plethora of social organizations representing ethnic, religious, women's, neighborhood, and other groups bargain with elected politicians for material resources, rather than being wedded to political parties, as remains common in Malaysia.

To illustrate how these distinctions matter for patronage politics, let us consider for a moment the lowest levels of community-cum-state organization in each country: the village and neighborhood. Each of our three core countries has governance units at these levels: villages (*desa*) and urban precincts (*kelurahan*) in Indonesia, as well as lower-level neighborhood and sub-neighborhood units; villages and urban wards (together referred to as *barangays*) in the Philippines; local authorities – including city councils and council-less city halls, municipal councils, and district councils – in Malaysia. (See Appendix B, which diagrams tiers of government in the three countries.) Yet these local organizations and the officials who run them are integrated into patronage networks through markedly different patterns in each country.

In Malaysia, the Barisan Nasional government abolished local elections in the 1960s, allowing state governments to appoint members of local councils and effectively transforming this level of governance into an extension of the state governing party. Council positions are often rewards for loyal party workers, and local councils do the bidding of governing parties in each state. By contrast, village leaders and councils are elected in both the Philippines and Indonesia (except in Indonesia's *kelurahan*) and ordinary citizens at these levels often have a great deal of engagement with – and sense of ownership over – community governance: they often first call on village and neighborhood leaders if they need help accessing government services or assistance. There the similarities end. Typically, *barangay* leaders are integrated into the governing local machine in the Philippines. They commonly take their cues from the mayor, coordinate their patronage strategies with him or her at election time, and earn meso-particularistic rewards for their community by demonstrating loyalty to the local machine. In Indonesia, elected community leaders are also highly prized vote-brokers, given the degree of social influence they exercise. But they retain significant autonomy, honing their bargaining skills when coaxing community projects from local-government politicians and bureaucrats. Much of the political dynamism at election time comes when such leaders negotiate and strike deals with candidates, typically entailing a promise of a bloc of votes in exchange for road extensions, lighting, drainage, or other community improvements. This contrast illustrates the general pattern (notwithstanding numerous exceptions) across our three cases: close integration of social organizations and networks into national party networks in Malaysia; close and often enduring integration of barangay governance into local political machines in the Philippines; relative autonomy and only negotiated and fleeting integration of social networks into enduring political networks in Indonesia.

KEY CONTRIBUTIONS

Our book makes a number of contributions to the literature on comparative clientelism/patronage, electoral systems, and party politics. First, central to our theoretical and conceptual contributions is our argument that patterns of patronage and the networks through which it flows are mutually constitutive – corresponding to what we have labeled as distinct electoral mobilization regimes. The strengths and limitations of a given mobilization network shape the mix of patronage strategies politicians pursue, and those strategic choices, in turn, can reinforce existing networks.

Second, our work also builds on and contributes to comparative work on state building, party development, and political institutions by exploring how these combine in different ways to produce coherent, self-sustaining patterns and systems for patronage. Specifically, we argue that the ways in which constituencies for patronage develop help shape (but also then reflect) which actors emerge as the primary players in patronage politics, the extent to which politicians have access to public patronage resources, and the types of mobilization strategies candidates prefer.

Third, our work helps refine our understanding of the meaning and motivation behind what we often label as clientelism and patronage. We argue that much of the behavior that scholars and commentators treat as contingency-based clientelism, is, in fact, not contingent at all. Instead, when candidates distribute patronage to individual voters and groups, they are frequently engaging in *credibility buying, turf protection,* or *brand building.* Consistent with a growing literature on what might be termed "noncontingent" clientelism (e.g. Kramon 2016; Muñoz 2019; Hicken and Nathan 2020), we show how and why such strategies are common, rational, and viable. This clarity and precision can help to move scholarship toward finer-grained, more revealing distinctions across polities – for instance, to understand better why candidates even in similarly weak-party systems might opt for divergent patronage strategies.

Fourth, as part of this analysis, we provide a conceptual framework for thinking about the types of patronage tools candidates utilize. Our framework separates the type of patronage being distributed from the strategic motivation behind such distribution. Thus, we distinguish among micro-particularism (patronage targeted at individuals and households), meso-particularism (patronage targeted at narrow geographic or associational groups), and macro-particularism (patronage hijacked from programs ostensibly targeted at broad swaths of voters). Depending on a candidate's motivation, micro-particularism may be a way to persuade swing voters to support a candidate (vote buying) or core supporters to vote (turnout buying), or it may serve as a form of political advertising (brand building), a signal of candidate viability (credibility buying), or an inducement to potentially promiscuous supporters to resist competitors' entreaties (turf protection). Similarly, candidates might distribute meso-particularism (club goods, pork, etc.) with varying strategic motivations and degrees of hoped-for contingency. Finally, under the umbrella of macro-particularism, we differentiate among types of programmatic hijacking – *credit-claiming*, *facilitation*, and *morselization* – while exploring the relative benefits of each for politicians and parties across contexts, offering both conceptual clarity and concrete examples.

Fifth, moving beyond parties and state structures, we also situate patronage politics within its wider societal framework: we analyze the ways in which patronage politics interacts with identity and group politics. To begin with, we find that regardless of the particular identity mobilized, the cohesion and hierarchy of the group matter for the choice of patronage strategy employed. Contingent distribution of meso-particularistic patronage is most likely where groups are cohesive and hierarchical. We also find that while identity politics varies tremendously in form across our cases, the architecture of patronage politics looks remarkably similar whether the networks through which resources flow are religious organizations, ethnic groups, or occupational associations. With the notable exception of class, patronage politics tends to work with and within existing identities and ultimately to reinforce rather than undermine them. That said, while patronage distribution can promote either bonding within or bridging across identity groups, we identified much more of the latter effect – that is, more pooling of voters across communities than intensifying in-group over out-group identities. In other words, we find the typical candidate strategy includes using patronage to mobilize identity-based groups of voters but that few candidates can afford to rely on a single identity group. As a result, they attempt to use patronage to mobilize a wide variety of identity groups, such that most groups can expect to receive something. In the end, we find that patronage politics simultaneously relies on and transcends identity politics – complicating a literature that has tended to assume a specific ethnicized aspect to patronage politics (for instance, Chandra 2004).

Finally, both our cross- and within-country analyses underscore the conclusion that there is no simple link between development and a decline in patronage politics – a finding that challenges foundational work in this area (e.g., Scott 1969). We do observe a link between more programmatic politics and rising incomes, but the strength of that relationship varies greatly and we find significant exceptions. This inconsistency leads us to unpack what mechanisms might foster declines in patronage. We find that the mechanisms at work seem less "development" per se than state capacity and reach, the local resource base, the character of social networks and leadership, the degree of discretion politicians enjoy, and the incentives embedded in electoral systems.

STUDYING PATRONAGE POLITICS IN SOUTHEAST ASIA

In this book, we explore the varied forms of patronage politics by focusing on three countries of Southeast Asia: Indonesia, Malaysia, and the Philippines. These are the countries where we conducted the bulk of our research and which we draw upon to build our core arguments. We also conducted supplementary research in three additional countries (Singapore, Thailand, and Timor-Leste) and draw on these cases intermittently through the volume for observations that sharpen our comparative arguments.

In most ways, this set of countries is extremely diverse. It includes both presidential (Indonesia, the Philippines, Timor-Leste) and parliamentary (Malaysia, Singapore, and Thailand) systems, electoral-authoritarian regimes (Singapore and Malaysia), as well as vigorous but low-quality democracies (Indonesia, the Philippines, and Timor-Leste), and one country that in recent times has fluctuated between military rule and electoral democracy (Thailand). Indonesia, with about 270 million people, is the world's fourth most populous country and its third most populous democracy. Timor-Leste, with about 1.3 million citizens, is among the world's smallest democracies. Indonesia has the world's largest number of Muslims, while Thailand and the Philippines are, respectively, among the most populous majority-Buddhist and majority-Catholic countries. Most of these countries are officially classified as middle-income economies, but Singapore has one of the highest GDPs per capita in the world while Timor-Leste is among the poorest countries in Asia.

At the same time, as we discuss in further detail later, these countries display highly varied patterns of patronage politics. For example, the distribution of cash to individual voters in the lead-up to polling day – a phenomenon popularly known as vote buying – remains very common in the Philippines, Indonesia, and Thailand. It also occurs, but at much lower rates, in East Malaysia (the Borneo states of Sabah and Sarawak), while it is far rarer in West (peninsular) Malaysia and Timor-Leste and entirely absent in contemporary Singapore. In other words, it is least common in both the wealthiest and the poorest of these countries, despite the fact that vote buying is often understood as being linked to poverty.

In trying to understand these and similar phenomena, students of Southeast Asian politics have long studied the mechanics of patronage. Two generations ago, Southeast Asia specialists produced much of the pioneering conceptual literature on patronage, clientelism, and allied phenomena. Carl Landé's seminal contribution (1965) described how pyramids of patron-client networks in the Philippines connected what was then a two-party system at the national level to bifactional competition at the local level. James Scott (1972) then took a comparative tack, examining the ubiquity of patron-client ties throughout the region. Analysis of patronage politics has been a recurring theme in studies of the politics of individual Southeast Asian countries ever since, including important studies of the role of patronage politics within the authoritarian regimes of the Cold War era (e.g. Crouch 1979), studies of the relationship between clientelism and parties in more recent times (e.g. Gomez and Jomo 1997; Tomsa and Ufen 2013), as well as a plethora of specialized analyses of topics such as vote buying (e.g. Callahan and McCargo 1996; Schaffer 2007a; Muhtadi 2019). Numerous scholars have highlighted the importance of patronage as a source of democratic dysfunction but without drilling down into how patronage politics actually works and how it varies.

Despite this wealth of research, we contend that the study of the comparative politics of patronage in Southeast Asia remains under-developed. For one thing, classic works such as those by Scott and Landé were written when Southeast Asia was primarily rural; succeeding decades have brought dramatic economic growth and urbanization throughout the region, undercutting the basis of traditional forms of patron-clientelism based on rural class relations, accompanied by significant transformations of national patterns of patronage politics. Equally importantly, with the notable exception of Scott (1972), most studies thus far have focused on a particular country, or even a particular institution or subnational region within one country (e.g. Tomsa's excellent 2008 study of Indonesia's Golkar party). Such studies provide valuable observations about the patterns and internal logic of patronage politics in the place or institution concerned but offer limited leverage for understanding broader variation. At the same time, we believe that the comparative study of Southeast Asian patronage politics has much to contribute to theory. There have been relatively few attempts to study comprehensively how and why patronage politics varies across or within countries (but see Berenschot and Aspinall 2020; Stokes et al. 2013; Hutchcroft 2014b).

Several principles guided our selection of the primary countries for our research. The four countries that were our initial focus (Indonesia, Malaysia, and the Philippines, as well as Thailand) are all middle-income countries with significant experience of electoral politics. (The 2014 military coup in Thailand, which led to the suspension of elections for the duration of our research, forced us to make Thailand a secondary case.) We knew they differed significantly in terms of dimensions we believed would be important in shaping distinctive patterns of patronage politics. These countries have at different times had very different political regimes, and levels of state capacity vary both across and within them. They are also socially diverse, encompassing three majority religions as well as subnational religious and ethnic diversity, providing scope for comparison of the effects of normative and cultural factors. We knew, too, that their patterns of political representation ranged from having relatively weak and fluid party systems to having well-established political parties. Existing literature tended to associate patronage politics with different political patterns in each country – strong parties in Malaysia, clientelism in the Philippines, social organizations in Indonesia – but we knew from our own research experience that all the components of patronage politics we were interested in could be found in each country. What we did not know at the outset of this project was precisely how these patterns differed and to what extent they cohered into distinctive amalgams.

OUR SCOPE AND METHODS

To compare these dimensions of politics systematically across Southeast Asia, and so develop broader theoretical and comparative insights, we embarked on an ambitiously large-scale, comprehensive, cross-national study of patronage politics in Southeast Asia. Since 2012, the authors have collaborated with large teams of researchers, totaling more than 200 persons, across the countries on which we focus. Much of our research effort centered on national and regional elections, notably national elections in Malaysia in 2013, Indonesia in 2014, Singapore in 2015, the Philippines in 2016, and Timor-Leste in 2017, as well as state elections in Sarawak, Malaysia (2016), and regional government (2017) and village elections (2018) in Indonesia. (Our original plan to include elections in Thailand, slated to occur in 2015, was – as noted earlier – scuttled by the 2014 coup.) In each case, we organized large teams of researchers who, either individually or in pairs or small groups, closely observed campaigning in one particular constituency. In the Philippines in 2016, for example, fifty researchers conducted research in forty-five locations spread through the archipelago.

Following each of these elections, our research partners submitted write-ups of interviews and campaign events along with reports presenting their observations and analysis. We then organized workshops at which subsets of the researchers presented draft papers on the constituencies they had studied, drawing on the data (detailed later) that they had submitted to our secure repository. We collectively discussed overarching findings and subsequently published a selection of those papers in a series of edited volumes that, together with other project-related publications (by these researchers and/or ourselves), provide a detailed series of case studies of the local dynamics of patronage politics in the countries concerned. The resulting works highlight both national patterns and subnational variation (for the edited volumes see Weiss 2014; Aspinall and Sukmajati 2016; Weiss and Puyok 2017; Hicken, Aspinall, and

Weiss 2019). When we cite chapters in these volumes throughout this book, we are thus drawing on our broader collaborative project – but doing so in a way that appropriately credits our research partners who gathered and initially analyzed the findings in question.

Given the scale of our collaboration, this part of our approach might best be characterized as a form of *extensive* political ethnography. While ethnographic research typically involves a researcher staying in one place for many months, our effort involved scores of researchers – many of whom originated from, lived in, or otherwise had local ties to the places they were researching – engaging in shorter bursts (generally two to six weeks) of intensive research. Through this method we were able collectively to interview over 3,000 political candidates, campaigners, party functionaries, vote-brokers, and other political actors;[10] to observe (and collect field reports on) thousands of campaign events; and to shadow hundreds of candidates and campaign workers as they planned and conducted their campaigns and interacted with voters. Along with our collaborators, we ourselves took advantage of many opportunities to observe distribution of patronage as it was happening and to discuss these strategies in detail with practitioners. Many of the candidates and campaigners with whom we interacted were very frank, generously explaining or allowing us to observe their activities, including some – such as distribution of cash payments to individual voters – that were formally illegal. These experiences provided us with insight into the strategic logic and cultural scaffolding underpinning patronage strategies. By spreading our efforts so widely, we were able to build a picture of how patronage strategies varied both among and within countries – across regions, parties, and candidates. This large-scale collective effort is the foundation of the analysis we provide in this book.

We supplemented these qualitative research methods with both national and local surveys (see Table 1.2 and Appendix A). In all, we commissioned four nationally representative surveys of citizens (two in Malaysia, and one each in Indonesia and the Philippines). These were conducted between four and six weeks after the national election in each country (and after the Sarawak elections in the case of one of the Malaysian polls) and asked respondents a wide range of questions about their political preferences, voting behavior, and social backgrounds and engagements, as well as their knowledge of, participation in, and attitudes toward various forms of patronage politics. The Indonesian and Philippines surveys were face-to-face, while the Malaysian surveys used telephone polling; we conducted all surveys in partnership with well-known political polling organizations in each country. In order to reduce social-desirability bias, we incorporated survey experiments that, by randomly assigning respondents to treatment and control groups when asking them about

---

[10] Given our supply-side focus, our research plan targeted candidates and party/campaign workers who might dispense patronage, rather than voters who might demand and/or receive it.

TABLE 1.2. *Data sources*

	Malaysia	Indonesia	Philippines
Elections	2013 general election 2016 state election	2014 legislative elections 2017 regional elections 2018 village elections	2013 midterm election 2016 general elections
Field research	60+ researchers (2013) 6 researchers (2016)	50 researchers (2014) 24 researchers (2017) 22 researchers (2018)	50 researchers (2016)
National surveys[a]	2013 & 2016	2014	2016
Additional surveys		Local broker and voter surveys, 2014	Local broker and voter surveys, 2016
Other data		Broker/voter focus group discussions, 2014 Brokers' voter lists, 2014	Broker/voter focus group discussions, 2016 Brokers' voter lists, 2016

[a] All listed national surveys included survey experiments.

certain sensitive issues (such as vote buying), allowed us to ascertain the extent of such practices without fear that respondents' reluctance to discuss them would taint our results. In addition, we have also been immensely helped by being able to draw on historical and recent data from surveys conducted by our research partners, Indikator Politik Indonesia, Pulse Asia (Philippines), and the Merdeka Center (Malaysia).

We also conducted two sets of local voter and broker surveys in the region, taking advantage of connections we and our research teams forged with candidates in national elections in Indonesia (2014) and the Philippines (2016). In both countries, some candidates were willing to share with us the lists of brokers and voters they had compiled in order to conduct vote-buying operations. We sampled Indonesian brokers from lists that eleven campaign teams in Central Java provided to us. These included candidates for national, provincial, and district seats. Our broker survey was more focused in the Philippines: we surveyed all the brokers working for two candidates for municipal office in two municipalities in the Bicol region. Because of the need to build up relationships of trust with candidates in order to convince them to share their lists, we were unable to select candidates randomly from across each country. (It is especially worth noting that the Indonesian lists were from the highly competitive legislative elections rather than less closely fought local executive races, a point we return to later.) Even so, our surveys – the first such conducted in either country – point to highly suggestive differences in brokerage structures and broker behavior between the two countries. We also paired these broker surveys with voter surveys specific to those constituencies. (Appendix A describes each survey in more detail.)

Given this combination of extensive political ethnography and surveys, including survey experiments, we have strong confidence in the validity of our findings. Moreover, we expect our findings to resonate beyond Southeast Asia, as earlier studies of the patron-client ties in the region did in previous decades (e.g., though the weakness of political parties is a common theme in many democracies, our study is one of relatively few that investigates patronage and clientelism in settings with weak parties[11]). Our comparative approach allows us to explore dynamics across three very distinct patterns of political networks, as well as identify the major types of patronage associated with each. As we have no reason to expect the electoral mobilization regimes we sketch to represent either a unique or an exhaustive set of types, we leave it to others to adopt our framework and method in investigating other cases. (We do, however, offer speculative first steps in that direction in our concluding chapter.)

Finally, having presented our approach and scope, it is equally important to emphasize at the outset what is *not* at the center of our analysis. Two elements stand out. First, we are most interested in the disbursement of patronage and not its sources. We fully acknowledge the importance of studies that examine campaign finance and the corruption and cronyism that frequently accompany, reinforce, and enable patronage-based strategies (e.g., Brierley 2020, on the conditions under which bureaucrats facilitate politicians' rent-seeking; Gomez 2012, on parties' own corporate ventures; Kapur and Vaishnav 2018, on the industries and regulatory loopholes most useful to resource-seeking politicians; and Mietzner 2011, on illicit campaign fundraising at the local level). We touch on such matters, but ours is not a study that homes in on where parties and politicians obtain resources. Where possible, we seek to identify broad categories of funds – whether public or private, licit or illicit – and we contextualize our findings by positioning local actors within regional and nationwide structures, which helps to explain how they access resources. But we do not provide a detailed account of the political economy of campaign finance.

Second, nor is our primary focus the impact of different types of patronage or patronage networks on either the quality of service delivery or on broader political outcomes such as the quality of democracy, the nature of the political economy, and the like. We touch on such topics in our conclusion and see them as a natural progression from the present analysis, but in this study we largely limit ourselves to the components of patronage politics, how they work, and how and why they vary within and across countries.

---

[11] But see the excellent book by Muñoz (2019) on clientelism in Peru, where parties are likewise weak, as well as works by Novaes (2018) and Hilgers (2008).

THE STRUCTURE OF THE BOOK

We develop our arguments in the remainder of the book. In *Chapter 2*, we provide the historical-institutional underpinnings of our explanatory framework through a broad-brush survey (going back to the late colonial era) of state structures, party and electoral systems, and the scope for discretion across our three core cases. Like Martin Shefter (1994), we are interested in understanding the emergence of "constituencies for patronage" and how the sequencing and intertwined development of electoral politics and bureaucratic structures shape them. We trace the roots of each country's contemporary electoral mobilization regime back through time: in the Philippines, to the early twentieth century, when American colonial authorities introduced local elective posts and national legislative bodies prior to the establishment of a strong bureaucracy, enabling major elite families to create local political machines that could be nourished with ample resources derived from the national level; in Malaysia, to the transition to independence and the emergence of a party with a strong ethnic mission and ability to win national elections and subsequently subordinate the bureaucracy to its own patronage purposes; in Indonesia, to the long period of authoritarian rule between 1966 and 1998, when the country's rulers centralized patronage distribution within the civilian and military bureaucracy and marginalized political parties, leaving a legacy that contemporary elected officials still confront. Careful analysis of distinctive historical patterns of state formation, party development, and state–society relations as they have transformed over time, we demonstrate, is essential to understanding cross-national differences in patronage and the networks through which it flows. These legacies continue to be the starting point for comparative analysis – complemented, we emphasize, with close attention to (a) how incentives are shaped by the particular design of electoral systems; and (b) the degree to which politicians enjoy discretionary control over public funds. Chapter 2 also provides historical and political context that will be especially helpful for readers who are unfamiliar with Southeast Asia and our cases.

Chapter 3 then examines the three distinct types of networks used for patronage distribution and election campaigning in our primary countries: a party-based national patronage machine in Malaysia, local machines in the Philippines, and ad hoc patronage networks in Indonesia. In each case – albeit in different ways and with varying degrees of effectiveness – these networks play critical roles in helping politicians to recruit, organize, and reward their brokers; coordinate access to patronage; and manage campaign activities. A further common feature of these networks is their resemblance to the classic brokerage pyramid associated with clientelistic politics. On closer examination, however, we find they differ significantly in terms of their geographic scope and degree of institutionalization or permanence. The chapter extends the analysis introduced earlier, by considering how these distinct network types map onto the three major types of patronage to produce distinct electoral mobilization regimes, and demonstrates how differences across these regimes stem from historical antecedents and institutional environments.

In the next section of the book, we proceed to deeper examination of different forms of patronage found across our three primary and three secondary cases, drilling down into how they function and are organized. *Chapter 4* focuses on micro-particularism, most common across Indonesia and the Philippines but not entirely absent in Malaysia (especially East Malaysia). Micro-particularism, it will be recalled, involves money, goods, or services given out to individual voters and households in hopes of obtaining their electoral support, often but not exclusively at election time. The micro-particularistic practice given the greatest attention in the literature is cash handouts; our research confirms that candidates (at least those in the Philippines and Indonesia) devote major attention to how to distribute cash most effectively (both in terms of trying to influence voter behavior and minimizing leakage into the pockets of campaign staff). While we do not entirely eschew the term "vote buying," we emphasize that it often obscures other important objectives and dynamics of cash handouts: they are rarely straightforward market transactions, either in how the disbursement of money is expressed culturally or in their anticipated outcomes. These payments are generally not, in other words, contingent patronage – that is, material benefits provided with relative confidence or expectation of electoral support. Our research reveals that candidates find cash handouts most valuable as a means of signaling that they are serious contenders (a process we term "credibility buying") and protecting their presumed turf, recognizing that most voters being targeted have, at best, tenuous loyalties. By comparison, where we have strong parties, commanding deeper loyalties, we find comparatively less individual-level distribution.

In *Chapter 5*, we examine the type of patronage we find most consistently across our primary cases: what we call meso-particularism, but which is also commonly referred to as pork, club goods, or local public goods. There are at least four ways that candidates may find this form of collective patronage to be advantageous. First, candidates may view meso-particularism as a useful means of overcoming resource constraints, given the high cost of dispensing cash to a wide array of voters. (Recall from the start of this chapter the roughly USD200,000 budgeted for a small-town Philippine mayoral race.) Rare indeed is the candidate who can afford payments to a majority of voters in a constituency. Second, meso-particularism carries far less social stigma than does micro-particularism. Giving out cold cash, no matter how accepted it may be in practice, is not something that can be broadcast as an achievement; it is illegal in each of our core countries and widely condemned as a subversion of democratic practice. When candidates bestow small infrastructure projects and other club goods upon a community, in contrast, they have something to boast about. A third advantage of meso-particularism is that it represents an opportunity to provide benefits to voters throughout the electoral cycle and not just on the eve of elections. The fourth issue to consider is monitoring. Whereas micro-particularistic cash handouts present monitoring challenges, as noted earlier, some scholars have argued that club goods promote more efficient monitoring since they put the focus on groups of voters rather than on individuals. In the course of our research, however, we found that meso-particularism – like micro-particularism – rarely involves a clear quid pro quo. Rather, its main value is in buying credibility, protecting turf, and building a brand. The only time it can be viewed as contingent patronage is when candidates are able to deal with group leaders (e.g., lower-level politicians, religious leaders, or social-network leaders) who can reliably deliver their members' votes.

Chapter 6 focuses on macro-particularism, or the hijacking of programmatic policies. We begin by acknowledging that it is inherently difficult to draw a clear line between programmatic politics and patronage; in fact, as this chapter highlights, they readily intermingle, as when an individual politician claims that their individual intervention is critical to the delivery of a benefit to an individual or community (credit-claiming), when they actually do intervene to help a beneficiary access an entitlement (facilitation), or when they break up a program into bite-sized chunks and allocate them according to political criteria (morselization). Our main case-study countries present different mixes of these forms, though all three countries display all three types. For example, hijacking under party-dominated systems such as Malaysia's centers, not surprisingly, on parties, and involves a great deal of credit-claiming and facilitation but relatively little morselization: a party-in-power that runs an entrenched and coordinated patronage system sees little benefit in providing significant leeway to individual politicians when allocating benefits. Morselization, the most permissive type of hijacking from the standpoint of local politicians, tends to be especially common in political systems that provide a high degree of discretion to individual politicians over resource distribution: the Philippines, with its system of deeply entrenched local machines, arguably exemplifies a political system founded on the exercise of discretion, and, hence, morselization. Indonesia represents a mixed case: some politicians, notably regional government heads, enjoy considerable discretion in allocating resources, while legislators have been engaged in a constant, multi-fronted battle to expand their access to state resources throughout the post-Suharto period, still without much success. The relatively low levels of coordination among politicians when it comes to accessing state patronage, at least when compared to Malaysia and the Philippines, also constrains the extent of programmatic hijacking in Indonesia.

The book's third and final section examines how variations in social context modify and complicate the national patterns we identify in earlier chapters. *Chapter 7* focuses attention on categories of identity, notably ethnicity, religion, gender, and class, as they interact with patronage structures in our three core countries. We present a story of a rich multiplicity of *forms* of patronage politics across these categories, coexisting with underlying similarity in the *functions* of patronage politics. Politicians cater to a wide range of social identities, showing immense creativity when doing so (providing, for example,

Qur'ans and prayer mats for some communities and Bibles and prayer beads for others). But the underlying goal across our highly diverse, multiethnic, and multireligious contexts is fundamentally the same: to capture more votes using offers or promises of patronage. This instrumental process generally reinforces rather than erodes existing social identities (except those based on class, which clientelist politics tends to undermine by connecting lower-class recipients of patronage to higher-status dispensers of it). Even so, particularly where electoral systems encourage broadly inclusive strategies, patronage distribution regularly crosses identity-group boundaries and thus tends to bridge divides rather than promoting deeper within-group bonding.

In *Chapter 8*, our attention turns to variation at the subnational level. For all our previous focus on cross-national variation in patterns of patronage and types of networks, we emphasize here how our research reveals very considerable inter-regional variation *within* the major three countries. This range is especially apparent at two extremes, both of which the chapter addresses: locales where politicians rely more intensely on patronage, including by combining patronage strategies with coercion; and "islands of exception," generally urban areas, where programmatic appeals supplement or may even begin to supplant patronage politics. In explaining this subnational variation, at both extremes, we focus on three variables: the degree of concentration of control over economic and coercive resources, levels of capacity of local state institutions, and the relative autonomy and egalitarianism of local social networks. The particular mix of these three factors can provide politicians and citizens with options for escaping from the cycle of patronage politics, or it may deepen citizens' dependence on patronage and make them more vulnerable to predatory politicians. A focus on these three key variables thus helps us to explain major elements of subnational variation, including an intensification of patronage politics relative to the rest of the country (e.g., in East Malaysia and Papua), significantly higher levels of coercion (e.g., Mindanao), and urban reform movements that provide at least some modest shift toward a more programmatic basis for politics (e.g., Penang in Malaysia, Surabaya in Indonesia, and Naga City in the Philippines).

The book concludes in *Chapter 9*, first by reiterating our core arguments and contributions, then by exploring the potential extension of our framework to other cases, including the possibility of expanding our typology of electoral mobilization regimes. Next, reviewing the implications of our findings for democratic governance, we discuss the opportunities for and limits of reform measures with potential to curtail patronage politics and improve the quality of democracy, including electoral-system reform to help shift polities from a candidate-centric to a party-centric focus. Additional reforms are also important, whether promoting bureaucratic capacity and autonomy or creating a more level electoral playing field. Throughout, we do not hide our normative bias for democracy, as it is concern for improving the quality of democracy that motivated our study in the first place.

2

Historical and Institutional Foundations

States, Parties, Constituencies for Patronage, and Electoral Systems

In Chapter 1, we provided a broad overview of variation in patronage and political machines across the three countries that are central to this study. Recall that we identified three distinct *electoral mobilization regimes*: those based on party machines (Malaysia), local machines (Philippines), and ad hoc teams (Indonesia). In this chapter, we provide an overview of the historical and institutional contexts from which these regimes have emerged and within which they operate, laying the foundation for the chapters that follow. What follows is a story of both convergence and divergence. On the one hand, all three countries have developed strong and enduring "constituencies for patronage" (to borrow a term from Martin Shefter's pioneering 1994 analysis), with the concomitant subordination of forces committed to bureaucratic autonomy. On the other hand, the historical processes by which these patronage-oriented constituencies emerged vary enormously. These differences are foundational to our three distinct electoral mobilization regimes. As we shall demonstrate, careful examination of historical patterns of state formation, state–society relations, and political party development is critical to understanding the significant variations across our three core cases in patronage and the networks through which it flows.

As important as these historical legacies are to understanding contemporary patterns of patronage politics, our explanatory framework goes beyond the *longue durée* focus on "political parties and the state" that Shefter expounds. Supplementing his analysis of the *historical timing and sequencing of electoral mobilization*, we add careful attention to the specific *rules that govern electoral contestation*, that is, the choice of electoral institutions. This choice plays a critical role in molding the incentive structures within which parties, candidates, and voters operate, and helps to determine whether a polity will be relatively more party-centric or candidate-centric. As recent Indonesian experience attests, even small tweaks in electoral systems can have huge impacts on the magnitude, location, and character of patronage. As such, this chapter focuses both on the historical development of states and parties and on the scope and rules of electoral contestation. Together, they help us understand critical differences among electoral mobilization regimes.

Furthermore, the goal of much recent comparative scholarship on patronage and clientelism (for instance, in Latin America, Japan, or Africa) has been to shed light on the microfoundations of patronage politics, focusing in particular on the relationship between candidates and voters. As explained in Chapter 1, we see this relationship as just one element of much more expansive formal structures and informal networks that extend from the centers of power in the capital down to the village level. Of particular importance is elected officials' access to and discretion in distributing public sources of patronage. As with our attention to historical-institutional factors, we assert that understanding cross-national variation requires a wide lens of analysis. In other words, our analysis rests upon both broad territorial and broad temporal scope.[1]

We argue that robust constituencies for patronage developed along three distinct historical pathways, cultivating distinct electoral mobilization regimes. These pathways helped shape not only whether parties or politicians emerged as the primary players in patronage politics, but also who had access to public patronage resources (and in what quantity). They further shaped the viability and appeal of party- versus candidate-centered mobilization strategies. In the Philippines, early in the twentieth century, the establishment of local elective posts and national representative structures preceded the development of a strong bureaucracy. American colonials granted political power to a landed provincial elite, whose access to national-level resources allowed them to consolidate their local machines. In Indonesia, during the period of authoritarian rule under President Suharto (1966–98), regime leaders worked to build a strong state apparatus, creating a bureaucracy that could serve both the administrative and patronage goals of the state. Suharto simultaneously undermined the capacity and autonomy of Indonesian parties, excluding them from systematic access to patronage resources. Finally, in Malaysia, a dominant ruling coalition captured what had been a relatively capable, autonomous bureaucracy as independence approached in the mid-1950s and remade it into a source of and conduit for self-serving patronage.

Understanding this mix of colonial legacies and postcolonial disjunctures clarifies both our analytical starting point and the continuing trajectories of the three countries on which we focus. From that premise, and drawing on extensive field-research findings, we offer evidence through this volume that three factors are key to the shape and character of electoral mobilization regimes:

---

[1] As essential as we deem historical and institutional foundations, we are by no means claiming historical-institutional determinism. Critical junctures – including colonial foundations and postcolonial transitions – may set countries on particular paths, but these paths are not fixed (as we discuss further later in this chapter).

historical-institutional underpinnings, electoral rules, and the extent to which politicians exercise discretion over disbursement of public funds.

We begin by putting our three countries in regional context, particularly for the benefit of readers with little previous background on the diverse states of Southeast Asia. The core of the chapter then examines the historical and institutional trajectories that produced the distinct patterns of patronage politics found in these countries, beginning with the character of states and (generally nascent) political parties as they transitioned from late colonialism into the early postcolonial era. We then shift the lens to political party systems since independence, surveying, too, the critical role of electoral systems in shaping patterns of patronage. Again for the benefit of readers new to the region, we outline key periods of postindependence politics in Indonesia, the Philippines, and Malaysia, and the range of democratic, semi-democratic, and authoritarian structures they present. (Appendix B carries this survey further, outlining territorial structures of government and the extent of electoral contestation in each country.) We conclude the chapter by reviewing the argument undergirding our analysis. Throughout this chapter, as well as in Chapters 3–7, our attention is primarily on cross-national variation; it is in Chapter 8 that we probe more deeply into subnational variation *within* each country.

INDONESIA, MALAYSIA, AND THE PHILIPPINES IN REGIONAL CONTEXT

Southeast Asia has always been a region of great diversity: in social structure, religion, topography, and more. Particularly germane here are the historical legacies of distinct systems of colonial rule that Southeast Asia experienced: British (in present-day Brunei, Malaysia, Myanmar, and Singapore), French (Cambodia, Laos, and Vietnam), Dutch (Indonesia), Spanish followed by American (the Philippines), and Portuguese (Timor-Leste), alongside the success of Thailand (formerly Siam) in remaining formally independent of European colonial rule. Across the region, Japan's wartime imposition of its "Greater East Asian Co-Prosperity Sphere" also had highly varied impacts on national political dynamics. Unlike in Latin America, where we find broad similarities in the legacies of Iberian colonialism and in the wave of independence movements that swept the continent in the early decades of the nineteenth century, the Southeast Asian experience of colonization and decolonization is far more diverse across many dimensions. Whereas historians can speak of "Spanish America" as a coherent category, there is simply no analog for a Southeast Asian region whose modern polities have been shaped by such a mix of colonial powers.

Striking as well are these states' divergent paths to the postcolonial era: from protracted wars of independence that ousted the old order (as in Indonesia and especially Vietnam), to years of negotiations and carefully calibrated distancing

from the colonial power (as in Malaysia and Singapore), to negotiated arrangements in which the former colonial overlord retained substantial sway (most of
all in the Philippines). Rivalries of the global Cold War further influenced
postcolonial trajectories, shaping new alliance structures and becoming the
dominant lens for understanding (often preexisting) societal fissures. The wide
array of contemporary political systems exhibits additional diversity, including
military dominance, personalistic authoritarianism, Leninist party-states,
monarchical rule, electoral authoritarianism, variants of populism, and democratic structures facing varying degrees of challenge and promise. In sum, the
backdrop to our study of patronage and political machines features tremendous
variation in both societal and institutional starting points and in modern-day
political systems.

INITIAL FOUNDATIONS: BUREAUCRATIC COHERENCE VERSUS
THE LOGIC OF PATRONAGE

Inspired by Shefter's approach to the study of patronage politics, our analysis
begins with a focus on historical sequencing – in particular, of the development
of bureaucracies and of opportunities for mass political participation. Where
strong and independent bureaucracies precede the mobilization of a mass
electorate, as in the historical experience of Germany, Shefter (1994, 21–60)
argues, one should expect the predominance of a "constituency for bureaucratic autonomy." Such a constituency – typically drawn from forces within the
bureaucracy itself as well as allies within the political elite and wider middle
classes – can promote the development of a professional civil service able to
allocate resources impartially, effectively keeping patronage out of the hands of
elected officials. Where electoral mobilization precedes the emergence of relatively insulated bureaucracies, as in the historical experience of Italy, one
should anticipate a tendency toward the predominance of a "constituency for
patronage" (Shefter 1994, 21–60). That said, even in polities with well-
developed constituencies for bureaucratic autonomy, assaults on the integrity
of the state may stimulate stronger patterns of patronage politics. Conversely,
in countries in which patronage politicians capture bureaucracies from the
start, reformers may still be able to challenge well-entrenched forces of a
constituency for patronage – but any such effort would be an uphill battle.

   A second critical dichotomy Shefter presents is between "externally mobilized" versus "internally mobilized" political parties. The former, he explains,
are established by elites and activists *outside the regime* who lack access to
patronage and instead rely on ideological appeals in their quest for a mass
following. This roster includes European socialist parties and anti-colonial
nationalist parties (Shefter 1994, 30). "Internally mobilized" political parties,
by contrast, are those "founded by elites who occupy positions within the
prevailing regime and who undertake to mobilize a popular following behind

themselves in an effort either to gain control of the government or to secure their hold over it" (Shefter 1994, 30). These parties may base their support on patronage resources: among Shefter's examples is the Nacionalista Party in early twentieth-century Philippines, for which close collaboration with American colonial officials provided extraordinary opportunities to use state resources for electoral benefit. Sequence matters a great deal. Internally mobilized parties established *after* the emergence of bureaucratic systems strong enough "to resist the depredations of patronage-seeking politicians" may orient less toward patronage (Shefter 1994, 28; see also Hutchcroft and Rocamora 2012, 100–1).

Of the three distinct historical pathways to the emergence of constituencies for patronage examined in this chapter, only the Philippines fits neatly within Shefter's framework (with, broadly speaking, a historical trajectory resembling that of Italy). All three countries experienced high levels of patronage in the wake of independence, but only in Malaysia did a single ruling coalition enjoy an effective monopoly over access to government resources. In the Philippines and in early postcolonial Indonesia, by contrast, access to patronage fragmented among a range of claimants, including the array of local political machines in the former and rival political parties in the latter. Over time, the three patronage-oriented states each developed very different – but similarly well-entrenched – constituencies for patronage.

Before we delve more deeply into this history, however, it is important to highlight briefly the impact that a dominant constituency for patronage has on the polity as a whole. Critical to our framework is the degree of discretion politicians enjoy, conferring not only ready access to resources but also the ability to bend laws and administrative procedures to their particularistic benefit. As Shefter (1994, 27) explains, the distribution of patronage is frustrated when "government agencies are protected by civil service statutes and other general laws that specify how public benefits and burdens are to be distributed and that thereby *prevent politicians from intervening in the administrative process on a case-to-case basis*" (emphasis added). He cautions, however, that civil service statutes "are not self-enforcing" and can be undermined in the absence of protection from a "sufficiently powerful" constituency for bureaucratic autonomy (Shefter 1994, 28). Where such a constituency has never emerged in the first place, internally mobilized parties enjoy substantial access to patronage resources and thus have "every incentive to acquire popular support by distributing patronage to notables and politicians who have local followings" (Shefter 1994, 35–36). This practice becomes effectively self-perpetuating, he suggests, as such a party "will only be able to maintain itself in office by heeding the demands of the patronage-seeking politicians who are affiliated with it" (Shefter 1994, 29).

What are these patronage resources, and how are they obtained? As we have observed in our research, they may include control over appointments and promotions (to give jobs to supporters and to exert control over those already holding bureaucratic positions), ability to manipulate budgets (most obviously through discretionary pork), and the capacity to influence the implementation of laws and administrative procedures (and thus opportunistically to skew government policies).[2] Where politicians enjoy substantial discretion, they can be expected to access resources with which to curry electoral support. Notwithstanding these common features, patronage-oriented polities diverge considerably: in the types and degrees of discretion over resources that politicians enjoy, in the targets of patronage distribution (from micro- to meso- to macro-particularism), and in the character and relative strength of the constituency for patronage that allows these practices to thrive and endure. We turn now to how such distinct constituencies for patronage have emerged across our three primary cases.

Indonesia

Applying Shefter's framework to the colonial legacies of our three major cases, we find the strongest constituency for bureaucratic autonomy in the Netherlands East Indies. After the Dutch consolidated this vast archipelagic realm in the early twentieth century, colonial officials proceeded to develop a "single state apparatus," with standardized regulations and rotation of officials among regions (Cribb and Brown 1995, 7). The colonial state increased its capacity for "vertical penetration" across realms of activity, explains Benedict Anderson (1983, 478–80), with "a rapidly expanding officialdom" that "unfolded more according to its inner impulses than to any organized extra-state demands." The proportion of officials from the metropole relative to the size of the native population was nine times that of British India. Even so, Indonesian colonial subjects comprised a full 90 percent of the bureaucracy. Though there were strong vestiges of patrimonialism in the developing colonial state (Sutherland 1979), through the decades leading up to the Japanese occupation of the Indies in 1942, "an ever more centralized and streamlined colonial *beamtenstaat*" emerged (Anderson 1983, 491). Meanwhile, the powerful state apparatus provided few opportunities for societal input. The *Volksraad*, a small and only partially elected national legislative body, was restricted to an entirely advisory role. The major political parties of the time exemplify the challenges of external mobilization: the Partai Komunis Indonesia (PKI) was banned in the 1920s, while the Partai Nasional Indonesia (PNI) advocated independence and likewise faced severe repression from the late 1920s until 1942, eventually losing its capacity to mobilize a large following (Brown 2003, 129–37). Even

---

[2] Our focus here is on the public weal, but (as noted in Chapter 1) patronage resources also commonly derive from illicit activities (e.g., revenue from illegal gambling operations, drug trafficking, prostitution, gun-running, or kickbacks from contracts and licenses). This mix only reinforces the point, highlighting as it does the extent to which politicians may engage in illegal activities with relative impunity from the state (of which they are at least formally a part).

so, Indonesia's vigorous associational life took root in this period, especially in the religious sphere, with the impact of Islamic modernism prompting an efflorescence of religious reform and educational organizations that soon prompted equal vigor on the part of traditionalist Muslims and non-Muslims alike.

In the eight years preceding Indonesian independence at the end of 1949, the *beamtenstaat* collapsed throughout much of the archipelago. First came the trauma of three and a half years of Japanese occupation, with separate territorial jurisdictions across the formerly unified Netherlands East Indies, the sudden removal of the Dutch from the upper echelons of the bureaucracy, economic collapse, and (in the latter stages of the war) popular hatred of "a native officialdom increasingly regarded as quisling" (Anderson 1983, 480). Next came the struggle for independence, stretching from the end of World War II in 1945 through 1949. While the Dutch worked to piece back together the old colonial state (Anderson 1983, 481), the authority of a rival republican state "was limited, conditional and widely fluctuating from region to region and time to time" (Cribb and Brown 1995, 27). An explosion of associational life saw militias, parties, religious groups, unions, and organizations of all stripes suddenly emerging and contesting for a stake in the new political order. By 1950, the civil bureaucracy was in tatters as it faced potential new competition from disparate military forces emboldened by their role in the war for independence, and from a diverse range of parties, mass organizations, and other civilian groups. Indonesia had departed from its late colonial path of growing bureaucratic autonomy, unable to sustain these foundational patterns in the context of a jarring anti-colonial upheaval.

Thus comes the dramatic collapse of a constituency for bureaucratic autonomy, which is, in larger perspective, hardly surprising. The *beamtenstaat* of the Netherlands East Indies was the product of colonial absolutism; those of its subjects struggling to end colonial rule were generally disdainful of collaborationist Indonesian officials. The reemergence of a coherent bureaucracy came much later, in the wake of the army takeover in the mid-1960s, at which point civil servants became the major vehicle for the distribution of patronage rather than part of a strong constituency for bureaucratic autonomy.

The Philippines

As Dutch colonials were creating a *beamtenstaat* and tightly restricting electoral mobilization, their American counterparts in the Philippines were doing the opposite over the first four decades of the twentieth century.[3] After easily defeating the Spanish in 1898, leading into a grueling and protracted counterinsurgency war against forces seeking Philippine independence, the American

---

[3] The following discussion draws on both Hutchcroft (2000) and Hutchcroft and Rocamora (2012).

colonials set out on a path of "political tutelage" quite unlike the strategies being pursued by other contemporaneous colonial regimes. As Governor-General William Howard Taft took the helm of a newly created civilian government on July 4, 1901, a core goal of his "policy of attraction" was to win over both the *ilustrado* (educated) elite and a broader group of local *caciques* who had backed the revolutionary effort. With anti-imperialist sentiment still strong in the United States, Taft wanted to demonstrate not only that the war was coming to an end but also that the United States was grooming Filipinos for eventual self-government. A distinctly American playbook instilled patterns of patronage politics not entirely unlike those then prominent in many US localities. The colonial government rapidly expanded elective positions: from the municipal level in 1901, to the provincial level in 1902, to the creation of a national assembly in 1907. At the same time, Taft and his successors' tutelary project included active encouragement for the creation of collaborationist political parties, eventually bearing fruit in the form of the Nacionalista Party, mentioned earlier, which came to be dominated by politicians emerging from the provinces (Cullinane 2003, 167–71, 335–36).

As suffrage was limited to a tiny elite, the ultimate result of American colonial rule was neither democracy nor mass electoral participation but the creation of a "national oligarchy" (Anderson 1988, 11; Hutchcroft 1998, 22). Because a legislature of powerful provincial-elites-turned-national-politicos was in place prior to the development of a strong colonial bureaucracy, these elected officials quickly moved to assert particularistic control over the emerging political system.[4] The Americans were simultaneously taking initial steps to establish a meritocratic civil service, but a constituency for bureaucratic autonomy had not yet begun to consolidate ahead of the 1907 convening of the Philippine Assembly.[5] On the contrary, enormous pressures for patronage soon overwhelmed administrative structures and budgets.

After the end of the Taft era in 1913, opportunities for "patronage-seeking politicians" of the Nacionalista Party to control appointments and budgets became even more plentiful – with the creation of the Philippine Senate in 1916 and all the more with the 1918 establishment of a Council of State (through which an American governor-general shared executive authority with the House speaker and the Senate president). As the bureaucracy rapidly Filippinized, explains Anderson (1988, 12), "civil servants frequently owed their employment to legislator patrons, and up to the end of the American period the civilian machinery of state remained weak and divided." These

---

[4] Hutchcroft (2000, 298, fn. 28) offers an amendment to Shefter's framework, recommending a focus on "the impact of the introduction of representative institutions" rather than on mass suffrage, in light of major colonial-era restrictions on the franchise.

[5] In 1910, the former American head of the Civil Service Commission lamented the shortcomings of his efforts, given "the struggle against the coercive power of patronage" (quoted in Holmes 2019, 57).

legislators also took the opportunity to create a state-owned bank in 1916, loans from which (ultimately derived not just from government deposits but also, eventually, currency reserves in New York) became such a rich field for patrimonial plunder for well-connected agricultural families that the bank collapsed – in the process endangering the financial stability of both the colonial government and its currency (Hutchcroft 1998, 66–68). As the national bank went into reorganization in the early 1920s, a new source of riches emerged with the genesis of the congressional pork barrel in 1922. In that year, two-thirds of the appropriations for a Public Works Act were slush funds distributed by a joint Senate–House committee (Holmes 2019, 64). Both initiatives demonstrate the high degree of discretion that Filipino politicians enjoyed as a powerful constituency for patronage.

Although subsequent American governors-general tried to reassert executive authority, the greatest success in this regard came after former Senate president Manuel Quezon himself became president of the newly created Philippine Commonwealth in 1935. But Quezon's power was based most of all on his consummate skills as master of patronage politics, as he astutely played local political clans against each other. "The first Filipino politician with the power to integrate all levels of politics into a single system," explains McCoy (1989, 120), "Quezon once confessed to an aide that '90 percent' of his dealings with politicians involved the disposition of patronage."

Under the occupation, the Japanese abolished political parties and replaced them with a so-called mass party sponsored by the Philippine puppet government in Manila. But the Japanese occupiers struggled to control the national territory, challenged as they were by US-backed guerrilla armies as well as the Hukbalahap (the People's Anti-Japanese Army, based in Central Luzon and battling both foreign occupation and landlord oppression). The war brought enormous destruction to many parts of the Philippines, but the population widely hailed the returning Americans as liberators (in stark contrast to the Dutch in Indonesia). The Americans formally reestablished the Commonwealth government – even as the state apparatus, not unlike Manila itself, was in ruins. Elections were held in April 1946 and independence followed three months later on the 4th of July (just one year behind the schedule the United States had promised in the 1930s). The essential continuity of a planned, structured transition helped, too, to ensure that many of the old patterns of patronage politics would quickly reemerge from the ashes. Amid continuity, however, were elements of major change – including growing ideological challenges from below, an expanded electorate, and the widespread proliferation of guns (the latter creating fertile terrain for postwar bossism).

Malaysia

In British Malaya, a strong colonial bureaucratic officialdom remained in place through the middle of the twentieth century, setting the course for the postcolonial state. This situation provides a clear contrast both with Indonesia, where the *beamtenstaat* collapsed, and with the Philippines, where such an apparatus never took hold in the first place. As we will see, however, internally mobilized parties, motivated and sustained by a politically dominant social cleavage, tilted Malaysia toward patronage politics. This outcome seemingly runs contrary to Shefter's expectations, as a constituency for bureaucratic autonomy was unable to resist the growing dominance of a constituency for patronage.[6]

Our major initial focus is on what is today peninsular Malaysia. It bears mention that the names and contours of territories under British colonial rule were in considerable flux in the wake of World War II – leading up to the 1957 granting of independence to the Federation of Malaya (composed of peninsular Malaya minus Singapore) and, in 1963, to an expanded Malaysia (comprising the former Federation of Malaya plus Malaysian Borneo, and, very briefly, Singapore).

The British entered what is now Malaysia through the British East India Company, which, in the late eighteenth and early nineteenth centuries, acquired Penang, Malacca, and Singapore. In 1826, the three were conjoined as a single British government administrative unit known as the Straits Settlements. Private interests predominated much longer in what is now East Malaysia, as the adventurer James Brooke established a family dynasty of "White Rajas" in Sarawak from the 1840s; in subsequent decades, the British North Borneo Company gradually extended its control over what is now Sabah. Meanwhile, from its base in the Straits Settlements, the British government started to intervene more systematically in the interior of the peninsula. This process of colonial intrusion led to the establishment of the (four) Federated Malay States in 1896 and subsequent control over the (five) Unfederated Malay States by the early twentieth century. Thus, the British government fully consolidated its control over the peninsula, which became known as "British Malaya" before achieving independence in 1957 as the Federation of Malaya (Andaya and Andaya 2001). Sabah and Sarawak had become British Crown colonies in 1946. They then joined in with the federal state of Malaysia when it was created in 1963 with fourteen states (twelve on the peninsula plus two in East Malaysia), reduced by one with the departure of Singapore in 1965.

Although the sultans of the Unfederated Malay States led state-level civil services (joined by British advisors), the Federated Malay States had a single, consolidated civil service as of 1896 (Yeo 1982, 18–23). Until independence in 1957, British staff dominated the Malayan Civil Service (MCS) that later came to form the core of the postcolonial state. These British administrators, explains Harold Crouch (1996, 131), were supplemented by "small numbers of

---

[6] In fairness, Shefter was not examining the impacts on the state apparatus of such momentous political shifts as transitions from colonialism.

Malays" who could rise up from an ethnically restricted Malay Administrative Service (MAS) that had been established early in the twentieth century as a "clerical and lower-level administrative" adjunct to the MCS. It was only after World War II that Malays could enter the MCS in larger numbers, and the fuller Malayanization of the civil service came well after independence (unlike the bureaucracy of the nearby US colony, substantially Filipinized half a century earlier). "Only in the late 1960s," notes Crouch (1996, 131), "were the British officials finally replaced." Meanwhile, the British excluded Chinese and Indians from the MCS until the 1950s, despite their comprising about half the Malayan population at independence; even after they were admitted, at least 80 percent of total civil-service positions were reserved for Malays.

As the British gradually edged toward departure, their primary negotiating partner was a multiethnic political coalition known as the Alliance, led by the United Malays National Organisation (UMNO) and including the Malayan Chinese Association (MCA) and Malayan Indian Congress (MIC). UMNO was formed in 1946, *before* Malaya's first general election in 1955 and independence in 1957, but *after* the establishment of a relatively strong bureaucracy. Driving UMNO was a powerful sense of mission: to benefit a particular ethnic group – the Malays. Toward that end, it cultivated a mass base. With its origins in an array of Malay-ethnic organizations, the party took root in heavily Malay rural areas. Its leadership remained largely aristocratic – UMNO's first "commoner" prime minister assumed office only in 1981 – but civil servants (especially teachers) and traditional local authorities dominated among the rank-and-file into the 1980s. By this point businesspeople and professionals, themselves largely products of UMNO-led programs to foster a Malay middle class, had assumed greater prominence (Weiss 2020c, 58–59).[7]

UMNO did not begin as an internally mobilized party, but its goal very clearly was to become one as quickly as possible. Based on Shefter's insights, we might expect this sequencing to favor a constituency for bureaucratic autonomy; after all, the internally mobilized party and mass enfranchisement came after the colonial-era emergence of a robust bureaucracy, and one that was absent a strong patrimonial element. Moreover, the Malayan Emergency (1948–60), a counterinsurgency campaign that substantially deepened the reach of the state at the local level, both demonstrated and heightened bureaucratic capacity (Weiss 2020a, 516). UMNO's drive to assert its dominance, however, slowly but surely eroded the autonomy of the Malaysian bureaucracy, trumping what we might expect merely on the basis of historical sequencing. Arising in the late colonial years, UMNO especially, but also its Alliance partners, mobilized internally through the state apparatus as soon as the British began incrementally to hand over power. The British policy of favoring Malays

---

[7] As late as 1981, schoolteachers still constituted a plurality (40 percent) of delegates to UMNO general assemblies; their share then declined precipitously (Funston 2016, 54).

over Chinese and Indians provided UMNO with a clear advantage relative to its Alliance partners: UMNO commanded unrivaled support among the mass of Malay voters, including among civil servants specifically, so UMNO and its core constituents benefited symbiotically with Malayanization and the expansion of ministries and agencies. Although the prior existence of a strong bureaucracy "diminished the space for patronage jobs" in the early postindependence years (Weiss 2020c, 71), the tide had started to turn by the late 1960s. As we will discuss later, this was when the largely UMNO-controlled state began to preside over a massive expansion in public-sector employment.

UMNO's determination to exert control over the state becomes especially clear when one examines trends at the subnational level. Even before it had substantial financial resources, UMNO built a strong party machine, penetrating the countryside where most Malays lived. With a colonial legacy of "hobbled local authorities" (Weiss 2020c, 71), lacking the fiscal capacity to deliver essential services, the UMNO leadership saw a postindependence opportunity to fill the void with its own machine and so extend its political influence downward. This effort came most dramatically with the abolition of local elections in the early 1960s, as posts on city, municipal, and district councils came to be filled instead via appointment by state-level officials, amplifying the latter's role in local affairs. To an increasing degree, as state governments favored local party leaders and other loyalists, "party offices came to serve as access points to state resources and programs" (Weiss 2020c, 71–73). The logic of patronage thus emerged very strongly at the local level, carefully orchestrated from the center by a ruling coalition of parties that had quickly and deftly shifted from external mobilization when they formed in the 1940s to internal mobilization in the lead-up to, but most dramatically after, independence in 1957.

PARTIES AND ELECTORAL INSTITUTIONS FROM INDEPENDENCE TO THE PRESENT

We have seen clear instances earlier, across all our three cases, of how mutually constitutive the historical development of states and parties may be. As we proceed further into the postcolonial era – still remaining for now at a high level of cross-national generalization – we give more focused attention to the character of both these countries' party systems and their means of organizing elections. These postwar political histories together reinforce the point that patronage can thrive not only in democratic but also in semi-democratic and authoritarian systems.

As we noted in Chapter 1, and as we elaborate upon later, parties' roles vary dramatically across our three primary cases in both their institutional strength and their centrality to patronage distribution. Parties are principal political actors in Malaysia and the most important dispensers of patronage.

Indonesia's party and candidate registration rules ensure that national parties play an important gatekeeping role, although recent changes to the electoral system have tilted the system in a candidate-centric direction. In the Philippines, local political machines thoroughly overshadow national political parties. Overall, party structures and ideological foundations have greater coherence in Malaysia, followed by Indonesia and then (by some distance) the Philippines.

In our analysis, three major factors have had the greatest impact on the character of political parties in each country: the historical evolution of party development, the social roots of political parties, and the electoral institutions states have chosen. We discuss each in turn to understand not only why we find varyingly focused and organized parties but also why parties take on such different roles in electoral mobilization across our cases.

First, drawing on Shefter and as already explained earlier, parties are shaped historically by their relationship to the state and the degree to which they are internally or externally mobilized, that is, whether they have access to state patronage resources or are obliged to develop other types of appeals. The second major factor homes in on the social roots of political parties, specifically the connection between societal cleavages and party-system formation. A massive literature details the connection between social divisions and identities, on the one hand, and political parties, on the other. Classic accounts, such as that by Seymour Martin Lipset and Stein Rokkan (1967), see parties as expressing the interests of key social groups. Their seminal analysis of the historical development of European parties focuses on four key cleavages (center vs. periphery, church vs. state, urban vs. rural interests, and labor vs. capital) as parties emerged at critical historical junctures in modern European history. To the extent that such cleavages are politically salient at key moments, Lipset and Rokkan (1967, 14, 52–54) argue, clashes among antagonistic groups can trigger the aggregation of interests and identities in parties. The advent of mass democracy then "freezes" cleavages into enduring party alignments. More recent accounts incline toward a constructivist approach, highlighting the capacity of electoral competition not merely to reflect existing social divisions but also to reshape them, with voters and politicians alike strategically orienting around identity categories most likely to ensure victory (and, thus, most likely to deliver access to patronage). This dynamic can make certain identities more politically salient than others (see, e.g., Chandra 2004; Posner 2005).

While concurring with scholars who emphasize the need to attend to the fungibility of societal cleavages, we nonetheless find Lipset and Rokkan's basic framework useful in examining how the relative salience of these cleavages can shape the character of contemporary political parties, mold their orientation to patronage, and, in particular, affect their capacity to endure and maintain coherence over time. Notably, we argue that the coherence of Malaysia's party-based system of patronage derives in large part from the close association of Malaysian parties with underlying ethnic and religious cleavages, and from the governing coalition's efforts over the decades to structure the state, and distribute resources, around those cleavages. In our other two cases, identity-based cleavages do less to structure patronage politics. It is common for political parties in the Philippines to span identity lines as they forge short-term alliances across the archipelago. Indonesia is an intermediate case, with some parties aspiring to represent particular identity-based (especially religious) constituencies, and others seeking a catchall appeal.

While these first two factors – the evolution and social roots of parties – are based on historical factors, and thus inherited, the third pertains to a matter over which contemporary political actors may have at least some measure of control: the choice of electoral system, by which we refer primarily but not exclusively to the formula used to convert votes to seats. The incentives different electoral systems present to politicians help to determine whether a political system is relatively more party-centric or candidate-centric, and whether parties themselves are oriented more to programmatic appeals or to patronage and clientelism (Hicken 2019a). As we shall see, electoral systems also help to shape the particular character and location of patronage as well as the networks through which it flows. We see this effect most sharply in Indonesia and the Philippines, where key features of electoral institutions combine to undermine the value and coherence of political parties. Yet in Malaysia, too, the electoral system has helped amplify and protect the electoral fortunes of the ruling coalition.[8] Notwithstanding an element of choice in the design of electoral systems, these systems also reflect historical legacies, including colonial inheritances and/or domestic power dynamics at the time they were established. Nor, as discussed further in Chapter 9, can we ignore how difficult it can be to change electoral systems. The choice of system inevitably favors some interests and not others, and any redesign process involves complex political dynamics (see Hicken 2019b).

Taking these three factors together, we can now trace how very different patterns of party politics and rules of electoral competition developed in each of our three countries. These patterns and rules gave rise to electoral mobilization regimes that, while sharing a basic orientation to patronage, differ greatly in terms of their degree of national coherence, the solidity of parties and other electoral vehicles, and the networks through which candidates deliver patronage to voters, among many other features.

---

[8] An additional feature of electoral institutions that affects coordination incentives is the timing of elections. For example, while Indonesian elections for legislative and local-executive offices have been on different calendars, in Malaysia and the Philippines, elections are simultaneous (the exceptions being barangay and youth council elections in the Philippines and some state elections in Malaysia). Simultaneous elections help to align the incentives of candidates from across tiers and allow them to coordinate efforts, either within strong parties, in the case of Malaysia, or via locally anchored alliances in the Philippines.

Indonesia

We can divide postcolonial Indonesian political history into four distinct periods: an initial stage of democratic structures under a parliamentary system, extending into the latter part of the 1950s; an authoritarian but pluralistic government under Sukarno, dubbed "Guided Democracy," from the late 1950s to mid-1960s; Suharto's authoritarian "New Order," from 1966 to 1998; and post-Suharto democratic structures from 1998 to the present.

By the time of independence in late 1949, the once-vaunted *beamtenstaat* had effectively collapsed, leaving no strong center of power. "It could easily be argued," writes Anderson (1983, 482, emphasis in original), "that parliamentary democracy survived in Indonesia until about 1957 simply because *no other form of regime was possible.*" Unlike UMNO, which played a lead role in negotiating the transition to independence with the British, the PNI had not played a dominant role in the struggle for independence; rather, the protracted effort had involved a wide range of societal forces with very different visions for the future of the country. Political parties representing different societal currents soon found themselves in pitched contention, first as part of a nonelected, multiparty parliament and then in a 1955 election when four parties split roughly 80 percent of the vote:[9] the PNI with 22 percent, followed in close succession by Masyumi (the party of "modernist" Islam, strongest in urban Java and the outer islands), Nahdlatul Ulama (NU, the party of "traditionalist" Islam, with its base in rural Java),[10] and the Indonesian Communist Party (PKI). Cooperating in multiparty cabinets, the major parties, apart from the PKI, controlled particular ministries and were able to funnel funds downward to their respective constituencies. At the time of independence, only the PNI was deeply rooted in the bureaucracy and could be considered internally mobilized, though the other major parties strove to mimic the PNI's position (e.g., Nahdlatul Ulama secured control over the Ministry of Religion and used its resources to benefit its members). Meanwhile, hostility from Islamic and other anti-communist parties left the PKI mostly excluded from national government.

At a time of "hypertrophic" swelling of the bureaucracy – eight-fold growth in the number of ministries between 1945 and 1965, and ten-fold expansion in

---

[9] The electoral system in 1955 was closed-list proportional representation with high district magnitude (i.e., a large number of seats within each district). This system allowed each of the four major parties to gain substantial representation, notwithstanding a highly fragmented party system.

[10] Nearly nine out of ten Indonesians profess Islam (and are overwhelmingly Sunni). A shrinking segment often described as "nominal Muslims" combine Islam with syncretic beliefs including Javanese mysticism. So-called "traditionalist" Muslims, strongest in rural eastern and central Java, combine scripturalism with practices (e.g. veneration of saints) that "modernist" Muslims – who seek to purify the faith by putting emphasis squarely on original textual sources – deem heterodox. Modernists have historically been prevalent in urban business communities in West Java, Sumatra, Sulawesi, and elsewhere.

the number of civil servants from 1940 to 1968 – parties found in the bureau-cracy opportunity to create "jobs for the boys" (Emmerson 1978, 87–89), using state patronage to cultivate their respective societal bases. The four major parties' general (but not complete) dominance of Indonesian political life fostered a system of "pillared clientelism" that stretched from Jakarta all the way downward to villages throughout the archipelago (Aspinall 2013). That parties largely controlled access to the bureaucracy fostered "an over-all increase in the dependence of civil servants on party leaders" (Feith 1962, 123, 366). In Shefter's terms, a constituency for patronage clearly dominated.

The perpetuation of parliamentary democracy could well have resulted in "a strongly party-focused system of patronage politics in contemporary Indonesia" (Aspinall and Berenschot 2019, 47). But several factors rendered the parliamentary system fragile: short-lived cabinets, the steady growth of the PKI (which other parties viewed as a major threat), an army keen to assert greater influence, and the weak fiscal basis of the state. Parties themselves "showed an often bewildering mix of obduracy and opportunism," explain Cribb and Brown (1995, 51), divided over matters of conviction (of importance to their respective social bases) while at the same time showing the capacity for "cynical and unprincipled horse-trading … over access to government posts and funds." Sukarno's 1957 declaration of martial law, in response to rebel-lions in the outer islands that were in part associated with Masyumi, effectively brought an end to parliamentary democracy.

Then, in 1959, Sukarno entrenched his so-called Guided Democracy after dissolving parliament and returning to the presidential-focused and more authoritarian 1945 constitution. While political parties no longer had an electoral function, they continued to have access to state resources and consid-erable latitude for popular mobilization – all, that is, except for Masyumi and the Indonesian Socialist Party, which Sukarno banned in 1960 for their role in the regional rebellions. Societal tensions mounted across several fronts in the 1960s, and Sukarno was unable to contain the escalating contention between an increasingly assertive PKI and an increasingly restless and empowered army (Crouch 1988, 43–96). His authoritarian government collapsed in the cata-clysm and mass killings of 1965–66, when the army and their anti-communist civilian allies targeted the PKI and its supporters.

This brief survey makes clear the enormous disjuncture between the *beam-tenstaat* of the late colonial era and the political dynamics of postindependence Indonesia, not only in terms of the character of the state but also the mobiliza-tion of societal actors and the central role of parties in national political life. The fall of Sukarno and the establishment of Suharto's New Order brought another momentous shift. As Anderson notes, the subsequent influx of foreign resources, assisted by surging oil revenues, "allowed Suharto to build, over the course of the 1970s, the most powerful state in Indonesia since Dutch colonial times." Whereas Anderson (1983, 488–89) portrays the New Order as "the strengthening of the state-qua-state," it should more correctly be viewed as a state in which a strongly patrimonial logic drove bureaucratic performance and national policy alike (Crouch 1979). And while the New Order led to the emergence of the first reasonably coherent bureaucracy since the colonial era, this same bureaucracy was also the primary vehicle for the distribution of patronage. Although the military accorded the bureaucracy a central role, it was by no means a polity with a strong constituency for bureaucratic autonomy. Rather, *contra* Shefter, a constituency for patronage emerged in a military-dominated polity, where both parties and politicians were generally supine but the bureaucracy was coherent.

The New Order thoroughly reshaped the relationship between the state and political parties. Particularly germane for our purposes was the reversal of the 1950s trend toward a system of party-focused patronage distribution. The new military-dominated authoritarian government instead pursued policies that systematically marginalized parties. In the early 1970s, Suharto and his generals forcibly amalgamated two major rival Islamic parties (NU and the surviving elements of Masyumi), as well as two smaller Islamic parties, into the Development Unity Party (PPP) – the name of which significantly lacked any reference to religion. They also created the Indonesian Democracy Party (PDI) by combining the PNI with several minor Christian and nationalist parties. Critically, however, the regime did what it could to sever the links between these parties and the social organizations and identities that had underpinned the vitality of the 1950s party system. Although important remnants of the associational pluralism of Indonesian society – especially in the religious sphere – survived through the New Order period, religious and other organizations were now increasingly delinked from party life (in striking contrast to Malaysia, where such linkages have persisted through the postindependence era).

Even as the New Order intervened heavily in the internal affairs of PPP and PDI, it also established its own vehicle, Golkar. Technically not even referred to as a political party, Golkar effectively served as "the electoral manifestation of the military and civilian bureaucracy" (Aspinall and Berenschot 2019, 55) and "existed wherever there was a government office, which included every village in the country" (Liddle 1999, 43). Organized along corporatist lines, Golkar aimed to exert central state control over a wide range of societal groups, foreclosing their mobilization by other political forces. This catchment included all state officials, who were required to shift to Golkar (and to move way from what had been, for many, historical linkages to PNI). This was part of the state edict of *monoloyalitas*, or singular loyalty (Emmerson 1978, 105–10; Liddle 1999, 42).

But beyond military dominance, central control, and suppression of political parties, the authoritarian New Order also relied heavily on the dispensing of patronage. Patronage served the specific interests of government leaders in ways that went far beyond its use as a tool of the state-qua-state. Indeed, officials could brand patronage as coming from Suharto himself, as with infrastructure programs and national revenue-sharing initiatives known as

"Inpres" or *Instruksi Presiden* (Malley 1999, 80). Unlike in the 1950s, the bureaucracy now took charge of distributing patronage; in addition, the timing of the handouts was often unrelated to the quest for electoral support and the range of beneficiaries was much narrower, focused largely on "senior military officers, civil servants, businesspeople, and other notables whose support was needed to maintain stability" (Aspinall and Berenschot 2019, 43).

While elections continued every five years – proclaimed, in Orwellian fashion, to be "festivals of democracy" – Golkar's victory was never in doubt. Nor was Suharto's regular reelection, not least given the high proportion of appointive posts in the assembly that chose the president. The only mystery was the precise percentage of votes that Golkar received, within an electoral environment that gave little scope for the assertion of local concerns. As in 1955, the electoral system was closed-list proportional representation with large district magnitude; unlike in 1955, the rules restricted voter choice to the three entities that remained standing after the restructuring of parties in the early 1970s (Golkar, PPP, and PDI). It was the duty of all civil servants, including village heads, to turn out the vote for Golkar (Liddle 1999, 41). Officials who failed to deliver could be punished, and their communities could miss out on development projects and grants.

Suharto's fall in 1998, and the subsequent transition to democratic structures, again brought monumental change to Indonesian politics – including, in 1999, the country's first free-and-fair elections since 1955. Across this gap of more than four decades, however, were initial elements of continuity. While the New Order systematically undermined many societal cleavages, some reemerged, albeit in modified form, in its wake. As Andreas Ufen (2013, 44–47) explains, "[T]he new party system seemed to be structured by some of the same cleavages that had marked party politics in the 1950s." For example, new parties aligned with modernist and traditionalist Islam emerged, while the largely nominally Muslim or non-Muslim constituency of the PNI gravitated toward the Partai Demokrasi Indonesia–Perjuangan (Indonesian Democracy Party–Struggle, PDI–P), headed by Sukarno's daughter, Megawati Soekarnoputri.

This alignment with societal cleavages never entirely disappeared (Fossati 2019), but it began to dissipate for three reasons. One was the rise of so-called presidentialist parties, such as the Partai Demokrat, associated with President Susilo Bambang Yudhoyono (2004–14). All these electoral vehicles had some linkage to the New Order's Golkar and were inclined to mimic Golkar's "catchall" appeals. By their very nature, these parties were less connected to any particular societal cleavage and were usually built around and subservient to specific presidential contenders. A second factor was the rise of cartel-like arrangements among parties. What Dan Slater called "collusive democracy" (2004) made it harder to differentiate among parties on policy grounds. In other words, the extent to which parties not only engaged in similar types of rent-seeking behavior but also colluded with one another in government blurred their linkages to distinct societal cleavages. Third, decades of crony capitalism under the New Order had produced a range of powerful national business conglomerates and local oligarchies, whose members were happy to trade financial support for political influence. This pattern, combined with the absence of an effective party and campaign financing system, made the parties less accountable to their respective societal bases, and more responsive to the needs of oligarchs (Mietzner 2020). In sum, the initial strong linkage between parties and social cleavages, apparent in the 1999 election and never entirely eliminated thereafter, began to weaken through the first decade after the fall of Suharto.

Viewed over a longer time frame, one enduring legacy of the New Order was thus a continuing autonomy, and to some degree, fragmentation, of associational life: a large number of religious and other organizations persisted from earlier periods in Indonesian history, and many new groups emerged in the aftermath of democratization. However, most lack structured links with political parties, unlike during the period of pillared clientelism in the 1950s. The continuing disarticulation, and complexity, of associational life, we shall see in later chapters, opened up a vast zone for bargaining over collective and other benefits between group leaders and politicians.

Aspinall and Berenschot (2019, 43–45) emphasize an additional authoritarian legacy, in the New Order's "institutionalizing and even universalizing patronage distribution as a key feature of the political order." Citizens in general were well aware "that civil servants, and their political bosses and allies, had been milking the state for private benefit" and "now wanted to take their share." As in Suharto's time, the bureaucracy retained considerable control over patronage distribution; while elected politicians gradually gained greater control, parties remained relatively marginal to the process. The major change came with a shift "from elite to massified clientelism."

Yet authoritarian legacies, they emphasize, only partially explain the continuing marginalization of parties. After the first post-authoritarian election in 1999, it seemed as if parties might reassume a central role in the patronage system. Indeed, more than a decade into the post-Suharto transition, certain parties were replicating patterns of the 1950s by exploiting government ministries for party gain. Two significant changes in electoral arrangements, however, undermined the centrality of parties: the introduction of direct elections of national and regional executives, starting in 2004 and 2005, and, especially, the shift from a closed- to an open-list proportional representation electoral system for legislative elections (started in 2004 and fully effective by 2014), such that voters could now vote for individual candidates on party lists. These changes each had a profound effect on the locus of patronage politics. Prior to these reforms, patronage distribution was primarily an intra-elite affair carried out among party leaders, bureaucrats, and other elites; after the reforms, "ordinary voters were a prime target of patronage" (Aspinall and Berenschot 2019, 64, 68).

This outcome might seem, at first glance, virtuous: advocates of the new system had, after all, wanted to make politicians more responsive to voters. In fact, we view the shift to an open-list system as a failed experiment, given its numerous negative impacts on the character of Indonesian democracy: broadening the scope of money politics at the grassroots (amply documented in the chapters that follow), intensifying incentives for engaging in corruption to finance patronage-oriented campaigns, shifting legislators' focus from national policy concerns to providing patronage projects in their respective constituencies, and strengthening personal networks at the expense of party institutions (Aspinall 2014a, 108–9).

In sum, as could have been anticipated, the open-list system induced a transformative shift from a party-centric to a candidate-centric system. While this change has led some to speak of the "Philippinization" of Indonesian politics (Ufen 2006, 16), remaining institutional safeguards have prevented a similar diminution in the importance of parties. These checks include prohibitions on independent candidates in legislative elections, strict registration requirements for parties, prohibitions on local or regional parties (with a special exception for the province of Aceh), rules that prevent party-switching by individual legislators, and steady increases in electoral thresholds to prevent the proliferation of small parties (Aspinall 2019, 107).

Moreover, the alignment of parties with broad social constituencies never entirely disappeared: PKB (National Awakening Party), for example, derives virtually all its support from the traditionalist Muslims of Nahdladtul Ulama; PDI–P (the successor party to the PNI) gains strongest support among syncretist Muslims in Java and non-Muslim minorities. Recent years have offered clear indications that old social cleavages still count. This resurgence was most apparent in the 2019 presidential elections, which saw polarization between two camps: defenders of pluralism associated with incumbent President Joko Widodo (known as Jokowi) versus proponents of Islamism associated with former General Prabowo Subianto. Strong momentum emerging from the grassroots bolstered both camps, pushing the presidential campaigns in antagonistic directions (Aspinall and Mietzner 2019). While the key issues in 2019 were in many ways distinct from those of earlier post-Suharto elections, the impact of polarization was to mobilize some (but certainly not all) of the same societal cleavages apparent in the 1999 and even the 1955 elections: Jokowi drew substantial support from both NU and PDI–P, and Prabowo enjoyed the backing of voters in regions where Masyumi had been strong in 1955. (Not surprisingly, catchall parties scattered across both sides of the divide, though most attached themselves to the patronage-rich incumbent.) Yet interparty collusion quickly reemerged in the wake of the election, with Prabowo joining Jokowi's cabinet as defense minister.

Importantly, survey data reveal a dramatic downward trend in the share of post-Suharto voters who feel themselves close to a political party: from 86 percent in 1999, 58 percent in 2004, 21 percent in 2009, and 15 percent in 2014, to a mere 10 percent in 2019 (Muhtadi 2019, 21). While parties continue to enjoy a major gatekeeping role, one can safely conclude that they have failed miserably in the task of endearing themselves to voters. This failure can be attributed to the factors explained earlier, notably the weakening of parties' alignment with social cleavages and their relative marginalization as the country shifted to more candidate-centric electoral arrangements (and, hence, grassroots electoral patronage).

Indonesia's experience thus leads us into a discussion of the nearby archipelago to the northeast, home to weak and generally incoherent political parties that rarely exhibit significant linkages to major societal cleavages. Far from being entirely static, however, Philippine political parties are arguably even weaker and more incoherent today than they were in the early years after independence.

The Philippines

Philippine political history since the end of World War II can also be divided into four major periods: the elite-dominated democracy of the postindependence years, 1946–72; the martial law dictatorship of Ferdinand Marcos, 1972–86; a return to elite-dominated democracy from 1986 to 2016; and illiberal democracy under populist *supremo* Rodrigo Duterte from 2016 to 2022.

Unlike the dramatic break that marked Indonesia's transition from colonialism, the Philippines' transition evinced a high degree of continuity. With independence, the constitution that had been drafted under the direction of incoming Commonwealth President Quezon in 1935 returned as the fundamental law of the land. Closer examination, however, reveals several important political shifts between the heyday of the Commonwealth in the late 1930s and the political system that reemerged postwar.[11] These include, first, threats from below: after Congress excluded members of the leftist Democratic Alliance from its ranks in 1946, the wartime Hukbalahap reconsolidated itself and went into full-scale rebellion against the government. Their fight peaked between 1949 and 1951, until the government was able to turn the tide through US-backed counterinsurgency measures (Kerkvliet 1977, 238).

Second was the continuing expansion of the electorate. Before the war, as the result of various reforms, the number of registered voters had steadily risen from 105,000 in 1907 to 2.27 million in 1940, three years after women gained the suffrage. After the war, this tally increased further, to 4.7 million voters in 1951 (after the removal of a constitutional literacy requirement), 7.8 million in 1959, and 10.5 million in 1969.

---

[11] Much of the following draws on Hutchcroft and Rocamora (2012), supplemented by Hicken, Hutchcroft, Weiss, and Aspinall (2019).

Third, the war had engendered a large number of intra-elite disputes. Most importantly, the 1944 death in exile of President Quezon left no single figure able to take on his role as the country's undisputed leader, triggering a split in the ranks of the formerly predominant Nacionalista Party (NP).[12] The 1946 election pitted two former Quezon associates against one another, with the victor running under the banner of the newly formed Liberal Party (LP). For the next twenty-six years, until the declaration of martial law in 1972, these two parties alternated in power.

Fourth and finally, the protracted wartime guerrilla struggles against Japanese occupation had encouraged the rampant proliferation of firearms (Mojares 1986, 28), providing a ready armory for emergent local bosses with "warlord armies." In the boss-ridden province of Cavite, for example, an estimated 3,000–5,000 firearms left behind by Japanese and guerrilla forces helped to fuel "an upsurge in violence and criminality" after the war. At election time, "relying on strong-arm tactics to guarantee his hold on provincial power," Governor Dominador Camerino supplemented his extensive private army (comprised in large part of municipal police forces controlled by loyal mayors) with bandits who suspiciously "escaped" from the provincial jail. As he used his coercive resources to deliver votes for LP allies at the national level, Camerino "was amply rewarded ... with patronage and special favors" from above (Sidel 1993, 127–28). Many other parts of the archipelago demonstrated similar patterns, fusing coercion with local bossism (see McCoy 1993; Sidel 1999).

Within this changed context, the Philippines remained very much a patronage-oriented polity. Given the country's long history of electoral clientelism, it is not surprising that postindependence Philippine politics provided the inspiration for Carl Landé's pioneering 1965 analysis of patron-client relations. Foundational to the system Landé described were family-based factions at the municipal level, led by local elite patrons (often landowners), who used a variety of means – kinship, personal ties, and offers of jobs, services, and other favors – to build a clientele composed of those from lower social classes. The goal was to build a strong vote bank, which local elites could then exchange for favors and projects from national-level politicians:

Strong local roots and an ability to survive independently give the factions considerable bargaining power in their dealings with the national parties. ... The result is a functional interdependence of local, provincial, and national leaders which promotes a close articulation of each level of party organization with those above and below it. (Landé 1965, 24, 82)

---

[12] Not unlike Malaysia's UMNO, but two decades earlier, Quezon's NP assumed control of the state in the process of decolonization and used it as a font of patronage resources. But whereas UMNO could count on inter-ethnic competition to encourage unity and support, the NP lacked so clear a unifying leitmotif. It fractured soon after the death of its leader.

In addition to being merely "loose federations ... among independent factional leaders in the provinces," the two rival parties were also indistinguishable on ideological grounds (Landé 1965, 24). This similarity led, unsurprisingly, to rampant levels of party-switching (known in the Philippines as "turncoatism") between the NP and the LP. Landé lamented the wastefulness of a system based on "[t]he competition of identical parties," lacking in programmatic vision and "[seeking] to maintain themselves in power through the haphazard, particularistic distribution of largesse to all individuals or groups." Yet he concludes that "these shortcomings" were tolerable, as the price of avoiding "dictatorial rule." The country, in his view, had "a lively yet remarkably united and stable democracy" (Landé 1965, 120). Landé identified, moreover, at least one further redeeming characteristic of the Philippine party system: how it "exerts a unifying influence by bringing together within each party politicians from all of the islands, whose diverse constituencies include voters representing every type of crop, industry, and linguistic or religious minority" (Landé 1965, 40). This characterization highlights the very weak connection between societal cleavages and political party alignments in early postindependence Philippines.

The electoral system helped produce this outcome. At the time, the Philippines used single-member district plurality (SMDP) or "winner take all" rules for the House, and a multi-member plurality system for the Senate (with the country comprising a single district). SMDP predictably helped to nurture the two-party system, as third-party challenges were disadvantaged by lack of access to patronage, inability to field local election inspectors, and legal exclusion both from House and Senate electoral tribunals and the powerful bicameral Commission on Appointments (Wurfel 1988, 94). The ability of presidents to run for reelection (i.e., the presence of an incumbent) encouraged candidates down the ticket to align behind the president or one major challenger; the concurrence of presidential and legislative elections, moreover, helped to reduce the number of political parties (Hicken 2009, 169). Meanwhile, the fact that the Senate was elected by a single archipelago-wide constituency helped encourage the two major parties' national orientation.

The elite dominance that Benedict Anderson (1988, 16) describes as "cacique democracy" had its "full heyday" in the period 1954 through 1972, when "the oligarchy faced no serious domestic challenges." Its genius, Anderson writes, was its capacity to "[disperse] power horizontally, while concentrating it vertically." This horizontal dispersal of power, he explains, drew "a partial veil over" the vertical concentration of power (Anderson 1988, 31). Put somewhat differently, the democratic structures of this period provided a convenient system by which power could rotate at the top without effective participation of those below.[13] The very substantial power of the president,

---

[13] And because political participation was mediated through local leaders, the two political parties did not even bother to cultivate a mass base, as UMNO did in Malaysia. See Landé (1965), 69–70.

explains Thompson (1995, 19, 23–24), made presidential succession "a crucial but fragile rule of the political game." Both parties were internally mobilized, but – in part due to American refereeing of the system – they were willing to take turns at the trough.

Ferdinand Marcos, elected president in 1965, pushed the limits of this rule until he broke it entirely in 1972. Unlike his predecessors, who busted the budget only in election years, Marcos "ran deficits even in off years to fund a massive infrastructure program that was parceled out for maximum political advantage" (Thompson 1995, 34–35). He augmented the Philippine presidency's already enormous budgetary powers with new discretionary funds that he could distribute directly to officials at the *barrio* level for "community projects." As Arthur Alan Shantz (1972, 148) explains, the Marcos administration "sought to broaden the flow of resources and executive contacts beneath the congressmen and into the municipalities, minimizing its dependence upon the political brokers in the legislative branch who have historically proven to be such a disappointment to incumbent presidents seeking reelection." Marcos became the first president to win reelection when, in 1969, he raided the public treasury and thereby hastened the arrival of a major balance-of-payments crisis. Grumbled his defeated opponent, "[We were] out-gooned, out-gunned, and out-gold" (Abueva 1970, 62).

Chafing at the 1935 constitution's two-term limit, Marcos declared martial law in 1972. The US supported the country's authoritarian turn with sizeable increases in grants and loans – in exchange for which Marcos provided continued unhampered access to its important military bases (Wurfel 1988, 184–91). Benedict Anderson (1988, 20) colorfully describes the resulting concentration of power:

> From one point of view, Don Ferdinand can be seen as the Master Cacique or Master Warlord, in that he pushed the destructive logic of the old order to its natural conclusion. In place of dozens of privatized "security guards," a single privatized National Constabulary; in place of personal armies, a personal Army; instead of pliable local judges, a client Supreme Court; instead of myriad pocket and rotten boroughs, a pocket or rotten country, managed by cronies, hitmen, and flunkies.

The absence of elections, combined with Marcos's monopoly of political power, left pre-martial law political parties severely weakened. Marcos had no allegiance to the Nacionalista Party on whose ticket he won the presidency in 1965 after a last-minute switch from the Liberal Party; neither did he show any inclination for creating a new type of highly institutionalized ruling party, such as Golkar in Suharto's Indonesia. It was not until 1978, in preparation for elections to the long-promised Interim National Assembly, that the Marcos dictatorship launched its own ruling party, the Kilusang Bagong Lipunan (KBL, or New Society Movement). Rhetoric of a "new society" notwithstanding, the old, informal patronage politics of the pre-martial law years remained the fundamental basis of the KBL.

The emergence of the KBL represented a major, albeit temporary, break from pre-martial law patterns. To a far greater extent than any Philippine president since Manuel Quezon and his Nacionalista Party in the 1930s, Marcos and his KBL masterfully centralized patronage resources. Throughout much of the country, politicians flocked to the Marcos political machine for the benefits that it could dispense (Thompson 1995, 60, 76). Local officials, whom the regime could replace at will, were particularly anxious to join the ruling party. The earlier "close articulation" Landé described of national, provincial, and local politics endured, but the balance of power tilted decisively in favor of the national. Significantly, however, even Marcos could not attempt a full-scale assault on local power; he was able to restructure and rechannel, but not undermine, the influence of clan-based factions in the provinces (McCoy 1993, 17–18). Moreover, to a degree unprecedented in Philippine history, the ruling *family* lorded over all formal political institutions, the ruling *party* included. Finally, there was considerable overlap between the structures of the ruling party and the crony abuses that defined the essential character of the Marcos dictatorship.

The electoral exercises of the late 1970s and early 1980s saw the emergence of new elite-led political parties to challenge the KBL. However, Marcos's major challenge came from an entirely new type of ideologically driven (and externally mobilized) party: the Communist Party of the Philippines (CPP). The CPP played a leading role in opposing the dictatorship but then chose to boycott the January 1986 snap elections that Marcos called in response to US pressure. At a critical juncture, the moderate opposition won the day – and installed a decidedly elite form of democracy once again.

The key opposition figure was Corazon Aquino, who entered politics after the assassination of her husband, opposition leader Benigno S. Aquino, Jr., in 1983. Her core goal was to restore the democratic structures and freedoms that had been in place prior to 1972; with those structures came the return of strong local clans, many of which soon reestablished their private armies. Unlike Golkar after the fall of Suharto, the KBL soon disintegrated. A multiparty system replaced the prior stable two-party system, one indicator of which is the large number of parties contesting the five post-Marcos presidential elections. Since 1987, a total of eighteen parties or coalitions of parties have put up candidates; three additional candidates have run as independents (see Casiple 2019, 113–16; Hutchcroft 2019a, 15). Neither the NP nor the LP recovered their previous stature, although the latter has had the most consistent presence in post-1986 presidential races and one of its candidates – Corazon's son, Benigno S. Aquino III – served as president between 2010 and 2016.

While the number of parties multiplied in the post-Marcos period, they emerged weaker than they had been before martial law. As in Indonesia, elements of the electoral system contribute to parties' fragility and incoherence, and encourage candidate-centric rather than party-centric behavior. But the four most important of these elements differ from those found in

Indonesia.[14] First, a multi-member plurality system (MPS), in which voters select as many candidates as there are seats available and those with the highest tallies win, is used to elect nearly 80 percent of the 18,000 electoral posts filled every three years – including the twenty-four members of the Philippine Senate as well as all members of provincial, city, and municipal councils. As Nico Ravanilla (2019, 171) explains, "Given that MPS fosters competition among co-partisans, and winning elections is all about building a personalized network of support, candidates have very little incentive to coordinate campaigns and policy stances along party lines." Second, presidents and vice presidents (as well as governors/vice governors and mayors/vice mayors) are elected separately rather than on joint tickets. Not surprisingly, this regularly breeds conflict between executives and vice-executives from the national level downward. Third, the Philippines has a very unusual party-list system for electing 20 percent of its House of Representatives. (Elections for the other 80 percent of seats continue to be through the same single-member district plurality system used prior to martial law.) This system is distinguished most of all by a three-seat ceiling that not only violates the principle of proportionality but also leads to a large number of small and ineffectual parties – an average of more than twenty-five between 1998 and 2016 (Teehankee 2019, 157). Fourth and finally, term limits further undermine politicians' incentives to invest in party building. Particularly important is the post-1986 imposition of a single (six-year) term limit on the presidency. This rule contributes to "less party discipline, more factionalism, and to a larger number of short-lived parties" (Hicken 2014, 322).

The election of Rodrigo Duterte in 2016 marked the end of the thirty-year dispensation that had been in place since the fall of Marcos. In its place came an illiberal democracy (Thompson 2019) that adopted much of the playbook of other populist governments, including removal of restrictions on executive power, erosion of civil liberties, and attacks on media freedom (Kenny, Hawkins, and Ruth 2016). Duterte's new style of presidential leadership combined reliance on patronage politics with both charismatic appeals and threats of coercion – the credibility of the latter greatly enhanced by government-sanctioned killings of thousands of alleged drug users and dealers. Unlike some other populists, however, Duterte has displayed little interest in popular mobilization and has not pursued a consistent party-building strategy. Immediately after he won the presidency came the usual postelection stampede of turn-coatism: while the PDP–LABAN[15] party under whose banner Duterte ran won only three seats in the House of Representatives, it soon claimed 93, supplemented by alliances that produced a supermajority (Hicken 2017, 41).

---

[14] The following draws on Hicken (2019a, 39) and Hutchcroft (2019a, 10–11).

[15] The merger of two leading parties forged in the struggle against the dictatorship created Partido Demokratiko Pilipino–Lakas ng Bayan, or Philippine Democratic Party–Strength of the Nation in 1984 (Casiple 2019, 112–13). Its origins, however, had largely been forgotten by the time it was revived to serve as Duterte's vehicle for the presidency.

Despite PDP–LABAN's success, however, Duterte paid it little heed. Other political vehicles soon rivaled PDP–LABAN from within the administration itself: first an early aborted attempt to build a cadre-based movement that would bypass local political clans (dubbed Kilusang Pagbabago, or Movement for Change) and then a national coalition that actively courted local political clans (called Hugpong ng Pagbabago, or Contingent for Change). Notwithstanding his new populist leadership style, therefore, Duterte has maintained the country's long tradition of weak and incoherent parties.

Stepping back to observe the broad historical sweep, we can see across these four distinct postwar periods two constant features of the Philippines political system: the permeability of the bureaucracy and the weakness of political parties. Politicians and their allies have commonly enjoyed direct access to state resources, exerted significant influence over bureaucratic decisions, and generally exercised an impressive degree of discretion over the distribution of patronage. Quite unlike Malaysia, to which we shall now turn, these political actors do not exercise their substantial control over patronage resources through stable partisan channels.

Malaysia

For over six decades after independence in 1957, Malaysian politics had an extraordinary degree of continuity under the dominance of the same coalition of ethnically based parties – known initially as the Alliance, as discussed earlier, and then since 1973 as the Barisan Nasional (National Front, BN). While the core parties are UMNO, the MCA, and the MIC, the BN added other partners, including state-based parties from Sabah and Sarawak. The dominance of this single longstanding coalition, however, experienced two principal disjunctures. The first came with postelection riots in 1969, after which the ruling coalition reorganized as the BN and oriented itself even more forcefully to the promotion of Malay welfare. UMNO supremacy within the now-expanded ruling coalition heightened, while the MCA lost much of its bargaining power. The second major disjuncture came with the May 2018 elections, when opposition forces formed the government for the first time in the country's history. Tenuous from the outset, however, that Pakatan Harapan (Alliance of Hope, PH) government collapsed in late February 2020. As discussed further later, neither the short-lived PH government nor the even shakier coalitional arrangements that brought UMNO back to power in PH's wake can begin to rival the original BN's enduring political weight.

UMNO, whose early postwar founding we described briefly earlier, stands out as the paradigmatic national patronage party in Southeast Asia. The names of UMNO and its core partners make clear the high degree of alignment between parties and societal cleavages, at least for the three major ethnic groups. The ethnic categories the British put in place prevail still: 69.6 percent are in the broad category of *Bumiputera* (literally "sons of the soil," including

Malays as well as smaller peninsular and East Malaysian indigenous groups), while 22.6 percent are Chinese and 6.8 percent are Indian. All Malays are, per norm and law, Muslim, the religion of 61.3 percent of the population.[16] Particularly for the Malay-Muslim majority, therefore, ethnicity and religion correspond very closely; ethnicity has historically coincided closely, too, with occupation and socioeconomic class in Malaysia. Affirmative-action policies, initiated in the colonial era and greatly expanded as of the early 1970s, have sought to reduce or eliminate that association, particularly by cultivating a Malay urban, entrepreneurial middle class – yet, as we explain later, the fact that ethnic preferences are such natural partisan lures has done more to transform the overlay of ethnicity with class (with many Malays now being state-, and seemingly UMNO-dependent, capitalists rather than farmers) than to eliminate it.

Indeed, it is this enduring identity and popular base, we argue, that has made the "communal" (ethnicity-based) party the core channel for patronage – a role that UMNO's internal mobilization made possible. In comparative perspective, the centralized disbursement of patronage through the party, rather than through local notables, political families, or individual politicians, stands out. In contrast to the fragmented pattern of locally rooted political families found in the Philippines, and the overshadowing of elected politicians by a dominant state bureaucracy found in Indonesia, the strong sense of ethnic mission that drove UMNO from before the transition to independence lent coherence to its party-building efforts and to its endeavor to capture and hold the state. Confidence in the stability of its voter base, which an ethnic or religious premise may especially enable (Birnir 2007), allowed UMNO to institutionalize not just as a party but also as a governing system. As UMNO's strong party machine put down deep roots in the predominantly Malay countryside, it adopted an approach that was "basically traditional, feudal, conservative, and religious."[17] UMNO expanded by establishing and nurturing branches in every Malay village, building a party machine that, even today, remains enormous in scope (as we discuss further in Chapter 3).

Malaysia's first-past-the-post electoral system, with single-member districts – the system used continuously at the federal, state, and initially local levels[18] – amplified UMNO and Alliance dominance. Malaysia's electoral rules, like those of majoritarian systems generally, encouraged centripetal coalition arrangements. As Donald Horowitz (2014, 9–10) describes, UMNO turned to correspondingly centrist Chinese and Indian partners prior to independence, when the party needed non-Malay votes to best a charismatic challenger.

---

[16] Department of Statistics Malaysia, www.dosm.gov.my (accessed July 27, 2020).

[17] Interview, former UMNO MP and minister, July 28, 2015, Kuala Lumpur.

[18] Sarawak and Sabah delayed introducing direct elections of state and federal legislators (instead selecting state legislators from among district councilors and federal MPs from among state legislators) until 1967 in Sabah and 1970 in Sarawak (Loh 2005, 75–78; Aeria 2005, 118–21).

The three Alliance partners saw mutual advantage in pooling votes, being "squeezed between Malay and non-Malay extremists on the flanks." "Electoral exigencies," in short, "induced politicians to behave in ways that could attract votes from both sides of a very contentious ethnic divide," even when seemingly against the interests of the subordinate partners (Horowitz 2014, 10). Over time, UMNO exaggerated its own advantage – vis-à-vis challengers, but also its own coalition partners – including (though not only) through successive redelineation exercises, which combined both malapportionment and gerrymandering. The result is an electoral system that has given increasingly disproportionate weight to rural (overwhelmingly Malay and other Bumiputera) votes at the expense of "cracked and packed" opposition-leaning districts (Weiss 2020c, 110–11) and regularly allowed the ruling coalition to turn a modest majority of votes into a supermajority of seats, or even to win with a popular-vote deficit. An increasingly Malay electorate, given differential birthrates, has compounded UMNO's "first-mover advantage" in being able to set the rules of the system in which it competes (Templeman 2012).

As UMNO entrenched itself in power, the lines between party and state apparatus blurred. After all, UMNO was the party that, with its much smaller partners, captured and then recrafted the early postcolonial state, and the party that could present itself as the (still genuinely popular) champion of the ethnic group favored politically since British days. This blurring deepened in the 1970s, when the UMNO-led state moved to expand and homogenize the civil service with the extension of preferential policies for Malays. A swollen federal civil service – the largest, proportionate to population, in the region – has comprised over 10 percent of the labor force since 1990, growing by nearly one-quarter from 2000 to 2009 alone (Woo 2015, 230, 232). Yet the Chinese share of civil-service positions declined from 18.8 percent in 1970 to a mere 6 percent in 2009; the Indian share declined in the same period from 15.7 percent to 4.3 percent. Reflecting how internalized that bias had become, fewer than 3 percent of applicants in 2011 were Chinese or Indian (Woo 2015, 229–30, 234). The issue in Malaysia is thus less a party-loyalty test for recruitment to the civil service than the UMNO-dominated government's normative reinforcement, codified in policies, of a (corruption-prone) "Malay agenda" within the civil service (Hunter 2019). Of course, this agenda aligns with that of the party. Given this symbiosis, after ousting UMNO in 2018, the Pakatan government complained of some civil servants being, as one politician judiciously put it, "bound by ties of friendships ... [with] members of the previous administration" (Bernama 2019).

Even beyond civil-service bloat, UMNO used its dominance of the state to become the primary source of patronage for rural Malay voters. Explains Jesudason (1999, 139), the party's strategy in the 1960s reflected a pork-barrel logic. "State patronage," he notes,

took the form of providing access to land for underemployed Malay agriculturists, supporting prices for rice production, subsidizing re-planting schemes in cash crops for smallholder farmers, and pouring in development funds, especially in UMNO-controlled constituencies, for road construction, electrification, and the building of mosques.

UMNO's control of the state has given it an unmatched advantage in providing such benefits.

Even so, some externally organized parties formed even prior to the Alliance parties – most importantly, the Malayan Communist Party (MCP), which was initially launched in 1930 out of the former South Seas Communist Party. It first took up arms in opposition to the wartime Japanese occupation, and then, as of 1948, against the returned British colonial government – which formally banned the party that year. The MCP thus faced constricted opportunities to pursue constitutional struggle, despite its official postwar policy promoting such a pathway (Weiss 2020a, 515). (Not unlike in the postwar Philippines, excluding the left from parliamentary politics allowed no obvious channel apart from insurgency.) Anxious to preserve substantial British economic holdings after Malayan independence, the British in 1948 launched the anti-communist Emergency against the MCP. The counterinsurgency campaign continued until 1960 – three years after independence. Testament to the strong coincidence of social cleavages and political parties, even the MCP, which was a firmly ideologically driven party, had a strong ethnic base in the Chinese community. Indeed, the state's ability to conflate "Chinese" with "communist" in public rhetoric throughout and after the Emergency had a substantial impact on the configuration of postindependence parties, delegitimating left-wing or class-based appeals and validating communalized, capitalist ones, thus helping to consolidate BN dominance (Weiss 2020a). Although 1960 marked the end of any significant threat from the insurgency, the government continued to find anti-communist and anti-socialist rhetoric "a useful foil to legitimate a strong state and a society concertedly depoliticised … and organised communally" (Weiss 2020a, 517). The extension of many of the internal security provisions the British put in place, including constraints on party registration and campaign activities, backed up that discourse.[19]

These controls, coupled with UMNO's command of resources, have served also to hamstring other parties that organized externally as of the 1950s–60s or subsequently; first the Alliance and then Barisan Nasional have vigorously protected their broad middle ground from encroachment by other parties. The Democratic Action Party (DAP), for instance – successor to Singapore's People's Action Party after the latter exited Malaysia – struggles still with being branded as "Chinese chauvinist" or too far left. On the opposite flank, Parti Islam

---

[19] It was not until 1989 that the MCP formally surrendered to the Malaysian government. While the latter finally repealed the 1960 Internal Security Act in 2011, the "entrenched logic of security through extraordinary powers has persisted." Special police powers directed against "loosely defined, including specifically political, threats," represent "a holdover from Cold War-era efforts" (Weiss 2020a, 522).

seMalaysia (PAS) courts Malay voters with piety and the moral value of "simplicity" or "moderation" (*kesederhanaan*) to validate its comparative penury and that of Kelantan state, its stronghold, which the BN federal government starved of resources. At other times (including following the dislocations of 1969 and 2018), PAS has joined forces with UMNO or other parties, anxious to obtain a toehold on federal power and to gain access to the resources that come with it. When opposition parties have captured state-level governments, they, too, have tended toward patronage politics, regardless of their core ideology, not least to win over voters whose self-interest otherwise lies with the BN.

Over time, UMNO therefore came to define its mission not only as defending and promoting Malay culture, including Islam, but also as promoting Malay economic and social interests. This is evidenced in efforts to improve the Malay community's welfare, education, and business opportunities vis-à-vis the more economically prosperous Chinese minority. This welfarist orientation became especially apparent in the wake of the 1969 riots, most of all with the 1971 adoption of the New Economic Policy (NEP). This policy framework entailed significant state intervention in the economy, with various positive-discrimination and redistributive schemes that were readily turned to clientelistic purposes (Gomez 2012; Gomez 2014; Funston 2016, 44–48; Jomo and Gomez 2000). With Malaysia's making the transition to middle-income economic status, and with many Malays' moving to urban areas and taking up professional and private-sector employment, the party supplemented its rural patronage strategy with approaches that made "UMNO protection and patronage ... vital for the creation of the new urban clientele of businessmen and corporate men" (Jesudason 1999, 140). At the same time, "it used the bureaucracy for partisan political purposes, and engaged directly in business on a massive scale" (Funston 2016, 11–12).

Attendant changes included rapid growth in the bureaucracy, as noted earlier, offering even more opportunities particularly for Malays. Bureaucratic and patronage constituencies overlapped and aligned: as the Malay share of civil service positions rose, the bureaucracy assimilated a "political rationale" that obviated blatant partisan intervention (Washida 2019, 76). The state, too, assumed the role of "trustee" for Bumiputera, investing on their behalf through trust agencies aimed at building up the community's wealth. As the state divested itself of public enterprises in the 1990s, it gave first dibs both to these trust agencies and to UMNO-linked investors, including those holding assets on the party's behalf (Weiss 2020c, 123).

UMNO's engagement in business increased the stock of patronage resources available to the party, especially for incorporating newly socially mobile Malay elites. By the 1980s, an "UMNOputera" (a play on Bumiputera) economic elite, owing its wealth to UMNO policies, had emerged. Both party and state office offered extensive access to rents, which, in turn, provided new opportunities for corruption. The rapid expansion of patronage programs also served to put the spotlight on an order increasingly skewed along communal lines; as these programs spanned domains from higher education access, to housing support, to small-business assistance, they alleviated public irritation with increasingly open corruption and abuse of public funds – at least among Malay voters who benefited most from these generous schemes. The culmination of this dynamic came with the unusually self-aggrandizing Prime Minister Najib Razak in the 2010s, as frustration with corruption and perception of a plausible alternative combined to propel the BN to an electoral loss in May 2018. As the former BN chief for Penang state explained, lamenting the coalition's loss in 2018: despite his party's efforts to "push up the number of major projects" they proffered during the campaign, the BN's "tainted image" from corruption at the national level undermined voters' trust that they would deliver.[20] This was, as noted earlier, the first-ever successful challenge to the ruling coalition's dominance at the federal level.

Replacing the BN was Pakatan Harapan (PH), a coalition of parties that were at least ostensibly more programmatic and oriented to fighting corruption. Comprising PH were ideologically non-communal parties (even if they were nonetheless prone toward an ethnic skew in membership) – Parti Keadilan Rakyat (People's Justice Party, PKR), the DAP, and Parti Amanah Negara (National Trust Party, Amanah) – as well as the Malay-communal Parti Pribumi Bersatu Malaysia (Malaysian United Indigenous Party, Bersatu). The last was launched and helmed by former UMNO Prime Minister Mahathir Mohamad, who once again assumed the premiership in 2018. Pakatan Harapan was not immune to the benefits of state capture; even prior to gaining control at the federal level, the component parties, individually or in a somewhat different coalition, had curried favor through strategically deployed state-level resources (in ways we detail in chapters to come). Moreover, what tipped the scales toward PH in 2018, especially among nonurban and Malay voters, was a vote *against* Najib that supplemented the coalition's not quite sufficient pro-reform constituency. After assuming office, PH rhetoric and policies revealed the coalition's reluctance to alienate a Malay constituency considered crucial to the coalition's continued electoral success. It would have been excessively risky for PH to attempt a substantial rebalancing of the pro-Malay state apparatus by, for instance, reframing affirmative action to be need-based instead of race-based. Similarly hazardous would have been an excessively aggressive effort to downsize the bloated, overwhelmingly Bumiputera civil service.

Indeed, claims that PH had been insufficiently attentive to the needs and status of Malay-Muslims offered validation for what was essentially a parliamentary coup in early 2020, spurred in large part both by pushback against efforts to curb patronage and by individual leaders' irreconcilable ambitions. While Mahathir proved reluctant to make good on a promise to stand down after a prescribed period, his designated successor and rivals in the coalition champed at the bit. After a series of twists and turns, former BN Deputy Prime

---

[20] Interview, January 3, 2015, George Town.

Minister and PH Home Minister Muhyiddin Yassin became prime minister. Muhyiddin's "Malay unity" coalition was able to secure a perilously slim majority comprised of not just his own Bersatu (minus Mahathir and a clutch of loyalists) but also patronage-oriented UMNO, its BN partners, and the Islamist PAS, together with mostly Bumiputera party blocs from Sabah and Sarawak. Collectively, their implicit promise was a reconstitution of the old BN logic of rule and a robust reconfirmation of the state's commitment to benefitting Malaysia's ethnoreligious majority. Muhyiddin's administration, in turn, folded under pressure in August 2021. The new government that came to power hardly differed, except that UMNO was now back at the helm.

Although Pakatan Harapan had promised to reform Malaysia's electoral system and other key components of Malaysia's institutional framework – which might have encouraged new electoral and outreach strategies – the government collapsed before it could do so. Discussion of possible electoral-system changes, including introduction of proportional representation or a mixed-member system, continued after the fall of PH, but with little traction. For that reason, we might consider the 2018–20 interregnum as marking merely a change of leaders rather than the installation of a new government, let alone of a new electoral mobilization regime (Weiss 2020b).

Formed in the context of cleavage-defined, internally mobilized, and firmly dominant parties, Malaysia's institutional order makes it hard to exit from or firmly eschew patronage strategies. In contrast to the Philippines and Indonesia, these strategies are structured around relatively coherent parties with strong national reach. Even so, the fact that voters still vote for individual candidates gives candidates incentives for particularistic spending, whether from personal, party, or state funds. That said, Malaysian candidates and parties do clearly tend to favor macro- and meso- rather than micro-particularistic strategies. Parties' alignment with social organizations and communal categories, which inclines them to pursue bloc votes, encourages forms of patronage that benefit large groups of voters. The party-oriented nature of patronage distribution (and politics more generally) also makes party-provided macro- and meso-particularism a more feasible mobilization tool than in either Indonesia or the Philippines, where parties lack the organizational coherence to be able to coordinate the distribution of state-derived patronage on a national scale. Patronage politics thus remains firmly embedded at the heart of Malaysia's system but centered around well-institutionalized parties to an extent that clearly differentiates Malaysian political patterns from those found in either Indonesia or the Philippines.

CONCLUSION

As the foregoing discussion makes clear, colonial legacies intersect with post-colonial disjunctures in sometimes hard-to-predict ways. This chapter has provided the historical and institutional context for comparing and contrasting patronage resources and networks across Indonesia, the Philippines, and Malaysia. While all three polities are strongly oriented to patronage, they diverge significantly in how that manifests. Understanding differences in electoral mobilization regimes requires examination of distinctive historical patterns of state formation, state–society relations, and political party development, complemented with careful attention to the scope and rules of electoral contestation and how much discretion politicians enjoy. Beyond offering an empirical survey of how these features have evolved in our cases, however, the discussion in this chapter offers the explanatory foundation for the analysis to come.

Our starting point is a twist on Shefter, whose dichotomy between constituencies for bureaucratic autonomy and constituencies for patronage, and his argument for how and when these develop, offers an apt entry point. Yet our focus is on colonial states and often-convulsive transitions to postcolonial orders – polities understandably peripheral to Shefter's analysis. While colonial states always depended to some extent on relationships with local elites, and frequently contained a highly personalistic element, they were also strongly inclined to restrict political participation and insulate themselves from the demands of the local population as a whole. It is not surprising that they tended to nurture strong constituencies for bureaucratic autonomy, especially as the twentieth century progressed. This was indeed the case in the Netherlands East Indies and British Malaya, where major political parties were by necessity externally mobilized. In the American Philippines, however, we find the unusual phenomena of a strong constituency for patronage as well as an internally mobilized political party emerging under colonial rule – all within the context of a highly circumscribed elite electorate. From early on, US officials failed in their effort to develop well-insulated bureaucratic structures. As the constituency for patronage evolved in form but endured intact into the postcolonial era, the Philippines accords broadly with Shefter's expectations.

We cannot say the same of Indonesia and Malaysia, where colonial-era constituencies for bureaucratic autonomy were undermined in the postcolonial era: in Indonesia via spectacular collapse and in Malaysia via capture by the dominant political party. Yet the strong constituencies for patronage that subsequently emerged in both countries differed markedly in character. In Malaysia, UMNO, now internally mobilized, gradually recrafted the state toward its own institutional, and Malay-ethnic, interests. In Indonesia, by contrast, after the dramatic collapse of the colonial *beamtenstaat* in the 1940s, then a kind of patronage free-for-all in the 1950s, the state reconsolidated under Suharto after he grabbed power in the mid-1960s. Although he built a more powerful bureaucracy, there was still no constituency for bureaucratic autonomy. In Suharto's New Order, patronage from state sources flowed through bureaucratic networks and civilian politicians remained almost wholly dependent on bureaucrats and military officers for access to these resources; the constituency for patronage was not rooted in parties and elected politicians. In the post-Suharto period, elected officials once again became important political actors, but the lingering strength of the bureaucracy – and the entrenchment of patronage politics within it – hampered parties' ability to seize control of patronage and its distribution. Still today, Indonesian candidates not only have limited access to party-based patronage, but many also lack easy access to the state resources that can build and sustain local machines.

These historical trajectories – occurring within authoritarian, semi-democratic, and democratic structures alike – led to the emergence of very distinct constituencies for patronage across the three countries. In Malaysia, the patronage system has revolved around party channels. In the Philippines, the major players have been politicians and local political machines, and access to patronage is much more atomized. In Indonesia, the role of the bureaucracy eclipses that of parties and politicians, however reliant the latter still are on patronage-based strategies for electoral mobilization.

Beyond historical inheritances, choices regarding electoral systems present a second key factor behind the three types of electoral mobilization regimes that we analyze in the chapters to come. The Philippines has, over time, had the strongest inclination to candidate-centered electoral systems. In Malaysia, the single-member district plurality system – in combination, critically, with an electoral playing field skewed against opposition parties – helps to facilitate single-party dominance without eliminating the salience of a personal vote. Recent changes to the electoral system in Indonesia largely explain a dramatic shift from a party-centric to a candidate-centric system, having substantially altered the magnitude and locus of patronage politics.

The third and final major factor we highlight is the extent of discretion politicians enjoy in their dealings with the bureaucracy. The stronger a constituency for patronage relative to a constituency for bureaucratic autonomy, the greater the leeway that politicians will enjoy. What matters for the character and prevalence of patronage politics is not just that a given politician would *like* to distribute largesse but whether they have access to public resources to do so: who controls the bureaucracy and whose interests does it serve? In none of our three countries has a strongly impersonal state developed, impervious to predation and the capture of patronage resources by political actors. But the forms of predation and capture vary greatly; once established, moreover, these patterns become very hard to break. The interruption of the BN's decades-long monopoly on power did not end the pattern of party-centered patronage politics in Malaysia; the Philippine state, over time, has exhibited a high degree of permeability; and, in Indonesia, more than two decades after the collapse of authoritarian rule, elected politicians still struggle to wrest control of patronage resources from bureaucrats. These questions of discretion extend also to enforcement of laws designed to prevent politicians from engaging in illicit activities to fund patronage.

This combination of factors helps to explain the emergence of our three types of electoral mobilization regimes. Malaysia's party-based regime probably has the greatest number of analogs, given the many dominant-party systems throughout the world. The Philippines' electoral mobilization regime is built around local patronage machines within the context of weak and poorly institutionalized political parties. And, in Indonesia, we find an electoral mobilization regime characterized by candidate-centered ad hoc teams alongside political parties that at least enjoy an important role as gatekeepers. With these insights in mind, we turn in the next chapter to our three types of networks for patronage distribution and campaigning, and to further analysis of our three distinct electoral mobilization regimes.

3

Mobilization Networks and Patterns of Patronage
National Parties, Ad Hoc Teams, and Local Machines

Consider the following scene. A few days before the 2013 election, in a small town in Malaysia's easternmost state, Sabah, a group of about a dozen women systematically sorted, coded, and collated papers at the office of a local candidate of the ruling Barisan Nasional (BN, National Front) coalition. They had printed a separate sheet for every voter in the constituency, including on it such details as the voter's name, address, and polling station, stapling to each a how-to-vote card and a pamphlet extolling the BN's policies and promises. The women were now coding each voter as white (a BN loyalist), black (a diehard opposition supporter), or gray (undecided). All these preparations were for a last-minute push, as the women and other party workers prepared to revisit all voters in the constituency except those coded "black," offering them personalized attention and, if necessary, final persuasion and assistance with getting to the polling station. The scene evinced orderly, systematic, and collaborative effort.

Female party workers and members of women's auxiliaries are often the backbone of party election campaigns in Malaysia; (male) party leaders frequently praise them for their selfless dedication and commitment. Members of the United Malay National Organisation's women's and young-women's wings (Wanita UMNO and Puteri UMNO, respectively), in particular, invest time "going from house to house to establish personal ties with voters" (Tony 2014, 226), but women's organizations affiliated with other parties also play similar roles. In the 2018 elections, Wanita UMNO's national leader claimed that the organization would mobilize more than 200,000 of its members to campaign for UMNO's reelection (Rohaniza and Babulal 2018). Through women's, youth, and other wings, as well as individual party members – many or most of whom join with the intent of a lifelong commitment – Malaysian candidates typically benefit from an array of dedicated volunteers who organize, monitor, and persuade voters. Party volunteers can expect to be rewarded for their service with recognition and praise, increasingly senior positions, government jobs, business opportunities, and other benefits over time.

Contrast this model with the quite different scene that unfolded in the early evening at a meeting outside the large home of an incumbent member of the provincial legislature in Palembang, the capital of Indonesia's South Sumatra province. The legislator – let's call him Agus – is a member of the Partai Gerindra (Greater Indonesia Movement Party) and is running for reelection in the provincial legislature. About 100 members of his *tim sukses* (success team), almost all women, are sitting on rows of plastic chairs under tarpaulins on his driveway. With the election in about two weeks, the women are preparing to act as polling-booth witnesses on voting day. Everyone is anxious to get onto the main business of the evening – dinner – but first, they have to sit through a training session run by a couple of young party activists and watch a party promotional video. Many of the women chat and gossip among themselves throughout the event. At the end of the session, the trainers ask if everything is clear. One woman shoots her hand up: "When do we get paid?" she shouts, prompting general hilarity. Another asks whether they will get enough toilet breaks when performing their duties on voting day. The candidate warns everyone that if they receive offers of cash from other politicians, they should not accept them.

In an interview just before the meeting, Agus explained that his biggest concern was that his team members would "run to other candidates."[1] He was trying to ensure this did not happen by monitoring their performance and keeping tabs on the voter lists they were compiling. He was also trying to build convivial personal relationships with them; a few nights earlier, he had hosted a big tambourine competition at his house – several hundred women had attended, everyone taking home free gifts, including big cash prizes for the winners. But his "secret weapon" was his skill at attaining government grants for microenterprises. Over the preceding five years, he had obtained such grants for hundreds of women's cooperatives in his constituency. Most of the women at his house that night had been beneficiaries. Though they were all getting small cash payments to cover their costs during the campaign, "their main reward is after the election." He explained that he tells his success team members that if he gets a sizeable vote at their booth, "I will come back after the election and we can sit down and make a program with you."

Thus, we see a clear contrast. In Malaysia, candidates can often rely on the voluntary labor of party loyalists whose work, while not always exactly selfless, is at least partly based on time horizons that might encompass years, even a lifetime. In Indonesia, candidates like Agus often have little choice but to motivate their supporters with short-term and instrumental rewards. Moreover, though Agus was formally running under a party label, the campaign team he built with these women was entirely personalized, consisting of

---

[1] This and subsequent quotations from Agus: interview, March 22, 2014, Palembang.

individuals who felt obliged due to the help he had already provided, or had an eye on postelection benefits, or were simply in it for the pay. And Agus was comparatively lucky: as an incumbent, he *could* rely, to at least some extent, on campaign workers with a sense of obligation to him, built up through the programs he had distributed; most of his challengers, lacking similar access to government programs and resources, had to rely mainly on guns-for-hire.

These two anecdotes illustrate that a key source of variation in patronage politics in Southeast Asia is the form of networks candidates use to connect with and deliver patronage to voters. Even when such networks have superficial similarities – as with the female-focused nature of both networks just described – close examination of how they function can reveal striking differences. In this chapter, we look closely at the three broad types of mobilization networks we find in Malaysia, Indonesia, and the Philippines. We first describe these networks and the dimensions along which they vary, then explain why each of these networks is linked to specific types and patterns of patronage distribution. In doing so, we show how these different networks and patronage patterns combine to produce three distinct types of what we dub *electoral mobilization regimes*. Next, we compare and contrast how these regimes operate in our three main cases and consider in more detail the differences between the local party machines in the Philippines and the ad hoc teams in Indonesia. Finally, drawing on the discussion in Chapter 2, we reiterate the importance of understanding the historical and institutional origins of these three regime types.

THREE NETWORKS OF MOBILIZATION

The different networks politicians use help to delineate the boundaries among the three electoral mobilization regimes we describe in this book. It is useful, we propose, to conceive of electoral patronage networks as varying along three dimensions: the degree to which parties are central to the network; the level of aggregation, including the degree to which these networks coordinate on behalf of multiple candidates; and their degree of permanency.

We begin by considering the *role of parties* in mobilization networks. Much of the comparative literature on patronage politics assumes that this form of politics is organized primarily by and through political parties (e.g., Calvo and Murillo 2004; Stokes 2005; Kitschelt and Wilkinson 2007; Nichter 2008; Kitschelt and Kselman 2013; Stokes et al. 2013; Gans-Morse et al. 2014).[2] Certainly, in each of the countries on which we focus, political parties have at least some prominence in both national and local politics (most obviously in Malaysia, then Indonesia, and far less solidly so in the Philippines). Members of national and subnational legislatures typically attach themselves to party labels, journalists and other observers generally analyze election campaigns and

---

[2] Important exceptions include Muñoz (2019) and Novaes (2018).

outcomes as contests among rival parties (though in the Philippines they often pay particular attention to clan performance), and local activists and campaigners usually organize under party banners.

But appearances can be deceptive. We show in this chapter that the networks used for patronage distribution and election campaigning approximate three distinctive modal patterns: national parties, local machines, and ad hoc networks. *National parties* are the key networks and agents of distributive politics in only one of our three main cases, Malaysia, though they also play a prominent role in our secondary cases of Singapore, Timor-Leste, and post-2001 Thailand. In the Philippines (and pre-2001 Thailand), while politicians typically identify themselves by party labels, the key networks they rely upon in organizing their election campaigns and connecting them to ordinary voters are *local machines*. These machines are usually organized at the municipal or provincial level; coordinate a slate of local candidates under the leadership of one or more subnational politicians (typically a mayoral or gubernatorial candidate); share resources, brokers, and information when executing their campaigns; and often endure between and across elections. In Indonesia, by contrast, the standard form of campaign organization is an *ad hoc network*. This is a personalized campaign team, typically established by a single candidate and existing only for the duration of a single election, with little coordination with or assistance from a larger party organization.

If we map these mobilization networks, each of these organizations resembles the classic brokerage pyramid associated with clientelistic politics, in which candidates connect themselves to voters via multiple tiers of intermediaries, using those brokers to identify, recruit, and cultivate sympathetic voters and to deliver patronage to them. Importantly, brokers' roles may vary, too. Some work as simple go-betweens who link candidates with individual voters during an election season. Others are representatives of collective groups in the community; some are designated, often party-based, problem-solvers who work to respond to community requests and fix problems throughout the electoral cycle. Despite the surface similarities, however, these organizations differ significantly in other regards, as we will see.

Second, the *level of aggregation* – what the geographic scope of the network is and who leads it – helps distinguish among these networks. In the Malaysian case, as in most party-based patronage systems, it is national leaders who sit astride party organizations, coordinating their activities – at least at the level of grand strategy and organization – across the entire country. In the local-machine model of the Philippines, it is a political grandee at the municipal or provincial level; such local bosses are typically connected, but often only loosely, to national-level party leaders and politicians, often viewing such relationships through an entirely instrumental lens. They do, however, typically coordinate the electioneering and other political activity of a raft of lower-level candidates. In the Indonesian model, it is the candidate himself or herself who recruits a personal "success team," typically viewing other candidates, even co-partisans, as competitors rather than potential partners in campaigning and patronage (though candidates running for executive posts always run as a pair, alongside a deputy, and candidates running for legislative seats at different levels may coordinate to some extent). Put slightly differently, we can consider the degree to which networks are vertically and horizontally integrated. Do networks merely connect an individual candidate with brokers, and voters? Or do they continue upward and downward, to connect the candidate with politicians at higher and lower tiers of the political system? And do they extend outward, to include political allies within the same or another constituency?

Finally, we distinguish among these networks on the basis of their *degree of institutionalization or permanence*. Malaysia's national parties have been established in many cases for decades, and party activists often pursue lifelong careers through their parties, first proving their loyalty to their superiors at the branch level then, potentially at least, working their way up through party structures until they can stand for senior party positions or legislative office. At the opposite extreme are Indonesia's *tim sukses*, which are highly ephemeral organizations, cohering only as long as the campaign lasts. A candidate might draw on some of the same individuals when establishing a new team in a subsequent election but most essentially start from scratch. Candidates themselves often do have long-standing attachments to a party, as might some of their campaign workers, but their campaign organization itself is a temporary arrangement. In between are Philippine-style local machines. Especially if built around a dominant political dynasty, such machines can be multigenerational, but they are generally much shorter-lived and more fluid in composition than parties in Malaysia, frequently splitting and reconfiguring as local political alliances change. Even so, relationships between candidates and brokers in the Philippines tend to be based on more enduring clientelistic ties than in Indonesia, with loyalties that often last over years; in Indonesia, by contrast, many brokers join success teams on a temporary and instrumental basis, lured by immediate material rewards – as in our opening vignette from Palembang.[3]

Mobilization Networks and Patterns of Patronage

These three features, in turn, affect how various networks and organizations help politicians pursue their patronage-based electoral strategies. It is useful to think of organizations – whether they be parties, machines, or more ephemeral networks – as providing this help in at least three ways. First, all three of the preceding network types help politicians *recruit, organize, and reward their brokers*, though we shall see that they do so in different ways and with varying levels of effectiveness. As the literature on the topic makes clear, politicians pursuing patronage strategies need to rely on brokers or intermediaries who

---

[3] See Nichter (2018) on the interplay between relational and electoral clientelism.

can identify potential recipients, deliver patronage to those constituents, and do what they can to monitor and enforce clientelistic exchange.

Second, organizations such as parties and machines can help multiple politicians to *coordinate their campaign activities*, capitalizing on economies of scale by allowing them to draw on the same teams of brokers, pool patronage resources if running more than one candidate in a single district, or concentrate campaign activities and patronage in particularly competitive or crucial districts. Again, a candidate who relies on an individualized campaign team will not be able to turn to a broader team for such purposes, and may not want to.[4]

Third, organizations and networks can help marshal politicians' *access to patronage*. Most obviously, a politician who is a member of a political party that controls or participates in government may be able to access state funds and resources that can be directed toward their constituents, and even reap rewards from government programs that target voters directly with benefits, perhaps without any personal involvement by the politician. A local political machine will likewise be able to access patronage resources – to the extent that those resources can be tapped at the local level or through bargaining with national politicians – and distribute them in a way that benefits all members of the machine, including at lower levels. An ephemeral campaign organization such as a success team, by contrast, is fundamentally about connecting an individual politician to voters and can play little role in providing access to resources. The candidate will need to attain those in other ways – from personal resources, direct access to state office, donors' personal networks, or party or other political connections.

Expanding on this point, patterns of access to government resources shape the distribution of patronage and – important for present purposes – the kind of networks politicians can foster. Patronage strategies are more viable options where politicians and candidates have access to and discretion over public funds (see Allen 2015). In Malaysia, the fusion of the party and state is nearly complete, providing ample funds to the parties in power, enabling them to shore up the party's mobilization network by directing meso-particularism and macro-programs to groups of supporters. The result is that, for individual candidates, party connections can even substitute for direct access to office. As a BN candidate in Sarawak explained, when he worked as the coalition's *penyelaras* (coordinator) in an opposition-held seat he had previously occupied, he had been able to "look after the area" even after his last defeat, readying the ground for his next attempt: while he received no official allocation for projects, he could "go straight to the PM's office" or other state agencies if he had one to recommend (and the sums involved would "obviously" be higher at election time).[5]

Such centralized coordination of patronage for party purposes is rare in the Philippines, but there local politicians can leverage their access to public

---

[4] Of course, parties and other organizations can also perform other functions. For example, they might aggregate interests, enhancing an image of a party as representing a particular social group or coalition of groups and presenting a program that appeals to that constituency.

[5] Interview, April 25, 2016, Meradong.

resources to distribute meso- and micro-particularism via their local machine throughout the electoral cycle. Doing so is the key source of the resilience of these local machines. By contrast, the still prominent role played by Indonesia's bureaucracy in allocating public resources, and the difficulties some politicians (especially legislators) have in freely accessing such resources, place limits on politicians' ability to engage in ongoing meso-particularism. This pattern makes it harder for politicians to build and maintain enduring local machines to the extent possible in the Philippines. As a consequence, the provision of micro- and meso-particularism is more likely to be both privately funded and concentrated during the election period. Throughout our research in Indonesia we encountered candidates who were mobilizing personal funds – for example, selling land, borrowing from family members, or seeking donations from wealthy supporters – in order to fund their campaign efforts, with the party providing at most a few posters and banners, or support for ballot-box witnesses. One Gerindra candidate, a former Dewan Perwakilan Rakyat (DPR, national parliament) member, rather ruefully described, for instance, having to sell a warehouse to fund his campaign-time distributions; his party contributed nothing.[6] Most candidates also lack the equivalent of a local-machine boss ready to provide them with the financial support needed to fund their campaigns. This pattern in Indonesia is slowly changing, especially in the case of local executive offices, where decentralization has increased access to funds, and where we are seeing the first inklings of Philippines-like local machines and dynastic politics. Yet even in these cases, the level of access and discretion that politicians possess pales in comparison to the Philippines.

THREE TYPES OF ELECTORAL MOBILIZATION REGIME

The combination of different types of mobilization networks and the patterns of patronage found in each produce what we have dubbed electoral mobilization regimes. As we have explained, we distinguish among three types of mobilization regimes: *party machines*, *local machines*, and *ad hoc teams*. Party machines are the dominant pattern in Malaysia, local machines predominate in the Philippines, and ad hoc teams are the norm in Indonesia. We emphasize that we are describing general patterns across our three cases. There is, of course, interesting variation within these three broad regime types (some of which we explore in Chapters 4–7), as well as exceptions to these patterns within each country (the focus of Chapter 8, on subnational variation). And, as we note in Chapter 1, we do not claim that these three regime types capture the full typology of mobilization regimes, nor are they unique to our three primary cases. We see similarly organized mobilization regimes elsewhere – a point to which we return later in this chapter and in Chapter 9.

---

[6] Interview, March 31, 2014, Jakarta.

As their names suggest, these electoral mobilization regimes rely on different mobilization networks. But they can also be distinguished along three other dimensions: their relative reliance on different forms of patronage (micro-, meso-, and macro-particularism), the timing of patronage distribution, and their relative reliance on public versus private resources. Table 3.1 (reiterating what we introduced in Table 1.1) sketches the variations across regime types along these three dimensions. The table notes how ubiquitous each mobilization strategy is under each regime – a designation based on our own interviews and observations, our local research partners' ethnographic research, and our surveys. The evaluations we make indicate the relative ubiquity of a given strategy within a given country and also its relative pervasiveness in one case, compared to the others. "Limited" indicates that candidates seldom deployed a particular strategy as a part of their campaign. "Moderate" corresponds to a strategy that many candidates employed routinely as an important part

TABLE 3.1. *Mobilization networks and patronage patterns in Southeast Asia*

	Party machines (Malaysia)	Local machines (Philippines)	Ad hoc teams (Indonesia)
Micro-particularism (Chapter 4)			
Ubiquity	limited	extensive	extensive
Main timing of distribution	–	between and during elections	during elections
Meso-particularism (Chapter 5)			
Ubiquity	moderate	extensive	moderate
Main timing of distribution	between elections	between and during elections	some between, mostly during elections
Macro-particularism/Hijacking (Chapter 6)			
Ubiquity of credit-claiming	extensive	extensive	moderate
Ubiquity of facilitation	extensive	moderate	limited
Ubiquity of morselization	limited	extensive	moderate[a]
Main timing of distribution	between elections	between and during elections	between and during elections
National public goods			
Ubiquity	moderate	limited	limited
Primary sources of patronage			
Public vs. private resources	public	public and private	private

[a] Limited for legislators; extensive for regional executives.

of their campaigns, while "extensive" strategies are those on which we observed most candidates relying, with relatively few exceptions. Likewise, the sources of patronage we identify predominate but are not exclusive.

In *party-machine regimes*, politics and electoral competition revolve around relatively institutionalized national parties. (Malaysia, but also Singapore and, to a lesser extent, Timor-Leste, are in this category.) National parties control access to patronage and distribute it downward through party networks and state organs they control. The predominant forms of patronage are macro- and meso-particularism, with micro-particularism being comparatively rare. The national party or parties able to capture power at the center will be able to monopolize and direct macro- and meso-particularistic patronage toward communities and voters identified as party loyalists. Distribution occurs over the entire electoral cycle, and not just during elections. Not surprisingly, too, it is in the party-based polities that we see a greater degree of programmatic and policy-based competition, either alongside or even preempting patronage-based competition.

At the other end of the spectrum is the *ad hoc-team regime*, the norm for Indonesia. In these regimes, candidates form campaign organizations almost exclusively for electoral purposes. These teams exist for the duration of an election campaign, then dissolve. The emphasis is on private and ephemeral forms of patronage, such as cash gifts to voters (micro-particularism) and electorally linked club goods or pork for small groups (meso-particularism), with the bulk of distribution concentrated around election time.

Between these poles are *local-machine regimes* (found, among our cases, not only in the Philippines but also at certain recent historical junctures in Thailand). Local machines lack the capacity or incentive to provide programmatic policies, but they are able to hijack national government programs (macro-particularism), distribute pork or engage in other meso-particularism between elections, and supplement with micro-particularistic handouts to voters between and during elections.

Across all three regime types, incumbents, of course, find mobilizing patronage easier than do challengers, but challengers' relative disadvantage may also vary by the nature of these networks. Challengers with national party networks may still have access to central-government or central-party patronage resources, while those with access to local-party networks may be able to tap patronage from the local machine. Individual challengers relying on their own ad hoc networks will need to rely on private resources (their own or from others) to fund meso- and micro-particularism. (Complicating the picture for Indonesia is that challengers are also often affiliated with national parties – indeed, electoral rules require such affiliations for legislative elections – but, as countless candidates and campaign workers conveyed in our interviews, their party connections provide little in the way of patronage resources.)

Figure 3.1 illustrates the relative levels of micro- and meso-particularistic patronage across our three cases, highlighting whether and how distribution changes over the election cycle – patterns we analyze in greater detail in the

(a)

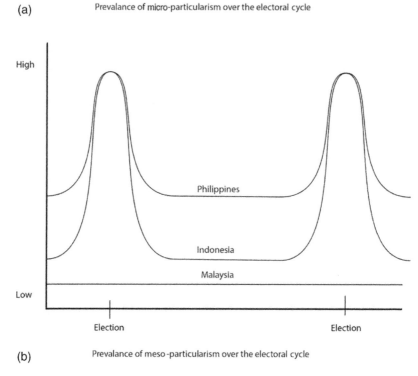

(b)

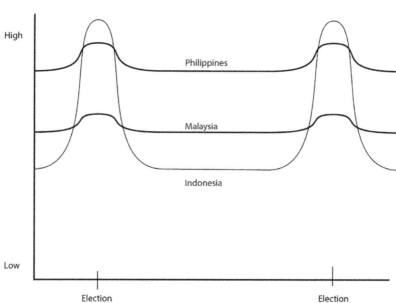

FIGURE 3.1. Levels of micro-particularism (a) and meso-particularism (b) over the electoral cycle

chapters to come. Variance across the electoral cycle is highest in Indonesia and lowest in Malaysia, while in the Philippines, the prevalence of electoral clientelism and the access to resources that can be used for meso-particularism between elections corresponds with a more pronounced electoral cycle for micro-particularism than for meso-particularism.

In summary, we argue that differences in the nature of mobilization networks correspond with differences in the mix and pattern of patronage – what together we call electoral mobilization regimes. To elucidate this argument, we next discuss each type of patronage network in turn – national parties, ad hoc networks, and local machines – drawing mostly upon the paradigmatic cases of Malaysia, Indonesia, and the Philippines to illustrate the three types of mobilization regime and explain how the nature of the mobilization networks available to politicians shapes choices over patronage strategies.

NATIONAL PARTIES: MALAYSIA

As noted earlier, parties dominate much of the discussion of patronage politics in the comparative literature but are the principal distributive network in only one of our three main cases. Of course, parties are present in all the countries that we study, but our focus in this chapter is the extent to which they are the *primary* vehicle for mobilization and patronage distribution in connection with elections. For example, in Indonesia, as we explain more fully later, parties play an important gatekeeping role during elections and in many ways dominate national politics. But in the actual organization of election campaigns, and in the distribution of patronage to voters, their role is secondary if not peripheral. All the more marginal are national political parties in the Philippines.

Distinguishing a party machine from a local machine is the former's nationwide and relatively stable organization. Most national parties in party-machine electoral mobilization regimes have identities beyond the personality of their leaders (though there are exceptions, such as Timor-Leste's CNRT, National Congress for Timorese Reconstruction, which was utterly dominated by its founder, former president, prime minister, and independence hero Xanana Gusmão). Moreover, within parties, national leaders rather than local-level functionaries or politicians strategically determine the allocation of patronage, though sometimes leaving considerable discretion in the hands of local officials and candidates.

Emblematic of these party machines is Malaysia's UMNO. As we explained in Chapter 2, from early in its history, UMNO built a strong party organization, penetrating the countryside where most Malays lived and binding rural voters to it through the distribution of agricultural and other benefits. This rural orientation and associated machinery have remained central to UMNO's identity and strategy to the present. However, in the 1970s, 1980s, and beyond, even as UMNO continued to treat its rural Malay base as its mainstay, under the impetus of the New Economic Policy, the UMNO-dominated government supported a series of policies to hasten the country's economic modernization and to improve

Malays' economic and social condition. It promoted preference for Malays in education, government employment, business, housing, and other fields, expanding its appeal to new generations of Malay businesspeople and urbanites.

Returning to the three functions that mobilization networks can play for patronage politicians (organizing brokers, coordinating campaigns, and marshaling resources), we note that UMNO has been persistently adept at playing all three roles. In the first place, UMNO – both through its own structures and through its influence over the bureaucracy, local government, and informal social networks – became a formidable grassroots political machine. By 2021, the party claimed 3.35 million members (over 13 percent of Malaysia's adult population), distributed across nearly 22,000 branches (Bernama 2021). (By contrast, as of two years earlier, it will be recalled from Chapter 2, only 10 percent of Indonesia's population said they even "felt close" to *any* party.) Though many of these members were inactive, often enlisted merely to support the ambitions of local leaders, the party's organization nevertheless penetrated society, with branches and sub-branches down to the village level. MPs generally run (and rely on support from) their UMNO branch (the level individuals join) and administrative division.[7] Wings for women (Wanita), young men (Pemuda), and, since 2001, young women (Puteri), mimic the overall party structure.[8] Overall, though, UMNO has remained much more densely organized in rural areas than in cities.

This structure has provided the party with a powerful means to reach ordinary voters, identify and monitor their preferences, and ensure they deliver a vote at elections. Our research revealed that a key component of UMNO's mobilization strategy, which longtime rival, and now partner, Parti Islam seMalaysia (PAS) mimics, is the Jalinan Rakyat (people's network or JR).[9] At JR's core are members of Wanita who are each responsible for ongoing, house-to-house outreach among a set of voters or households, as our opening example illustrated.[10] Members of the network know their communities intimately, from their family trees to their economic hardships, so are well-placed to explain government policies and programs, respond to concerns, and provide small-scale support throughout the electoral cycle. During outreach visits, they tout the party's manifesto, record, and plans as elections approach; urge voters to support the party (to vote UMNO or not vote at all); and monitor the leanings of voters in the community. One UMNO MP explained to us that his first step upon assuming

---

[7] Interview with UMNO MP, July 31, 2015, Kuala Lumpur.
[8] Puteri formed to counteract sharp declines in youth support. Pemuda's age cap is 40; Puteri's, 35.
[9] Formerly known as *kepala sepuluh* (head of ten).
[10] It is likewise PAS's women's wing, Muslimat, that does house-to-house outreach. Puteri has increasingly supplemented Wanita's role, focusing more on online outreach and not overtly political events to engage with and lure in more skeptical younger voters – for instance, sports or cross-party civic education or volunteerism – though Puteri also gears up for door-to-door outreach as elections approach (interview with Puteri activists, October 12, 2016, Kuala Lumpur).

office was to appoint the local Wanita chief to run his local office and distribute his constituency allocation; she "knows all leaders downstream, down to every village." Moreover, showing his "full trust in Wanita," he explained, will "trickle down," ensuring his "effectiveness." In normal times, each of 120 Wanita branches in the constituency monitors 500–1,000 voters, identifying both individual inclinations and strategic groups to target, like teachers. In a disaster, within three days, Wanita can mobilize 5,000 volunteers.[11] Parties delegate these roles to their women's wings, given women's reputation as both polite and persuasive – though in fact, they can be quite aggressive in their efforts – but also because women have readier access to homes and housewives are presumed to be able to sway their husbands' and children's votes (see Chapter 7 for more details; also, from our team's fieldwork: Chiok 2014, 23–24; Tony 2014, 226; Teo 2014, 70–71). Combined with such practices as counting votes at the level of the polling station and hiring party workers to intensify mobilization efforts at election times, this outreach has long given UMNO detailed insight into and influence over its electoral map (Pepinsky 2007, 116).

Despite being well-positioned to act as brokers for the distribution of electoral patronage to individuals and households, these party organizations are rarely employed in this fashion in most of Malaysia. In fact, given the presence of local party workers throughout the country, coupled with the ruling party's ready access to resources, we expected to find far more evidence of handouts and other types of micro-particularism than we did. But, as we explain further in the next chapter, our extensive research – triangulating field-research findings with interviews and surveys, and taking social-desirability bias into account – turned up very little evidence of election-related micro-particularism in peninsular Malaysia. Sabah and Sarawak are a different story. There, mobilization strategies more closely resemble what we observe in the Philippines, with rampant cash handouts during elections; we explore the reasons why in Chapter 8. But otherwise, while Malaysia's party-centered mobilization networks connect people with government services, facilitate the distribution of meso-particularism, help ensure voters credit the party and candidate for what benefits flow their way, and visit households to get out the vote during election season, they do *not* systematically distribute money or goods to individual voters as part of that mobilization effort, as far as we have been able to determine.

Let's take a closer look at how these party machines function. The lynchpin of party organization and strength at the local level is typically the MP (or aspirant for that office, if another party holds the seat), who often heads the local branch and runs a "service center" (*pusat khidmat*). At least since the 1970s, these centers have taken on increasingly important and expansive social-welfare functions, becoming contact points for citizens who need help from the state. Run by salaried staff generally drawn from the party, and financed in large

---

[11] Interview with UMNO MP, April 24, 2013, Kemaman.

part by constituency development funds the ruling party has allocated to its own MPs (but withheld from opposition-party MPs, as explained later), these service centers are places where citizens can obtain help in accessing government assistance programs: a scholarship, say, or an old-age pension, or healthcare. Service center staff, or sometimes the MP in person, provide advice, help fill out forms, or put constituents in touch with relevant government agencies and bureaucrats. (See Chapter 6 for more on this type of facilitation.) Sometimes the MP or their staff disburse cash or groceries for the needy. MPs also often hold regular drop-in days, sometimes with relevant state officials such as local councilors or bureaucrats from relevant government departments also present.

Successful MPs work hard to cultivate a "personal touch" – getting to know their constituents; spending time at weddings, funerals, and other community functions; and having a reputation for being responsive to needy constituents. Being in power for so long enabled UMNO, along with its coalition partners, to entrench a role as the first point of contact for citizens needing assistance with a wide array of welfare, educational, health, and other personal needs – though as we explain later, the same basic strategy now characterizes opposition and government parties alike. In an important distinction from the Philippines and Indonesia, even though they strive for that "personal touch," Malaysian MPs are first and foremost representatives of their parties: they derive authority and resources from the party and represent the face of that party to their constituents.

We might look to a secondary case, Singapore, for insight into whether what we see in Malaysia is unique to UMNO or applicable to other party-machine regimes. Indeed, we see a very similar pattern in Singapore: the ruling People's Action Party (PAP) penetrates society down to the grassroots level and distributes assistance of various forms through party and party-linked channels, with MPs and their staff engaged in extensive constituency service.[12] In fact, in both Singapore and Malaysia the line between state and party remains blurred (even after the Barisan Nasional's federal-level loss in 2018).

Part of the reason why party organs play such an important intermediary role between state and citizens is that, as discussed in Chapter 2, not long after independence, the apparatus of local government ceased to function as an independent layer of the Malaysian state. It was largely supplanted by partisan political machines, as authorities phased out elections for local-government posts (a development paralleled in Singapore, also). Instead, the state-level government in Malaysia appoints local councilors; these posts have effectively become patronage rewards for loyal party workers and up-and-coming party

---

[12] Like their Malaysian counterparts, Singaporean ruling-party MPs meet regularly with voters as representatives of their party (weekly constituency-outreach sessions have been a PAP mainstay since the 1950s), field requests from voters in their constituency, and bring the resources of the state to bear to help petitioning voters. As in Malaysia, too, opposition-party MPs also now hold similar sessions and "walk the ground" assiduously. Though they have fewer material resources to offer, they engage in advocacy and facilitation work resembling that of their PAP counterparts (see Ong 2015; Weiss 2020c, especially 105–6, 191–96).

leaders. (In Singapore, MPs head unelected town councils.) This situation contrasts dramatically with both the Philippines and Indonesia, where elections for local-government posts down to the neighborhood level continued (with significant interruption and some variation) even at points during authoritarian rule – and became especially lively and competitive after democratic transition. In both Indonesia and the Philippines, elected officials at the national or provincial level must deal with a whole array of potentially quite independent local-government leaders positioned between them and their constituents, requiring complex negotiations and deal-making. In Malaysia and Singapore, by contrast, the only layer between state and national parliamentarians and citizens consists of appointed, party-aligned local-government functionaries.

The lowest tier of government in Malaysia therefore amplifies the party's centrality. When citizens need help, they turn to the local party branch, seeking assistance as often from party workers as from representatives of the local government. Hence, for instance, when in 2012 the BN government introduced the unconditional cash-transfer scheme Bantuan Rakyat 1Malaysia (1Malaysia People's Aid), eligible citizens could collect their checks from BN party offices – in many cases from MPs themselves. At the same time, long-lasting single-party dominance gradually eroded bureaucratic autonomy, not only leaving the government near-complete freedom to allocate state programs in ways that favored the BN's electoral interests but encoding a "bureaucratic norm" such that the civil service designed programs to reflect partisan preferences – for example, rewarding BN constituencies with development projects while withholding them from opposition-held ones (Washida 2019, 76–77).

The result of this long dominance over both central-government resources and local machinery was that UMNO and allied partners became very effective at performing the second organizational task noted earlier: facilitating access to patronage for supporters. However, our research revealed that these parties did so largely in ways that involved the cultivation of long-term relational clientelism with citizens (see also Weiss 2019a) and the dispensation of government resources – welfare payments, social assistance, and the like – rather than one-off private gifts or cash handouts. Exemplifying governmental patronage politics are constituency development funds, budgets allocated annually to individual MPs for infrastructure projects and welfare needs in their constituencies. Unlike in most countries, however, these funds, totaling about 5 million ringgit (USD1.2 million) after a dramatic increase as of 2016 (Malaysiakini 2015), were available *only* to BN parliamentarians; in constituencies held by members of opposition parties, the federal government instead directed the funds to appointed BN *penyelaras* (coordinators).[13] The Pakatan Harapan government largely continued that practice in 2018, allotting opposition MPs only a token allocation, as have the subsequent administrations since 2020.

---

[13] Interviews with Gerakan activist, January 3, 2015, George Town; UMNO MP, July 31, 2015, Kuala Lumpur.

In summary, the patterns of patronage we observe in Malaysia's party-machine regime involve various forms of hijacking of government programs (see Chapter 6) along with the distribution of meso-particularism (Chapter 5) – all organized by and routed through national (or in Sabah and Sarawak, also state-based) parties. By contrast, we see comparatively little in the way of micro-particularism – handouts to individual voters – outside East Malaysia.[14]

As for the third function mobilization networks play, UMNO and its coalition partners in Malaysia have also been highly effective at coordinating election campaigning: selecting candidates and placing them in the most appropriate seats; supplying them with funds, volunteers, and campaign paraphernalia; organizing and funding media coverage; managing the release of policies and programs, including the channeling of patronage; allocating seats among coalition-member parties to avoid "three-cornered" contests; and so on. This role allows a far more nationally structured effort than disparate parties with either distinct or overlapping catchments would allow, and certainly than politicians without strong party organizations could achieve.

In addition, though UMNO is the paradigmatic model, we find that other parties in Malaysia have mimicked its approach (see Weiss 2020c for a fuller development of this argument). This is certainly the case for parties within its BN coalition. In particular, ruling parties in Sabah and Sarawak became patronage machines, adapting the UMNO model (in Sabah, including as UMNO Sabah from 1991) but drawing much more on funds from natural-resource rents (i.e., from timber, palm oil, and land) in order to trade infrastructure development and other collective benefits for electoral support. Village and longhouse leaders, generally the local party head or a stand-in, came to monitor loyalty, bar opposition campaigners, and otherwise curry favor for their BN parties. When Sabah's state government fell into opposition hands in 1990, speeding the BN's comeback in 1994 was the federal government's channeling resources through its own (partisanized) bureaucratic agencies rather than through the state government (Chin 2001, 41–43; Loh 2005, 98–101).

Since the tripartite Alliance (the progenitor of the BN) first formed in 1955, UMNO's core partners have been the MIC (Malaysian Indian Congress) and MCA (Malaysian Chinese Association). Each has played a similar role, not only representing the communal interests of the ethnic groups they claim to represent when it comes to negotiations over government policy (the feature most emphasized in past scholarly literature on these parties: e.g. Heng 1996; Hilley 2001; Ng 2003; Shekhar 2008) but also acting as conduits for the delivery of patronage to prominent organizations, community leaders, and ordinary members within these groups. Particularly important among these beneficiary groups have been well-established Chinese guilds and associations, such as Chinese education associations, *wushu* (martial arts) organizations, and Hungry Ghost

---

[14] Vote buying has also been common in internal party elections, particularly within UMNO (Weiss 2020c, 116).

Festival committees. From the 1950s until around the 1980s, these organizations were especially politically important, including in delivering blocs of votes. While their partisan loyalties have been increasingly divided since then, Chinese-based parties still see these groups as important to court.[15] The legacies of these patronage-oriented networks thus have longer-lasting effects, continuing to structure a system in which they are coming to play a less active role.

Opposition parties have long been severely disadvantaged under this system. UMNO and other BN parties have enjoyed a near monopoly on government patronage resources by virtue of their strong political control at the national level and in most states – and it is this government patronage, delivered as partisan but impersonal, collective benefits throughout the electoral calendar, that most clearly distinguishes praxis in Malaysia from that of our other cases (see Chapter 6). When opposition parties took control of state governments, particularly as of 2008, they could try to steer policy and resources in ways that benefited their own interests, but the BN's centralization of resource control left state governments with relatively few such levers. As early as 1959, when the opposition Pan-Malaysian Islamic Party (PAS) gained control of two east-coast state governments, the Alliance coalition in control at the federal level withheld all but the "constitutional minimum" in development funds (Smith 1962, 153). The pattern has deepened since then: central-government revenues were only four times the sum of state-level revenues in 1985, but by 2010, federal expenditures were over ten times higher than those of the states. States are severely hampered in their ability to raise more revenue, as through taxation and fees, and federal distributions to states totaled only 2.48 percent of the 2010 federal budget (Yeoh 2012, 20–22, 140–42).

On the whole, the opposition's lack of access to state resources, in a context of competing with a coalition heavily reliant on them, made opposition parties generally more programmatic in orientation than most parties throughout Southeast Asia – emphasizing varying mixtures of communally oriented policies, welfarism, and calls for democratic reform. This pattern corresponds to findings in other country contexts, where externally mobilized opposition parties that are cut off from resources for patronage develop a programmatic orientation as an alternative mobilization strategy (Shefter 1994, 1977; Cox and Theis 1998; Samuels 1999; Golden and Chang 2001). For instance, PAS has drawn on an alternative Islamist discourse of "moderation" (*kesederhanaan*) and spirituality in contrast to the developmentalism on which the BN staked its core claim, emphasizing a certain wariness of "modernization," crony capitalism, and crassly consumerist aspirations (e.g., Hooker 2004; Stark 2004, 60–61). That position proved useful both for underlining PAS's emphasis on Islam and for vindicating its inability to emulate BN-led states in the sort of development benefits it could offer in the states that it controlled.

---

[15] Interview, Teng Cheng Yeow, January 3, 2015, Penang; Ho 1992.

But although they tend to be patronage starved, these parties have also tended to replicate the BN approach when given the opportunity to do so (c.f. Piattoni 2001). After opposition coalition Pakatan Rakyat – the Democratic Action Party (DAP), Parti Keadilan Rakyat (PKR, People's Justice Party), and PAS – took control of a growing number of state governments in 2008, they distributed constituency development funds as small grants to local NGOs, religious organizations, and schools; introduced new programmatic but party-branded welfare schemes for the bereaved, youths, seniors, and other population segments; offered free legal aid or medical services; and more (see Weiss 2020c, 127–28). And upon winning national power in 2018, the former opposition adopted a party-based patronage approach similar to the one BN had relied on for decades, albeit with new checks on corruption.

Dynamics in our secondary cases mimic these patterns. In Singapore as in Malaysia, it is parties that structure campaigns and resources. The dominant PAP claims credit for both large-scale development and smaller-scale intercession to help constituents secure state services and other assistance, while opposition parties do what they can to mimic the PAP's outreach, writing letters of support to state agencies and service-providers, marshaling volunteers and donations to provide support (from food aid to private-sector jobs), mediating disputes among neighbors, and more (Weiss 2020c, 192–93). That said, while PAP preelection budgets and "packages" aim to give all key voter segments cause for gratitude, strict (and enforced) campaign-finance rules prohibit the sort of campaign-time beneficence (free meals, etc.) in Singapore that we tend to see in Malaysia; PAP and opposition campaign costs alike are astonishingly low (Weiss et al. 2016, 870–71). We found similar, if less institutionalized, patterns in Timor-Leste, where political competition, mobilization, and patronage distribution are also very much party-based (see Aspinall et al. 2018 for more details). The largest parties have networks of loyalists (*militantes*) deployed down to the village level, and patronage tends to flow through these party networks.

Above all, these patterns reflect a context of strong parties, fostered by historical factors, as detailed in Chapter 2, and sustained by electoral rules – Malaysia and Singapore's majoritarian single- or team-centered multi-member districts and Timor-Leste's closed-list proportional representation, both of which systems can favor coordination through parties and discourage or disallow independent challenges. Parties matter not just because they are the flags under which candidates stand; they also play central roles in coordinating brokers and campaigns while marshalling resources and structuring citizens' access to the state and its services throughout the electoral cycle.

AD HOC TEAMS: INDONESIA

Having reviewed Malaysia's relatively robust and effective patronage parties, we jump to the opposite extreme. In Indonesia, most political candidates are essentially on their own when they run for office. Most of them opt to build personalized campaign structures, commonly known as "success teams," to connect them with voters and to organize their campaigns. Typically, they start by recruiting a number of close confidantes (relatives, friends, business partners, and the like) to form the team's inner core. Some of these individuals take care of specialist campaign functions – finances or advertising, for example – while others establish geographically organized teams of brokers. While some candidates draw on party structures and members in building these teams, most have minimal party support. Strikingly, these success teams are generally not merely personalized, but also short-lived, organizations. Formed on an ad hoc basis in the lead-up to an election, they typically dissolve shortly thereafter, being based frequently on relationships that are, at least in part, equally short-term and instrumental. Most people who get involved as candidates or success team members more or less openly recognize that these teams are about the mutual exchange of short-term benefits. A candidate in Central Java, for instance, identified the key to a success team that worked well as being "operational costs": finding small payments for transport and gifts of food, drink, and other items essential to building "friendship" within his team.[16]

The irony of this situation is that Indonesia has a relatively strong tradition of party organization and parties remain important players in national politics. As explained in Chapter 2, in the 1950s, Indonesia made the transition to independent statehood with competitive elections and a series of parties that were based on deeply rooted socio-religious "streams" in Indonesian society – so-called *aliran* (Geertz 1959; Fossati 2019). Though Indonesia was subsequently ruled by an army-based authoritarian regime between 1966 and 1998 that did what it could to cripple party politics and uproot parties from their moorings in Indonesian society, the country's re-transition to democracy at the end of the 1990s revealed that parties had been relatively resilient. Several parties formed that could trace their lineage back to the 1950s and the various streams of secular nationalism, traditionalist Islam, and modernist Islam that had dominated the country at that time. A new era of party politics seemed to be dawning.

Over subsequent years, however, several factors conspired to undermine parties' cohesion and to motivate aspiring politicians to establish their own ad hoc brokerage networks when running for office. One factor was the rise to political prominence of a new layer of local elites – many of whom had one foot in the world of business and another in the bureaucracy – who, having gained private wealth and social stature during the New Order or in its aftermath, mostly lacked traditional loyalties to parties and, when they engaged in politics, simply sought whatever electoral vehicle would be most convenient in their locale (see Hadiz 2010 for one elaboration of this argument). A similar story played out in the arena of presidential elections, where leading candidates organized personalized party vehicles to support their presidential aspirations.

---

[16] Interview, April 3, 2014, Pati.

Even more important were changes in Indonesia's electoral system. Indonesia made the transition to democracy with electoral rules that placed parties at the forefront of political life. Legislative elections, which were held simultaneously at district, provincial, and national levels, used a closed-list proportional-representation system. Candidates ran on party lists for legislative seats in multi-member districts. Whether an individual candidate won a seat depended on the total number of votes for the party (was it enough for one or more seats?) and where they were ranked on the party list (was it high enough to attain one of the seats the party won?). The system aligned incentives among candidates from the same party: the higher the party vote, the greater their individual chances of winning a seat.

Before long, however, Indonesia changed its electoral rules to embrace a more candidate-centered system. Just ahead of legislative elections in 2009, it adopted an open-list arrangement. Citizens could now cast a vote either for a party or for an individual candidate on the party's list. These votes were then added together to determine how many seats the party would win in the electoral district concerned. The candidates on each party's list with the highest number of personal votes secured those seats. This shift meant that, suddenly, candidates began to view candidates from their own party list as their greatest rivals – they were competing directly to attain the largest number of personal votes – dramatically reducing their incentives to cooperate. Prior to this shift, in 2004–05, the country had also introduced direct elections for executive government posts: district heads, provincial governors, and, at the center, the president. This change toward a candidate-centered system also tended to downgrade the role of parties because candidates with enough name recognition, money, or other advantages could bypass or eclipse established parties when building their campaign infrastructure. In general, parties do little to assist candidates, whether in terms of resources, mobilization, or coordination assistance. In fact, the flow is commonly in the opposite direction: parties, taking advantage of their still-important gatekeeping role, are more likely to predate upon candidates, including by extracting resources from them.

In most cases, parties hold the key to standing for elected office. In legislative elections, candidates must be members of registered parties, and the requirements for parties to register have become more onerous over time, not less. In regional executive elections (*pilkada*), though it eventually became possible to stand as an independent candidate, the rules for doing so are quite demanding and most candidates generally prefer to patch together coalitions of parties to nominate them. Often, they simply purchase those parties' support, paying them large sums to sign off on the relevant nomination forms, and expecting little or no concrete support in terms of actual campaign infrastructure. Although some parties do take ideology and party loyalty seriously, it is not uncommon for candidates in legislative elections to purchase a position on the list of a party with which they otherwise have only tenuous connections. The overall result is a system in which parties continue to occupy an important place in legislative bodies and in national affairs in general, but where they often are of decidedly secondary importance when it comes to organizing election campaigns.

One incumbent DPR candidate we encountered in 2014, an influential figure within Golkar and province-level chair of the body within this party charged with coordinating its election campaign, acknowledged that he was "not relying on the party at all" in coordinating his own election campaign. The problem, he explained, was that the open-list PR system meant that it was "hard for the party to control competition among candidates within the party." So although the body he chaired produced policies, it was,

hard to apply them in the field, because the candidates are hard to control. The party can try to be firm about something, with the goal of increasing votes—for example, dividing up the territory [of an electoral district so as to minimize competition among candidates]. But the fact is that it's extraordinarily difficult to coordinate them. They are all motivated by the fear that they won't be elected. ... Even the party leaders can't concentrate on coordinating the campaign or the election strategy, because they are themselves candidates.[17]

The solution for political candidates is to establish the sort of ad hoc success teams described earlier – even this senior Golkar member drew largely on people he had supported through various government programs, rather than party cadres. Such teams can be immense, mobilizing thousands of members for large-scale elections, or include mere dozens for a low-level post, such as a seat in a district parliament. Functionally, however, the teams are generally similar. Depending on the sophistication and funding of the campaign, some core members of the team perform specialist tasks – for example, organizing media campaigns or monitoring the performance of base-level brokers. Every candidate hopes to form teams that are led from top to bottom by persons who are personally loyal, typically because they have benefitted from that candidate's assistance or largesse in the past, or are connected through organizational ties or other social networks (Tawakkal et al. 2020). But the bulk of team members are generally rather ordinary members of the community with little direct connection to the candidate. Each is charged with enlisting a number of other voters – from a handful to a few dozen – to vote for their candidate.

To facilitate the organization of such base-level brokers, these success teams are generally pyramidically structured and geographically organized (see Figure 3.2). For example, in an election for a district-level position, the candidate and their advisors divide the district into subdistricts and appoint a coordinator for each one; the subdistrict coordinators recruit village coordinators, who recruit hamlet coordinators, who then recruit a large number of base-level brokers tasked with approaching voters and convincing them to support the candidate. One of the key functions of the base-level brokers is to collect lists of names of voters who (purportedly) pledge to support the candidate and pass

[17] Interview, April 3, 2014, Pati.

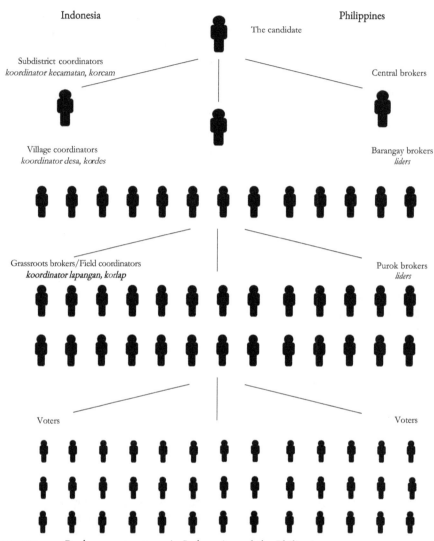

FIGURE 3.2. Brokerage structures in Indonesia and the Philippines
Source: Aspinall and Hicken (2020).

these lists up the pyramid to the candidate and his or her core team. They, in turn, collate the lists in the lead-up to election day, allowing the candidate to get a picture of his or her electoral strength in advance of the vote. Approaching election day, money – typically doled out in plain envelopes – makes its way to voters through the same layers of coordinators, eventually being delivered into voters' hands by the base-level brokers. (See Chapter 4 for more details about the make-up and function of these broker networks.)

It should be noted that some candidates do draw on party structures in organizing their campaigns – for instance, candidates who hold positions of influence within the local party organization. But in legislative elections, most candidates cannot direct the local party organization to support their candidacy, precisely because candidates from the same party and electoral district compete against each other. Very often, the majority of party cadres in the district work for the most senior party leader standing for election there; on other occasions, party members are themselves divided, supporting whichever candidate they owe most loyalty, or whom they view as their most promising future patron. As one candidate for Gerindra in Central Java explained: "You can't rely on the party at all: the party is something we fight over. All candidates fight to use the party."[18] A PDI-P candidate in Northern Sulawesi likewise complained that members of his party in his province either wanted to campaign for their local branch head, or else "just want money, and are quite pragmatic about it."[19] The result of this intra-party competition is that few candidates end up relying on parties alone, and some do not rely on their parties at all. Parties are therefore not inactive during election campaigns; they are simply one network among many being mobilized (indeed, when describing their success teams, many candidates will refer to their "party team" alongside their "family team" and so on), and they rarely serve the coordinating function across candidates that we observed in Malaysia.

Even in regional government head elections (*pilkada*), for which each party can nominate a maximum of one candidate pair, these candidates almost never rely exclusively on parties to organize their campaigns. Very often, such candidates need to purchase (with cash payments) their nomination from one or more parties (Hendrawan et al. 2021), and they generally view the parties as either too expensive or too fickle to rely on them for campaigning. Most thus opt to build personalized *tim sukses*, incorporating their nominating parties as more or less active components of the campaign structure, but not pinning their hopes on them to get out the vote.

We find almost infinite variations on these ad hoc mobilization networks. In particular, candidates often outsource at least part of the brokerage function to leaders of social organizations at the community level – for example, a village head, an influential preacher, the head of a farmer's cooperative, or a women's microenterprise cooperative (see Chapters 5 and 7). Significant negotiation may be involved, with the candidate delivering some sort of club good – such as a village road, a new minaret, a hand tractor, cooking equipment – to cement the bargain. Sometimes such deals on club goods are separate from systematic distribution of cash to voters (donations that confer some sort of collective benefit tend to be viewed as far less morally and legally suspect in Indonesia than individualized payments), but very often they supplement electoral handouts; candidates often fear that if they provide *only* club goods, many beneficiaries will choose to freeride and fail to deliver the expected vote.

Overall, then, success teams are primarily purpose-built, short-term structures designed to organize election campaigns and mobilize brokers. Success teams play few if any of the other roles parties play in Malaysia, such as helping candidates gain access to patronage resources or coordinate with other candidates. Even though most are at least weakly affiliated with a party, candidates are typically on their own when it comes to organizing the funds needed for patronage strategies. Those who are incumbent legislators or, especially, regional government heads can certainly access state resources; they might engage in corruption and fund their vote buying and similar efforts that way, or they might divert development projects and other government programs to reward supporters (see Chapters 5 and 6). But many candidates are self-funded or take campaign donations from business sponsors who expect special favors should they succeed.[20] Nor do success teams play much role in raising funds – they are machines for dispensing electoral patronage, not for accumulating it. Unsuccessful candidates in Indonesia often struggle for years to repay campaign debts, and, as we have already mentioned, many candidates bemoan the heavy financial burden they are required personally to bear. One candidate, who would go on to win, had previously been elected under the old closed-list system. He noted the complete lack of support from the party and expressed his dismay at what the election was costing him. "If I had it to do over," he conceded, "I would not have run."[21]

This pattern translates into a norm of patronage distribution focused largely on elections. In the run-up to elections, patronage resources flow through success teams to individual voters in the form of electoral handouts, with very little in the way of micro-particularism between elections. Elections also bring a flowering of club goods and other forms of meso-particularism targeted to groups of voters, though candidates also aspire to provide some club goods between elections as a way to build and/or maintain their reputation, and certain categories of incumbents have considerable capacity to do so. We explore this practice in greater detail in Chapter 5.

With regard to coordinating across campaigns, what coordination occurs is the exception rather than the rule. In legislative elections, an Islamic party, Partai Keadilan Sejahtera (Prosperous Justice Party, PKS) has attempted to avoid geographic overlap and competition by divvying up legislative electoral districts into distinct zones, allocating a different candidate to each zone. With that one exception, most such efforts have been ineffective: other parties lack the means to restrain the ambitions of candidates who want to maximize their personal vote by recruiting brokers and voters in zones notionally allocated to

---

[20] Of course, poorly resourced challenger parties may provide little by way of campaign funds even where parties are strong – for example, Malaysia's PAS and DAP have long tithed their members in elected office. Yet those parties still perform mobilizing and coordinating roles, and presumably *would* subsidize campaigns if they could.

[21] Interview with DPR candidate, March 31, 2014, Jakarta.

other candidates. Candidates who are running at different levels in legislative elections – national, provincial, and district – and thus not in direct competition for votes, sometimes share brokers and otherwise cooperate. But these arrangements, known as *tandems*, are vulnerable to free-riding and deceit, relatively rare, and, according to those we interviewed, usually ineffective. In any case, even such cooperative arrangements involve coordination among individual candidates' success teams – teams quintessentially focused on individuals – and are not a collective effort.

To sum up, Indonesia's pattern of ad hoc teams has been conditioned by the collapse of a long-dominant authoritarian regime. When that regime collapsed, locally powerful political figures, most of whom had been nurtured by the informal networks that infused the state, were well-positioned to stand for elected office. To organize their campaigns, they could turn to a range of formal and informal networks and leaders who exercised influence in their local communities, piggybacking on their resources and connections, and trying to buy their loyalty with offers of patronage and short-term pay-offs. At the same time, the post-2009 electoral system provided these newly empowered political actors with few incentives to rely upon parties to coordinate their campaigns. Parties still have little to offer in terms of access to patronage or campaign support. On the whole, all they offer many candidates is a spot on the ballot. The result is a pattern of electoral competition dominated by ad hoc vote-brokerage structures and focused on micro-particularism and meso-particularism that is mostly – but not entirely – dispensed during elections.

LOCAL MACHINES: THE PHILIPPINES

In the Philippines, the dominant mode of electoral organization is best conceptualized as something that combines elements of both Indonesia's ad hoc campaign teams and Malaysia's highly coordinated and institutionalized parties. As in Indonesia, candidates for political office in the Philippines organize hierarchical teams of local brokers. These networks – which may call themselves parties or at least "teams" – are less ephemeral than their Indonesian counterparts, often lasting over several electoral cycles and being based on enduring forms of relational clientelism. They typically also involve collaboration among groups of candidates rather than being centered solely around a single candidate or candidate pair. In contrast to the Malaysian pattern,[22] the machines are, in general, local or provincial rather than national in scope. They bring together local elites – often from a single political dynasty in a particular area – and engage in fluid negotiations and ever-changing alliances with national parties (themselves more shells than functional

---

[22] With the partial exception of East Malaysia: given their physical and substantive distance from the peninsula, Sabah and Sarawak *have* historically supported strong state-specific parties, with regionally bound machinery; see Chapter 8.

organizations). In short, they are true *local machines*, aggregated and institutionalized at a higher level than in Indonesia but a lower level than in Malaysia.

As discussed in Chapter 2, and as in our other cases, we locate the origins of this distinctive form in the country's history and political economy. Unlike in Malaysia, where a strong national party captured power early on during the transition to independence, turning the state and its resources to its own patronage purposes, or Indonesia, which was long ruled by a military and bureaucratic-based authoritarian regime, in the Philippines, the dominant forces that emerged at the local level in the early twentieth century were family groups that organized strong and enduring local political machines. Since independence, these local machines have attached themselves to national political parties, generally through short-term arrangements intended to maximize their access to national patronage resources. In doing so, they benefit from a system that tends to give well-connected politicians a high degree of discretion over the regulatory and allocative processes of the state.

Throughout the early postwar period, from independence in 1946 to the declaration of martial law in 1972, the Liberal Party and Nacionalista Party alternated in power within a two-party system. However, the local power blocs that constituted the core of the system positioned themselves opportunistically vis-à-vis these parties. Carl Landé's description, a classic in the field of clientelism studies, is worth quoting at length:

Formally, each party is an association composed of those who have become party members. In practice each party, at any point in time, is a multi-tiered pyramid of personal followings, one heaped upon the other. Each link in the chain of vertical dyads is based upon personal assurances of support and conditional upon the downward flow of patronage and spoils. But even this description of a party exaggerates its coherence. For as has been noted, political leaders wander into and out of parties with personal followers in tow, feeling no strong obligation, and being under no real pressure, to support their party mates. Party membership is not a category but a matter of degree.

If one wishes to discover the real framework upon which election campaigns are built, one must turn away from political parties and focus one's attention upon individual candidates and the vertical chains of leadership and followership into which they arrange themselves at any given point in time. While tending to tie together persons who claim the same party label, these chains must in fact be viewed as independent structures resembling a network of strong vines which variously cling to or twist back and forth between two great but hollow trees. (Landé 1973, 116)[23]

Though the two-party system broke down under the Marcos dictatorship (1972–86), and has since been replaced with a multiparty system (Hicken 2009), the country still has an "absence of strong and credible parties" (Teehankee 2012, 187) perpetuated by a decidedly candidate-centric electoral

---

[23] On subsequent amendments to, and critiques of, Landé's framework, see Hicken, Hutchcroft, Weiss, and Aspinall (2019), 13–17.

system (as discussed in Chapter 2). One indication is the regular party-switching that takes place when newly elected members of Congress (and other office holders) associate themselves with the party of the president so as to gain greater access to patronage. This practice has led to the emergence of a succession of dominant parties in Congress, each associated with a particular president (Teehankee 2012, 186–87). More deeply, it is not merely that clientelistic networks of the sort Landé describes persist as a fundamental basis of political alignments, undergirding the parties, but so too do political clans, which Teehankee (2012, 195) describes as the "building blocks of politics."

Given this context, the key organizations during elections are local political machines. In their basic structure, local machines in the Philippines look very similar to the brokerage structures used in Indonesia. Both adopt the same pyramidal form (see Figure 3.2), with an apex team recruiting and organizing large teams of brokers whose functions are to map voter support, enlist sympathetic voters, and distribute cash payments and other inducements. As in Indonesia, candidates are especially keen to recruit informal community leaders into their teams, and to use their brokers' personal networks and social influence to generate support. As one senior broker put it, these are, "people who they [residents] look up to in the *purok* [neighborhood]; if there is a problem, they are the ones who go to the mayor and ask him to intercede."[24]

Barangay officers, especially barangay captains, are particularly prized as brokers, given their close association with voters. Although barangay officials are elected separately in what are purportedly nonpartisan races, captains usually ally with a local machine and mobilize voters' support. The machine then reciprocates at the next barangay election. The same broker explained of barangay captains: "if they are doing their job well, the people will follow them. For example, if they have medical needs, need a fare, or whatever they go to the barangay captain, if the barangay captain can't help, they go to the mayor. The barangay captain is the 'first line of defense.'"

Not only does the structure look similar in the Philippines and Indonesia, but brokers also employ many of the same techniques. For example, they draw up very similar lists of voters to whom cash should be delivered, divvying up the responsibility for collecting names and distributing funds by neighborhood. As in Indonesia, brokers pass lists of names up to the central campaign, where they may be reviewed; as election day draws near, the central campaign then passes money down to brokers for distribution to individual voters.

More generally, campaign organizers in the Philippines and Indonesia often speak in strikingly similar terms about the challenges they face in building reliable teams, ensuring broker discipline, recruiting voters, ensuring that brokers deliver votes, and responding to the vote-buying efforts of rivals. The similarities are such that it sometimes seems as if the two groups must have

---

[24] Interview, senior broker, May 4, 2016, Tagbilaran.

learned from each other, though the general lack of regular interaction between subnational Philippines and subnational Indonesia makes that unlikely. Instead, the similarity of vote-buying networks in Indonesia and the Philippines is an example of similar forms emerging when political actors confront comparable problems.

The obvious similarities in form and style of brokerage structures in the Philippines and Indonesia, however, mask two main differences that help define and delimit local party machines vis-à-vis ad hoc teams: the degree of cooperation and coordination among candidates, and the degree to which structures endure between and across elections. We consider each of those differences in turn, and then discuss reasons behind them.

Cooperative vs. Adversarial Campaigning

Local machines in the Philippines tend to be more cooperative enterprises than campaign organizations in Indonesia. In Indonesia, candidates form success teams that either work to elect just one candidate pair (in *pilkada*) or are distinct from, and compete against, the teams of their co-partisans (in legislative elections). Occasionally, candidates from the same party will engage in limited coordination or cooperation for different offices (e.g., seats in national, provincial, and district legislatures), but such arrangements are the exception rather than the rule. By contrast, in the Philippines, local machines typically mobilize on behalf of an entire slate of candidates. This list can include candidates for governor, mayor, provincial and municipal councilors, and, to a lesser extent, candidates for national offices.[25] These machines generally operate under the leadership of one or more local leaders (usually a mayoral or gubernatorial candidate) and share resources, brokers, and information when executing their campaigns. The leaders of the machine also frequently negotiate with higher-level candidates, including presidential candidates and their parties, to leverage electoral resources and future patronage. However, as noted earlier, their relations with national parties are generally flexible, with the local-machine boss frequently shifting the machine's alignment as opportunities at the national level change.

Campaigns usually print sample ballots (to which they often staple cash), listing all the candidates linked to the machine – from president to municipal councilors – and urge voters to support the entire slate: to "vote straight." (Occasionally, they even promise voters bonuses if the whole slate wins.) Of course, as the vignette at the beginning of Chapter 1 recounted, the focus tends to be on local-level offices, with national offices a secondary consideration, and brokers always emphasize voting for *their* individual candidate first, then the rest of the slate if voters are so inclined. (In the heat of electoral battles, it is not

---

[25] The same machines also mobilize to elect allied barangay councilors during separate elections.

uncommon for others on the slate to be unobtrusively ditched.) Individual candidates often supplement the machine's efforts with their own personal campaign organizations.

These local machines also tend to play a role in coordinating access to patronage among candidates. Again, this pattern diverges from what we see in Indonesia, where candidates are typically on their own when it comes to fundraising and sourcing patronage (and in Malaysia, where the party provides most resources). The difference arises from the fact that teams in the Philippines are fundamentally collective enterprises. The key figure at the top of the slate – behind whom is often a wealthy and powerful local family – has an interest in having allies in other village, municipal, and provincial positions. Common purpose makes it easier to consolidate and defend their local base, pursue their agenda, and generate resources for patronage. As such, the candidate at the head of the machine will typically want to support candidates across positions. Likewise, the candidate will see obvious advantages in aligning with sympathetic politicians in Congress, able to direct pork-barrel spending and other benefits to the locale. There are thus strong incentives for collaboration up and down the ballot, with both lower-level and higher-level candidates, and coordination across candidates for the same office (e.g., for provincial boards).[26]

If already entrenched in local government, the machine will be able to direct government projects and other resources to support the slate. For example, many of our interviewees reported a biased distribution of municipal projects in favor of barangays with leaders allied with the mayor. Similarly, Hicken, Atkinson, and Ravanilla (2015) find that political ties shape the distribution of congressional disaster assistance to municipalities. The machine leader will sometimes also take responsibility for financing the bulk of electoral handouts and other campaign expenditures for the whole group (though, again, individual candidates may also augment such efforts with their own funds), or several leaders (e.g., mayoral and gubernatorial candidates) might jointly cover the slate's campaign costs.

Data from our surveys of brokers in the Philippines and Indonesia (see Chapter 1 and Appendix A for details) illustrate the higher level of coordination and cooperation in the Philippines. We asked brokers whether or not they had worked for any other candidate, besides the one we were discussing. Only 8.1 percent of Indonesian brokers reported doing so. By contrast, a majority of brokers we surveyed in the Philippines (52.6 percent) worked for at least one other candidate in the same election (Table 3.2). Of these, most reported working for candidates at higher-level or parallel positions (e.g., governor and provincial board) on the same slate, indicating that they were doing at least some campaigning for teams of candidates linked to the same machine.

---

[26] As discussed earlier, loyalty and links to the president's team tend to be much stronger in the wake of, rather than prior to, elections.

TABLE 3.2. *Philippine and Indonesian brokers compared*

	Philippines	Indonesia
Did brokers work for at least one other candidate during the same election?		
No	47.4	91.9
Yes	52.6	8.1
Brokers' expected compensation		
None	58.1	29.9
Salary or expenses	7.5	62.9
Job or patronage	34.5	6.9
Did brokers expect to be rewarded for high performance?		
No	28.0	91.1
Yes	72.0	8.9

Source: Authors' surveys of brokers in Central Java, Indonesia (2014), and Sorsogon Province, Philippines (2016). Survey details available in Appendix A.

Enduring vs. Ad Hoc Organizations

The second difference between campaign organizations in the Philippines and Indonesia is linked to the first but is more subtle: local machines in the Philippines are based on much more enduring forms of relational clientelism than are the usually more ad hoc and ephemeral Indonesian success teams (for more details see Aspinall and Hicken 2020). Though Philippine machines are mobilized and deployed during election season, at their core are clientelist and/ or family relationships that can and do last a lifetime, and are often even passed down from one generation of politicians and brokers to the next.[27] They operate between elections along more traditional patron-client lines: brokers expect to receive assistance (jobs, development projects, help with school fees, etc.) from their politicians, in exchange for staying on as vote mobilizers. Almost all candidates we interviewed were either already part of enduring local machines or were working to build them, with plans to keep these machines alive and operating long-term. For this reason, despite an increase in the provision of micro- and meso-particularism around elections, we do not see nearly so big a spike in the Philippines as in Indonesia. This is because the baseline level of patronage distribution is simply much higher in the Philippines. Even "new" candidates rarely have to start from scratch, being instead able to rely on established local machines to mobilize on their behalf.

One way to illustrate the differences between these two types of mobilization networks is to look more closely at the nature of the brokers in each. To be sure, most local machines in the Philippines employ some instrumental

---

[27] See also Hicken, Aspinall and Weiss (2019) and Mangada (2019).

brokers – those with weak ties to the candidate, for whom the work is temporary and transactional – but data from our two sets of broker surveys confirm that the ratio of loyalists to instrumentalists is much higher in the Philippines than in Indonesia. For instance, we can consider how campaigns compensate brokers for their labor (Table 3.2). Where brokers are guns-for-hire, we would expect broker employment to be transactional, with brokers receiving immediate payment for their services. Where brokers are part of enduring political machines, however, we would expect more brokers to work as volunteers, demonstrating loyalty and gratitude to the machine for past assistance, or to work with an expectation of future rewards. This divergence is exactly what we see in our surveys. The large majority of our Philippine brokers did not expect immediate compensation for their work. A substantial majority (58.1 percent) reported expecting no compensation at all, while 34.5 percent expected to garner jobs or other forms of patronage. By contrast, in Indonesia, brokers were more commonly paid directly and immediately for their work (62.9 percent), though the majority of respondents only expected reimbursement for expenses and did not receive a salary.[28] Fewer than 7 percent of Indonesian brokers expected to receive jobs or other types of patronage (such as access to government programs) after the election in compensation for their work. Also indicative of the more enduring nature of campaign machines in the Philippines are brokers' beliefs about the possibility of rewards for high performance. Most brokers (72 percent) expected such recognition in the Philippines. But in Indonesia, fewer than 10 percent of brokers expected to be rewarded for exceeding expectations, suggesting they truly viewed campaigning as a one-shot transaction (Table 3.2).

In summary, the structures and purposes of Indonesian success teams and Philippine local political machines have certain basic similarities. In both countries, these personalized organizations substitute for strong national parties. Their primary purpose is to link the candidate with voters at the grassroots, by creating a network of brokers connected to individual voters in villages and neighborhoods. These structures are constructed from a mix of affinity or loyalty ties and opportunistic or instrumental relationships. (Chapter 7 explores the differences between these two types of networks.) However, important differences distinguish these otherwise similar organizations. Philippine local machines tend to be more stable and enduring, with a higher ratio of loyalists to instrumentalists, corresponding to a steadier flow of patronage between elections. By contrast, Indonesian teams are constructed only for the campaign period and rely much more heavily on guns-for-hire, while the distribution of patronage between elections is much lower. And both these patterns differ from

---

[28] Specifically, 6.3 percent expected to be compensated with salary and expenses, while 56.6 percent expected to be reimbursed for expenses only. As we discuss in more detail in the next chapter, Indonesian brokers are also "compensated" in other ways. Most campaigns assume the brokers will pocket some of the funds intended for voters, and many do so.

what we find in Malaysia: there, national parties structure campaign organization and mobilization. Although candidates may mobilize their own supporters, whether party members or not, to support their campaign effort, the party brand is almost always front and center. Parties provide at least a share of campaign resources and materials, coordinate among candidates, and deploy strategic meso-particularism between elections to help build and bolster the party's brand.

CONCLUSION: WHY THESE DIFFERENCES AND DO THEY TRAVEL?

In this chapter, we have described and analyzed three distinct types of electoral mobilization regimes. In the subsequent chapters we explore the ways in which different types of mobilization regimes shape candidate electoral strategies. To summarize, we see real differences in types of mobilization networks across our three cases. These span a rough continuum, from party-based networks in Malaysia; to relatively enduring vehicles of cliques, factions, or dynasties in the Philippines; to personal, ephemeral teams for individual candidates in Indonesia. In Chapter 2, we examined how key historical-institutional factors – the (co-)evolution of the state and political parties, the emergence of distinct constituencies for patronage, features of the electoral system, and rules and norms governing politicians' discretion over state patronage resources – have shaped contemporary electoral mobilization regimes within each country. We return to these issues in Chapter 9.

To what extent is our conceptual framework useful for understanding other cases? While we don't presume our three regime types are exhaustive of the ways candidates for office might mobilize for elections, we do contend that they have corollaries in other contexts, as discussed in Chapter 9. We believe our conceptual approach is appropriate for studying electoral mobilization in a variety of contexts. The questions we ask in this chapter are as useful for analyzing mobilization networks in Mauritius and Peru as they are in Malaysia and the Philippines. These questions include: How central are parties, particularly national parties, in electoral mobilization? To what extent are mobilization machines enduring organizations? Who has access to state resources? To what extent do politicians have access to state-based patronage resources between elections? To what extent can parties or machines help politicians coordinate that access, or are they on their own? The answers to such questions help us map the kinds of mobilization networks that operate within a given context.

By examining the types of networks involved in structuring competition, determining access to resources, and mobilizing voters, we gain insight not only into the shape of the campaign itself but also the type of patronage distribution that accompanies it. In the next three chapters, we turn our focus to describing and analyzing these dynamics as they relate to, respectively, the distribution of micro-particularism, meso-particularism, and macro-particularism.

4

Targeting Individuals: Don't You Forget about Me

A few months prior to Indonesia's 2014 legislative election, Ahmad was resign-edly preparing for his reelection campaign. A member of the local parliament in the Javanese city of Yogyakarta, representing an Islamic party, he did not like the direction the country's electoral politics were going. The introduction of open-list voting in 2009 had given rise to a new pragmatism on the part of voters and candidates alike. People didn't care anymore about a party's "vision and mission," he complained; now they only cared about "financial resources and social networks." In the preceding election, he had won reelection but had had some bad experiences. In one village, he gave a large donation to help renovate a mosque, but the village had voted *en masse* for another candidate. Curious about why they had done so, he visited the village after the election and talked to the community leaders, with whom he thought he had reached a deal. It turned out that a rival candidate had given the people in the village 10,000 rupiah (less than USD1) each. One of the locals explained the problem to Ahmad: "It's not the mosque who votes, it's the people."[1]

Ahmad learned his lesson, and he knew he was facing a tough challenge if he wanted to be reelected in 2014. Another candidate, number four on his party's list in his electoral district, was going to "fight to win," using money to do so. In response, Ahmad was busy building his own success team, down to the grass-roots: "It's very costly, but unavoidable." Now, when he went to visit voters, if they told him that another candidate had visited and given them material benefits, and asked him to do the same, he always complied. On election day, he was expecting the price of a vote to be 25,000 rupiah per person (about half a day's wage for a laborer). He still preferred to provide collective benefits, but he was getting ready.

---

[1] Interview, September 13, 2013, Yogyakarta.

Ahmad's discomfort with providing individual gifts is widely shared. Among patronage strategies, the distribution of money, goods, and services to individual voters or households often produces the most concern among good governance advocates and the most sensationalist headlines at election times. It is to these activities that we turn in this chapter. Building on Hutchcroft (2014b), we label these kinds of activities *micro-particularism* to distinguish them from the practice of targeting resources to larger groups of voters (meso-particularism such as "pork," club goods, and local public goods, the subject of Chapter 5) and from the at least ostensibly more programmatic macro-particularism we explore in Chapter 6.

The variety of micro-particularistic handouts we witnessed during elections was astonishing, bounded only by the creativity of the politician or broker involved. Cash was the most common offering, but other examples included food, construction materials, fuel, household goods, school books and other educational equipment, religious paraphernalia, bill payments, scholarships, medical assistance, and public-sector jobs (spoils). Looking across our primary and secondary cases, micro-particularism is a ubiquitous strategy in the Philippines, Indonesia, and East Malaysia (the Borneo states of Sabah and Sarawak), as well as Thailand (e.g., Penchan 2019).[2] By contrast, the targeting of individuals and households is less common in Peninsular Malaysia and rare in Singapore and Timor-Leste. In Chapter 3, we discussed the factors that shape preferences over different types of mobilization strategies across and within countries. In this chapter, we focus on data from our cases where micro-particularism is common.

By far the most common form of micro-particularism in our cases is the distribution of cash to voters. Sometimes, participants attempt to turn electoral handouts into formal market-like transactions. One candidate in Indonesia had recipients sign contracts pledging to vote for him and voters sometimes directly ask brokers what they are offering for a vote. More commonly, though, handouts are framed in culturally acceptable ways that imply an act of generosity or assistance. This gloss is apparent in the terms used, which are as numerous as they are creative. In the Philippines alone, terms for cash handouts include:

- "allowances" (Pampanga)
- *uwan-uwan* or "rain showers" (Bohol)
- *tag-tag* or "distribution" (Compostela Valley)
- *salu-salo* or a gathering where food is shared (Laguna)

In Indonesia and Malaysia, too, we heard references to cash (*uang* or *wang*) to pay for trivial items, such as *uang cendol* (a dessert), *uang es* (an ice-drink), or *uang bensin* (gas money), income replacement, bus money, and pocket money

---

[2] In the words of a Thai aphorism: "if the money doesn't come, voters can't vote" (เงินไม่มา กาไม่เป็น).

(*pesangon*). As we detail in this chapter, these softening euphemisms correspond to broader candidate and broker behavior; very little about what they do suggests that they consider these offers to be the opening salvo in a quid-pro-quo transaction.

We begin this chapter with a closer descriptive look at practices of micro-particularism in our cases to give a flavor of how they appear on the ground. What is being distributed? How is distribution carried out? When in the electoral cycle is micro-particularism distributed? What are the notable differences across our cases? We focus especially on the two settings in which national parties are commonly eclipsed by individual politicians and local machines. That is, we draw particular attention to the comparison between mobilization regimes in Indonesia (focusing on legislative rather than regional government-head elections) and the Philippines, and analyze how the nature of these regimes shapes the ways in which micro-particularism is organized and carried out in each country. We then turn our attention to what these handouts do and do not represent, to consider how what we observe in our cases stacks up against some of the classic models of clientelism in the literature. We show that handouts are rarely contingent exchanges – that is, vote buying or turnout buying – though there are some exceptions. Instead, we show that candidates offer voters electoral handouts as part of efforts to build a candidate's brand (*brand building*), demonstrate credibility (*credibility buying*), and keep contingent loyalists loyal (*turf protection*). This chapter thus contributes to a growing body of scholarship that considers patronage politics in circumstances lacking significant monitoring and enforcement (see Hicken and Nathan 2020).

WHAT DOES MICRO-PARTICULARISM LOOK LIKE?

Early on in our project, we were sitting in the house of a candidate for the DPR (Indonesia's national legislature) in Central Java trying to understand the mechanics of giving handouts to voters. "How do you decide who to offer money to," we asked, "and how do you get the money to them?" We were initially taken aback at how freely the candidate discussed the details of his operation with us – though the conversation proved to be representative of what we and our team later heard from hundreds of candidates and brokers across Indonesia and the Philippines. The candidate described how he divides up the electoral map, pointing out which areas he prioritizes and which he views as lost causes. He explained the process by which he decides how much to give and shared his formula for calculating the ratio of wasted handouts per vote (*margin error*), openly discussing his fear that brokers and voters would defect, and explaining what he was doing to minimize those defections (this turned out to be very little, apart from hoping for the best). He even brought out a binder listing the names and locations of each of his brokers in one subdistrict. Under each broker's name was a further listing of the voters they were assigned to target with offers of cash – complete with addresses and identity-card numbers.[3]

The brokerage networks described in the last chapter comprise the backbone of an electoral mobilization strategy relying upon micro-particularism. As we discussed, brokers compile lists of voters to be targeted and pass those lists up the organizational chain to the campaign headquarters. Money then flows back down the network to local brokers, to be passed along to voters. The timing of the distribution varies, but the distribution of cash usually occurs in the day or two before the election and often the evening before – during the "*oras de peligro*" (the critical moment) in the Philippines or in a "*serangan fajar*" (dawn attack) in Indonesia.[4]

The distribution of cash to voters was near-ubiquitous in both the Philippines and Indonesia. One of the goals of our project was to document just how common (or uncommon) this practice was. We did so using both national and local surveys that included a variety of questions designed to estimate the degree to which candidates targeted voters with electoral hand-outs. We asked voters about their personal experience in the most recent election. Lest social desirability bias cause voters to underreport the incidence of handouts, we also asked less personal questions about how common the practice was in their area, among their neighbors, etc. Concerns about social desirability bias also motivated our decision to include list experiments (also known as item-response experiments) in both countries to try to ascertain the "true" level of handouts (Corstange 2009; Gonzalez-Ocantos et al. 2012). In list experiments, the treatment and control groups each view the same list of items (e.g., of factors that influenced their vote), with one exception. The treatment group's list includes the addition of a potentially sensitive item – in this case, whether they received an offer of cash or goods before the election. Respondents are asked how many listed items apply to them personally. The difference in the average number of counts across the treatment and control groups serves to estimate the frequency of electoral handouts.

These surveys tell remarkably similar stories. In Indonesia, our national survey revealed that between one-quarter and one-third of voters were offered handouts by at least one candidate, results consistent with survey results from other researchers (e.g., Muhtadi 2018, 2019). Our survey in Central Java (where we sampled voters that brokers reported targeting, rather than a fully random sample) showed 35 percent receiving payments or goods from one candidate and a further 18 percent receiving such contributions from multiple

---

[3] We later used his lists, along with those from other candidates, as the basis for broker and voter surveys in Indonesia and the Philippines.

[4] While electoral handouts were comparatively rare in peninsular Malaysia, small payments on polling day, to reimburse for travel costs or lost work time to get to the polls, were somewhat more common. (As we detail in Chapter 8, the political economy of East Malaysia supports comparatively more endemic micro-particularism.)

candidates. The numbers are similar in the Philippines, where Pulse Asia has found that 22 and 23 percent of all respondents to national surveys in 2016 and 2019, respectively, reported receiving offers and one-quarter of respondents who had actually voted reported being offered handouts (Pulse Asia 2019b; see also Canare et al. 2018). Our own two local surveys there in 2016 revealed even higher rates in some areas – up to 60 percent. Likewise, we found very little social stigma associated with handouts in either country. Most candidates, brokers, and voters we met spoke openly of the practice. In both countries, we found the reported incidence of electoral handouts to be nearly identical, whether we asked about them directly, indirectly, or via the list experiment.

The amount of money offered varies widely. In both the Philippines and Indonesia, amounts are higher in closely contested races, or, e.g., where control of resource rents is at stake (see Chapter 8). Amounts also differ by office. In Indonesia, the general pattern is that candidates paid more per voter in lower-level contests in which they needed fewer votes to achieve victory. By contrast, in the Philippines, mayors and governors tended to offer the most, with candidates below and above them on the ticket offering less. In both the Philippines and Indonesia, candidates for national-level office (especially the presidency in both countries, and the Senate in the Philippines) generally find electoral handouts an inefficient way to mobilize the large number of voters needed, so offer less than candidates for lower-level office do (and may not offer anything). The amount per handout also varied. In Indonesia, we observed offers from 5,000 to 200,000 rupiah (approximately USD0.35–14), and heard reports of payments up to 1,000,000 rupiah (USD69) in some areas, though most offers were within the 20,000–50,000 range (approximately USD1.40–3.50). Amounts from individual candidates in the Philippines ranged from 20 pesos (USD0.40) for municipal councilor candidates to 1,000–1,500 pesos (USD20–30) for mayoral or gubernatorial candidates. (Amounts for an entire team of candidates can in some cases balloon into some thousands of pesos.) In Malaysia, handouts could be as low as a token 10 ringgit (USD2.50) "transport allowance," for instance, to 160 ringgit (USD39) for vouchers our team heard campaign workers in Penang were distributing, to be redeemed for cash after the election if the candidate won (Teo 2014, 73) – and we received reports of payments ranging from 50 to 1,000 ringgit (USD12–244) in East Malaysia.

The technicalities of distribution vary, but the process tends to be roughly as follows. Brokers personally deliver payments to each targeted voter or head of household, often in envelopes with the voter's name and address; less commonly, voters go to a central location to collect their handout. Sometimes brokers give food or other small gifts along with the cash (for instance, a bag of rice or packages of instant noodles). Also included in the envelope is some sort of information indicating the candidate or slate the voter should support. Candidate cards are common in Indonesia. In the Philippines, sample ballots are the norm, with the candidate's name highlighted, as part of a larger roster of other candidates from the same party or machine.

Candidates devote a great deal of time and thought to strategizing about how to get the most bang for their micro-particularistic buck. To illustrate, one afternoon we sat with a candidate for local office in the Philippines as a steady stream of brokers filed in to pick up cash and cases of instant noodles to distribute to voters. As we chatted, the candidate pulled out a stack of sample ballots – his own and several from other candidates on his team, but also some from his competitors. He then proceeded to give us a tutorial on the most effective way to attach cash to the sample ballot. First, he showed an example of a sample ballot with the cash stapled to the back. Rookie mistake, he explained. Voters won't see the name next to the cash, which weakens the association between cash and candidate. Next, he showed us a ballot with a single 500-peso note stapled to the front. An improvement, he conceded, but the ballot would have been more striking if the candidate had opted for five 100-peso notes. Finally, he showed us two ballots, each with 300 pesos. The first had a 200-peso and 100-peso note, each stapled to the front, one on top of the other. The second, the best ballot of the bunch – and, not coincidentally, his own – had three 100-peso notes fanned out across the top of the ballot, with his name clearly visible in a large, bold-print font below.

We and our research team saw less evidence of electoral handouts in practice in Malaysia, though lawsuits as well as candidates' and campaign teams' descriptions, plus abundant anecdotal evidence, confirm its prevalence in East Malaysia. There, the practice thrives in less readily accessible places: indigenous-community longhouses, palm-oil plantations, and the like. One example testifies to how taken-for-granted the process is. A local grandee in a rural, but not so remote, district in Sabah – who had recently "hopped" to the national party under which he now contested, reputedly recruited specifically for his ability to fund a successful campaign – slipped a Malaysian member of our team who happened to be his constituent 600 ringgit (about USD150) as "lunch money" after we interviewed him. Our discombobulated colleague politely demurred, but the incident underlined how normalized micro-particularism is in this part of Malaysia.

These are just a flavor of the types of strategies and behaviors that accompany elections in the Philippines, Indonesia, and Malaysia. In the next section, we put these strategies into broader theoretical and comparative contexts.

THE CHARACTERISTICS AND CONTOURS
OF MICRO-PARTICULARISM

We define micro-particularism as money, goods, or services distributed to individual voters or households in anticipation of electoral support. Three key characteristics distinguish micro-particularism. First, micro-particularism is discriminatory: it targets some voters and not others. Second, the handout is given in anticipation or hope that the recipients will feel an obligation to support the candidate. Third, while much of the activity on which we focus occurs during election season, micro-particularism can occur outside that temporal window. In fact, as we discuss in more detail later, our cases intriguingly vary in the extent to which election-related handouts build on or reflect more enduring clientelist relationships.

As the rich comparative literature on electoral clientelism has documented, election-related micro-particularism spans a number of different types of handouts, distinguished by the purpose behind them. These types include:

- *Vote buying*: targeting undecided voters and weak opponents in hopes of persuading them to support a candidate
- *Turnout buying*: targeting weak supporters in hopes that they will show up to vote
- *Abstention buying*: targeting opponents in hopes they will not vote
- *Brand building* (our term): non-targeted distribution meant to signal viability or generosity
- *Turf protection* (our term): targeting presumed supporters to hedge against defection
- *Credibility buying* (our term): targeting presumed supporters to signal viability as a candidate

The existing literature has tended to focus on the first three items, grouped under the rubric of "electoral clientelism" (Gans-Morse et al. 2014). Each of these three strategies approaches the distribution of cash and goods to voters as *contingent* clientelism, whether persuading swing voters through vote buying, targeting core but unmotivated supporters through turnout buying (Nichter 2008), or convincing opponents' supporters to stay home (abstention buying).[5] The expectation is that having accepted money, the voter will support the candidate or party (or abstain) *in exchange*. The chief concerns of candidates employing electoral-clientelist strategies are thus monitoring and enforcement of brokers and voters. Where they can, candidates tie future rewards (jobs, other forms of patronage) to both broker and voter performance. This requires campaign teams to collect systematic information about who turns out to vote, and to ascertain *how* they voted. The former information is not hard to track, though it can still be costly. Where there is a secret ballot, however, the latter is elusive. Brokers use a variety of strategies to deal with this challenge, from relying on dense social networks where people are more likely to know how others in their network vote (Ravanilla et al. 2021), to violating ballot secrecy (one campaign worker in the Philippines related a surely wishful tale of installing periscopes through the ceilings of schools used as polling centers), to merely implying the ability to ascertain how voters vote (Cruz 2019).[6]

---

[5] "Double persuasion" combines turnout buying and vote buying (Gans-Morse et al. 2014).

[6] In settings with high levels of coercion, a topic discussed further in Chapter 8, the tactics of bosses erase any fiction of ballot secrecy. For historical examples from the late 1940s and early post-Marcos years, see Sidel (1999), 82–83, 122.

Regardless of the strategy employed, systematically monitoring vote choice is difficult and costly – and according to recent studies, relatively rare (Hicken and Nathan 2020). This reality shapes candidates' and brokers' strategies. For example, brokers have an incentive to target disproportionally their candidate's most reliable or core supporters because they are both less costly to identify and less likely to defect, even when party leaders would really prefer to target swing voters (Stokes et al. 2013). Candidates and brokers may also leverage dense social networks or target community or group leaders who can reliably deliver a bloc of votes (Cruz 2019; Ravanilla et al. 2021). Finally, Finan and Schechter (2012) find that brokers systematically target voters who are more likely to feel a moral or social obligation to vote for someone who gives them a handout (e.g., candidates in Malaysia and Indonesia who make their pitch at places of worship, implicitly or even explicitly invoking voters' sacred commitment to follow through).

To what extent is candidate, broker, and voter behavior in Indonesia and the Philippines consistent with these types of electoral clientelism? On the one hand, there is much that looks similar. As we discussed in Chapter 3, candidates rely on extensive brokerage networks to deliver targeted handouts to individual voters and households. Candidates and brokers clearly give in the *hope* that voters will feel an obligation to reciprocate. On the other hand, much of what we observe in these two cases is inconsistent with the standard vote buying or turnout-buying story, and is instead more in line with handouts representing something other than contingent exchanges between candidates and voters. To better understand this, let's look at who gets targeted for handouts, the extent to which campaigns engage in monitoring and enforcement, and the degree to which voters defect.

Who Gets Targeted?

In the course of our field research, candidates and their campaign staff regularly claimed to have detailed information about the voter landscape – who were their supporters, who were persuadable, who were pledged to rival candidates, etc. For example, in Bohol, Philippines, one campaign divided voters into four categories (Macalandang 2019). The group that was first in line to receive electoral handouts were *ato* (ours), loyal supporters who could be reliably expected to vote for the candidate. The next category were *bali-bali*, or flexible. These voters received cash from more than one candidate but did not align with any, remaining overtly neutral in order to benefit from both or all sides. Some *bali-bali* voters received handouts. The third category were *palitunon* (to be bought): undecided voters who vote according to which campaign offered the most money. Finally, *pusilunon* (to be "shot") or *dili ato* (not with the party) voters were the last in line to receive handouts. These voters were known supporters of rival campaigns. While they were the lowest priority, resources permitting, they might still be "shot" with last-minute handouts in hopes of changing their minds.

Voter-classification schemes varied from campaign to campaign, though a three-fold categorization of loyal, swing or undetermined, and hostile was by far the most common. Overwhelmingly, campaign strategists prioritized for handouts the first group: core or loyal supporters. This core goes by various names – the aforementioned *ato* in Cebuano-speaking parts of the Philippines, *basis* in Indonesia – and consists of those individuals or households the campaign believes are predisposed to vote for the candidate. Almost without exception, the candidates and campaign staff our team interviewed insisted these voters were their top priority for handouts and other forms of micro-particularism. A campaign operative in the Philippines put it this way: "Why are we giving to those undecided, when we have our own supporters? [That would] waste our resources."[7] Only if funds suffice do campaigns explicitly target swing or undecided voters.[8] Given this preference, the actual distribution of funds may seem puzzling. Despite teams' reportedly prioritizing their core or base, in fact, most electoral handouts end up in the hands of voters with, at best, tenuous loyalties to those candidates. This paradox is particularly evident in Indonesia (see also Muhtadi 2019), but is very common, too, in the Philippines.

This discrepancy appears puzzling until we remember how, in environments with weak party loyalties such as the Philippines and Indonesia, candidates define their base. In our interviews with candidates, we found that campaigns defined this base to include personal networks, patronage networks, and brokerage networks. We can think of these networks as a set of concentric circles around the candidate. Networks further from the candidate encompass more voters but with diminishing loyalty. We discussed the structure of these networks in the last chapter. Here, we delve into how candidates use them to distribute electoral handouts and how the nature of the electoral regime shapes the kinds of risks campaigns associate with these mobilization networks.

In a candidate's inner circle are personally loyal family members and close friends. These individuals usually make up the core of a candidate's campaign team, and because of their close personal ties with the candidate, do not need a monetary inducement to secure their loyalty. Still, the candidate may compensate some core campaign staff for their time and give others token payments to signal that their loyalty is valued.

The next set of voters in a candidate's base are voters they have helped in the past – those in the candidate's patronage networks. This category could include, in the Philippines, barangay officials whom the machine supported in village elections or voters to whom the candidate or machine provided financial assistance or public-sector jobs. (As we have explained, such enduring support is especially salient in the Philippines, though we do also see these ties in

---

[7] Interview with senior campaign staffer, May 2, 2016, New Bataan, Compostela Valley.
[8] We found relatively little evidence of abstention buying – paying voters not to vote – although there were a few reports of all-expenses-paid beach outings' being arranged on election day for likely supporters of rival candidates in the Philippines (dubbed "kidnapping" in local parlance).

Indonesia, sustained by both personal and public resources.) Such voters are likely to view electoral handouts as merely one component of an ongoing clientelist relationship with the candidate or machine (Nichter 2018). In Indonesia and the Philippines, we found that candidates routinely target such voters, believing them inclined to be loyal. One campaign worker in southeastern Mindanao, who had received a job from the candidate that enabled her to pay for her children's education, told our researcher that fighting for the candidate was the "least she could do" to repay that help (Aquino 2019, 306). Similarly, when we asked the campaign manager for a mayoral candidate in Sorsogon, Philippines, how he kept his brokers (*liders*) loyal, he replied simply, "KBL": the tradition we described in Chapter 1 of giving cash for weddings (*kasal*), baptisms (*binyag*), and funerals (*libing*).[9]

However, we discovered that while campaigns considered such voters to be relatively loyal, by no means did they assume that loyalty to be absolute. Indeed, they viewed these voters as contingent loyalists – perhaps favorably disposed to the candidate but willing to defect if neglected. Consistent with this understanding, we found that most campaigns offered loyalists the same payment as non-loyalists to discourage defection, a practice Muhtadi (2019, 161) confirms in a survey of winning teams in Indonesia: 39 percent of successful candidates surveyed believed that "a lot" or "quite a lot" of loyalists would defect to other candidates if they did not receive ongoing assistance; another 47 percent thought some would. In our own survey of brokers, 44 percent predicted at least "quite a lot" of voters would defect. Though we lack comparable survey data for the Philippines, our interviews and focus-group discussions revealed that candidates and brokers consistently reported targeting their own loyalists first, usually with the same amount they offered to non-loyalists,[10] and expected that not distributing money to core supporters would induce many to defect. One broker, for example, lamented that "among the 80 percent of the voters that [we] expected would vote in [the] party from the barangay ... only 56 percent of the voters voted for the candidate."[11] The solution, she and others said, was to be sure to give enough money to solid supporters or allies (*kakampi*) to keep them loyal. We discuss motives for targeting ostensibly loyal voters further when we turn to our discussion of turf protection.

Finally, some of those whom candidates consider part of their base are tied to the candidate only through the candidate's broker network. Candidates generally seek to assemble as large a broker network as they can afford; the more brokers, they reason, the more voters to whom the campaign has direct, personal access. Candidates count on each broker using campaign-supplied

[9] Interview, May 8, 2016, Sorsogon province.
[10] A few campaigns did report offering more to supporters of the other side (*kalaban*) to induce them to switch. However, the priority for distribution remained unchanged: core supporters first, undecided voters next, and then, funds permitting, opponents' supporters.
[11] Focus group discussion (FGD), Broker Group #1, Sorsogon province, July 17, 2016.

handouts to mobilize their own personal core for the candidate. However, the larger the brokerage network grows, the more tenuous the connection between the candidate and broker becomes, all else equal, and the more likely brokers are to be guns-for-hire rather than loyalists. As a result, although most of the voters who receive handouts have some personal connection to a broker, they may have little to no direct connection to the candidate, leading candidates to have little confidence in their loyalty.

As we detailed in Chapter 3, in the Philippines, campaign organizations are most commonly built on established networks of relational clientelism within local machines, while success teams in Indonesia are more likely to be transactional and ephemeral. As a result, not only is the ratio of loyalists to guns-for-hire larger among brokers in the Philippines, but the number of voters with personal or patronage ties to the candidate is also higher. Still, even in the Philippines, many voters who receive handouts have weak or no loyalty directly to the candidate. In consequence, most voters that make up the candidate's "base" in either country are, at best, conditionally loyal. Much of what drives candidate behavior is underlying uncertainty about these loyalties, despite confident assertions to the contrary (Rohman 2016). This pattern echoes what Diaz-Cayeros et al. (2016) describe in Mexico: party loyalty is conditional on benefits received (see also Dunning and Stokes 2007). Because contingent voter loyalties in the Philippines and Indonesia are not to parties but rather to local machines and individuals, they are all the more fragile.

So, to summarize, consistent with what we would expect from much of the existing literature, when it comes to electoral handouts and other forms of micro-particularism, candidates prioritize targeting their core supporters. But despite this stated preference, most recipients of electoral handouts end up being individuals without personal loyalty to the candidate. This pattern reverses what Stokes et al. (2013, 76) identify in Argentina. There, parties attempt to sway undecided voters by targeting swing constituencies, but within those constituencies, brokers tend to target core supporters in order to maintain their own base of influence and hence capture greater rents. By contrast, in Indonesia and the Philippines, candidates prefer to target core supporters, but, because of weak party loyalties and the importance of broker ties with voters, most funds end up in the hands of those with tenuous loyalty to the candidate.

Monitoring and Enforcement

If most recipients of electoral handouts have, at best, weak loyalty to the candidate or party distributing them, we might expect campaigns to invest in capacity for monitoring and enforcing voter behavior. For turnout and abstention buying, what matters most is monitoring whether or not individuals turn out to vote. For vote buying, enforcement requires getting information about *how* they voted. Surprisingly, though, we see minimal monitoring or enforcement efforts in Indonesia and the Philippines – much less than we would expect if electoral handouts were the kind of contingent exchange standard models of electoral clientelism describe. Candidates make some attempts to monitor broker behavior but expend almost no effort to monitor or respond to that of voters. To understand this pattern, we begin with campaigns' limited attempts to monitor brokers, and especially how the nature of the mobilization regime shapes the risk of broker shirking; we then turn to the (lack of) evidence of voter monitoring or enforcement.

Mobilization Regimes, Broker Risk, and Broker Monitoring

Let's start with broker monitoring. A major concern of almost every candidate we interviewed was brokers' shirking. Brokers shirk in myriad ways, including constructing voter lists without speaking to voters, not doing enough to encourage votes for the candidate, diverting some or all of the funds intended for voters to their own pocket, and double-dipping to work for rival campaigns. Hence, candidates make every effort to recruit brokers they can trust.[12] But as we discussed in Chapter 3, the size of brokerage networks is such that, inevitably, many of the brokers recruited to work on a campaign will have scant personal ties or loyalty to the candidate. This problem is most acute in Indonesia, where the ratio of mercenary to loyalist brokers is higher than in the Philippines, with its more commonly ongoing clientelist relationships and enduring local political machines.[13] (The far more limited prevalence of vote buying and other micro-particularism in Malaysia makes it harder to identify broad patterns there. However, interviews with candidates and campaign staff in East Malaysia suggest parties supplement their own workers with hired brokers, the latter offering access to specific communities being targeted, such as longhouse residents or oil-palm workers. They, too, expect brokers to shirk.)

The greater proportion of instrumental brokers associated with Indonesia's ad hoc teams comes through in our broker surveys. These surveys reveal information on how brokers assembled their lists of voters to be targeted (Table 4.1). Overall, brokers in Indonesia put in significantly less effort when assembling their voter lists than did their Philippine counterparts. Nearly all brokers in the Philippines reported speaking with voters before adding them to the list in order to confirm their vote choice, while only three-quarters of Indonesian brokers bothered with this step. Indonesian brokers were also much less likely to talk to voters about the candidate for whom they were working. A quarter of Indonesian brokers said nothing about the candidates' policy platforms, and nearly 60 percent said only "a little." By contrast, nearly all brokers in the Philippines spoke to voters about their candidate before listing

---

[12] For more on broker recruitment and types, see Aspinall (2014b), Auerbach and Thachil (2018), and Holland and Palmer-Rubin (2015).

[13] This section draws on Aspinall and Hicken (2020). See also Hicken et al. (2022).

TABLE 4.1. *Effort by brokers in the Philippines and Indonesia (% of brokers surveyed)*

	Philippines	Indonesia
Did the brokers confirm with voters before putting them on the list?		
No	4.2	24.8
Yes	95.8	75.2
Did brokers speak to voters about their candidates' policy platforms?		
No	2.7	24.8
A little	33.3	59.6
A lot	64.0	15.7

TABLE 4.2. *Number of names on brokers' lists (% of brokers surveyed)*

	Philippines	Indonesia
0–15 voters	11.6	34.5
16–50 voters	21.6	42.0
51–100 voters	23.2	12.5
101–200 voters	21.2	5.3
More than 200 voters	22.4	5.7

them: 64 percent spoke "a lot"; 33 percent, "a little." (See Appendix A for survey details.)

This difference between electoral machines also plays out in how campaigns attempt to monitor and reward or punish broker behavior across the two countries. Due to the high number of guns-for-hire in Indonesia, we see a much greater emphasis on making sure that brokers do not pad their voter lists with people with whom they lack strong ties. Candidates and campaign staff repeatedly told us that they viewed overly large voter lists (beyond around thirty names per broker) with suspicion, as they doubted brokers' ability to secure commitment from voters beyond their immediate circle. Campaigns often capped the number of voters per list or verified individuals' location and voter-registration status before dispensing funds to brokers. By contrast, while we heard of similar strategies in the Philippines, caps were much less common. Our broker survey results bear this out. In Indonesia, few brokers had more than 50 voter names on their list, while fully two-thirds of Philippine brokers were responsible for more than that number (Table 4.2).

Candidates concerned with minimizing the risk of broker shirking accordingly engage *lots* of brokers. A common strategy for campaigns in Indonesia is to blanket constituencies with their brokers even as they limit the number and types of individuals brokers put on their lists. While we heard of similar strategies in the Philippines, blanketing and limits were much less common.

TABLE 4.3. *Limits on brokers (% of brokers surveyed)*

	Philippines	Indonesia
Brokers' area of operation		
Sub-village unit only (*purok* or ward)	30.3	76.6
Village-wide	62.5	20.7
Multiple villages	7.3	6.7
Who was on brokers' lists?		
Only family, friends, and neighbors	26.9	84.9
Also acquaintances and strangers	73.1	15.1

Our survey results bear this contrast out. Consistent with the blanketing strategy, nearly three-quarters of brokers in Indonesia operated in a single small neighborhood or ward within a village, while a majority of the Philippine brokers in our survey operated across multiple neighborhoods (*purok*) within the village (Table 4.3). (Few brokers in either country reported having people on their list from outside their own village.) The survey results also support what we heard from candidates: campaigns in Indonesia are skeptical of lists including people who are distant from the broker. The vast majority of Indonesian brokers reported *only* having direct family members, friends, and neighbors on their lists (Table 4.3). By contrast, Philippine brokers were far more likely to report enlisting at least some distant acquaintances and strangers.

Despite efforts to choose loyal brokers and limit the number and type of voters for whom they were responsible, brokers' shirking remained a big concern for virtually all candidates we interviewed in Indonesia, and for many in the Philippines, as well. Some campaigns claimed to have developed elaborate strategies for cross-checking and monitoring brokers. For example, some campaigns employed teams – dubbed "invisible teams" (*tim siluman*) by some Indonesian candidates – to spot-check the lists brokers furnished, confirming that voters knew they were on the list and had spoken with the broker. In both Indonesia and the Philippines, some candidates sent brokers out to deliver handouts accompanied by higher-level campaign staff. One Indonesian candidate bypassed local brokers altogether at the handout stage, employing a specialized team to carry out this task.[14] Almost all candidates centralized the task of putting cash in envelopes, seeking to minimize leakage of funds. But at the end of the day, most candidates said they had few mechanisms for monitoring and disciplining brokers.

---

[14] The candidate who adopted this strategy was also the only candidate we encountered whom brokers explicitly criticized in focus groups. Several of his brokers said this approach suggested the candidate did not trust them; they blamed his poor performance on their resulting reciprocated distrust.

TABLE 4.4. *To what extent do brokers feel they were monitored? (% of brokers surveyed)*

	Philippines	Indonesia
Never	57.7	69.0
Sometimes	32.2	11.8
Often	10.1	18.7

Broker surveys confirm the somewhat surprising lack of effort in broker monitoring and enforcement we noted in interviews, along with the subtle differences we observed between common practices in Indonesia and the Philippines. Overall, in both countries the majority of brokers reported that they were never monitored. Monitoring was more common in the Philippines, where about 42 percent of brokers felt they were monitored at least sometimes, compared to around 30 percent in Indonesia (Table 4.4), consistent with the idea that Philippine brokers were more likely to be part of larger, enduring local political machines.

Among the minority of brokers who were monitored, we find a notable cross-national difference in the degree to which they expected to be held accountable. Fewer than 5 percent of the Indonesian brokers we surveyed thought they would be punished for poor performance, while nearly 25 percent of those in the Philippines believed they would be.[15]

Voter Monitoring

While campaigns may find it difficult to monitor brokers, their capacity for and investment in monitoring voters is even weaker. One reason why many observers find electoral clientelism problematic is that it has the potential to reverse the nature of the democratic-accountability relationship between voters and politicians, enabling politicians to hold voters accountable for their behavior, rather than the other way around (Stokes 2005). It is for this reason that "voters in patronage-democracies are unlikely to *believe* that their vote is secret" (Chandra 2004, 53, emphasis in original), because, so the argument goes, politicians need to know how citizens vote in order to punish those who fail to deliver on clientelistic deals. However, there is little sign of such "perverse accountability" in Indonesia or the Philippines. With few exceptions (see Ravanilla et al. 2021), we found scant evidence that candidates or brokers

---

[15] In terms of type of punishment, the 25 percent in the Philippines breaks down as follows: 9.3 percent believed they would not be invited to be a *lider* in the future; 8.6 percent believed they would not receive future jobs, assistance, projects, or other forms of help; 4.5 percent believed they would be verbally abused; and 3 percent believed they would not receive money or goods that they were promised. None of our respondents reported fearing physical violence.

TABLE 4.5. *Do brokers believe voters can be punished for failing to turnout or voting for an opposing candidate? (% of brokers surveyed)*

	Philippines		Indonesia	
	Not voting	Defecting	Not voting	Defecting
No	70.1	64.6	87.5	87.2
Yes	29.9	35.4	12.5	12.8

either systematically tracked who turned out to vote or actively tried to determine how voters voted. While surprising at some level, this finding is consistent with other recent work in the field. A lack of evidence of monitoring and enforcement is actually the norm in studies of electoral clientelism, despite what the predominant theories might lead us to believe (Hicken and Nathan 2020).[16]

Starting with our broker surveys: we found that most brokers saw no way to penalize voters who shirked. Seventy percent of brokers in the Philippines and 87 percent in Indonesia believed they could not punish voters for failing to turn out to vote (Table 4.5). And even if they learned that a voter had voted for another candidate, a large majority of brokers (65 percent in the Philippines and 87 percent in Indonesia) reported that their hands were tied – nothing could be done. (Among brokers who felt otherwise, most saw being removed from future broker lists as voters' likely punishment – meaning they would not receive future cash payments – while a few said other forms of future patronage could be withheld.) These findings were confirmed by our interviews and focus-group discussions with brokers and candidates about punishing voters who reneged. A common story emerged from campaigns in both countries: even if the campaign had reliable information about voter misbehavior, candidates and brokers believed punishing those voters would damage their own reputations and ultimately do more harm than good. A candidate in Southern Luzon summarized, "Voters really aren't worried about punishment."[17] Note, too, that the differences between the Philippines and Indonesia are consistent with more Philippines brokers' being connected with enduring local machines that are in a position to provide or withhold ongoing patronage.

Voters confirmed the stories we heard from candidates and their brokers. Across all our voter surveys, large majorities reported believing their votes to be secret. For example, in our postelection national surveys, slightly less than 3 percent of respondents in either Indonesia or the Philippines believed a

---

[16] Another line of work considers how candidates' communal or collective monitoring can underpin clientelist exchange (Gottlieb and Larreguy 2016; Nathan 2016), but we found little evidence of such practices in our cases. We discuss why this is so in Chapter 5. For more on collective monitoring, see Cruz (2019); Kitschelt and Wilkinson (2007); Larreguy et al. (2016); and Rueda (2015, 2017).

[17] Interview with candidate, May 8, 2016, Sorsogon province.

candidate could ascertain how they voted. (Interestingly, those numbers were higher in Malaysia: 13.2 percent thought it very likely, and another 32.4 percent somewhat likely, that "powerful people" could do so.)

Our local surveys of voters shed additional light on ballot secrecy and how it might be violated. Only 18.3 percent believed it was at least "possible" for a campaign to learn how they voted in Indonesia. (While still a minority, this is a higher percentage than in our national survey – not surprising, given that these were voters who appeared on broker handout lists). As for *how* politicians might get that information: 75 percent of that minority of voters said that they would willingly tell, if asked. In the Philippines, our local surveys revealed that only 5 percent of voters believed brokers (and by extension, the campaign) knew how they voted. However, this assessment varied by voters' positions in social networks. Voters who were centrally located in dense village family networks were much more likely to believe that brokers could figure out how they voted – among these voters, up to 23 percent thought brokers knew how they had voted (Ravanilla et al. 2021).

But even those voters who believed campaigns could tell whether they had shirked evinced relatively little fear of reprisal, particularly in Indonesia (Table 4.6).[18] A large majority of voters in our local voter survey in Indonesia believed a candidate would do nothing if they failed to turn out to vote or voted for a rival candidate. About one-fifth said they would feel embarrassed for not having voted as promised, but few feared actual consequences. We see a similar pattern in the Philippines, though with some intriguing differences consistent with the type of mobilization regime found there. Again, the largest percentage of respondents, nearly a majority, reported no fear of consequences for not voting or defecting, while about a third said they would feel some embarrassment. However, unlike in Indonesia, a sizable minority of voters did anticipate penalties for reneging; these consequences reflect the fact that Philippine voters are more likely to be linked to enduring local machines via clientelist ties. A little more than a quarter of Philippine respondents believed they would not be able to ask the candidate for help if they did not reciprocate with a vote, and about 20 percent feared being excluded from handouts in future elections or being verbally scolded (presumably by the local broker).[19] In neither Indonesia nor the Philippines did many voters express fear of physical violence.

---

[18] Our surveys were done in areas where election-related violence was uncommon in 2016, but we note that we would expect localized departures from this pattern in each country, in areas where violence and coercion are a regular part of electoral politics (e.g., parts of Mindanao in the Philippines). We discuss some of these areas of exception in Chapter 8.

[19] Here again, though a voter's relative position within a network matters, voters more centrally located were more likely to believe they could be reprimanded or lose access to future patronage, though the overall number of voters fearing reprisal was still very low (Ravanilla et al. 2021).

TABLE 4.6. *Consequences of reneging. Suppose you received an envelope or foodstuffs/goods from a candidate but did not turn out to vote/voted for a different candidate on election day. What might the consequences be? (% of voters surveyed)**

	Indonesia		Philippines	
	Not vote (%)	Defect (%)	Not vote (%)	Defect (%)
None, the candidate would not do anything	76.7	79.6	46.2	49.3
I would feel embarrassed but the candidate would not do anything	21.2	20.4	35.4	34.2
I would not be able to go to the candidate and ask for help from him/her if I needed it	3.2	4.3	29.5	27.4
I would not get any envelopes/gifts from that candidate in the next election	7.3	4.6	18.7	20.4
The candidate or a member of his team would ask for the money/gift back	1.5	0.6	1.2	1.4
I would be the target of verbal abuse	1.5	1.1	22.1	19.9
I would be physically threatened or targeted with violence	0.6	0	0.7	1.7

* *Note*: Respondents could pick all the consequences that applied, so totals may exceed 100 percent.

To summarize, candidates and their campaigns are well aware of shirking by brokers and voters. That risk among brokers is more severe in Indonesia, with its ad hoc mobilization teams, and we thus see greater attempts to restrict broker behavior there. But even in Indonesia, investment in broker monitoring is limited, and almost completely confined to restricting the scope of voter lists and the types of voters included. Campaigns do little in either country otherwise to monitor broker effort or behavior. Similarly, campaigns worry a lot about voter shirking, but our interview and survey data show that they invest almost nothing in monitoring voter behavior (including vote choice), and are not inclined to punish voters even if they do find out that voters shirked. For their part, a substantial majority of voters do not think campaigns can learn how they voted – but even among the minority who believe otherwise, relatively few fear any sort of costly reprisals for shirking.

Voter Reciprocity

We have shown how campaigns, while attempting to target core supporters, end up distributing funds to many with weak or no loyalty to the candidate.

We have also demonstrated that campaigns invest very little in monitoring voters and that voters neither report being monitored nor appear to be very concerned about punishment should they fail to deliver. Given such scant monitoring and enforcement, it is perhaps not surprising that voter shirking is common. Whether speaking in terms of "mortality rates" in the Philippines or the *"margin error"* in Indonesia, the candidates and campaign staff we interviewed recognized that there would be a sizeable gap between the number of voters to whom they gave payments and votes received. One national DPR candidate in Indonesia explained, "There is a consensus among candidates: If you only get a third of the total envelopes you distribute, that's a good result. First, set your target. If you want to receive 100,000 votes to get elected, you must distribute envelopes tripling that. That's the rule" (quoted in Muhtadi 2019, 154). Expected yields ranged from a low of 33 percent to a high of 70 percent, although most campaigns appeared to estimate a 50 percent return when calculating how many voters to target with handouts. Even the leader of one exceptionally disciplined and well-funded local machine in the Philippines – one that closely monitored its brokers and worked hard to build and maintain lasting clientelist relationships with voters – explained that he expected a yield rate of only two-thirds. He targeted 41,000 voters with handouts of 3,500 pesos each, in hopes of yielding 27,000 votes.[20]

In short, many recipients of electoral handouts take the money and run – a fact that all campaigns recognize and attempt to adjust for (see also Greene 2021). In fact, our work on broker yields in Central Java suggests that yield rates were actually much lower than even conservative campaign targets: 20–22 percent, on average.[21] This number corresponds with Muhtadi's (2018, 221) finding that only 20.8 percent of those voters who deemed it appropriate to accept cash handouts said they would vote for the candidate who gave them the most. Likewise, in the Philippines, only 18 percent of those who accepted handouts from candidates in 2016 voted for all those candidates, though 31 percent reported having done so in 2019 (Pulse Asia 2019b). Of the rest, 49 percent voted for some but not all of the candidates from whom they received handouts, and 28 percent didn't vote for any of them. In our local survey of voters in one Philippine municipality, we found that yields ranged from a high of 83.7 percent for one mayoral candidate to a low of 54.7 percent of voters for another.

Given this low return on investment, why do candidates continue to rely on electoral handouts, and why do they not invest more in monitoring and enforcement? We turn now to this seeming paradox.

---

[20] Interview, May 5, 2016, Visayas.
[21] See Aspinall et al. (2017) and Hicken et al. (2022) for more details on handout yields in Indonesia.

BRAND BUILDING, CREDIBILITY BUYING, AND
TURF PROTECTION

As in many other democracies, candidates and their electoral machines in Indonesia and the Philippines invest significant resources in direct handouts to voters in the run-up to an election. Yet, what we observe in these cases looks different from the standard stories of electoral clientelism, as described in much of the existing literature. Candidates and brokers expect many if not most voters to defect, and most voters do in fact fail to vote for candidates who give them electoral handouts. Many voters, too, receive more than one handout – a fact of which candidates are aware and around which campaign teams strategize as they calibrate the "market rate" for initial and last-minute payments. As explained earlier, presumed-core voters are the most likely to be paid. Despite known endemic shirking, candidates and brokers invest only minimally in voter monitoring and enforcement efforts, and evince very little interest in doing more. In the end, the primary purpose of handouts does not appear to be about persuading swing voters (as vote-buying models assume) or rallying core supporters on election day (as in turnout-buying models). Rather, we argue that the micro-particularistic distribution of handouts to voters serves three purposes: it builds the candidate's name-recognition (*brand building*), signals to voters and brokers alike that candidates are credible contenders (*credibility buying*), and helps secure the votes of weak loyalists (*turf protection*).

We start with *brand building*: non-targeted spending to help raise awareness of the candidate among voters. In all our primary and secondary cases, except for Singapore, brand-building efforts such as the distribution of campaign paraphernalia or handouts at campaign events, or of bags of rice to neighborhood residents during a campaign sortie, are ubiquitous during elections. (In Singapore, we see scattered souvenirs like party pens or hand fans – useful for outdoor rallies in the tropics – but handouts beyond party literature are otherwise rare.) Functioning as a form of political advertising, these activities are primarily designed to raise the profile of a candidate and signal something about their viability and perhaps their generosity (Kramon 2016). However, unlike micro-particularism, these efforts *are not targeted or discriminatory*. Everyone at the campaign rally gets a free meal, everyone along the road gets a t-shirt, and everyone in the neighborhood gets a bottle of water emblazoned with the candidate's name and face. There is no real expectation on the part of the candidate that handout recipients will vote for them, nor do recipients feel any particular moral or cultural obligation to reciprocate. The goal is to build the candidate's brand by distributing these types of handouts as widely as possible. In this way, brand building looks more like a special form of political advertising than like a targeted handout.[22]

---

[22] Even in peninsular Malaysia, despite the relative lack of vote buying, we heard tales of enterprising "aunties" who strategized to dine for free at different parties' spreads throughout the campaign.

Unlike brand building, *credibility buying* and *turf protection* target individual voters or households, using networks of brokers, in a way that looks a lot like contingent electoral clientelism. However, they have very different implications in terms of the degree and focus of monitoring and enforcement. Whereas contingent electoral clientelism implies campaigns monitor voter behavior to secure targeted voters' cooperation, credibility buying and turf protection require little or no such investment. Candidates give handouts to signal their viability and competitiveness and to reassure core supporters who might otherwise be tempted to stray.

Credibility Buying

First, distributing money to voters functions like an entry ticket: it allows candidates to compete by signaling to voters and brokers that they are credible contenders. We build here on the work of Muñoz (2014) and Kramon (2016), who explore how electoral handouts help apprise audiences of the dispenser's viability. Muñoz and Kramon describe such handouts as centered around campaign rallies.[23] In Muñoz's account, politicians in Peru distribute handouts to poor voters to induce them to attend campaign events. Turning out large numbers signals the candidate's viability to a number of important audiences, including voters, donors, activists, and the media (2014). As for Kramon, he finds that handouts during Kenyan elections occur during campaign rallies themselves, and allow candidates to convey information about their generosity and reliability (2016).

While the arguments these two authors make resonate to some extent with our cases, what we observe in Indonesia and the Philippines diverges in two respects. First, the timing of distribution is different. In Kenya and Peru, handouts occur in the midst of electoral campaigning, while in our cases, monetary handouts largely occur in the day or two prior to the election. Second, neither Kramon nor Muñoz describes much discriminatory targeting in the distribution of handouts. Every rally attendee gets a handout in Kramon's account, while Muñoz concludes that campaigns indiscriminately target poor voters to get them to campaign events. By contrast, in both Indonesia and the Philippines, the process of distributing handouts is discriminatory by design. Campaigns target certain voters for handouts and not others.

We agree with Muñoz and Kramon that handouts convey important information to key audiences – in our case, voters and brokers. But, *contra* Kramon, we suggest that these payments need not signal anything about prospective generosity or reliability. In fact, given that nearly *all* (viable) candidates engage in the practice and studiously attempt to match what their competitors give,

---

[23] Szwarcberg (2012) likewise suggests that campaigns use rally attendance to gauge broker effort and quality. We saw some evidence of this strategy at work in Timor-Leste but not elsewhere.

electoral handouts contain very little information about how one candidate's generosity or reliability compares to another's.[24] Instead, we argue that distributing money to voters is simply the price of admission. In a context in which party affiliation at best only weakly differentiates candidates, contenders need to stake their claims and attract attention. Where other candidates are distributing largesse, not doing so can be fatal, especially if there is a mass of names on the ballot – as there is in Indonesia's open-list proportional-representation system. Brokers and voters will judge candidates who fail to distribute funds as not serious contenders. Those candidates will find it difficult to recruit reliable brokers, the brokers they do recruit will be more likely to shirk, and voters will likely dismiss the candidate altogether. In effect, candidates find themselves trapped in a Prisoner's Dilemma: choosing to be the only candidate not to distribute money ensures the sucker's payoff (Chauchard 2018; Canare et al. 2018; Muhtadi 2019; Hicken and Nathan 2020).

Brokers frequently talked about cash payments in this way. Commented one Indonesian broker: "If you don't have money, you can't stand."[25] Another concurred, "So the minimum a candidate needs to do is provide *sangu* [pocket money, a local euphemism for these payments], Sir. That's all."[26] Viewed this way, what we see appears less a market for votes than barriers to entry, to help voters and brokers screen out unserious contenders. This reading reflects the fact that electoral handouts have become an expected part of the electoral process for many voters. If candidates don't pay, they cannot play. As one voter from the Mindanao province of Lanao del Sur put it, "The election is harvest time for us, so we take advantage of the blessings as much as we can" (Latiph 2019, 312).

Turf protection

Distributing resources also serves to protect a candidate's presumed turf. Candidates are well aware that the majority of the voters they target are weakly loyal at best; some may have only tenuous ties even to their broker. And even presumably solid loyalists can be poached by other candidates, given the right conditions. Thus, campaigns see a need to target payments to loyalists in an effort to insulate them from competing offers. We are not the first to note that "core voters" might not actually be so loyal. In explaining why parties may

---

[24] We presented several reasons why candidates might distribute money to voters in our Central Java survey. Only 9 percent responded that money was used to signify that a candidate had a charitable or socially concerned character; 37 percent opted for the conventional local explanation that the money is compensation for loss of a day's work; 24 percent described it as a sign of gratitude on the part of a candidate for a vote; 23 percent deemed it a form of bribery directed at voters.

[25] FGD, August 21, 2014, Rembang.   [26] FGD, August 23, 2014, Blora.

choose to target core supporters, Dunning and Stokes (2007) refer to support-ers' *conditional loyalty* and Diaz-Cayeros et al. (2016) speak of the *endogeneity of partisan loyalty*. But the problem of disloyalty is even more acute where partisan attachment is weak to begin with, as in both Indonesia and the Philippines.

To elaborate, recall that when calculating their base or core, candidates generally count voters they have helped in the past. They might have provided such help to voters as individuals, families, or as part of functionally or geographically defined groups (e.g., organizations or neighborhoods). This group of voters is potentially quite large, since clientelism broadly is a year-round activity, particularly in the Philippines, where this ongoing practice is known in Cebuano-speaking areas as *pangulitaw* (courtship). Candidates, particularly incumbents, frequently bemoaned the need for such continual wooing, believing that in order to build and preserve their reputations they had to respond positively to most requests (see also Nichter and Peress 2017). Most Philippine incumbents had staff dedicated to dealing with constituent demands at their office, and sometimes their homes.[27] One of the researchers with whom we collaborated in Laguna, for instance, described a two-term incumbent who entertained a steady stream of visitors at his house each day:

These visitors asked for resources or financial assistance – sometimes to process legal documents, to cover ceremonial fees, or a little for *merienda* [snacks]. The candidate would hand them cash, ranging from PhP50–500, depending on the amount requested. (Sta. Romana 2019, 108)

A member of our research team working in Muntinlupa captured the frustra-tion many politicians feel at being held hostage to voter demands for patronage.

People ask for virtually everything from their politician, even for trivial things such as money for fares, vehicle fuel for an outing, money for snacks, or for a movie, and so on. Sometimes people just approach a candidate and ask for money outright; if the candidate asks, "What for?" the person might smile and say, "*Wala lang!*" (nothing really) as an answer. (Rocina 2019, 155)

Given that many of the voters campaigns target for electoral handouts are also embedded in such ongoing clientelist relationships with politicians, it is under-standable that some scholars view electoral clientelism as simply a reflection or outgrowth of relational clientelism. Nichter (2018), for example, describes how enduring economic vulnerability drives voter demand for clientelist services from politicians. For their part, politicians would like to exchange those

---

[27] This practice mirrors closely prevalent praxis in Malaysia and Singapore, where constituency service far exceeds what electoral imperatives would seem to demand. The logic there is somewhat different, though: incumbent and aspiring politicians intend these efforts to bolster reliance on and faith in the party – but also to top up what is mainly a party vote with fortified personal support (see Weiss 2020c).

services for electoral support. However, the fact that voters lack information about the credibility of politicians' promises to provide future services, and that politicians lack information about how voters truly vote, exacerbates the potential for market failure. One solution to this collective-action problem, Nichter suggests, is that voters publicly and visibly declare their support for a candidate (as by working for the campaign), coupled with requesting help from politicians between elections.

While arguments like Nichter's usefully remind us that electoral handouts may be part of a larger clientelist context, we are still left with a puzzle: Why do politicians spend so much time and scarce resources wooing those clients who should already feel most indebted to them? Given that, all other things being equal, voters should prefer (i.e., find more credible) politicians who have provided a steady stream of benefits in the past over challengers offering one-time electoral handouts, why do political patrons have to offer their client-voters anything at all? At the very least, should not voters be willing to give their patron-politician a home-town discount? In fact, more than one campaign claimed that, given the candidate's history of service, electoral handouts were not strictly necessary – voters would choose to vote for them anyway. Similarly, respondents to our voter surveys and focus groups consistently listed constituency service and patronage as more important than electoral handouts in deciding their vote.

And yet, not only did each of the myriad campaigns we observed prioritize the client-voters in their base when it came to electoral handouts, but also, most candidates and brokers with whom we spoke stressed that they offered loyalists the *same payment* as non-loyalists. The reason, of course, is that candidates fear these loyalists are actually quite fickle and prone to defection, ongoing clientelist relationships notwithstanding. Candidate after candidate, and campaign worker after campaign worker, expressed the same sentiment in our interviews: if loyalists are not paid during the election, they will cease to be loyalists. Loyalists will defect for the right price. Muhtadi's survey of winning campaigns in Indonesia confirmed how widespread this fear of even loyalists' defection is: 86 percent of candidates thought at least some loyalists would defect without a handout (2019, 161). Two (typical) statements that members of our research team gathered encapsulate this effect:

[I]f voters can't get cash or incentives for electoral support from one candidate-politician, they will vote for the opponent who can have [a] better offer. (Candidate in Camarines Norte, Philippines, quoted in Nolasco 2019, 86)

Blood is thicker than water; but money, especially if it's a bundle of 1,000 pesos, is much thicker than blood. (Candidate in Lanao del Sur, Philippines, quoted in Latiph 2019, 323)

One candidate we interviewed in Central Java, an incumbent member of a city legislature in Rembang, explained in 2014 how he had spent the preceding five years cultivating the loyalty of a *basis* of voters by directing government funds toward small farmer and fisher cooperatives in a group of target villages. But he still needed to give them cash in the lead-up to elections because, he explained, "It's a real competition. We give them money just to bind them, so they are not pursued by others." But he was fatalistic: for candidates to hand out large sums, even to loyal voters, he explained, was "like herding goats into a holding pen. You can be sure that some will run off, tempted by the green grass over there."[28]

Together such findings suggest that candidates and brokers understand payments to loyalists primarily as turf protection: reassurances that the candidate still has their back. In an environment of pervasive uncertainty about *any* voters' loyalty, candidates need to shore up support against the ever-present threat of defection. Much of what looks like contingent vote or turnout buying, then, is actually intended to signal viability and to prevent the straying of voters attached to the candidate through brokerage networks (Hicken and Nathan 2020).

Finally, while we found evidence of credibility buying and turf protection in both Indonesia and the Philippines, there is a difference of emphasis across the two countries: credibility appears to be the dominant motivation for Indonesian candidates, and turf protection the primary concern of Philippine candidates. This divergence is again a consequence of different types of mobilization regimes. Lacking access to durable political machines, often deprived of ready access to the kinds of resources that could fund patronage between elections, and facing high levels of inter- and *intra*-party competition, Indonesian candidates have smaller cores to protect, to begin with. They therefore focus their attention on using funds to buy brokers' networks, and signal their viability to those brokers and the voters each will target. By contrast, the presence of enduring local machines in many parts of the Philippines, with access to abundant sources of patronage from a more permeable state, means that it is easier for candidates to build a core of contingent loyalists through the ongoing distribution of benefits. It is this contingent core that needs protecting when election season rolls around.

CONCLUSION

In this chapter, we have explored the role that micro-particularism plays, particularly in two of our cases, Indonesia and the Philippines. Significant percentages of voters in each country report being targeted with handouts of money or goods, and a large proportion of the campaigns we interacted with over several years and numerous elections admit participating in the practice. In terms of its organization and structure, much of what we see in Indonesia and the Philippines looks at first like the broker-facilitated electoral clientelism commonly described in the literature. But, in line with other recent studies, we find that the distribution of electoral handouts lacks the degree of

---

[28] Interview, April 4, 2014.

contingency traditional models of electoral clientelism imply. Campaigns invest very little in monitoring brokers and voters, and are reticent to punish voters whom they know have defected. For their part, voters feel little obligation to vote for candidates who target them with cash and express little fear of consequences if they do renege.

Based on these observations, we argue that targeted micro-particularism goes beyond an initial investment in brand building to focus on credibility buying and turf protection. Candidates distribute handouts in order to signal their credibility and viability to voters and brokers, and to insulate their loyalists against poaching. We also demonstrate that the nature of mobilization regimes in Indonesia and the Philippines shapes both the severity of the risk that brokers will shirk and the relative weight of turf protection versus credibility buying as the core motivation for targeting voters with handouts. But the nature of the electoral regime does more than shape the hows and whys of micro-particularism; it also shapes the *mix* of mobilization strategies candidates choose to pursue. We turn in Chapter 5 to a second major strategy: meso-particularism.

5

Targeting Groups

Pork Barreling and Club Goods

Herman was running for the local parliament in an eastern district of Central Kalimantan province in Indonesia in 2014. A retired village head, Herman was a first-time legislative candidate for one of the country's nationalist parties. He had decided that the best way to get his constituents' support was by funding their community groups and social activities. When we visited him at his campaign office a few days before voting day, he showed us a booklet in which he had been recording the donations he had made over the preceding few months. It listed an array of gifts, including a total of twenty-four separate sums of money for committees that ran mosques, prayer halls, churches, and prayer groups; fifteen donations at weddings; five televisions for village security groups; seven grass cutters for farmers' cooperatives; three generators for village halls; and so on. The document neatly recorded his expenditure on such items, which added up to about 150 million rupiah (roughly USD10,300). It also listed how many votes each donation would yield. Each television, he thought, would generate fifty votes, a total of 250; each donation to a house of worship would generate thirty votes, a total of 720; each generator would yield fifty votes, and so on. Through this means, he calculated, he would get a total of 7,465 votes. He knew that other candidates were making cash gifts to individual voters, but he did not want to do so, both because it was illegal and because he thought his donations were more socially beneficial. When he gave these donations, he said he told the recipient he felt *ikhlas*, an emotional state implying a clear conscience, and the absence of expectation of reward. If the recipients did not vote for him, he would not ask them to return his gifts – as unsuccessful candidates in Indonesia occasionally do. In fact, Herman thought distributing such benefits was the best way to generate support. It helped him to promote his image as a "figure" (*figur*) who really cared about the community. It was a good thing that Herman felt this way, because he was roundly defeated.

In some of the villages where he gave donations, he received only a handful of votes. Overall, he fell far short of his target.[1]

In Sibu, in the East Malaysian state of Sarawak, an incumbent BN member of parliament – a wealthy ethnic-Chinese businessman – was courting Muslim voters.[2] Like the majority of his constituents, he was *not* himself Muslim, but 5–10 percent of local residents were, and he needed those votes. Hence, he found himself on a walkabout to a Malay *surau* (prayer hall) and adjacent community center one morning during the 2013 campaign. After chatting casually with local residents outside the hall, he joined the small crowd in moving indoors to enjoy a light meal provided by the community. A local master of ceremonies kicked off the proceedings, averring that the ninety-six local families stood behind this MP and his party, whatever their differences. But they could use "*sedikit bantuan*" (a bit of help) to fix up the courtyard and this community space. Specifically, they would appreciate air-conditioning for their mosque, some support for local poor children, resurfacing the area out-side, and general renovation for the *surau* itself. He pointed out the spots that would most benefit from a fix. Next up was the candidate. He reminded the assembly that politics is important – and the opposition had won this state constituency in the last election: their votes mattered. He heard their requests, he assured them, and if he won, "I will try my best to help." The host of the event closed out the event by reiterating his hope that the candidate would fulfill their wish-list, in exchange for which the community would give full support with their votes. Unlike the candidate in our first example from Indonesia, however, the MP was an incumbent. Everyone in the audience expected him to use government resources – perhaps sourced from the discretionary constituency development funds he could access as a member of the ruling coalition – to pay for the improvements they wanted. He was not providing them as private gifts in the lead-up to the election like Herman was; it was assumed that he would be able to provide them after the election was over.

Both these examples illustrate a rather different strategy from what we have just seen in Chapter 4. There, we detailed the ways in which candidates target individual voters with micro-particularistic strategies as part of their mobilization efforts. In this chapter, we turn our attention to strategies that target *groups* of voters – villages, religious associations, occupational organizations, and the like. The nomenclature in the literature for such targeting strategies varies: pork barreling, group patronage, distributive policies, collective goods, local public goods, and club goods.[3] We label this range of strategies

---

[1] Interview, April 7, 2014, Kuala Kapuas.   [2] Field notes, May 1, 2013, Sibu.
[3] See Golden and Min (2013) and Stokes et al. (2013) for a review of these terms and how they are used in the literature.

"meso-particularism," though we also refer specifically to club or collective goods for ease of exposition.[4]

What distinguishes meso-particularism from other distributive strategies is its beneficiaries. Programmatic goods target large groups of citizens who match objective criteria for eligibility (age limits, income levels, illness, and the like), while micro-particularism targets individuals and households. Meso-particularism lies between these two extremes; it refers to the allocation of goods to "specific localities and to correspondingly small constituencies" (Golden and Min 2013, 76). Instead of, or as well as, selecting recipients on the basis of objective eligibility criteria, those allocating benefits target groups on political grounds. The initiatives in question, and hence their key recipients, may be defined geographically – for example, improving a village road, a bridge, or another infrastructure project that primarily benefits members of a local community. Or they may specifically help members of a targeted formal or informal organization: repairs to a particular congregation's house of worship, as in Sibu, for instance; equipment or uniforms for members of a sports team; or a hand tractor for members of a farmers' cooperative.[5] Unlike micro-particularism, which is prominent only in Indonesia, the Philippines, and East Malaysia, we find meso-particularism throughout our cases, though with important variations that we will discuss.

In this chapter, we explore the factors that shape politicians' incentives and capacity to incorporate meso-particularism as part of their electoral strategy. Why do they choose this approach rather than, or in addition to, programmatic promises or cash handouts and other micro-particularistic alternatives, and what factors shape the ratio of micro- to meso-particularism a candidate deploys? We offer two answers to these questions. First, parallel to our argument in the last chapter about electoral handouts, we suggest that much of what candidates provide in terms of club goods should not be considered contingent patronage. Relatively few of these goods are provided on a contingent basis – that is, with a clear expectation that recipients will reciprocate. Instead, as is the

---

[4] We find the use of the term "club goods" particularly apt because it captures the collective but limited nature of distribution, and because the recipients of such benefits frequently are, indeed, clubs or other organized groups. As we note in Chapter 1, however, we recognize that our usage is somewhat different from that found in the economics literature, in which (as we explain there) a club good is a benefit that is excludable but non-rivalrous. By this definition, some of the benefits we look at in this chapter would not be club goods (e.g., a village road accessible to all users or a set of sports uniforms that, once distributed among members of a club, are fully exhausted). These distinctions are not relevant here, given our focus on electoral dynamics; for us, it is the unit of aggregation and the perceived political impact that is key. If a limited collective of persons is *supposed* to appreciate the benefit, then we classify it as a club good.

[5] These categories are sometimes treated separately in the literature because infrastructure or other benefits targeted at particular locales are frequently publicly funded. We combine these categories because, as we found in the field, that is what Southeast Asian politicians often do: numerous public allocations go to clubs and associations; politicians likewise may fund (publicly or privately) small-scale, locally targeted infrastructure projects.

case with electoral handouts, candidates allocate collective goods as a form of brand building, credibility buying, or turf protection.

Second, we argue that where club-good provision *is* a form of collective patronage, carrying expectations of contingency (most common in Indonesia), it is almost always mediated by representatives who claim to speak authoritatively for a beneficiary community or social network. Most candidates who distribute collective patronage do so because they feel confident in the capacity of that group representative to be an effective broker: to deliver promised votes from their network in exchange for their gift, even though such confidence is frequently misplaced. Building on Aspinall and Berenschot (2019, 133), we distinguish between two sorts of networks, *networks of affect*, oriented around religious, cultural, or other social purposes, and *networks of benefit*, tied to participants' income-generating, employment, or other material needs. We argue that both types are generally less effective than political candidates hope. However, we also explain when and how community-level elected officials have emerged as key brokers in clientelist club-goods exchange.

In the remainder of this chapter, we first set the scene by considering how the patterns of meso-particularism we encountered vary across our countries, noting that while meso-particularism is ubiquitous in all three, it differs somewhat in terms of intensity, and differs greatly in terms of timing, form, and specific targets, with consequences for its visibility. Next, we consider the *functions* of meso-particularistic distribution, arguing that it is frequently distinctly not contingent clientelism, and analyze as well the *reasons* for why it is nonetheless so common. We next argue that meso-particularism is typically associated with different sorts of networks, with different consequences for its utility. Networks based on a shared material benefit are the most fruitful – and the foundation of the most enduring and effective patronage networks we see in Southeast Asia.

PATTERNS ACROSS COUNTRIES

Our fieldwork findings suggest that meso-particularism is a very common strategy across all three of our core countries. It is an essential feature of political life in all three of our countries (see Figure 5.1). We and our teams of field researchers observed distribution of a huge and inventive range of benefits, among them, balls, nets, new courts, uniforms, and other equipment given to sports clubs; crockery, carpets, tarpaulins, tents, plastic chairs, and cooking equipment and implements for women's groups; ambulances, garbage trucks, fire water-pumps, mobile health clinics, street lights, and bridge or road repairs for neighborhoods; and irrigation apparatuses, drainage canals, fertilizer, livestock, water pipes, nets, boats, and jetties for farmers' or fishing collectives.[6]

---

[6] Note that some of these collective gifts also have individually targetable components.

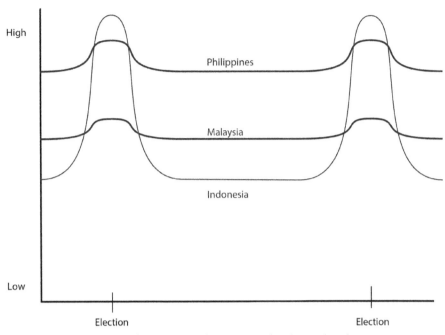

FIGURE 5.1. Prevalence of meso-particularism over the electoral cycle

Yet the mechanisms, funding, timing, and public understanding of such gifts vary considerably across our countries. For example, in our national Indonesian survey in 2014, just under one-third of voters (31.3 percent) said that their community had received collective gifts of some sort from candidates or parties; in contrast, 28.9 percent said members of their community had received individual gifts, including cash. The proportion of voters reporting similar collective gifts was much lower in the Philippines – less than 5 percent. (Unfortunately, we did not include a question about collective gifts in our Malaysia surveys, though our field research there suggests a much higher prevalence than the 6.8 percent who report having been offered money, food, or other items individually.)

What might account for the difference in survey responses between Indonesia and the Philippines? As Figure 5.1 (reiterating what we introduced in Figure 3.1) indicates, we do not believe that it means meso-particularism is more intense in Indonesia than in the Philippines. Instead, the difference can be explained in large part by differences in the funding, presentation, and timing of collective benefits. In both the Philippines and Malaysia, meso-particularism primarily involves politicians' distributing publicly funded goods, most commonly to geographic entities (municipalities, congressional districts, etc.), and doing so between elections, which might explain why the respondents to our Philippines survey did not highlight this phenomenon: even those who lived in communities showered with pork-barrel projects and similar collective gifts may think of such benefits as ordinary products of government, rather than associating them with the electoral strategies of particular parties or candidates. That same presumption would likely confound accurate measurement in Malaysia, especially given how much of the distribution of such benefits in both Malaysia and the Philippines occurs between elections.

By contrast, in Indonesia the distribution of meso-particularism tends to be more closely tied to the electoral cycle than in either Malaysia or the Philippines, with much of the collective gifting that stands out to voters occurring in the lead up to elections. In addition, meso-particularism organized and funded by the government tends to be somewhat less dominant in Indonesia than in Malaysia and the Philippines, for reasons we explain shortly. Indonesian meso-particularism is often organized by individual politicians and candidates rather than parties, frequently with private rather than public funding. Candidates may be especially inclined toward group-targeted club goods, given the proliferation of promising identity-based and other networks – though they also do engage in geographic targeting. This is part of what makes electioneering such a challenging experience for so many Indonesian candidates: they not only have to find their own private funds to pay for their patronage strategies, but they also have to decide how to allocate those funds between micro-particularistic and meso-particularistic distribution. (To be clear, Indonesian incumbents do draw on public sources, but much less systematically than their counterparts in the Philippines and Malaysia. Candidates in these latter countries, particularly incumbents, can rely on public funds to support the distribution of local public goods, enabling them to devote more of their private resources to micro-particularism. This reflects the high degree of discretion that Philippine politicians enjoy in their dealings with the state, and the substantial control that the Malaysian ruling party has had over the organs of the state.) We encountered many Indonesian candidates who agonized over the choice, and many others who were adamant that favoring collective gifts over individual cash payments was the superior strategy – or vice versa.

Figure 5.1 illustrates the differences in patterns of meso-particularist distribution across our three cases. While we did observe somewhat more meso-particularism in the Philippines (we labeled it "ubiquitous" in Table 3.1), compared to in Indonesia and Malaysia (where we labeled it as "common"), the main purpose of Figure 5.1 is to represent differences in the timing of distribution across the three countries. Across all our cases, we observe increases in collective-goods provision around elections, but in Indonesia, the distribution of collective goods is more highly concentrated around elections than in the other two cases.

What explains these differences? As already anticipated in Chapters 2 and 3, differences in the nature of patronage networks across our country cases, and the varied opportunities politicians have to access state resources, provide the main explanation. In the Philippines, the pork barrel has been a major binding force in the political system since the period of American colonialism. The vertical alignment of Philippine politics, from the president's office down to the remotest municipality, has been largely built around bargaining over and distributing chunks of funding from the national budget: in return for access to pork-barrel funds for their locales, community-level elected officials provide national-level politicians the help they need at election time – even though such alliances of convenience are notoriously fluid. Pork also serves as a critical lubricant, enabling presidents to pass measures through Congress (Holmes 2019, 18). Over the years, members of Congress have worked hard to expand and regularize the pork-barrel grants they can access, through numerous schemes repeatedly reconfigured over the years. The result is that, "across the congressional districts of the Philippines, one sees the names of politicians etched on public school buildings, waiting sheds, street lamps, ambulances, public markets, and multi-purpose halls" (Holmes 2019, 1), in a practice known as *"epal"* (a colloquial term derived from *"mapapel,"* or self-promotion). A major side-benefit of pork comes in the form of kickbacks, the extent of which major scandals both in the mid-1990s and in 2013 exposed. These resources help politicians finance electoral campaigns (Holmes 2019, 25, 157–58, 342).

Out in the provinces, the mayors who run local political machines, meanwhile, have enormous discretion to allocate the budgets and national programs provided to local governments – often through a process known as morselization, which we describe in Chapter 6 – in accordance with their own political priorities. In doing so, they often collaborate closely with members of Congress and other national political figures to increase their access to funds and programs. At the grassroots, mayors tend to allocate many of the projects and public works they control – everything from sewerage improvement to harbors, roads, basketball courts, and community-gardening projects – to reward or entice supporters. Mayors typically direct such projects disproportionately to barangays run by captains who are already part of their machine, or to help allies in areas where they are trying to entice support (e.g., council-members in a barangay captained by a member of a rival team). In short, much of the provision of club goods occurs *within* the networks that make up the local machine. What's more, given the ready access to publicly funded patronage resources, the distribution of club goods occurs throughout the electoral cycle, though there is certainly an uptick around election time, coupled with an intensive effort to remind voters of the source of the patronage.

The Malaysian system is similar, except that the primary organizers of meso-particularism are parties rather than individual candidates or even incumbents, and the overall greater preponderance of programmatic delivery in the country tempers the extent of discretionary allocation of projects and other benefits. Compared to Indonesia, far fewer individual candidates invest their own money in community gifts, because – as we have explained in previous chapters – so much patronage politics in Malaysia is coordinated through parties and provided by the state. As in the Philippines, funds for discretionary allocation by sitting legislators – a classic example of constituency development funds (Van Zyl 2010) – are prominent and are invariably deployed with electoral considerations in mind. A portion of the funds is generally allocated for small-scale infrastructure projects, through which those legislators with access to these funds (a caveat to which we turn in a moment) might highlight certain signature initiatives, such as improving local parks or upgrading a community market. They then tend to divvy up the balance among welfare payments to needy constituents (though more of this micro-particularism comes out of pocket, if only because legislators often feel the paperwork isn't worth the effort); small grants to local mosques, churches, and temples; project grants to community associations, local schools, festival committees, cultural festivals, and the like; and whatever other requests come their way. Few legislators with whom we spoke had developed an orderly system for these disbursements: most were first-come, first-served, though BN legislators could appeal to their party for supplemental funds, if needed, and members of other parties supplemented state resources through fundraising appeals.

Technically, each federal or state constituency receives the same allocation. In reality, all legislators do not enjoy the same access to those funds, underscoring the party-focused nature of the Malaysian electoral mobilization regime. For opposition members of parliament, constituency development funds have been "available but not accessible," in the words of one such legislator. The BN parked opposition constituencies' funds with a state development officer rather than the relevant legislator, to ensure that the central (BN) government rather than an opposition MP could take credit for what they provided.[7] Explains a former BN politician, giving opposition MPs access to government funds would give them "a weapon."[8] In constituencies where the ruling BN was not in power, the state development officer typically disbursed these funds at the direction of a nonelected party *penyelaras* (coordinator) in that seat.[9] When Pakatan Harapan came to power at the federal level, they, too, granted opposition legislators only token partial allocations (as they had earlier done, as Pakatan Rakyat, at the state level).

More generally, both national and state governments have substantial ability to reward key constituencies with projects and other benefits (Weiss 2020c, 130). Some government-linked companies (GLCs) reportedly even shifted their "corporate social responsibility" investments in response to BN requests before the 2018 election, targeting not BN leaders' safe home districts (the standard

---

[7] Interview, April 24, 2013, Pahang.   [8] Interview, April 28, 2013, Perlis.
[9] Likewise in Singapore, the parastatal People's Association "grassroots adviser" is from the PAP even in opposition-held constituencies, ensuring the ruling party maintains control of the People's Association and the disbursement of benefits through it; see Weiss (2020c).

approach, used to curry favor) but swing seats. Sometimes, members of opposition parties work to counter such advantages – for example, the DAP and PKR raised funds in peninsular Malaysia to finance small-scale solar-power and hydroelectric projects for under-developed areas in Sarawak and Sabah, to prove that they, too, could deliver, even without federal funds. But the BN government quickly and decisively trumped such efforts by rolling out larger and more impressive projects in the same communities.[10]

In Malaysia, as in the Philippines, much of the disbursement of such projects and benefits occurs throughout the electoral cycle, but there is also a discernable uptick during the campaign period, punctuating the consistently fairly high levels we indicate in Figure 5.1. At these times, both government and opposition parties organize teams of volunteers to engage in community-improvement projects like painting public housing blocks, while the government issues new licenses for school expansions or breaks ground for new facilities, as well as rolling out roads, bridges, electrification, streetlights, and so on – typically with the incumbent MP present.

Indonesia features patterns reminiscent of Malaysia and the Philippines. Regional government heads – especially *bupati* in rural districts and mayors in municipalities – have considerable leeway over local-government allocations, and we have evidence that distribution of projects maps onto electoral outcomes, with incumbents rewarding communities that provided them with votes and withholding projects and other benefits from communities that did not (Aspinall and As'ad 2015). Moreover, certain budget items – notably so-called grant (*hibah*) and social assistance (*bantuan sosial*) funds – are particularly notorious for the extent to which regional government heads dispense resources for political purposes to such beneficiaries as religious and other community organizations, local preachers, and schools.[11] Legislators, too, have tried hard to wrest a greater degree of discretionary control over government budgets. In some parts of the country, they have struck deals with local government heads to attain an Indonesian version of constituency development funds in the form of set annual funding allocations – often known as "aspiration funds" (*dana aspirasi*) – that they can direct to their constituencies in the form of project grants, assistance for groups, or infrastructure improvements. Others try hard to intervene in budget-making processes in order to direct the allocation of such resources, and there is often significant competition to join the most rewarding parliamentary committees or commissions (*komisi*) – ones that deal with government ministries and programs that distribute substantial material benefits

---

[10] Interviews with Pakatan legislators, December 31, 2014, Kuala Lumpur; July 29, 2015, Selangor; April 23 and 24, 2016, Sarawak; and BN advisor, July 20, 2016, Sarawak.

[11] Sjahrir et al. (2013) show that spending on this category of expenditure and other discretionary allocations aligns strongly with the electoral cycle in Indonesian regions, peaking in years in which an incumbent faces reelection.

(for details, see Aspinall and Berenschot 2019, 164–68; on aspiration funds see Mahsun 2016).

Overall, however, the amount of discretionary control that elected officials in Indonesia exercise over government resources is substantially lower than in the Philippines or Malaysia, and, perhaps even more significantly, politicians coordinate much less when it comes to sharing out projects and resources for meso-particularistic purposes. As a result, there is somewhat less space for government-funded club goods in Indonesia than in the other two countries, accounting for the lower quantum of meso-particularism in between elections, as expressed in Figure 5.1. The national government has designed numerous funding initiatives in ways intended to reduce the discretionary role politicians exercise – for example, transferring national education grants directly to schools without channeling them through local government (Widoyoko 2010) or transferring village development funds directly to villages (Antlöv et al. 2016). Members of the national legislature have been unable to develop a major constituency development fund program, despite trying several times; the proposals have always been shelved after encountering significant media criticism and public opposition. Overall, unelected bureaucrats still have considerable influence over the allocation of spending (though this balance may shift over time, as elected politicians gradually wrest greater control out of their hands).

To the extent that Indonesian politicians face constraints in their ability to direct publicly funded club goods to constituents, they are frequently forced to fall back on privately funded distribution at election times and thus have additional incentives to engage in corruption in order to fill their war chests in anticipation of the next election. For example, members of legislatures may extract fees, often called "gavel money," from government heads and agencies in the regions in exchange for passing sponsored legislation or approving bureaucratic budgets. Lacking the strong parties or entrenched local machines that are major channels for the distribution of meso-particularism in Malaysia and the Philippines, respectively, and still wishing to win over blocs of votes at the community level, politicians and political candidates are required to fund many of their club goods themselves and to engage in transactional processes of bargaining with community and group leaders who can demand such benefits as the price of their support at election times.

In these circumstances, the allocation of club goods in proximity to Indonesian elections is understandable. Providing club goods is expensive, and voters tend to have short memories. With five years between elections in Indonesia, voters are unlikely to remember or give electoral credit for benefits distributed three or four years earlier. Candidates – even incumbents – thus prefer to concentrate their community gifting close to elections. While there are also modest spikes in Malaysia and the Philippines, the fact that such benefits are overwhelmingly provided through government budgets, and with more permanent local machines, makes it easier to remind voters of their source.

(The greater frequency of elections in the Philippines – every three years – also helps in this regard.) Politicians' and political aspirants' supply of club goods in both countries thus tends to be less volatile and discontinuous. Whether for weekly water distribution, a traveling notary service, mobile health clinics, or road repairs, club-goods provision tends to be a normal and expected part of everyday life in the Philippines, as in Malaysia, despite the difference in their formal political-party structures. The fact that club goods are less explicitly tied to the electoral cycle in the Philippines than in Indonesia may help explain why fewer survey respondents in the Philippines report having observed their distribution during the campaign: what happens endemically may not stand out as an election approaches.

CLUB GOODS AS NONCONTINGENT ALLOCATIONS

All else being equal, candidates might well prefer providing collective patronage to individual handouts – even if entirely funding these benefits out of their own pocket. The expense and other difficulties that enforcing individualized clientelist exchange entail may make exchanges with groups more attractive. Explain Kitschelt and Wilkinson (2007, 17): "Monitoring groups of voters – or having them monitor themselves and then rewarding or punishing the group – is much more efficient than monitoring and then rewarding and punishing individuals, especially where party organizations are weak and in elections with large numbers of voters dispersed over a wide area." However, clientelistic exchange with groups presents an additional problem: free-riding. Voters who receive some benefit as a member of a collective may assume other beneficiaries will repay the giver with their support, freeing them to back some other candidate or not to vote at all. Complaints about free-riders were common among the candidates and campaign workers we interviewed across all three countries. Most recognized that the exchange rate for converting money into votes is lower for club goods than for individual patronage. Recall from Chapter 4 that targeted yields for individual handouts are fairly modest: campaigns target an average yield of 50 percent, but actual yields are often considerably lower. Politicians almost always expect the yield for club-goods spending to be lower still. One candidate in Kalimantan, for instance, an incumbent, claimed that his yield rate for club-goods spending last time around – the percent of the vote he secured in communities he targeted with such gifts – was merely 10 percent.

Given such challenges, why are club goods so ubiquitous? While candidates anticipate that provision of the good in question will increase their chances of securing recipients' votes, neither candidates nor recipients seriously expect the supply of the club good to be contingent on future (or past) electoral support. There is no explicit or implicit quid pro quo in most cases. This is not to say that club goods are somehow programmatically distributed. Rather, candidates are guided by strategic political calculations in choosing which groups to target.

They allocate club goods to core areas or groups in order to shore up their base and reward past support, and they direct club goods to new groups or swing areas in a bid to expand their base. They distribute club goods with the goal of increasing their probability of securing recipients' support, but, again, there is no credible expectation of reciprocity, at least in the short term. There is only hope.

Lack of investment in monitoring and enforcement at the time of exchange reflects the noncontingent allocation of club goods. The absence of enforcement is particularly telling. Every election, examples appear in the Indonesian national media of candidates who, angered by the lack of votes from a community they targeted with club goods, move to withdraw their gifts – pulling out water pipes they have installed, taking down street lights, or even ripping out tiles from mosques (see, e.g., Mubarakan 2014). However, these stories make headlines not just because they are rare but also because they so directly violate the popular conceptions of generosity and fairness that supposedly underpin the gifting of such benefits. For the most part, the only recourse candidates have when their investment fails to yield hoped-for votes is to reduce or end their distribution to those areas or groups in the future. And for their part, most voters do not feel morally or socially bound to support a candidate who has provided a club good to their locale or group, though they may be more inclined to do so than if the candidate had not provided the collective benefit.

If club goods are often not collective, contingent patronage, then what are they? We find our framework of brand building, credibility buying, and turf protection developed in Chapter 4 useful also for thinking about the motivations behind the noncontingent allocation of club goods. Candidates' provision of these goods signals to voters that the candidate has a "social" orientation – that he or she cares about the community and is likely to deliver future benefits (brand building), and that the candidate is viable (credibility buying). For incumbents, collective goods are also a marker of performance, designed to prevent voters' defection to competitors offering a similar mix of individual and collective patronage (turf protection).

Since individual patronage fills many of these same functions, why bother with club goods? There are at least three reasons why they are attractive, even if they fail to produce hoped-for vote yields. First, and perhaps most simply, given resource constraints, many candidates cannot distribute enough handouts to individual voters to win an election. This is particularly true of candidates for higher offices. Distributing individual handouts can be immensely costly, both because of the cumulative expense of the gifts themselves and because of the investment typically required to build the extensive patronage networks needed to distribute them. The latter issue in particular helps to explain the relatively greater prevalence of club goods in Indonesia than in the Philippines during elections: Philippine politicians can build machines that draw on ongoing ties and relational clientelism, whereas Indonesian politicians often need to build success teams from scratch and somehow win over voters with whom they do not share direct connections. Given the costs of individual targeting, candidates must supplement micro-particularism with other strategies designed to reach more voters. Club goods are one way to provide benefits to a broader set of voters and build one's brand in the process. In addition, the fact that at least some politicians are also likely to be able to access funds for club goods (but not for individual patronage) through the government budget – thus saving themselves the expense of privately funding their patronage strategies – makes them particularly attractive.

Second, candidates also favor club goods because they help to fortify and expand one's base between elections. It is a mistake for candidates to rely solely on club goods to mobilize voters, but relying only on handouts at election time is also a sub-optimal strategy. The most effective candidates are those who pursue a mixed, layered strategy, cultivating a target area or group with pork-barrel spending and other kinds of club goods on an ongoing basis, then fortifying those efforts with individual handouts as election day nears. Many incumbents we encountered in the Philippines and Indonesia spoke in precisely these terms. Alternatively, particularly where parties are comparatively strong, as in Malaysia, club goods help the party maintain visibility and appeal between elections; as polls approach, candidates might supplement not with individual payments but with programmatic promises, drawing on their party's record and platform.

Regardless, club goods help plow the ground and plant the seeds that, with some last-minute showers of electoral handouts, yield votes candidates can then harvest at elections (see also Miranda 2019; Macalandag 2019). Candidates in Indonesia talked about club goods as either "entry doors" (*pintu masuk*) or ways to "open the road" (*membuka jalan*) to voters, while individual electoral payments are intended to "bind" (*mengikat*) voters to them (Aspinall and Berenschot 2019, 145–46). (In fact, voters show little evidence of feeling bound, as we discussed in Chapter 4.) In the Philippines, a common saying captures this logic: "money is for the election, projects for regular days" (Pancho 2019, 294). Individual electoral handouts, in short, pack a bigger punch when the distribution of club goods precedes them.

Finally, despite the general lack of social stigma attached to micro-particularism in Indonesia, the Philippines, and East Malaysia, candidates cannot publicly boast about the electoral patronage they distribute to individual voters, only about the (legal) assistance they provide. Electoral handouts, particularly cash, are technically illegal. Just as important, not all voters will receive cash payments, so talking about them risks rubbing salt in the wound of those not targeted with a handout. Consistent with this scope for inequity, voters generally view candidates who provide club goods more positively than those who only spend money on handouts.

Our voter surveys in Indonesia suggest clearly that voters view club goods more favorably than individual gifts, especially cash, and prefer candidates who distribute the former to the latter. A majority of respondents to our Central

Java voter survey (see Appendix A for details) – all of whom campaigns had targeted for vote buying – agreed that voters in their community favored candidates who use club-goods strategies. Fully 58 percent agreed that voters would be most inclined to support a candidate who "has helped the people of this village or precinct [*kelurahan*], for example, by helping repair a *mushollah* or other house of worship, building a bridge, giving assistance to a farmers' group, and so on." Only 12 percent of respondents stated that their neighbors would likely support the candidate who made the largest cash payments to voters, while 26 percent believed that the candidate with the best program for the district as a whole would win.

Stated differently, club-goods provision has a social legitimacy not accorded more individualized forms of patronage. All our cases have seen increasing public condemnations of "money politics" in recent years. The media, electoral monitoring and anti-corruption NGOs, religious organizations, electoral commissions, and other institutions have publicly denounced vote buying and other forms of clientelist exchange. Banners and media advertisements exhort voters and candidates alike at election time to abjure "money politics" and not sell or buy votes. Moreover, vote buying and similar practices are legally proscribed, however rarely or ineffectively these bans are enforced.

By contrast, many candidates and voters view gifts of club goods, either positively or ambiguously, as a form of charitable giving (*sedekah* in Indonesian or Malay) or as a form of community service or development. Indeed, in Malaysia, these gifted club goods are frequently proudly and prominently branded with party logos or signboards: their provision is highly public, not illicit. In the Philippines, the candidate's name and often photo are usually boldly on display (with parallels to India; see Auerbach 2019). Accordingly, in interviews, candidates who might deny that they distribute cash or other gifts to individual voters would often readily admit to distributing club goods and defend such gifts as being part of their normal charitable behavior. One candidate in Aceh, Indonesia, the wife of wealthy local contractor, explained that she viewed her donations for mosques, prayer halls, cooperatives, drainage, and the like – her biggest campaign expenditure by far – as very different from "just handing out money." It was a form of religiously sanctioned charity, which brought its own rewards in the afterlife: "That's why you should be well-off if you want to be a candidate ... At least, if I lose I won't carry any burden, I won't end up in the hospital" (here she was referring to the bankrupted candidates who reportedly suffer mental breakdowns when they lose in Indonesia).[12] In one survey of Indonesian candidates after the 2014 legislative election, a majority of candidates agreed that club goods of various sorts should not be classified as "money politics," whereas large majorities of respondents

---

[12] Interview, March 18, 2014, Bireuen.

classified all the many forms of individualized patronage, what we term micro-particularism, in this way.[13]

To summarize, while club-good expenditures do not seem to instill a sense of moral obligation or indebtedness on the part of beneficiaries, they do help promote the candidate and their reputation to voters (brand building), signal to voters that a candidate is viable (credibility buying), and fortify the candidate's base against poachers (turf protection). When choosing between two candidates offering similarly sized electoral handouts, voters unsurprisingly might favor the candidate with a record of also providing collective goods and services. Club-goods spending is a way to prepare the ground so that last-minute electoral handouts bear fruit and, where parties are salient, to keep the party useful and valued between elections. Indeed, viewing club-goods strategies in this way may help explain why so many unsuccessful candidates over-invest in club goods: lacking an established reputation in targeted social networks and among the local grassroots, they are trying to burnish their images as caring politicians among voters with whom their name recognition is low.

CLUB GOODS AS CONTINGENT PATRONAGE: SOCIAL NETWORKS AND THE ROLE OF GROUP BROKERS

While much of the provision of club goods that we observe is noncontingent, we do see examples of candidates' attempting to use club goods as a way of building reciprocity. That is, they explicitly tie the provision of collective goods to support for their candidacy. In this section, we explore the conditions under which candidates might try to make collective goods contingent. We argue that contingent collective patronage is most viable where there are groups of voters who vote as a bloc or who can be induced to do so (see also Spater and Wibbels 2018). Absent the kinds of social networks that produce such groups, candidates find it very difficult to make the provision of club goods contingent.

Clientelist exchange raises critical problems of trust.[14] Politicians investing large amounts in gifts for voters, whether as individuals or groups, would ideally be confident that the recipients will reciprocate with votes. We know from literature on social capital that trust is largely a product of the interpersonal interactions that people experience within social networks (Fukuyama 1995). When politicians try to mobilize voters by drawing upon the social networks that connect them, they are simultaneously trying to coopt the social trust these networks generate (Rohi 2016). A candidate who gives a group of voters a collective gift – let's say a new asphalt surface on the neighborhood basketball court – may have little hope of making the beneficiaries feel obliged to repay this generosity with their votes, especially if they have few other social

---

[13] Unpublished survey of Ahmad Muhajir, Australian National University.
[14] The following passages draw on Aspinall and Berenschot (2019), 129–37.

contacts connecting them. But if the candidate recruits a broker – in this example, the captain or coach of the basketball team – to persuade them and explain the deal, success is more likely. Another way of putting this is that what generates the norms of reciprocity that scholars see as being so essential to clientelist exchange (Schaffer 2007b; Finan and Schechter 2012) is primarily the interactions individuals have through social networks (Ravanilla et al. 2021).

This situation applies equally to individualized patronage, which a social-network leader might distribute on behalf of a candidate, and to club goods, for which the social-network leader endorses the gift, highlights its benefits to members, and encourages them to provide their support in response. But the fact that club goods benefit, and thus implicitly invoke, a discrete community, potentially undergirded or knit together by trust and norms of reciprocity, may amplify beneficiaries' sense of social obligation to comply. The pressure is especially germane when the group as a whole risks losing the benefit should some members defect (Cruz 2019). For example, we encountered candidates in the Philippines who offered barangays additional community infrastructure were they to "vote straight" (i.e., to elect a local machine's full slate). It requires a high level of coordination on the part of social-network leaders (in this case, barangay leaders) and compliance (on the part of residents) to pull such deals off. We have encountered local community leaders in all three countries who expend considerable effort – including organizing community meetings to explain the terms of their deals – to try to ensure such an outcome.

It is important to note, however, that the relationships and networks that politicians access come in different forms. In particular, we can distinguish among networks on the basis of the purposes for which they are created, that is, what individual needs they seek to address. Many of the networks politicians target can be considered *networks of affect*: they primarily serve religious, cultural, or other social purposes. (We examine the role such networks play in combining patronage and identity politics in Chapter 7.) *Networks of benefit*, in contrast, center around economic and occupational relationships, and cater directly to members' material needs.

Networks of affect can be useful entry points for political mobilization, especially if they are structured in a hierarchical manner. Kitschelt and Wilkinson (2007, 17), for example, discuss "cohesive ethnic groups with clear hierarchies" (referring specifically to the example of the Lubavitch Hasidim in New York state), to liaise with whom "the politician needs only to contract with the group leader to be assured of the support of the entire group."[15] Candidates in Southeast Asia attempt to court a variety of networks of affect with offers of club goods. Traditional communities and their leaders are common targets of contingent club goods in all our cases. In the Philippines,

---

[15] See also work that that considers the use of collective monitoring to enforce clientelist exchange (e.g., Gottlieb and Larreguy 2016; Nathan 2016).

candidates may seek the votes of particular indigenous upland communities in Mindanao and Luzon. Similarly, the Orang Asal are often targets in East Malaysia (Sabah and Sarawak), as are *paguyuban*, or self-help groups among Indonesian ethnic-minority internal-migrant communities (e.g., Javanese residing in Indonesia's outer islands). But perhaps the most common targets are religious networks. An Indonesian example is certain *tarekat*, or Sufi religious orders, headed by revered *syekhs*. Such networks can be very close-knit, requiring demanding initiation procedures and oaths of obedience from members; the adherents of such orders will generally obey their *syekh* in all things, including by voting for whatever party or political candidate he endorses. We have encountered election campaigners – from a *bupati* in Nagan Raya district, in western Aceh, to workers for Prabowo Subianto's presidential campaign in East Java – who cultivated such Sufi orders precisely because they believed their followers to be more obedient than members of comparable groups, including followers of other traditionalist *ulama*, or *kyai*. These groups thus seemed better worth the investment of time and effort than did looser networks. Similarly, in the Philippines, Iglesia ni Cristo (INC), an indigenous Christian sect, has a reputation for reliably delivering the votes of 80 percent of its members. For this reason, both national and local political aspirants aggressively court INC support.

Politicians seeking the support of such groups will often go to great lengths to court their leaders, backing their flattery with donations of club goods. Often, these will come in the form of funds or building materials to help with the construction of a house of worship, religious school, orphanage, or other physical infrastructure owned by the group. However, candidates may also donate other useful material, such as a sound system, rugs, kitchenware, or other paraphernalia that will help a religious or other community group hold meetings.

As we look across our three main cases, we can readily note that the supply of cohesive groups with clear social hierarchies is not the same across states, nor is it evenly distributed within them. This heterogeneity helps explain why the reliance on contingent club goods varies across countries and locales. All three cases feature myriad societal organizations – mainly autonomous from political parties in Indonesia and in the Philippines but more frequently aligned with them in Malaysia. The level of cohesion and hierarchy of these groups, however, varies greatly. Notably, the extent and durability of Malaysian groups' affiliation with parties make it harder to assess the extent to which parties proactively coopt them, versus being instead comprised of them.

In Malaysia, processes of economic modernization and the breakdown of communal solidarities means that many identity-based groups are no longer able to deliver bloc votes as in the past, as among the Chinese community organizations (chambers of commerce, festival committees, and the like) that formed the reliable backbone of Chinese communal parties in decades past. The closest parallels now are likely to be among indigenous ethnic, religious (perhaps especially Christian), and longhouse communities in East Malaysia. Hence in Malaysia, politicians and parties tend to target geographic, rather than affective, communities with club goods (e.g., with infrastructure projects) as part of a more general effort to build and defend their reputation for looking after their constituency. Likewise in the Philippines, networks of affect tend to be weak, with the exception of, for example, a few religious organizations and some traditional indigenous upland communities. Thus, most club-goods provision is, in practice, noncontingent.

It is in Indonesia where we see the most overt reliance on networks of affect, in part due to the prominence of autonomous ethnic and, especially, religious organizations; in part because the relative weakness of parties and machines drives candidates to seek alternative means to reach voters. However, even here, development and modernization have eroded cohesive social groups. In addition, electoral incentives push candidates toward a greater reliance on individual patronage. Thus, we find accumulating evidence that relying on contingent exchange with such groups is not so productive a strategy as it once was (see Muhajir 2009; Aspinall and As'ad 2015; Ismanto and Thaha 2016; Rubaidi 2016).

This reality raises an interesting question. If mobilization of this sort is often so ineffective, why do politicians still so commonly court religious and other identity-based networks, splashing out on club goods with such low confidence in the rate of return? One explanation is that candidates who are seeking an access point (or an "entry door," as it is often called in Indonesia) to reach voters misapprehend the political influence of the social or religious leaders and networks to which they themselves have some connection. They mistake religious and social authority for political influence – and those community leaders, of course, have no cause to disabuse these politicians of their assumption. In our interviews, we found that candidates, especially inexperienced ones, often imagine that it is a relatively simple process to transform their social-network connections into votes, or that courting the leaders of religious or similar networks is a sure way to drum up blocs of votes. It is true that local religious leaders and community networks are obvious points of contact for voters, as they are for candidates – but even candidates with preexisting links to such networks often find out that they were mistaken to believe they could readily convert them to political capital by attending a few meetings, seeking endorsement from a community leader, and supplying some club goods.

Focusing in on religious networks of affect specifically, in the context of a growing commodification and pluralization of religious life (Fealy 2008), it is far from clear that the religious networks in which people participate are as all-encompassing as they once were or that the followers of a particular preacher or *ulama* will be unable to separate their participation in religious activities from their voting choices and other political behavior. Indeed, one recent survey in Indonesia found that only 12.6 percent of Nahdlatul Ulama members and 10.7 percent of Muhammadiyah members said they would consult religious elites on political matters, a much lower figure than would consult them on socioreligious matters – 48 and 47.5 percent, respectively (Fealy and Bush 2014, 551–52). For their own part, religious leaders are often cautious about being drawn too obviously into political campaigning on behalf of candidates, reluctant to alienate members of their congregations who have differing political loyalties or who would look askance at engagement by a religious figure in the dirty world of politics.

So, to summarize, where they are present and robust, networks of affect can provide opportunities for candidates to use club goods as a form of contingent patronage to woo leaders and their groups. But candidates can find it difficult to make political use of such networks: their members' interests, even oriented as they are around a religious or social identity, will be aligned partially at best with those of the politician providing the benefit. Members commonly have a lot of other things they also care about and that influence their vote choice. An authoritative network leader can overcome such obstacles, but sufficiently cohesive, hierarchical groups are increasingly rare, even in Indonesia. Instead, if politicians want to make club goods contingent on votes, they often turn to an alternative type of network and a different type of broker.

NETWORKS OF BENEFIT: ALIGNING INTERESTS AND COMMUNITY MEDIATION

A starting point here is to think of *networks of benefit* as ones directly linked to their participants' immediate material needs. Most obvious here are networks that are themselves based around livelihoods, which can be distinguished between those that are relatively more horizontal and vertical in structure. Horizontal organizations are based on common occupation or economic interest (e.g., a farmers' self-help group, a wholesalers' cooperative, or a women's sewing collective). Some are organizations that play a broadly representational function; these are often attractive to candidates. For example, in the Philippines, leaders of transportation groups (e.g., tricycle drivers) are popular targets. In Malaysia, candidates often especially covet the support of organizations of taxi drivers and hawkers. Such groups not only include substantial numbers of potential voters, but their members have potentially far-reaching ability to influence the mass public, given the nature of their work. These groups are sometimes targets of club-goods distribution; in some cases, we have seen explicit attempts to make those goods contingent on the delivery of an agreed-upon number of votes.

But as is the case with networks of affect, the groups most appealing to political candidates are those that are vertical and cohesive. In other words, for contingent club-goods distribution to be viable, there must be a clear leader with whom candidates can negotiate and that leader must be credibly able to deliver their group members' votes. These networks are based on more personalized and hierarchical relations between employers and employees, wholesale traders and suppliers, foremen and plantation workers, funders and farmers' cooperatives, and so on. Given the element of economic dependence they entail, these relationships are especially amenable to being used for clientelist purposes.

However, even where these groups are (still) relatively cohesive and hierarchical, candidates in all three countries frequently bemoan organizational leaders' inability reliably to deliver votes. As in the case of networks of affect, the influence of the heads of occupational groups over their members' political behavior is generally weaker than it once was (and it may never have been so unequivocal as often presumed). At the same time, there are reasons why organizations based on horizontal patterns of solidarity among groups, particularly lower-class groups, are fundamentally ill-suited to the vertical social connections inherent in patronage politics – as we explore further in Chapter 7. In consequence, much of what we observe in the way of club goods to such groups really lies more in the realm of noncontingent than contingent patronage: an effort to boost one's profile or demonstrate one's viability with a group's members, without necessarily commanding reciprocal support.

But numerous other networks of benefit exist more or less for the purpose of patronage distribution and feature prominently in candidates' campaign efforts. This phenomenon is perhaps most obvious in Indonesia, where many politicians direct their club-goods strategies through a wide array of farmers' groups, micro-enterprises, fishers' cooperatives, communal savings groups, and the like. Their members often describe these groups as relying on an ethos of mutual assistance and self-help, but in fact, the groups are often established precisely in order to access government programs. In turn, politicians – including nearly all successful incumbents – direct patronage to these groups in hopes of electoral support. One illustrative example was a Golkar DPR member we encountered in Central Java during the 2014 election. He indicated that his success team consisted mostly of "farmers' groups, village heads, housewives' groups, fishers and the like" whom he had been helping to set up fish ponds, rice mills, and reforestation and training programs, and providing with agricultural equipment, cattle as breeding stock (a trademark of his), and other benefits. He had been able to mobilize substantial government funding for these activities because he sat on the relevant parliamentary commission (we return to these bodies in Chapter 6) and had been able to direct chunks of programs to his constituency. With each village getting a minimum of 100 million rupiah (about USD6,900) in assistance, he was able to mobilize a large team of several thousand beneficiaries to help his re-election effort.[16]

One striking feature of this candidate's patronage strategy, typical of many candidates we encountered, is the social location at which it occurred: the porous boundary connecting village society with the state's development and

[16] Interview, April 3, 2014, Pati.

welfare efforts. This picture suggests a departure from earlier patterns, as detailed in many first-generation studies of clientelist politics. In the mid-twentieth century, the landlord–tenant relationship was the prototypical patron–client tie in Malaysia and the Philippines, though these have always been somewhat less important in Indonesia, in part because it has a relative absence of large-scale landlordism. The centrality of the landlord–tenant relationship has faded in much of contemporary Southeast Asia as a result of economic growth and modernization, including agricultural mechanization and development of an increasingly mobile industrial and services workforce. At the same time, another type of patron – one linked to the state – and state-linked networks of benefit, have risen to take its place. Through these patrons and networks, the state and its agents, rather than traditional sources of authority such as landlords, become increasingly important in shaping people's access to economic and welfare opportunities.

Throughout Southeast Asia, as an outgrowth of state building, economic development, and modernization, access to state assistance and official welfare programs of various kinds increasingly affects popular welfare (e.g., on Thailand, Walker 2012, 49–55). And yet, capacity remains sufficiently low that many citizens are unable reliably to access state services and benefits. This persistent vulnerability drives the demand for individuals – Berenschot (2014) refers to them as "fixers" or "problem solvers" – who can mediate access to state resources (see also Nichter 2018). The identity of these problem-solving mediators varies somewhat both across and within our cases. In Malaysia, local party service centers and their staff, as well as the current or aspiring state and federal legislators who commonly hold weekly drop-in outreach days there, play this role. In the Philippines and Indonesia, it is the heads of the lowest-level government units who typically mediate such access. In the Philippines, these are municipal mayors and councilors, and, below them, barangay captains and councilors. In Indonesia, these mediators are village heads and their staff in rural villages and *lurah* (ward chiefs) and their staff in towns, and, beneath them, the heads of neighborhood units (*rukun warga* and *rukun tetangga*).

Across our cases, these officials provide citizens with, or facilitate their acquiring, the letters, identity cards, and endorsements they need to access public healthcare, senior-citizen or new-parent subsidies, and other services. They often exercise informal influence on whether citizens can get cash transfers, subsidized rice, scholarships, or other benefits, and they often negotiate on their citizens' behalf in dealings with state authorities, such as police or land-title offices. They are also typically the first point of contact for higher levels of government when providing small-scale infrastructure and development projects at the community level – precisely the type of projects that are commonly turned to patronage purposes, as demonstrated in our earlier example of the Golkar politician in Central Java. In Indonesia and the Philippines, local communities elect these problem-solvers (with the exception of *lurah*, the heads of Indonesia's urban wards); in Malaysia, the state and federal legislators

involved are elected (and function in this guise very much as *local* representatives), though local councilors and executives, as well as service-center staff, are
not. (See Appendix B for more detail on subnational structures across the three
countries.)

We will say more about these activities in Chapter 6, when we discuss
facilitation, but the inherently mediational functions of these leaders and their
close connections to voters make them especially suited to negotiating deals
over club goods (see also Auerbach and Thachil 2023). Electoral mobilization
through bargaining with community-level government leaders tends to be much
more effective than working with traditional or religious elites, in part because
it typically occurs in a much more explicitly transactional mode. In Indonesia
and the Philippines, political candidates, especially those running for local-
executive posts, frequently state that community-level elected officials are the
best sorts of persons to recruit into their campaign teams, precisely because of
the authority they wield in their communities and, therefore, their ability to
deliver votes. As one of our collaborators in the Philippines explains:

[Barangay officials] were especially sought as campaign coordinators for two major
reasons: first, barangay officials have usually earned the trust of the people because of
the work they perform in managing community affairs and solving people's problems
and, secondly, they are familiar with the voters in their barangays, and know how to
convince people to vote for their candidate. (Nolasco 2019, 216)

In Indonesia, likewise, a PPP candidate on Jakarta's peri-urban fringe explained
that he tried to bring as many village heads as possible into his campaign,
precisely because he knew villagers were dependent on these figures: "In marginal communities, the people still hold on to the village head. They need them
for subsidized rice, for health care cards, to participate in PNPM [a participatory development program run by the central government]. So dependence on
the village head is high."[17]

Courting such community leaders typically entails donating small-scale
community infrastructure: construction of or repairs to bridges, meeting halls,
irrigation ditches, village roads, lighting, sports fields, and the like, or sometimes support for community services such as garbage collection or healthcare.[18] One campaign worker in the Philippines, for example, reported that his
candidate offered barangay officials 3 million pesos' (USD62,000) worth of
projects and the chance to pick the projects they wanted in exchange for their
support (Tumandao 2019, 229). In fact, it is very often the community-level

---

[17] Interview, March 30, 2014, Tangerang.
[18] In Malaysia, candidates for state and federal office make similar donations directly, rather than
via lower-level officials. The party in control of the state government appoints the latter,
rendering their loyalty up the chain fairly assured. At the same time, precisely because they are
not themselves elected, their ability to deliver votes is likely limited.

official who approaches the candidate rather than vice versa, knowing that election time represents an excellent opportunity to extract benefits (see again, on India, Auerbach 2019).[19] Thus, the aforementioned PPP candidate explained that throughout the campaign period, he had been approached by numerous village heads, many of whom were offering 1,000 or 2,000 votes in exchange for new roads, irrigation pumps, village halls, or other improvements for their village. Incumbents – especially local executives, but also legislators – are especially well positioned to lock in the support of village heads (or, in urban centers, neighborhood heads), precisely because they can build a track record of delivering such projects.

That such strategies are explicitly transactional is a particular advantage. In contrast to donations to religious leaders, little ambiguity surrounds a donation of infrastructure to a village or urban community at election time. In fact, candidates in Indonesia often draw up a written "political contract" that details precisely what they promise to deliver to the community concerned in exchange for support, reflecting the relatively strong bargaining power community-level elected officials there enjoy (Sulaiman 2016, 63–64; Rohi 2016, 380; Savirani and Aspinall 2017); we return to this topic in Chapter 7. Similarly, candidates in the Philippines often set explicit vote-quotas for local officials in exchange for the provision of club goods. In Malaysia, this practice is equally unambiguous: billboards may proclaim the number of low-cost homes to be built in a community, or the hospital that might soon occupy that space – should the candidate in question win.[20]

This sort of networking around benefits works to align the incentives between candidates and voters far more perfectly than occurs when candidates reach out to religious or ethnic leaders. It creates a clear common interest ("if you win, I win"), without having to hang anything on the more uncertain and partial connection of a shared affective characteristic. Known in the literature as self-enforcing clientelism (see Gallego 2015; Albertus et al. 2016; Mares and Young 2018), such connections are an important foundation of both the patronage parties of Malaysia and the local machines of the Philippines. They are institutionalized in the latter case when a particular mayor backs a set of barangay captains over repeated election cycles, cementing their support through a steady stream of projects and other benefits, and by backing them in their own electoral contests. Though the overall pattern in Indonesia is of

---

[19] Candidates have also been known to offer barangay officials personalized inducements. One incumbent mayoral candidate reportedly gave each barangay captain a new car as a quid pro quo (Miranda 2019, 127). Candidates for higher office also agree to support the barangay official in their own (later) election. We heard similar stories in Indonesia of gifts of cars, motorbikes, or pilgrimages to Mecca or Rome.

[20] In our secondary case of Singapore, parties take such bidding to extremes, encouraging voters to decide their vote on hyper-local issues – a promised swimming pool or community-center upgrades, for instance – rather than per issues of national policy (see Weiss 2020c, 181–82).

more transient and negotiated electoral teams, there, too, we are seeing the beginnings of more enduring personalized machines of this sort, as when incumbent politicians cultivate the support of community-level leaders with ongoing projects and other benefits, boosting those leaders' credibility in the community, helping them financially or with projects when their elections occur, and, in turn, calling on their support in their own election campaigns (Paskarina 2016).

In sum, the contingent distribution of club goods is a viable strategy for some candidates, but only when group leaders can reliably deliver their members' votes. In all our cases, the influence of religious, cultural, or occupational group leaders appears to be on the wane, even as the presence of such figures remains an ever-present temptation for politicians seeking contact points in the community. In their place, community-level politicians and elected officials have increasingly become key mediators between candidates and groups of voters under their charge, at least in Indonesia and the Philippines. Where we observe the contingent distribution of club goods, it is these leaders – or in Malaysia, higher-level politicians in an ersatz-local guise – who are more often than not at the center of the transaction.

CONCLUSION

However common it is for candidates to employ club goods as part of a strategy for mobilizing voters, *how* they do so, or how they wring efficacy from the strategy, may be less than obvious. We suggest that much of the distribution of collective patronage falls outside clientelist, contingent exchange. Instead, club goods serve as signals to voters of various desirable attributes on the part of the candidate – specifically, their care for the community, assiduity, and ability to deliver. Collective patronage also demonstrates to voters that a candidate is a credible contender, while shoring up a candidate's base against tempting offers from rival politicians. Club goods take on a more contingent bent, we suggest, only where group leaders can credibly deliver a command vote from group members. As leaders' control of vote banks within their networks of affect have declined across our cases, candidates have come to favor networks of benefit. Thus, in our cases we are most likely to see contingency in transactions between candidates and community-level elected officials serving as vote-brokers.

While we have not focused on how candidates fund club goods, it is useful to remember that the provision of club goods is a costly strategy. Where club goods can be sourced from government budgets and programs, the candidates best placed to pursue this strategy are obviously incumbents (see Chapter 6 for more details) – even if ambitious aspirants still do invest in these goods independently. (Incumbents may also be well-placed to raise funds through illicit means, as we discuss further in Chapter 8.) Incumbency advantages are the most pronounced in Malaysia, where club-goods funding for sitting ruling-party politicians comes almost entirely from government sources. Politicians in the Philippines, too, have access to abundant government resources, thanks to the high levels of discretion they enjoy, but also regularly draw on private funding. Indonesian incumbents have the fewest advantages, on this account. They do have access to some streams of government funding that can be used for club-goods purposes. For example, sitting legislators in regional legislatures may tap "aspiration funds" to assist with development programs or aid community groups in their constituencies. But due to the greater autonomy of the Indonesian bureaucracy over budgets and projects, and the relatively low levels of machine-based coordination in the allocation of such benefits, opportunities for Indonesian politicians to generate publicly funded club goods are somewhat more limited than in Malaysia and the Philippines. As a result, many Indonesian candidates are forced to rely heavily on private sources to fund club goods and, hence, to concentrate their distribution strategically around elections. Further support, of course, can be sought from well-heeled businesspersons willing to bet on those candidates' electability.

However, even in Malaysia and the Philippines, the fact that well-resourced incumbents pursue a meso-particularistic club-goods strategy tends to encourage challengers to follow suit. In Malaysia, opposition parties (including those in Pakatan Harapan) have explicitly tried to use club-goods provision, not only emphasizing prospective promises but also investing in donation-funded projects to enable positive retrospective assessments, to build a base that could eventually compete with UMNO and the Barisan National. Challengers in the Philippines and Indonesia, too, regularly fund club-goods provision out of their own pockets to build their reputation, hoping to recoup their expenses if elected.

In short, collective goods are a weapon in almost all candidates' arsenals. But this weapon often misses the mark, deployed on its own. Collective goods are most effective when accompanied by gifts to individual voters and/or more macro-level appeals. And most importantly, where meso-particularism is to have independent impact, it must be grounded in longer-term relationships. Otherwise, as some candidates we encountered learned the hard way, the appeal may well misfire. We have already considered in Chapter 4 the sorts of micro-particularism that might bolster club-goods-based appeals. We turn next to another promising alternative, especially where parties are strong: macro-level patronage strategies.

6

Hijacked Programs

Using Public Policy for Patronage Purposes

In a May 1, 2018 campaign speech, incumbent Malaysian prime minister Najib Razak offered the residents of low-cost public-housing flats on the outskirts of Kuala Lumpur a bargain: vote for his Barisan Nasional (BN) coalition in the upcoming general election and he would allow them to purchase the flats in which they lived. The price was to be announced post-polls; if it were a big win, they could bargain over it, with the implication being that they would get a nice discount. "I have not forgotten you; don't forget me," he cajoled his audience. The provision of affordable housing in Malaysia – including in this *Projek Perumahan Rakyat* (People's Housing Project, PPR) community – is fragmented and complex, but it represents a substantial national program (see Iga 2017). What determines eligibility is household income, not party membership or voting record. And yet it is hardly unusual for a candidate to treat affordable housing as an electoral carrot in Malaysia. This incident embodies a similar electoral logic to the individualized and collective efforts described in the preceding two chapters, but with a twist. It is similar to those efforts insofar as Najib was seeking to link the provision of a particular benefit with support for him and his party, including by implying that receipt of the benefit was contingent on voter reciprocity. The difference, however, is that the benefit being provided was a national or *macro-level programmatic policy* that the candidate was seeking to *hijack* for partisan or personal advantage. This chapter investigates this intermingling of programmatic and patronage politics.

As the opening example suggests, while in principle it is possible to distinguish between programmatic policies and patronage targeted at groups or individuals, in practice the line is often blurred. This is because parties and candidates aggressively and creatively work to coopt programmatic policies in a bid to turn them into (or portray them as) more targetable and contingent benefits. We return to our framing of a continuum from fully particularistic to fully programmatic practices: here we near the latter end of the continuum, where the extent of actual discretion tapers off – even if enterprising politicians often pretend otherwise. In this chapter, we explore three different forms of such hijacking that we label *credit-claiming, facilitation,* and *morselization.* They are distinguished by the degree and type of discretion exercised at the point of distribution, and demonstrate how the form of hijacking and the identity of the hijackers (parties, local political groups, or individual candidates) is a function of the type of mobilization regime in place and of the discretion politicians have over the distribution of programmatic benefits.

Each form of hijacking occurs in each of the three states, but with differing frequency and in differing mixes. Briefly, in Malaysia, where parties have been relatively strong and the ruling coalition has had unchallenged and unfettered access to the state, hijacking has taken the form of party-focused credit-claiming (which favors the ruling party) and facilitation (which involves both government and opposition politicians). By contrast, in Indonesia, where parties are weak and legislators have more limited discretion over the distribution of state resources, individual legislative candidates work to facilitate access to state-provided benefits, while making sometimes feeble attempts to link the provision of benefits to their personal intervention. (Regional chief executives, however, have greater discretion and, hence, ability to morselize government programs and direct them to favored communities and individuals.) Finally, with weak national parties, strong local political machines, and abundant discretion to influence the provision of public benefits, candidates in the Philippines are much more likely to morselize programmatic benefits (explained in detail later), while also engaging in personal and machine-focused credit-claiming and facilitation.

In the remainder of this chapter, we first describe the logic of programmatic hijacking, and then define and describe its three distinct forms. As will become clear, what defines all three is a claim to, or exercise of, discretion in allocation of benefits from macro-level programs. Voters may experience these distributions, however, as either micro- or meso-particularism. Next, we explore how the degree of discretion politicians have over resource distribution, along with the type of mobilization regime, shapes the mix of forms of hijacking that predominate as well as the identity of the hijacker. Finally, we look more closely at how each type of hijacking operates across our three cases.

THE LOGIC OF PROGRAMMATIC HIJACKING

The goal of programmatic hijacking is to turn the benefits of a given programmatic policy to the advantage of a particular party or politician. Even where allocation decisions really are centralized and neutral, politicians assiduously work to make them *seem* contingent on their personal or partisan intervention and discretion. As a result, from the voter's perspective, a programmatic policy appears particularistic or partisan – when in reality, it may not be.

Most germane here are genuinely programmatic initiatives, access to which is technically neither legally excludable nor contingent on one's vote – a government pension, for example, that is available to all citizens over a certain age, or a scholarship provided to children from all poor families – but which politicians nonetheless attempt to distribute for political benefit. Citizens may technically have access to the good or service, according to fixed, public criteria, but parties and/or individual politicians find ways to take credit and appear responsible for that "gift," whether or not they were responsible for it in reality. (Within this category, too, are ostensibly programmatic initiatives, for which politicians *may* in fact exercise some degree of discretion – a national disaster relief or highway maintenance fund, for instance, with known, impartial, but disregarded criteria – and likewise seek to exploit for partisan advantage.) When the effort succeeds, politicians or parties effectively hijack programmatic policies and turn them to their own particular benefit.

We emphasize that we are not referring to the normal practice by which politicians and political parties produce policies and programs in hopes of winning the support of voters, and then work to make voters aware of their record after having delivered those programs. What distinguishes programmatic hijacking from regular, retrospective credit-claiming is the imputed contingency. With hijacking, parties and/or politicians work to convince voters that the (promised) provision of a given good or service that arises as a result of a national or regional program is contingent in some way on those voters' electoral support. Voters believe that they must support the party or politician in question to access the benefit.

What makes hijacking slippery to pinpoint is that it often entails more perceived than actual patronage. Even where all citizens formally have equal access to state-provided goods and services, it may be the case that, as Wilkinson (2014, 268) describes of India, "most believe that they can only secure the services of the state via patrons," rather than trusting the state to be "a socially neutral political entity" (see also Weitz-Shapiro 2009). Such beliefs arise naturally in polities where voters know that politicians routinely make deals and distribute benefits of various kinds on the basis of favoritism. Across political contexts, politicians find it advantageous to stoke this belief by attempting to claim credit for spending they did not influence or direct. Some politicians are especially adept at or focused on encouraging constituents to believe it was their intervention that mattered, with such attempts at credit-claiming especially likely to be successful when obliging bureaucrats facilitate them (Grimmer et al. 2012, 705).[1] What matters is not just the amount spent on particular programs and benefits, since voters are seldom able to tabulate and

[1] Hence, we might expect the historically BN-dominated Malaysian civil service, for instance, to have set BN politicians up for self-serving claims.

attribute expenditures correctly, but effective messaging, such that voters believe politicians' claims (Grimmer et al. 2012).

Hijacked programs may come into sharpest relief at the moment of elections but tend to entail ongoing interactions (Wilkinson 2014, 273–74). Where politicians or parties have, or claim to have, some discretion or power over the provision of benefits, they frequently use such provision to help establish or maintain relational clientelist links with voters in between elections that they can then leverage or reinforce during election season (Nichter 2018). The programs and distributions to which we now turn, then, track the electoral clock far less closely than did the micro- and meso-particularistic strategies explored in the preceding two chapters.

THREE TYPES OF PROGRAMMATIC HIJACKING

Our focus in this chapter is mainly on government programs that are national in their orientation and scope, but which are occasionally regional-, state-, or provincial-government programs. In principle, the rules governing qualification for and distribution of benefits of these programs are intended to be clear, public, and respected (Stokes et al. 2013, 7–8). In all our cases, we observe at least some provision of benefits through such programmatic policies. Indeed, the urge to generate such policies is a universal feature of contemporary political life, with notions of equal citizenship and public interest providing strong normative and legitimating underpinnings for all modern states – no matter how frequently violated in practice. Governments of all stripes thus have strong incentives to be seen as acting fairly when designing policies and distributing their benefits.

Moreover, in each of the countries on which we focus, national policy-makers are surrounded by technocrats, policy advisors, and bureaucrats working in relevant government agencies whose job it is to devise policies that will allocate resources in order to achieve specified policy outcomes: poverty alleviation, better health, improved economic growth, or other objectives. In some cases, these technocrats view the misuse of public money for personal use – whether in the form of corruption or diversion for political purposes – as a primary impediment to the achievement of development goals, and consciously design programs in ways that reduce discretion on the part of politicians (e.g., allocating block grants to regions on the basis of mathematical formulae using objective criteria rather than political calculations, or transferring cash assistance to indigent households directly rather than channeling it through local governments). These circumstances generate an immense range of programmatic policies across Southeast Asia, the most important of which, for our purposes, include conditional or unconditional cash-transfer schemes, scholarship programs, health-insurance schemes, infrastructure-development plans, and the like.

If national governments have incentives to design policies and programs that are seen as allocating government benefits fairly and pursuing greater public benefit, it is equally the case that politicians have incentives to use such programs for their own electoral purposes. In all our cases, and to varying degrees across place and policy, we see politicians attempting to turn such programs to their political advantage – hijacking programmatic policies for their personal or partisan political benefit.

The hijacking of government programs comes in three distinct forms – *credit-claiming*, *facilitation*, and *morselization* – differentiated by the degree of direct intervention in the actual distribution of the benefit they entail. *Credit-claiming*, in general terms, is "acting so as to generate a belief in a relevant political actor (or actors) that one is personally responsible for causing the government, or some unit thereof, to do something that the actor (or actors) consider desirable." It occurs frequently in democratic politics since "an actor who believes that a member [of the legislature or other politician] can make pleasing things happen will no doubt wish to keep him in office so that he can make pleasing things happen in the future" (Mayhew 1974, 52–53). The credit-claiming actor may be an individual politician or a political party. We are interested in a particular form of credit-claiming, which occurs when these actors attempt to tie – in the minds of the recipients or of some broader audience – the provision of some government benefit to a constituent or group of constituents to the actors' direct action or intervention.

We are not so much interested in whether actors claim to have been instrumental in passage or provision of a government program, which would be encompassed by Mayhew's definition. Claiming credit for government programs is, after all, the basic stuff of politicking. Our concern is when politicians and parties alter the character of a programmatic initiative by attempting to claim credit for providing a *particular benefit* to a *particular beneficiary*. As Weitz-Shapiro (2014, 29) puts it, "Voters are most likely to change their political behavior in return for some valued good when they believe that a given politician is indeed the gatekeeper who controls access to that good," motivating politicians to "effectively appropriate credit for goods they do not personally fund and, perhaps, whose distribution they do not control" (see also Cruz and Schneider 2017).

In patronage democracies, actors go beyond merely claiming credit for delivering pleasing projects. They may also attempt to create the impression that they skewed the timing or targets of a program to benefit that specific constituency, group, or individual. In other words, whether or not the political actor *does* in fact exercise discretion (which they will if they can), they attempt to create the impression that provision or continuance of benefits under a program is contingent on continued electoral support. Perhaps the most weighty examples of credit-claiming we observed in our cases concern programmatic policies addressing social welfare and poverty alleviation. As we describe later, even when distribution really occurs according to objective criteria, politicians go to great lengths to present these disbursements as *their* doing, not just by insisting that a challenger would cancel the program were they elected (standard fare of electioneering) but also by such means as requiring recipients to collect their checks from party branch offices. As one Malaysian ruling-party politician explained the distinction, "When you deposit the money straight into their account, then there's no political mileage."[2]

Whereas credit-claiming involves little to no effort or value-adding on the part of the political actor, *facilitation* is a different story. Facilitation involves connecting individuals or groups of voters with resources that are publicly provided and not contingent on support for the politician and party – and to which the individuals or groups concerned would be eligible even without the politician's help. Politicians can facilitate such access in response to direct requests from constituents for assistance and often do so as a form of constituency service. For example, politicians may direct constituents seeking assistance to an applicable government program or administrative office, perhaps contributing a letter of support. They might employ assistants who help constituents fill out necessary application paperwork. Politicians and parties may also be proactive – for example, organizing meetings to sign up constituents for a new government program or offering to help a community group apply for a government grant.[3]

With credit-claiming and facilitation, politicians attempt to benefit from the provision of public goods or services over which they, in reality, have little control. By contrast, *morselization* involves the carving up of public projects or programs so that they are produced and distributed according to political rather than economic or programmatic criteria (Cox and McCubbins 2001, 47–48). The process of morselization transforms ostensibly programmatic policies into goods and services over which politicians have actual discretion – politicians decide who does and does not get access to those resources. In other words, morselization involves a politician taking a programmatic good and turning it into micro- or meso-particularism.

---

[2] Interview with BN MP, January 6, 2015, Kuala Lumpur.

[3] An example from one of our secondary cases, highly programmatic Singapore, illustrates facilitation especially well. Here, at usually weekly meet-the-people sessions, MPs and party volunteers help constituents with everything from applying for work permits, to navigating state-run employment agencies, to seeking special dispensation from public-housing authorities, to negotiating down traffic tickets. As one opposition-party politician complained, the system, which encourages voters to see MPs as powerful "rule-benders," is "disempowering on many levels"; constituents speak of being "bounced back" from state agencies to their legislator when they seek redress directly (interview, June 29, 2015, Singapore). At the same time, politicians' letters are not, in fact, likely to "move the needle" beyond perhaps helping to speed things up (interview, Gillian Koh, July 9, 2015, Singapore). Or as a ruling-party legislator elaborated, what he and his volunteers provide are *party* services in connecting voters with government (and charitable) resources; he attends as an MP, he explained, but with his party machinery rather than his legislative office staff (interview, July 7, 2014, Singapore).

In Cox and McCubbins's colorful reading, morselization entails representatives' biting off what they can from the "carcass" of national programmatic policies – such that resources and benefits end up being distributed more to meet political objectives than according to standards of optimal efficiency or overall public benefit (Cox and McCubbins 2001, 47–48; see also Stokes et al. 2013). That distribution may be at the collective level, as with the geographic placement of a new university, or at the individual level, such as distribution of scholarships to study there: in other words, morselization can involve distribution of national programs in the form of meso-particularistic or micro-particularistic goods, with the key being that the politician has discretion over who gets what. We might think, too, of programs designed not to be contingent on votes but which may still be morselized for partisan advantage. For instance, a candidate might be able to deliver on a promise to push their constituents to the top of the list for enrollment in a national social-welfare scheme being newly rolled out. We detail later, for example, how a legislative candidate in Indonesia assured local voters of priority access to a new health-insurance scheme. Such a promise sits between facilitation and morselization.

MOBILIZATION REGIMES, POLITICAL DISCRETION, AND HIJACKING

While we find examples of all three forms of hijacking in each of our primary cases, two factors shape which forms of hijacking predominate and which actors are the hijackers: the degree of discretion politicians have over resource distribution and the type of mobilization regime. First, whether or not morselization is an option depends on the degree to which politicians have discretion over the distribution of funds. Legislators are generally not involved directly in the implementation of government programs, so their ability to engage in the more interventionist forms of hijacking – facilitation and morselization – tends to be more limited than that of their counterparts in the executive branch. Nevertheless, their leverage over government budgets can provide them with considerable bargaining power in accessing government programs. Where they exist, elected local chief executives (mayors, governors, etc.) tend to have more resources and more discretion than legislators, but the amount of discretion even they exercise varies greatly.

Harkening back to our discussion in earlier chapters, the amount of discretion that politicians have is shaped to a significant extent by the relative capacity and autonomy of the state. In other words, politicians operating in weak and porous states have the greatest opportunities to intervene to ensure their constituents can access programs that might not otherwise trickle down to them, however technically entitled they may be. In such polities, where state agencies offer erratic, partial, ineffective, or unpredictable access to programmatic benefits to intended beneficiaries, politicians will have greater scope to be useful to constituents by either facilitating access to those programs or capturing chunks of them to distribute themselves – and to claim credit accordingly.

Among our cases, politicians in the Philippines generally have the greatest discretion over government expenditures. Mayors and governors receive large transfers from the national government, some of which are tied to specific programs, but many of which are not. Likewise, members of Congress have until recently had their own constituency development funds[4] and can also influence how government agencies allocate some funds within their constituencies. This authority produces ample opportunities for the morselization of public programs, in addition to more routine facilitation and credit-claiming. One Liberal Party (LP) member of Congress, for instance, explained the situation back when her party was dominant. Prior to an election, her local LP-affiliated machine ran projects and programs for healthcare, the poor, and so on, not from campaign funds but secured through access to national programs, knowing that her constituents would "consider that as our machinery."[5] Likewise, a mayor described in matter-of-fact terms her jump to the Liberal Party: joining it gave her an advantage in accessing national projects she previously could not, from pensions for indigent seniors, to healthcare programs, to bottom-up-budgeting schemes. Now she was finally getting better police facilities, for instance, as part of a national project; her constituents were no longer "deprived" as before, when the national government sidelined her requests.[6]

Legislators within Indonesia generally have less access to and discretion over government resources than do their counterparts in the Philippines. They can influence government programs during the drafting and budgeting stage, but once programs are in place, it is largely executive government officials and bureaucrats who determine the distribution of resources. In some regions, legislators do have access to constituency development funds, as discussed in Chapter 5, and at all levels they can use their budgeting and review powers to bargain with relevant government agencies for chunks of programmatic goods for their constituencies. Almost every incumbent legislator we encountered during the course of our fieldwork averred that bringing home "programs" – whether in the form of infrastructure projects, livelihood projects, or other resources – was important to their political success, though it was often difficult to know the precise role that politician played in determining the allocation of these programs. Thus, morselization by legislators does occur in Indonesia,

---

[4] The shift came with a 2013 ruling of the Philippine Supreme Court, declaring constituency development funds unconstitutional. In their wake came another form of pork barrel: budget insertions, or earmarks, whereby congresspersons could have projects in their districts funded through the General Appropriations Act. These changes came in the wake of a major 2013 scandal, revealing previous (2007–2009) abuses in the Priority Development Assistance Fund, or PDAF. See Holmes (2019), 347–48, 305, 297–98.

[5] Interview, May 2, 2016, Mindanao.   [6] Interview, May 4, 2016, Central Visayas.

though credit-claiming and facilitation are relatively more common. The opacity of budgeting and allocation decisions makes it often very difficult to assess exactly which strategy is at play. By contrast, local Indonesian executives enjoy significant discretion over budgets, thus enabling them to morselize government programs and reward powerful vote brokers (such as village heads) or communities (such as villages) with a disproportionate share of infrastructure and other programs.

In Malaysia, though government MPs do have access to constituency development funds, the size of those budgets is generally less than in Indonesia or the Philippines, and individual politicians have much less individual discretion otherwise over how resources are allocated within their constituencies. Rather, a comparatively high-capacity bureaucracy implements infrastructure, healthcare, education, and other programs, even if parks and roadways are peppered with signs proclaiming "Another project of the Barisan Nasional government." (As we discuss later, though, MPs from the ruling party can, at times, leverage party connections to direct more resources to their constituencies.) As a result, we see limited opportunities for morselization for MPs; most hijacking in Malaysia entails credit-claiming and facilitation.

A second factor that shapes the dominant form of and actors behind hijacking is the nature of the electoral mobilization regime. Where parties are strong and policymaking comparatively centralized, credit-claiming and facilitation are relatively straightforward for members of the ruling party. Indeed, truly systematic hijacking of programmatic policies arguably goes hand-in-hand with party-based machines because, as Kitschelt (2000, 849) explains, this sort of strategy generally requires "heavy investments in the administrative infrastructure of multilevel political machines that reach from the summits of national politics down to the municipal level." Such investments provide a party machine with the capacity to divvy up and channel macro-level public goods (or to make a credible claim to having done so).[7] Hijacking under party regimes will be substantially party-centered, with programmatic benefits funneled through or adjacent to the party, so the party can facilitate access and claim maximum credit. However, where parties are weak or policymaking is highly decentralized, politicians lose the ability to reap rewards from collective party efforts. If individual politicians do attempt to claim credit for the passage of programmatic policies, such claims will generally not be credible. And so, politicians search for ways to hijack those policies for their *personal* benefit. Ideally, they are able to morselize those programmatic policies and exercise true discretion over distribution; when they cannot do so, they work to facilitate access to and/or claim credit for state-provided resources.

---

[7] As Kitschelt further elaborates, investment in "administrative-technical infrastructure" may be at the expense of similar investment in "modes of interest aggregation and program formation" (2000, 849).

Malaysia's party-based regime centers political activity on the ruling coalition, which has unfettered access to state resources. Morselization is generally not a priority. The ruling coalition designs policies in a way that maximizes its support across constituencies, leaving less room – and relatively little need – for individual MP discretion. Instead, hijacking commonly takes the form of party-oriented credit-claiming. For instance, federal-government-provided COVID-19-relief food aid for families in opposition-held constituencies was distributed through local ruling-party representatives, rather than a government agent (let alone the local opposition MP) (Ngu 2021).[8] Facilitation is also common, including through local party service centers. The ruling party and its members work to convince voters that government programs are really party programs and that access to those programs is contingent on continued support for the party. In short, in Malaysia, programmatic policies are *partisanized*, in a manner that goes far beyond merely extolling the ruling party's achievements to voters.

By contrast, in the ad hoc mobilization regime in Indonesia and local political-machine regime in the Philippines, parties rarely do the hijacking. Instead, individual politicians seek to personalize the distribution of public resources – working to ensure that voters link the provision of resources to the intervention of the politician in question. In Indonesia, local regional heads thus work hard to ensure that local people associate new infrastructure projects, welfare programs, and other services with them personally, by ensuring their photos appear frequently on government-sponsored billboards and in newspaper advertisements touting such initiatives. In the Philippines, this hijacking may also include tying resource provision to the capabilities of the local political machine (of which the politician in question is a crucial part). For example, it is common for most local projects to include signage linking that project to an incumbent politician, directly paralleling the similarly common signage in Malaysia crediting the ruling party. Some posters not only bear the name (and often the picture) of the relevant politician but also the pictures of family members or other members of the local political machine who are also running for office, but have nothing to do with the project in question. One incumbent candidate, for example, posted a sign next to local infrastructure projects, attributing them to his whole clan's "love" for the constituency (Tumandao 2019, 236).

Table 6.1 summarizes the general pattern of hijacking across our three primary cases. Credit-claiming is common in all our cases, though somewhat less so in Indonesia, given the more limited role of politicians in policy provision, and the fact that multiple legislators represent each electoral constituency. For these same reasons, facilitation is more limited in Indonesia, while being

[8] Individual ruling-party politicians also benefit, though, in their own constituencies: several distributed government-provided rice, hand sanitizer, and other pandemic relief, for instance, decorated with their own name and photo, along with their party logo (Sarawak Report 2020).

TABLE 6.1. *Patterns of hijacking*

	Credit-claiming	Facilitation	Morselization
Malaysia	Extensive, party-focused	Extensive, party-focused	Limited
Indonesia	Moderate, candidate-focused	Limited, candidate-focused	Limited (legislators) Extensive (local chief executives)
Philippines	Extensive, candidate- and machine-focused	Moderate, candidate- and machine-focused	Extensive

extensive in Malaysia, and moderately common in the Philippines. Whether we focus on credit-claiming or facilitation in Malaysia, provision is substantially *partisanized* (even if individual politicians also coast on that spin, touting their place within the party), while in Indonesia and the Philippines it is *personalized*, or, in the case of the Philippines, hijacked for the advantage of the local political machine. Finally, morselization is extensive at all levels in the Philippines, where politicians have ample discretion over the distribution of state resources. It is less common in Indonesia, though still a prominent strategy for local executives, and the least common in Malaysia, where the broader focus on party-based appeals reduces the attraction of morselization.

In the next section, we explore the three types of hijacking in more detail and demonstrate how they operate in our cases.

PATTERNS OF PROGRAMMATIC HIJACKING

The specific mix of programmatic hijacking strategies, as well as their fit among the alternative patronage strategies we detail in Chapters 4 and 5, varies across and within countries. Yet deployment of at least some type of hijacking strategies is near-universal. Whether the target is an individual or group is not the key distinction. Rather, what most clearly differentiates among hijacking strategies is the range of discretionary intervention exercised, from credit-claiming absent an actual effect on a policy's development or implementation, to facilitation in making a government program accessible, to actually being able to direct morselized benefits. Along our wider continuum, credit-claiming verges on the fully programmatic end; morselization falls closer to the fully particularistic end.

As such, we find it helpful to categorize programmatic hijacking less by place or category of beneficiaries than by type of program. We distinguish among broad, generally national-level programs for which individual politicians claim credit for themselves or their party, such as cash-transfer programs; individually or collectively targeted benefits, for which a politician's intervention is not technically required, such as expedited or easier access to disaster-assistance or education benefits; and individual or collective benefits delivered as morsels of national programs, such as healthcare vouchers or infrastructure projects.

Credit-claiming

Even if politicians' ability to shape or direct delivery of some national-level welfare and other policies is actually minimal, it is to their advantage to overstate their or their parties' powers of procurement. These programs may have known, published, and followed criteria for distribution – that is, they may be programmatic rather than particularistic (Stokes et al. 2013, 7) – but their design can offer politicians and parties opportunity to play up their own roles. They can do so, for instance, by distributing noncontingent state payments personally or at party offices, or highlighting their instrumental efforts to bring a given program to their constituents. In their attempt to court voters, politicians may make a programmatic policy appear more particularistic and contingent than it actually is. Examples of credit-claiming activities are ubiquitous across our Southeast Asian cases (see also Cruz and Schneider 2017). Politicians are often front and center at the launch of new infrastructure projects or the opening of a new hospital or school in their constituency – with signage to bear witness to their crucial intervention. These efforts shade into simply bragging about programmatic achievements, from a healthcare scheme to a new highway – as any incumbent might do – but cross the line when the intent is clearly to obfuscate for voters whether it was the state or rather the party or politician that provided the initiative in question, suggesting therefore that the continuance of such achievements is contingent on their reelection.

Conditional or unconditional cash-transfer programs are especially prone to opportunistic credit-claiming. Popular among both recipients and international donors, these programs are found in dozens of countries, especially across Latin America, but increasingly also in Asia. They are not specific to any constituency and can be an effective means of addressing broad policy goals, especially intergenerational poverty alleviation as well as the achievement of important targets in the realms of education and health (Baez et al. 2012, 2; Hall 2012, 26). Nevertheless, these programs' implementation and distribution allow opportunities for personalization and partisanization.

The political potential of cash transfers is well-known globally. In some cases, implementation specifically pursues political goals. A prime example is Guatemala's *Mi Familia Progresa* scheme, launched in 2008. Partisan politics pervaded the rollout, from efforts to enroll vote-rich municipalities first and to tweak poverty lines to ensure a crowd of beneficiaries at distribution events featuring the first lady, to using benefit-payment events for party propaganda, to threats to exclude defectors from the program (Sandberg and Tally 2015, 509–12). Yet the programs' inherent political benefits do not require such stark manipulation. Cash transfers have been associated with increased support for the incumbent party or president in a variety of countries, including Colombia (Baez et al. 2012, 5), Honduras (Linos 2013, 865), Brazil (Fried 2012, 1049), Mexico (De La O 2012) and, among our own cases, Indonesia (Mietzner 2009). While programs generally advantage incumbents, where the implementation of the program has been free of political capture, this incumbent advantage has come without undermining "healthy democratic habits" (De La O 2012, 9–10, 12).

We find unconditional or conditional cash-transfer programs, and associated credit-claiming, in all our cases. But specific variations distinguish not just the policies themselves but also their political implications. In the Philippines, for instance, mayors' central position in political networks plays out in the politics of the country's conditional cash-transfer scheme, known as *Pantawid Pamilyang Pilipino Program* (4Ps, translated as Bridging Program for the Filipino Family). The program, which offers payments to poor households contingent on their meeting health, nutrition, and education requirements, is centrally, not locally, administered: funds flow from the central government to recipients' accounts and mayors have no say in whether their municipality is included or who the beneficiaries are (Labonne 2013, 75–76). The program was "designed to minimise input from elected officials" precisely in order to undermine clientelism (Swamy 2016, 76). Even so, the extent of mayoral credit-claiming was so great that the central government in 2012 barred local officials from including their own name or photo on program materials (Labonne 2013, 74). In competitive environments, incumbents enjoyed a significant boost in vote-share from implementation of the 4Ps program, even though those officials could not influence whether the municipality, or which people within it, were able to participate. Candidates campaigned on the resources they claimed to have secured, shaping voters' (retrospective) decision-making (Labonne 2013, 84). Indeed, one incumbent mayor we interviewed explained that she had, in fact, commissioned a report to learn why some families dropped out of the 4Ps program, the better to channel support toward complementary assistance (in this case, job creation for parents of enrolled children). However, her constituents thanked her party for the program, an impression her party's presidential candidate played up in posters touting how he had helped the municipality, and thanked her for administering it.[9] At the same time, exclusion errors in the rollout of the program gave rise to widespread "suspicion that clientelism plays an important role" (Swamy 2016, 81) among community members.

However central the roles of mayors may be, credit-claiming is not limited to them. Politicians from the barangay to national levels need at least to appear to bring resources and projects to their constituents. An exemplar is a congresswoman from Mindanao who, as she described to us, plainly and purposefully played up 4Ps payments, as though she had been instrumental in the program's

---

[9] Interview, May 4, 2016, Central Visayas.

passage (which occurred before her time) or to the benefits delivered. She clarified that how one "translates" the program to local voters matters. Politicians from the president's Liberal Party (as she was) could explain that, lacking legislative institutionalization, 4Ps relies on the president's giving an annual allocation. Congress and the president could well opt for discontinuation. Thus, it is a "matter of letting them understand the possible consequence of a new administration."[10] Reflecting not just the strength of the (dynastic) local machine but also her party's efforts at institutionalization (which evaporated once they lost the presidency), the local party team would also give first-time candidates "access" to projects, as for healthcare or the indigent, so they, too, could claim credit.[11]

She noted that in her politician father's time, credit-claiming and morselization were even easier because members of Congress had direct access to constituency development funds (dubbed the Priority Development Assistance Fund, PDAF) that they could use to fund local programs at their discretion. For instance, her father collaborated with a funeral parlor for constituents in need of burial assistance: the funeral home provided a prearranged package, for which the government paid directly with PDAF funds, upon presentation of a certificate from the barangay. However, after a 2013 scandal revealed grave abuses in PDAF disbursements, the Supreme Court ruled that constituency development funds were unconstitutional (Holmes 2019, 347). Meanwhile, the 4Ps conditional cash-transfer program was designed to reduce opportunities for morselization. 4Ps, she noted, makes it "harder now to say it's from me," but even so, "there are so many ways of telling" – and even when it is government money involved, voters still take it as assistance from their governor or member of Congress, who can "personalize it." That this congresswoman had a social-welfare-related committee appointment, too, made it all the easier for her to claim credit for 4Ps assistance.[12]

In a similar vein, a campaign strategist in the Central Visayas explained how he and his team worked to claim credit for 4Ps benefits. Recognizing the mobilizational possibilities of 4Ps, they organized recipients into family development councils for monthly meetings. He would then invite attendees to a party meeting next door that just happened to be beginning as their 4Ps meeting ended. While many within his party had initially resisted such credit-claiming, they eventually realized the potential electoral advantages and began emulating these efforts as elections approached.[13]

In Indonesia, the urge to *appear* to direct benefits in order to credit-claim is also ubiquitous. It is relatively difficult for Indonesian local-level elected officials to claim credit for cash-transfer payments. These programs have been designed, as in the Philippines, to keep allocation and distribution of benefits

[10] Interview, May 2, 2016, Mindanao. [11] Interview, May 2, 2016, Mindanao.
[12] Interview, May 2, 2016, Mindanao. [13] Interview, May 5, 2016, Siquijor.

out of the hands of elected officials (though village heads have some sway: see Aspinall and Berenschot 2019, 155–56). More broadly, it is very common, for example – much as among local officials in the Philippines – for district heads to advertise the rollout of national programs in their regions by way of large billboards and newspaper advertisements that feature their own images prominently, thereby implying that they played some role in devising the program or winning it for their region. Incumbents frequently boast of their ability to "lobby" successfully in Jakarta for projects, and challengers often criticize them for their ineffectiveness in doing so. In fact, many of the grants the government makes to particular districts are negotiated through bureaucratic rather than political channels, in which regions' needs are assessed against technical formulae. But everyone knows that some political intervention does take place in the allocation of such assistance – whether in the executive branch or the legislative budgeting processes – such that district heads' claims to have played personal roles in delivering particular projects can appear credible even when not warranted.

Indonesian legislators generally have fewer opportunities than district heads to determine the allocation of resources and must compete with other legislators in their same constituency who are also eager to claim credit. Nonetheless, they try to associate themselves with allocations that do occur – for example, they will often achieve advance warning of distribution of village projects, agricultural extension schemes, and the like – especially if on friendly terms with the local district head. They then try to make sure that they appear at the ceremonies launching these programs at the community level. One very senior education ministry official explained how it was relatively easy to placate members of the national legislature: "The key thing they want is to be told when the money [for new projects in their constituencies] will be released and when the program will be launched, so they can be there."[14] A great deal of ambiguity surrounds such activities, with it often being difficult for citizens to know what exactly the politician's role was in the allocation of a benefit, facilitating credit-claiming. For example, members of Indonesian legislatures at every level typically claim credit for benefits delivered to their home constituencies – especially when those benefits have been allocated through spending programs overseen in legislative commissions of which they are members. As we explain later, it *is* possible for legislators to morselize at least a portion of programs delivered through this process, but we also witnessed plenty of occasions in which legislators claimed credit for local welfare initiatives and infrastructure projects that probably would have been delivered to their constituencies regardless of their personal role.

Lastly, Malaysia has had an *un*conditional cash-transfer scheme, Bantuan Rakyat 1Malaysia (1Malaysia People's Aid or BR1M, renamed Bantuan Sara

[14] Interview, November 29, 2015, Canberra.

Hidup, Cost of Living Aid, in 2018) at the federal level since 2012, along with cognate state-level programs. Unlike much redistribution in Malaysia, these programs are race-blind; they use income criteria (and for some component or auxiliary programs, age or, for instance, student, parental, or other status). To make them explicitly dependent on political criteria such as support for the ruling coalition would invite electoral backlash. They *are*, in short, programmatic. Yet the parties that crafted and implemented each of these policies eagerly and prominently claim credit, as do individual politicians from within those parties, regardless of their own personal role. Making that link all the more blatant initially was the mode of distribution. The government commonly disbursed checks through BN party offices, with the legislators themselves or party "coordinators" in opposition-held constituencies often personally handing checks to recipients.[15] In other words, distribution was designed in such a way as to suggest partisan involvement and add a whiff of imputed contingency. By 2018, the government shifted to direct-deposit, purportedly to avoid the appearance of partisan manipulation.

Although opposition candidates could stress to voters that the funds they received were "the people's money" rather than BN beneficence, or that these payments were vastly overwhelmed by the sums lost to government corruption, such messages were a hard sell.[16] Moreover, not only did the Pakatan Harapan (PH) government elected in 2018 maintain BR1M (albeit rebranded), but its state-level governments in Penang and Selangor already had developed cognate welfare programs to BR1M and associated "1Malaysia" programs, for which their politicians, too, claimed credit. After Parti Islam seMalaysia (PAS) left PH progenitor Pakatan Rakyat in 2015, the coalition berated a PAS state legislator in Pakatan-governed Selangor for including his image and party logo on envelopes with programmatic state healthcare assistance. His defense: the same thing had "been done by other assemblypersons before" (N. Faizal 2017).

Meanwhile, BR1M was a focal point of the BN's election campaigns in both 2013 and 2018, from billboards and posters to slogans of *janji ditepati* (promises kept): BN rally speakers, for instance, reminded voters that the incumbent BN government had promised and delivered BR1M payments, whereas, they argued, the opposition was not only inclined to cut BR1M but also less reliable in its pledges (they were merely *pancing undi*, fishing for votes).[17] As one BN incumbent cabinet minister explained, it was only contractors who had, in years past, enjoyed most of the pecuniary benefit from the BN's focus on infrastructure. With BR1M, voters benefit directly – and cash payments trickle out to the local economy, offering positive spillover effects that subsidies on staple goods cannot. He acknowledged, though, that distribution is "a bit

---

[15] Interview with opposition legislator, April 29, 2013, Perak.
[16] Interview with Pakatan MP, April 24, 2013, Pahang.
[17] For example, BN ceramah, April 23, 2013, Segamat, Johor.

politicized," as when accompanied by a *ceramah* (political speech).[18] Even so, it bears repeating that the macro-particularistic aspect of these programmatic policies is electorally useful spin rather than substance. The fact that, by 2018, most voters received their BR1M payments via direct-deposit rather than from their local BN party service center may well have weakened the credibility of those imputations of partisan credit.

We observed similar credit-claiming attempts around other policies during our fieldwork in Malaysia; given the pervasiveness of such efforts, it was entirely plausible for voters to assume that BR1M was a party, not government, handout. For example, in mid-2014 – about a year after the last election, and with the next still several years out – an MP from the Malaysian Indian Congress (MIC), part of the ruling BN coalition, arrived at his party's head-quarters in his constituency in Selangor state.[19] The building doubled as a service center. A handful of party members, activists in the party's youth wing and close to this MP, relaxed in the lobby, while local residents found their way to a large room upstairs. The MP was there to meet a roomful of around fifty mostly Malay constituents from across this peri-urban constituency. This event was a happy one, as the MP was distributing checks to support small businesses. He called each person up in turn, asking them what enterprise they were undertaking, handing them an envelope, and posing for a photograph, against BN-logo-peppered wallpaper. A federal-government fund for small-scale entrepreneurs, particularly connected with agriculture, over which the MP and his party had no discretion, provided the checks. But at this event, the MP was the warm, amiable, generous face of the program and his party, the visually unmissable backdrop. Again, the purpose was to tie distribution to the party as closely as possible.

Indeed, especially aggressive credit-claiming has tended to dominate the campaign strategies of the BN's non-Malay parties. The Malaysian Chinese Association (MCA) routinely papers the landscape with banners touting how much the party has secured for the Chinese-Malaysian community, for instance, by way of federal-government support for Chinese-medium schools and institutions of higher education, while MIC candidates claim credit for government support for Tamil schools and Hindu temples. These messages reverberate through campaign speeches and other materials, as candidates visit local community institutions and point out the new extension "they" have funded, or the scholarships their party has wrested for the community, raising the specter of reversal should voters elect other parties.[20] Such investments are clearly part of larger programmatic strategies, and entrance to those schools or other institutions is not contingent on one's vote. But the implication is clear:

[18] Interview, April 24, 2013, Terengganu.   [19] Field notes, July 12, 2014, Selangor.
[20] For example, interviews with BN candidate for state legislature, April 22, 2013, Malacca; incumbent MP, April 23, 2013, Johor; BN candidate for state legislature, April 25, 2016, Sarawak.

the community should be grateful to the *party* (as well as their local MCA or MIC politicians specifically) for securing these programs and channeling resources to the local Chinese school or Hindu temple, not to a neutral government functionary.

Meanwhile, the centralization of fiscal resources and policy authority in Malaysia has made it easier for the BN as central government to claim credit for local development, even when opposition legislators for those areas have been those projects' chief advocates. For instance, although a PH MP raised the issue of, and lobbied for, the introduction of a bus service (under federal-government purview in Malaysia) for her constituency in Pahang state, she found it difficult to get any credit when the BN federal government finally acceded to her request.[21] The very nature of programmatic policies – that they are government initiatives – makes credit-claiming inherently more available as a strategy to politicians in government than to opposition parties, regardless of who within either camp was really responsible.

Facilitation

Our second form of hijacking involves actions beyond simple credit-claiming. Facilitation is when politicians or parties work to connect constituents with government programs and resources for which they are formally qualified, but to which they may not in practice have access or know about without the politician's help. Beneficiaries may be either individual voters or groups; the outcome may thus take the form of either micro- or meso-particularism. These are programs and resources over which politicians have no real discretion, but for which they can use their position to inform citizens, cut red tape, and influence who gets prioritized. These programs have public, meaningful, non-contingent criteria for eligibility, and many citizens are likely to apply to or partake of the program through the "official" route rather than with a politician's assistance. But the criteria and procedures for accessing these programs can be opaque to voters, and in some places voters may be unaware that they qualify, or they may be distant from the relevant government offices, lack adequate literacy skills to fill out the application forms, or otherwise face difficulty gaining access. This provides an opportunity for entrepreneurial politicians and their brokers.

Access to national education and healthcare programs aptly demonstrates this pattern of central or provincial/state government programs, aimed at broad policy goals and not contingent on votes of the individual or community, but for which dimensions of their institutional design and access may be turned to partisan advantage. What we consider to be facilitation are not devolved-by-design allocations – we turn to those in the next section – but rather, national

---

[21] Interview, April 24, 2013, Pahang.

programs leveraged for political advantage. Specifically, we focus on situations where the politician or party assumes a facilitating or mediating role: connecting their constituents with available government resources, even though such intervention might not be strictly necessary.

Falling under the category of facilitation is lots of what we might describe as constituency service. Politicians learn of the needs of their constituents, then work to respond to those needs and solve those problems by putting constituents in contact with appropriate government agencies and programs. For example, it is not uncommon in the Philippines for politicians to have staff dedicated to helping connect constituents with government programs. One incumbent congresswoman, for instance, explained that she set up her office right next to a municipal health center, which allowed her more easily to connect her supporters with available, publicly funded medical assistance. While she provided very little in the way of her own funds, the goal of such intercession was still to produce constituents who felt personally loyal to her. She described as "more facilitating than providing," too, her role in helping constituents access Crisis Intervention Programs, a social-welfare initiative funded through a congressional appropriation. The congresswoman's office helps constituents apply, and so long as the applicant's papers are in order and funds are available, there is "no reason for them to say no." Later, when she comes to a beneficiary's barangay at election time, "they'll be the one to tell that story; they're the ones campaigning."[22]

In the Philippines, distribution of emergency food or disaster aid often flows through local government offices, allowing incumbents to act as the intermediaries, facilitating constituents' access to these nationally funded resources. While the aid is supposed to be available to all those in need, politicians inject themselves in the process, identifying recipients, setting distribution priorities, and, most importantly, making sure that voters understand the crucial role the politician played in securing that assistance. For example, politicians are quick to slap their image on boxes of food, emergency supplies, and bottles of water that actually come from the Department of Social Welfare and Development or the Red Cross.

Disaster relief has also provided opportunities for facilitation in Malaysia. Explained an incumbent BN MP, the state and federal governments had each contributed 500 ringgit (approximately USD120) per person toward relief after a recent monsoon that affected over 8,000 people in his constituency. Over 1,000 were still awaiting their funds as the campaign proceeded; he needed to iron those payments out before the election. The issue was not his discretion in determining recipients – he did not indicate having such authority – but he needed to be seen helping to fix distribution bottlenecks, so that he could benefit personally from any electoral bump the aid conveyed.[23]

In Indonesia, we find cognate patterns. Because the rollout of programs necessarily involves sequencing, politicians and candidates can claim credit for determining who gets covered first. A typical example of this process of politicization comes from West Java. There, a candidate for office, the son of a wealthy Golkar Party cabinet minister, had brought in training and other government-funded programs through the Golkar youth organization, giving himself the appearance of an incumbent. He was also able to ensure his constituents were in a "fast lane" in the queue for a new national health program, organizing members of his success team – again through the youth organization – to collect residents' data and help them arrange their payments. Not yet then in office, he had no discretion over whether they qualified, but he was confident local voters would know he had helped to speed their way to approval.[24] In a poor neighborhood in Surabaya, local campaigners for the PDI–P also worked collectively to organize enrolment in and payments for the new national health-insurance scheme, with local candidates touting this achievement as a major community contribution during campaign meetings. (Party-led efforts remain the exception rather than the rule in Indonesia, however.)

In West Timor and Sumba in the province of East Nusa Tenggara – one of Indonesia's poorest, most rural, and ethnically complex regions – an incumbent legislator of the Partai Demokrat was, in the leadup to the 2014 legislative election, engaged in perhaps the largest-scale facilitation effort we witnessed in any country. In order to enlist their children in a large-scale national-government scholarship scheme for poor children, members of this politician's success team collected data from poor families when they visited villages – while also engaging in normal micro-particularism (distributing packets of coffee, sugar, and betel nuts house to house). According to a team member, they were distributing 22,000 enrollment forms and helping people fill them out; two months prior to the election they had enrolled another 10,000 students whose families had already received two payments of about USD40 each. Mixing a large dose of credit-claiming into their appeal, the success team members told recipients that the legislator had boosted the allocation of these scholarships to their province from 20,000 to 40,000 – assisted by his close connection to incumbent president Susilo Bambang Yudhoyono. Further muddying the water, some also seemed to be suggesting that the politician was funding these scholarships out of his own pocket.[25] While some voters may not have believed the latter claim, the fact that many residents of the province themselves had very

[23] Interview, April 24, 2013, Terengganu.
[24] Interview with candidate for national parliament, April 2, 2014, Cirebon.
[25] We are grateful to our research partner Rudi Rohi for providing details, in part based on interviews he conducted in Sumba in April 2014.

low levels of educational attainment and were often very poorly served by government offices presumably made them very grateful for the assistance they received in acquiring an unlooked-for government benefit.

Where politicians derive substantial electoral rewards from facilitation, the practice can generate interesting and perverse incentives. Politicians benefit from riding to the rescue of their constituents, helping to navigate the bureaucracy, cutting red tape, and making government services legible. Efforts to improve public service access and delivery, then, represent a threat. One BN advisor explained East Malaysia's relative underdevelopment to us in precisely those terms: the BN federal government has an incentive to curb these disproportionately seat-rich states' development budgets, so these voters would remain dependent on the BN. However frustrated they might get as the development gap with peninsular West Malaysia widened, it is "better to negotiate with the wife than the ex-wife." By this, he meant that legislators from the ruling coalition (presumably the BN) would have more bargaining power with the federal government and could proceed to woo low-income voters through strategic deployment of social-welfare programs.[26] More broadly, politicians have incentives to keep government capacity low and the rules opaque so they can step in and offer "compensatory constituency services," thus earning the loyalty of potential voters (Golden 2003, 189).

Morselization

Lastly, politicians and parties may hijack programmatic policies by carving them into smaller, particularistic morsels over which they have some discretion. In effect, morselization is the process of turning programmatic (macro) goods into micro- and meso-particularistic benefits that can be distributed according to the logics discussed in Chapters 4 and 5. Even the most programmatic policies can present opportunities for morselization. For example, a government may increase spending on higher education in pursuit of goals of expanding access and developing a more skilled labor force. But how does it spend that money? Many sites are likely suited to hosting a university. Lots of students are deserving of scholarships. Which constituency gets a university and which students secure scholarships? If the allocation of those benefits is based on clear and public criteria, following Stokes and her coauthors (Stokes et al. 2013), we consider the policy programmatic, even if some receive the benefits and others do not. But, if allocation relies on political criteria or allows politicians' discretion, those ostensibly programmatic policies have been morselized.

Infrastructure-development projects are emblematic of this sort of discretion-tempered distribution across our three countries. Governments generally implement projects to develop infrastructure or designated sectors

---

[26] Interview, July 20, 2016, Sarawak.

according to larger policy or development goals, and in tune with some level of strategic, overall planning. However, politicians often intervene in various aspects of infrastructure projects – from sequencing to contracting to place-ment – in order to maximize their political benefit. Returning to our example of higher education: a politician may succeed in directing a piece of a national program to her constituency, in the form of, say, a scholarship program specific to a local ethnic community. Doing so might be justifiable in terms of central-government targets (to which any of several paths might lead), but it also has the potential to produce substantial political benefits.

Among our main cases, morselization is most central to the practice of politics in the Philippines, where politicians have substantial direct and indirect influence over how resources from public programs are distributed, notwith-standing the banning of constituency development funds in the wake of the 2013 PDAF scandal. For example, each year the Philippines passes a General Appropriations Act that, among other things, allocates money to the Department of Public Works and Highways (DPWH) for the construction and maintenance of the country's public infrastructure. For many years, a significant portion of that budget was a set-aside for members of Congress. Between 2000 and 2010, the total amount allocated for members of Congress amounted to USD155–540 million per year, or 4–12 percent of the national discretionary budget; each member received an equal share, regardless of party, ranging over the period from USD47,000 to 1.2 million.[27] Funds for the program flowed through and were administered by DPWH, but members of Congress had "the authority to identify specific projects for a given location and to release the funds for that project" (Hicken et al. 2015, 83–84). Thus, politicians could effectively hijack an ostensibly national program for address-ing infrastructure needs, reducing it to morsels over which they could exercise discretion. Evidence that such discretion follows a political logic is ubiquitous (e.g., Coronel 1998; Chua and Cruz 2004; Cruz and Chua 2004; Hicken et al. 2015; Ravanilla 2017; Holmes 2019). We see similar dynamics at the local level, where mayors can prioritize certain infrastructure projects, favor certain constituencies, and channel projects to certain contractors.

Indonesian electoral politics also offers space for discretion in parceling out benefits. As we explained in Chapter 5, Indonesian district heads and mayors enjoy significant discretion over the allocation of their own budgets – though less so than in the Philippines – and often distribute benefits according to political rather than technical criteria. Indonesian legislators also have some ability to intervene in the allocation of projects and other benefits distributed as part of national (or regional) programs. Members of provincial and district legisla-tures, too, often have access to budgetary allocations – so-called aspiration

---

[27] See Holmes (2019) for a detailed description of how these programs, and the level of morseliza-tion, have changed over time.

funds (Mahsun 2016) – which they can allocate on a more or less discretionary basis. They use these not only for local infrastructure projects but also to support local community groups (religious groups, farmer cooperatives, micro-enterprises, and the like) with government grants.

Legislators' influence, at both national and regional levels, comes also from their authority to deliberate upon government budgets and scrutinize the work of ministers, regional heads, and bureaucrats through the commission system found in both the national and regional legislatures. Legislative commissions specialize in discrete policy areas and are matched with relevant ministries and agencies, reviewing and approving their budgets and activities (Sherlock 2010). Frequently, legislators simply monetize this process, using their leverage to extract corrupt payments from their counterparts in the executive branch in return for passing relevant legislation or approving budgets, or to insert themselves as project brokers (*makelar proyek*), linking private contractors with their executive counterparts and taking fees in the process; many of the most spectacular and best-publicized legislative corruption scandals of the post-Suharto period have involved project-brokering of this type.[28] In doing so, they can build up war chests that they can use to fund private distribution at election time – a particular concern for Indonesian legislators, given the cost of micro-particularism in the country's elections. At the same time, legislators can also use the authority they derive from their commission positions to claim credit for national programs in the course of election campaigns, and they can also bargain in order to carve out slices from national projects for their own constituencies.

Most incumbent legislators spend a great deal of time boasting of their successes in using their positions to benefit their constituents when it comes time to recontest their seats. For instance, an incumbent member of Indonesia's national legislature we met in Sumatra not only bragged of national programs his commission had approved but also noted with pride that people thanked him for building a bridge in the district under one of those programs (which he advertised on local television, to be sure it wasn't missed).[29] Another incumbent member of parliament from Tangerang, just outside Jakarta, used his post (in the DPR commission concerned with transportation, telecommunications, public works, housing, village development, and disadvantaged communities) to morselize the budget on behalf of his constituents. He noted that he could explain to a ministry that a particular area was in need of services, and get what

---

[28] For a typical example, see Dongoran (2021) on a scandal involving members of the DPR's Commission VIII on social affairs, working with officials from the Ministry of Social Affairs, to extract fees from the provision of COVID-19 social-assistance packages in 2020.

[29] Interview, March 22, 2014, Palembang. He also practiced facilitation, helping constituents secure funds for education costs under another program that parliament had enacted. Voters took this intervention as "proof of what he has done," but he demurred. Because it didn't involve his personal funds, he shouldn't be viewed as "Superman."

they needed delivered.[30] A legislator in Central Java not only claimed credit for the health-related programs cleared through his parliamentary commission but also spoke of "injecting benefits" into his district – not only health-related benefits such as medications, support for nursing mothers, and hospital access but also benefits such as access to a gas line and free LPG tanks. He explained that the key to his reelection was the practice of *sering turun*: getting out often and mingling with the people to ensure they knew him, plus explaining and publicizing his efforts in local media. While he was pleased with his previous work on a commission focusing on policing and laws, that assignment gave him little he could take home to his voters: the work was "very manly," he joked, but did not help him much electorally, and for that reason he had requested transfer to his current commission.[31] Of course, it is often difficult to tell whether such legislators are morselizing public programs or merely claiming credit for benefits that would have been delivered to their constituencies anyway; lack of transparency in formal allocation rules and implementation produces a form of productive ambiguity that is highly advantageous for them.

Morselization is less common in Malaysia, where a strong party regime is adept at crafting policies that secure its electoral majority, with less incentive and opportunity for individual legislators to carve out discrete chunks of programs for their personal purposes. There is certainly a high level of meso-particularism, as outlined in Chapter 5, but most is coordinated and distributed by the ruling coalition, with less discretion for legislators than in the Philippines and Indonesia. The main exception is distribution of their constituency development funds (to which only ruling-party legislators have typically had access) to support small-scale infrastructure projects supplemental to larger schemes.[32] In effect, the additional step of morselization is superfluous in a setting where policymaking is already partisanized – designed to benefit the ruling party and is politicians – and enacted by a state apparatus with credible capacity to carry out government plans.

CONCLUSION

Efforts to hijack macro-level programmatic policies for partisan or personal advantage thus vary, depending especially on the relative primacy of parties versus persons in elections and systems of government, and the amount of discretion politicians have over the distribution of government resources. In the party-based regime, Malaysia, hijacking in all its forms is largely carried out by, and done for the benefit of, the ruling party. Programmatic policies are

---

[30] Interview, March 30, 2014, Tangerang. [31] Interview, April 3, 2014, Pati.
[32] E.g., interview with PH MP, December 23, 2014, Subang Jaya.

partisanized, made to appear more patronage-based than they actually are, with credit primarily to the parties to which the politicians touting these messages belong. By contrast, the object of hijacking in Indonesia is personalization. Personalization is also a focus of Philippine politicians, along with hijacking programmatic policies to help support local party machines.

Unsurprisingly, credit-claiming is ubiquitous in all our cases, though largely a rhetorical device. Credit-claiming has been the most straightforward in Malaysia, where the BN, with its control of the state, could credibly assert responsibility for the provision of governmental benefits and insist or imply that these were contingent on support for the coalition and its candidates. In the Philippines and Indonesia, such claims by individual politicians are, on their face, less persuasive, but politicians work hard to highlight their own key contributions and insert themselves into the distribution of government resources – and thus to make their claims more plausible. Facilitation is a similarly common hijacking strategy, but again, the type of mobilization regime shapes how it unfolds. In the Philippines and Indonesia, individual politicians work to connect their constituents with government benefits and to ensure that voters understand the politician's help as irreplaceable. In Malaysia, it is the party and its politician-agents that are the key facilitators. Morselization is most common in the Philippines, where the permeability of the budgetary process provides politicians with abundant opportunities to personalize the distribution of resources and convert ostensibly programmatic policies into discretionary patronage. Politicians use these morsels to help build their own personal support, and to build and maintain local party machines. We do find many examples of morselization in Indonesia, too, particularly among local executives, as well as among legislators who either (at the local level) have access to personal constituency funds or (at both local and national level) can carve out resources from programs their parliamentary commissions oversee for projects in their home districts, burnishing their personal political stars in the process.

Three closing caveats are in order. First, we have described broad patterns in each case and have shown how those patterns relate to the type of mobilization regime in place. However, as we attempted to detail throughout the chapter, we can and do find elements and examples of all three types of hijacking in each of our cases. Second, while we consider each type of hijacking separately from meso- and micro-particularism, in practice the boundaries between these concepts are blurred. Is an infrastructure project a regular club good, or a morselized piece of a broader, programmatic policy? Is it credit-claiming, facilitation, morselization, or something else when a legislator secures or supplies funding for a particular group or project? To answer these and similar questions requires us to look carefully at the details of the policy or project as well as the context in which the distribution occurs. And lastly, the line between credit-claiming and the "normal politicking" to be found in any electoral regime is a hazy one – governments anywhere want voters to attribute all good outcomes under their administration to their enlightened leadership. It is the effort to make programmatic policies *appear* not to be programmatic, but contingent on voters' political loyalties – shading, in turn, to the actual substitution of political for technical criteria in allocating resources – that leads us to consider this full range of hijacking modes as varieties of macro-particularism. This places them at least a notch off the fully programmatic end of our continuum of government outputs.

7

Patronage and Identity

Domesticating Difference

In the Compostela Valley of the Philippines' southern island of Mindanao, a first-term local councilor was running to become mayor of his town. He seemed to have a shot, not least because he had the advantage of being an incumbent office-holder, with the result that people came to his door all day seeking assistance for this or that personal or professional problem. More importantly, he was an indigenous, or Lumad, candidate, in a community that is 40 percent Lumad, and running with the backing of his Mandaya ethnolinguistic community against a nonindigenous opponent. If elected, he would have been the town's first Lumad mayor – a possibility his campaign team played up avidly in their campaign appeals. Hoping to mobilize Lumad voters, he promised to direct more patronage to the community, even tailoring his stump speeches differently for upland (more heavily indigenous) and valley crowds. To Lumad voters, he emphasized that upland areas lacked good roads, for instance, and he promised to improve them. Despite securing almost 46 percent of the vote, he lost, but his strong focus on his indigenous heritage and directing resources to that community was enough to ensure he was subsequently reelected as councilor.[1]

Meanwhile, in a nearby town, a businesswoman was making her second bid for election as councilor. Like most candidates, she cultivated relationships widely through community service and provision of patronage, targeting everyone from business groups to banana farmers to educators. But she gave special focus to networks of women within her community, combining the championing of issues they care about with patronage designed to demonstrate her empathy and commitment, as a fellow woman. In campaign speeches, she stressed that mothers could use their vote to defend their families, and her team

---

[1] Interview, May 2, 2016, Mindanao.

arranged for her to offer talks or livelihood trainings for women in her constituency. But beyond rhetoric, she also built a local machine designed to co-opt local networks of women, funneling patronage to and through these networks. For example, she supplemented party support with a private campaign team, composed primarily of barangay-level female leaders of co-ops and daycare centers. She made sure poor women in the town knew to call her when they needed assistance – for instance, when a 17-year-old gave birth in her car, she called the candidate for help, then named the child after the candidate's husband (in the process, cleverly obligating the candidate to buy the baby gifts). As councilor, she also intervened to help local women secure government-funded rehabilitation and counseling services for their addicted children, giving her real appeal, she explained, among women who found the police unhelpful in addressing problems of rampant drug use in the community.[2]

In this chapter, we move from explaining particular types of patronage to exploring the interaction of patronage politics with social identities and the specific networks these entail – focusing on ethnicity, religion, gender, and class – in the context of the social pluralism that scholars have long considered to be characteristic of Southeast Asian societies (Furnivall 1956). The candidates just discussed both exemplify politicians' mixing of patronage and identity politics, offering targeted assistance to constituents in exchange for (or expectation of) their support, while tailoring that assistance to particular identity groups – Lumad in the first case, women in the second – and stressing their shared identity. As we show, the intermingling of identity and patronage politics is widespread across all three countries that are our focus.

Identity politics, sometimes known as the politics of difference, has inspired a massive literature on how it can involve policing of group boundaries and zero-sum competition for resources and recognition (among many others, Horowitz 1986; Fraser 2000; Gurr 2000; Eifert et al. 2010). What struck us as we encountered the entanglement of patronage and identity politics through Southeast Asia, however, was not a politics of difference but an underlying similarity of structure. We found, in other words, a modular character to patronage politics that is replicated across groups and contexts. In one locale, a patronage politician might mark herself as distinctive by providing Christian congregations with grants for church improvements or keyboards for community choirs; in another, a politician promotes himself as a stalwart of one ethnic-minority community by sponsoring renovations of vernacular schools and scholarships for co-ethnic students. These appeals to distinct groups with little in common follow the same logic and have the same structure.

Moreover, while we encountered many examples of politicians using patronage to make *"bonding" in-group appeals* that solidify identity groups (ethnic-Chinese politicians' donations to Chinese-medium schools in

---

[2] Interview, May 2, 2016.

Malaysia, for instance, where ethnoreligious identity is central to the party system), politicians also frequently deploy patronage to broaden their political base and make *"bridging" appeals to members of out-groups* (as when ethnic-Malay politicians provide well-publicized donations to those same Chinese-medium schools). Even in the examples provided earlier from the Philippines, the politicians concerned did not exclusively target their assistance at their core constituency but also reached out to other groups. Overall, our findings suggest that mobilization on the basis of identity is not a substitute for patronage politics, but rather, patronage generally subsumes and even domesticates the politics of identity. The patterns we identified much more frequently involved opportunistic bridging and coalitional dynamics than zero-sum competition for patronage and exclusivist patterns of distribution.

As we show through this chapter, these homogenizing and generally pacifying effects reflect the structural logic within which patronage-wielding politicians operate, and the electoral incentives they face. Identity groups are attractive for patronage politicians precisely because – as we saw in Chapter 5 – such politicians are always on the lookout for social networks through which to distribute their patronage. Shared identity expressed through what we have called "networks of affect" imparts a sense of group cohesion that can make targeting easier, and might make recipients feel more obliged to repay that patronage with political support – especially if the identity group in question has recognized and authoritative leaders to whom the politician can outsource distribution, monitoring, and enforcement. This underlying similarity in function accounts for the modularity of the forms of patronage politics we see across identity groups: patronage flows through whatever veins and arteries constitute social life in each respective country.

Meanwhile, the mix of bonding (in-group) versus bridging (out-group) appeals we encountered can largely be explained by electoral institutions and the incentives they provide: when parties and politicians can realistically expect to achieve electoral victory by targeting patronage at one particular group they will do so. In such circumstances, zero-sum mobilization and inter-group conflict can occur. But such opportunities are relatively rare. Politicians generally face varying degrees of competition for the votes of the group in question, and that group may in any case be insufficiently large to assure victory on its own. In such circumstances, parties and politicians typically target their core group while also mobilizing cross-cutting appeals, often using patronage to reinforce relatively weak identity links with other groups or to substitute for them if absent. This pattern is especially common in Indonesia, accounting, for example, for the Christian politician we encountered in Central Kalimantan who provided money to mosques attended by members of his clan, the female candidate in Central Java whose campaign relied mostly on women's sewing and other cooperatives but who also provided funds to male-dominated farmers' groups in her home village, or the Hindu female candidate in Medan, North Sumatra, who reached out to her mostly Muslim female constituents by hosting fashion and beauty sessions and providing them with headscarves and other fashion items. The very complexity of the identity map of Southeast Asia lends itself to such bridging and hedging strategies.

We develop these arguments through the remainder of this chapter, turning first to the widely applicable identity categories of ethnicity and religion. Doing so allows us to explain the basic patterns of interaction between patronage and identity politics encountered in Southeast Asia, and to emphasize how these patterns vary across our three core countries. Historical patterns, once again, help us to understand cross-national differences in the politicization of identity. Second, we turn to gender, specifically, the mobilization of women *qua* women. While structural reasons might lead us to expect that female-focused patronage politics in Southeast Asia will be relatively rare, it is in fact quite common – at least when the right social networks and organizations are available. Next, we examine the one identity, social class, that is generally more resistant to co-optation through its inclusion in networks of patronage. Clientelist politics is fundamentally about connecting high-status patrons with low-status clients through vertically aligned social and political connections, and is therefore at odds with the horizontal forms of solidarity essential to class identities and mobilization. However, we do note hybrid forms of mobilization, especially in Indonesia and the Philippines, in which lower-class political actors attempt to wring concessions from patronage politicians in exchange for their votes. We conclude by noting both the fundamentally conservative character of patronage politics and its tendency to reinforce patterns of social hierarchy.

BONDING AND BRIDGING: ETHNIC AND RELIGIOUS IDENTITY NETWORKS

A longstanding theme in the comparative literature (e.g., Lemarchand 1972) is that clientelism goes hand-in-hand with, and tends to reinforce, exclusive forms of ethnic and religious identity politics. There are numerous strands to this literature, but the underlying insight is that by segmenting a population into discrete groups, ethnic and religious divisions help politicians to target some groups as recipients of patronage while excluding others (see, for example, Alesina et al. 1999; Fearon 1999). Building on this insight, some scholars emphasize the signaling function of identity for patronage politics. In one influential analysis, Kanchan Chandra (2004) argues that patronage politics elevates the role of ethnicity in political life because a party's or a candidate's ethnic affiliation can be a convenient signal to voters about where that party or candidate will direct patronage if elected. If voters are habituated to politicians using their positions to benefit in-group members, voters will have patronage-based reasons, not merely affective ones, for supporting ethnic parties or co-ethnic candidates (see also Hale 2007). Both Chandra (2004) and Posner (2005) further argue that in a democratic polity, the ethnic identity categories that become salient are those that allow adherents to form a "minimal winning coalition" – in other words, those that are sufficiently large to secure electoral victory but not so oversized that scarce patronage resources will be wasted on surplus members (see also: Ichino and Nathan 2013; Huber 2017; Auerbach and Thachil 2023). Another plausible connection between ethnicity and patronage politics lies through a pathway of social trust: a significant body of work in political psychology and economics demonstrates that people are less likely to trust other citizens in conditions of multiethnicity, a factor that encourages them to favor the immediate pay-offs of clientelist exchange via an ethnic patron rather than trusting politicians to deliver on programmatic policies (e.g., Alesina and La Ferrara 2002; Habyarimana et al. 2007).

However, as we have already alluded to, politicians who wield patronage can use it not only to promote in-group "bonding." Should circumstances encourage, they can also use it to work across ethnic (or other) group lines, using patronage to perform a "bridging" function. This distinction borrows from the language of scholars of civil society and social capital (particularly Putnam 1993; Varshney 2002). We can think of forms of patronage politics as serving a bonding function when patronage is funneled in an *exclusive* manner toward members of an in-group, reinforcing in-group solidarity, while (implicitly if not always explicitly) excluding those outside the group. It is this mode on which the literature tends to focus. In contrast, the bridging function occurs when politicians distribute patronage across ethnic lines. We might expect vote-maximizing politicians to focus on in-group identity when that is sufficient to provide a winning coalition in which they can be confident, but to downplay it and make bridging appeals when they need to shore up their base (e.g., on Indonesia, Aspinall 2011, 299). Of course, bonding and bridging strategies need not rely exclusively on the provision or promise of patronage; in a patronage-oriented polity, however, for a candidate to present herself as a communal champion she needs to convey an expectation of more than normative allegiance.

The basic demographic composition of our three countries (Table 7.1) tells us little about the highly varied ways in which patronage politics interacts with ethnicity and religion across them. The politics of ethnicity and religion largely structure the party system in Malaysia; religion is important at all levels of electoral competition in Indonesia, while ethnicity features most in local elections; both are rather marginal to electoral politics in the Philippines, outside of Mindanao and certain upland regions. The explanation for this variation lies in the historical origins of these countries' party systems and associated systems for patronage distribution, and the early critical junctures we discussed in Chapters 2 and 3.

In Malaysia, as we saw in Chapter 2, the politics of ethnicity and religion[3] have been hardwired into the country's party system since independence, despite the equally long-standing presence of multiethnic coalitions and

---

[3] These categories overlap: all Malays are Muslim by law, and most Malaysian Muslims are Malay.

TABLE 7.1. *Pluralism in Indonesia, Malaysia, and the Philippines*

	Ethnic fractionalization*	Population share of largest ethnic group**	Population share of largest religious group	Cultural fractionalization*
Indonesia	0.766	40.1% (Javanese)	87.2% (Islam)	0.522
Malaysia	0.596	62% (*Bumiputera*)***	61.3% (Islam)	0.564
Philippines	0.161	24.1% (Tagalog)	80.6% (Catholic)	0.116

* Fractionalization data from Fearon (2003), 216–17. Counting ethnic groups per a list of "prototypical" attributes, he defines *ethnic fractionalization* as "the probability that two individuals selected at random from a country will be from different ethnic groups" (201–2, 208). *Cultural fractionalization* assesses "the cultural distance between ethnic groups," assessing "cultural resemblance" in terms of language (212).
** CIA World Factbook, www.cia.gov/the-world-factbook/countries/ (accessed 23 January 2021).
*** Official statistics subsume ethnic Malays, with just over 50 percent of the population, under the umbrella category, *Bumiputera*, together with smaller other "indigenous" communities (see Nagaraj et al. 2015, 152–53).

repeated attempts to transcend communal politics altogether. In particular, identity-reinforcing exclusive rather than inclusive appeals were inherent to the strategy of communal parties first within Malaysia's Alliance, then within the Barisan Nasional (BN) during the long years of that coalition's political dominance; they remain the BN and its allies' chief lever against Pakatan Harapan and other opponents. We would expect, therefore, for patronage to be used in ways that further identity-bonding rather than bridging strategies. Indeed, as we describe in Chapters 3 and 6, BN component parties especially claim credit for programs that benefit "their" community.

The core party within the BN, the United Malays National Organisation (UMNO), has long made its history of providing special benefits to Malays and other Bumiputera – agricultural assistance, scholarships and other educational assistance, small-business grants, and so on – central to its electoral appeal. Many of these programs are, in fact, programmatic, with publicly stated, adhered-to criteria (which might include ethnicity); BN politicians have "hijacked" them, to encourage voters to believe they entail meaningful discretion (see Chapter 6). UMNO justifies its approach by way of an elaborate ideological defense of "Malay supremacy" (*ketuanan Melayu*), the claim that Malays deserve special status within Malaysia as the majority "indigenous" group. Likewise, efforts by the Malaysian Chinese Association and its candidates, for instance, to tout the extent to which they have brought selective benefits to Malaysia's Chinese community – federal support for Chinese-vernacular schools, funding for ethnic-Chinese entrepreneurs and businesses, even closer alliances with mainland-Chinese business and political elites – aim at bonding, not bridging (even when these appeals, too, rely substantially on spinning programmatic policies as particularistic). These parties and politicians build support within the ethnic community, although they have historically been careful to avoid antagonizing support outside it. So how might we interpret an UMNO politician in a particular electoral district granting benefits to a Chinese organization? Strictly speaking, as discussed further in the following sections, this is an example of bridging. But the Malaysian Chinese Association (MCA) is likely still to tot up those concessions as part of what its participation in the BN has yielded, and thus to maximize bonding.

A continuing emphasis on communal voting underpinned even the historic, if short-lived, 2018 change of government. The BN's main competition, Pakatan Harapan (PH), had previously adopted a less ethnicized approach, but in 2018 it tipped the balance in its favor with a more concerted bonding effort. PH made assurances of sustained support for the Malay community both explicit and more credible by dint of *who* made these assurances: known ethnic champions, including former prime minister Mahathir Mohamad, in the new component party Parti Pribumi Bersatu Malaysia. Part of what brought the BN down was UMNO's increasingly exclusive emphasis on bonding appeals (and its neglect of bridging strategies) in a competitive, multiparty, multiethnic environment. Although it was aware that BN had lost most of its non-Malay support, "UMNO shifted its survival strategy from recovering lost ground to consolidating the overrepresented rural Malays and lower income electorates who were more susceptible to distributive inducement" (Washida 2019, 198).

However, the context of Malaysia's complex multiethnic population, its single-member district electoral system, and its coalitional politics undercuts parties' ability to rely exclusively on bonding strategies. As noted earlier, Malaysia has a high level of ethnic fractionalization, and even if many seats have (or were carved out to have) a clear demographic majority, such seats – especially in urban areas – typically also include significant minorities. In this context, as Donald Horowitz has argued, the Alliance/BN formula has always relied upon cross-ethnic vote-pooling (Horowitz 2014, 9). This means that parties and their candidates often mix ethnicity-blind programmatic messages with communal strategies and that candidates will often make meso-particularistic offers to ethnic communities other than their own. In most electoral districts, while a candidate from a BN component party would typically cultivate especially close ties with their community of origin (Malays for an UMNO candidate, Chinese for an MCA member, and so on), that candidate would be able to rely on coalition partners to rally support among the other communities, and would devote some of their own time and resources to helping them in turn.

Consider, for example, the Chinese candidate in Sibu we described in Chapter 6, who fielded a Malay community's request for funds to improve a *surau*. By the same token, incumbent prime minister Najib Razak visited a private Chinese-community-established university college in Johor during the 2013 election campaign, with local UMNO Youth branches there to cheer him along. At the college, he detailed his ongoing negotiations with Malaysia's linchpin Chinese-education organization, his grant of a tax exemption for donations toward a new building for the campus, and his efforts to preserve

Chinese-medium schools. The UMNO incumbent for the seat (also the state's incumbent chief minister) then touted his own record as an "old friend" of the Chinese community and defender of Chinese community and cultural interests (Ho 2014, 171). These efforts represent bridging – and their framing as *personal* intervention and fruitful allyship means they extend beyond what the MCA can claim credit for, per its own bonding strategy. In fact, to maximize the BN's presumed advantage, given its vote-pooling capacity, BN-era exercises in drawing the boundaries of constituencies ensured an increasingly significant share of seats *were* mixed. (BN's advantage was whittled away when previously polarized opposition parties managed to coalesce in their own coalition in order to mimic its vote-pooling capacity.)

That Malaysian politics, whether under the BN, PH, or now Perikatan Nasional (of which BN is part), leans more heavily toward programmatic distribution than we find in Indonesia or the Philippines *does* complicate the picture, however much parties hijack these programs to claim partisan credit. On the ground, this complex map often produces a precarious balancing in the types of appeals candidates make. Politicians from parties such as UMNO as well as Parti Islam seMalaysia (PAS) often try to convince voters that they will remember their ethnic roots when distributing concrete rewards, while simultaneously emphasizing race-blind development policies; others reassure voters from beyond their own ethnic core that they, too, are in line for patronage. Consider the campaign of Ahmad Zamri bin Asa'ad Khuzaimi, a candidate for an urban seat in Kuala Lumpur in 2013. On one poster, he appeared in a *songkok* (a distinctive cap worn by Malay men), with the logo of his Malay-centric party (PAS) and a slogan about preserving the local community's stake in the exclusively Malay settlement of Kampung Baru (*"Selamatkan Kg. Baru"*) – not itself necessarily an issue of patronage, but clearly signaling his role as a communal protector. On an adjacent banner, he had traded his songkok for a baseball cap, featured the logo of his non-communal coalition (Pakatan Rakyat) alongside PAS's, and included a programmatic promise to reduce the cost of cars for everyone. His UMNO opponent, Johari Abdul Ghani, similarly appealed across audiences (likewise also via costume), both promising to uphold Malay rights to community lands, and, for instance, speaking at state-subsidized-housing blocks dominated by lower-income Chinese and Indian voters, to make sure they saw him as also promoting means-tested (programmatic) policies. He also provided services at his own expense for those needy minority communities (Choong 2014, 130–32). Mixing these bonding and bridging appeals was particularly useful in this urban seat, which includes a swathe of valuable Malay reserve land then under threat, but where Malay votes alone were unlikely sufficient to win.

Indonesia's parties are generally less communally based than those in Malaysia; to the extent that there is currently an ideological spectrum ordering Indonesia's party system, it centers on an Islamic–pluralist divide (Mietzner 2013; Fossati et al. 2020). In each post-Suharto legislative election, about

30 percent of the electorate has supported Islamic parties – parties that either explicitly aim to strengthen the political and social role of Islam or that are associated with major Islamic social organizations. Of the latter parties, Partai Kebangkitan Bangsa (PKB, National Awakening Party) is informally linked to Nahdlatul Ulama (NU), the major "traditionalist" organization, while Partai Amanat Nasional (PAN) is linked to Muhammadiyah, the organization of generally urban "modernist" Muslims. At the other end of the ideological spectrum, Partai Demokrasi Indonesia–Perjuangan (PDI–P) consistently promotes pluralist positions and has historically enjoyed strong support from members of religious minorities and nominal or syncretist Muslims – notably the so-called *abangan* of Java. The personality-oriented "presidentialist" parties that have emerged over the past two decades hew mostly to pluralism but have a catchall orientation and accommodate persons with a wide array of views on the proper role of Islam in the polity.

In contrast to religion, which is important to the party system, ethnicity is all but irrelevant to party positioning. Party registration rules require parties to show that they have a broad national presence before they can participate in elections. This rule has effectively prevented regionally concentrated ethnic parties from emerging; the only exception is the province of Aceh, where special-autonomy arrangements allow such parties. Whether candidates run as individuals for regional executive positions, or as party candidates in legislative elections, they often mobilize ethnic ties – but as a matter of personal positioning rather than party alignment.

This structuring of the party system, and the ubiquity of patronage, produce a fusion of patronage and identity politics. Candidates for Islamic parties, for example, tend to concentrate their patronage efforts all but exclusively on various segments of the Islamic community. An obvious example is PKB, which, as noted earlier, is largely based on the traditionalist NU community, which in turn rests on a vast, sprawling network of Islamic boarding schools (*pesantren*) led by religious scholars (*kyai* or *ulama*). At the national level, PKB-affiliated ministers and other senior officials try to use their positions to benefit this network, for example by funneling projects to regions where NU is strong and promoting government programs that deliver educational assistance, development projects, and the like to pesantren. PKB legislators at all levels take the same approach, directing constituency development funds or intervening in budgetary projects to direct assistance to pesantren and NU-affiliated organizations. Indeed, many PKB politicians think of helping *nahdliyin* (NU followers) as being among their primary tasks.[4]

However, in the context of Indonesia's increasingly candidate-centered electoral system, the interplay of identity with patronage politics varies greatly

---

[4] See Mahsun et al. (2021) for one recent analysis of how female candidates affiliated with NU mix identity-based and patronage appeals in their election campaigns.

according to the nature of the election, electoral district, and demographic composition of the district in play. The open-list proportional-representation system makes it possible for some legislative candidates to win by targeting a very narrow slice of the electorate. This factor tends to facilitate bonding strategies, with ethnic and religious targeting. Accordingly, during the course of our research in the 2014 and 2019 elections, we encountered numerous candidates who identified their *basis* (base) as supporters of Muhammadiyah or NU, or as deriving from a specific ethnic community in a given area. But most candidates supplement this approach. Especially in urban settings and provinces with complex ethnic and religious maps, it is common to meet candidates in legislative elections who, when designing their strategy, will first try to lock in the support of one or two key identity-based groups to which they are connected: their own kinship group, their spouse's relatives, the members of a particular church or Islamic organization, and so on. Importantly, such candidates often target their patronage at these core groups, attempting to secure the votes of their *basis* by providing the bulk of their vote-buying payments, club goods, or other largesse to that group rather than to others. This pattern is especially common in parts of eastern Indonesia, where clans are an important element of social structure and where candidates typically begin by trying to lock in their extended kinship group's backing. As explained by one candidate in Kuala Kapuas, Central Kalimantan, every candidate in this region starts by securing the support of their clan. They do so because, in a setting where individualized vote-buying is high, it is reassuring to recall that "family beats money." Even so, he hastened to add, it is still necessary to make cash payments to clan members: "If you don't, they might defect [to another candidate]."[5]

But such narrowly focused identity strategies have their limits in Indonesian elections. The open-list PR system for legislative elections means that there are so many candidates that it is almost certain that multiple candidates will target any particular identity group providing enough votes to secure a seat. Consider, for example, the NU heartland in East and Central Java: in these regions, numerous candidates from PKB and other parties target NU voters, each trying to cultivate ties with particular *kyai* and with leaders and followers of the various NU-affiliated youth, women's, and other organizations. While most candidates attempting this approach will themselves have NU backgrounds, it is also possible for non-NU candidates to reach out, offering patronage, by way of other ties. The result is a splintering rather than solidification of the NU base at election times, as well as a blurring rather than a crystallization of communal divisions (Rubaidi 2016).

In sum, the main effect of Indonesia's open-list PR system is to fragment identity-based electoral strategies: even more than in Malaysia, candidates try to make the most of whatever intimate social ties they have with this or that

---

[5] Interview with incumbent member of district parliament, April 7, 2014.

ethnic leader or association, preacher, or devotional group, but they also engage in substantial cross-identity hedging, supplementing an identity-based core with any friendship, associational, or other ties they have. Patronage thus trends to trump identity in Indonesia's legislative elections.

Indonesia's regional executive elections, or *pilkada*, are different insofar as these are less complex elections, pitting a small number of candidate pairs (for regional head and deputy). In areas in which two or three ethnic or religious groups are finely balanced, such as West Kalimantan or Southeast Sulawesi, this structure can lead to more or less zero-sum competition among candidates representing competing ethnic groups or coalitions and generate significant inter-communal tension (see, for example, Prasad 2015).[6] Rival communities in these areas believe they have much to lose in terms of patronage jobs, control over local institutions, and government projects. Even in *pilkada*, however, such cases are exceptions that prove the rule, with the dominant patterns being cross-ethnic and cross-religious coalition-building rather than exclusive ethnic and religious targeting. Facilitating coalition-building is the fact that candidates run as pairs – giving rise to a dominant pattern in which a candidate for regional head representing the largest religious or ethnic group in the region pairs up with a candidate for deputy drawn from the second- or third-largest group. The complex patterns of cross-ethnic pairings so produced in a single race often effectively cancel each other out, neutralizing the effect of identity politics and elevating the importance of other attributes: the candidates' patronage resources, their bureaucratic and other networks, their records of development achievements, and so on (Aspinall 2011, 296–99).

In striking contrast to the centrality of religious and ethnic identities in Malaysia and their importance in Indonesia, ethnic and religious affiliations in the Philippines play a comparatively minor role in political organization and elections. The two most politically salient political divides in the Philippines are between the dominant lowland Christian (over 80 percent Catholic) majority and the Muslim minority, largely based in Mindanao; and between lowland and upland populations, as found especially in Mindanao[7] and in the Cordillera region of northern Luzon. The cleavages have nurtured movements for autonomy in both Muslim Mindanao and the Cordillera, and have secured special recognition in the 1987 constitution.

Within the dominant lowland Christian population, we find a relatively low degree of politicization of what are in fact very substantial ethnolinguistic and regional divides. Several factors help to explain these patterns. Most important is the common experience of Christianization under 350 years of a Spanish

---

[6] Much of the ethnic violence that accompanied and followed the downfall of the Suharto regime also had a strong patronage-competition component (van Klinken 2007).

[7] It is this distinction that motivated the ethnic appeals of the Mindanaoan candidate with whose story we began this chapter, as he sought to capitalize on his indigenous heritage to become the first Lumad mayor of his town.

colonial regime in which ecclesiastical forces exercised substantial power at the national and especially local level. This imparted a shared religious identity that remains important today. In addition, as Anderson (1988, 11) suggests, the creation of a national oligarchy under American colonial rule brought high levels of interaction (including intermarriage) among lowland Christian elites from diverse regional and ethnic backgrounds, making localized ethnic identities less politically salient. Rotation of power at the top of the political system (except during the Marcos years), has also given local actors a stake in the national system and the patronage it offers. Indeed, once patronage politics became entrenched – which happened earlier in the Philippines than in our other cases – it undermined incentives to mobilize along other lines. This provided a basic political cement binding the Philippines together on a territorial basis (see Hutchcroft 2014b).

That said, there are indeed circumstances in which ethnic, religious, and/or regional identity becomes more electorally salient in the Philippines. This is evidenced, in its most basic form, by the common practice of ensuring that a slate of candidates for the Senate – elected, it will be recalled, from a single national constituency through a multimember plurality system – includes representatives from all three major island groups (Luzon, Visayas, and Mindanao) and, if possible, vote-rich subregions as well (e.g., the Bicol peninsula of Luzon or the Central Visayas). In a patronage-saturated polity like the Philippines, the implicit message is that the ticket will distribute pork across all three regions.

Even so, we rarely observe the sort of ethnic balancing in mayor–deputy tickets that we find in Indonesia – if one candidate in the pair is lowland Christian, the other almost always will be, as well. Being "local" helps a candidate, as in all our cases, but needs to be understood far more in terms of regional than ethnic identity (bearing in mind that, with certain important exceptions, such as urban centers and around former US military bases, congressional districts are commonly comprised of one dominant ethnic group). Voters assume that a candidate elected to the House will bring pork to the district, usually without favoring particular ethnic groups within it, and also – although less strongly – that a candidate elected to the Senate, based in part on regional appeal, will pay some degree of special attention to the needs of that region (Ravanilla 2019, 171). And while we do see candidates target the potent Iglesia ni Cristo vote-bloc, that segment of voters is never solely sufficient, nor are most candidates who make such appeals themselves from that religious sect.

So what can we conclude about the bridging and bonding effects of patronage politics across our cases in Southeast Asia? On the one hand, the availability of networks of affect based on ethnicity and religion, particularly when echoed or magnified by regime features such as candidate-centered electoral rules or communal political parties, encourages political candidates to tailor meso- and micro-particularistic appeals to defined communities. Contrary to common expectations regarding ethnicity-based mobilization, however, those appeals may not be (only) to one's own community. At the very least, such

patterns encourage politician-patrons to structure appeals differently for different communities: in Indonesia, we encountered some candidates who provided
very different patronage goods to villages depending on whether they were
majority-Muslim or majority-Christian. But the need to court votes wherever
they may be found encourages candidates to cast a wider, not narrower, net,
even when candidates *also* reassure their own community of its special access
to benefits.

This opportunistic patchwork of appeals, alongside pillarized patterns,
makes clear the extent to which ethnicity and religion may determine what
specifically a politician offers. In general, the primary consideration is likely to
be what gift or promise would most appeal to a specific community – not which
groups should be given patronage. The latter still figures into the equation,
however, and is determined more by how exclusive or instrumental a candidate's relationship with a given group is, and the electoral map in which they
operate: can they rely primarily or solely on that group, will that group offer
undivided or only partial loyalty, and so on. In other words, the fact that appeals
to identity work *within a patronage framework* – and are subsumed by rather
than substitute for that framework – means the expected payoff in votes tips the
needle toward a combination of both bonding and bridging appeals.

A POLITICS OF MATRONAGE?

Surprisingly little scholarly attention has been given to the interplay of gender
and patronage politics, especially with regard to the phenomenon we might dub
"matronage" – the funneling of patronage through female-centered clientelist
networks. Given the importance of informal norms and social networks in
clientelist politics, it seems obvious that gender relationships, and the gendered
distribution of political and economic power, would play a critical role in
structuring how this form of politics operates. The few scholars who have
examined the topic suggest as much. In one important study, based on a close
analysis of Thailand, Elin Bjarnegård (2013) argues that clientelism reinforces
gender disparities in politics, buttressing male dominance in parliaments,
parties, and other political institutions. The reason, she argues, is that the
subterranean, and often illegal, character of clientelist exchange places a premium on trust and informal relationships among powerful actors, who most
often are men. Consequently, clientelism has "many characteristics of a homosocial network" in which relations among powerful men are preeminent
(Bjarnegård 2013, 151).

By contrast, "if a majority of women are found in low-key positions, with
little access to information exchange and important resources, they will also not
be considered crucial in informal political networks" (Bjarnegård 2013, 26).
Mariela Szwarcberg Daby's research in Argentina offers further evidence that
women might have lesser stature in clientelist networks, including
"working longer hours on an everyday basis for fewer benefits than male

brokers" (2016, 13). As she explains, "The near-exclusive dedication and involvement of female brokers in political networks that target children – by definition a nonvoting constituency – precludes them from building, enlarging, and sustaining their political networks" (Daby 2020, 216–17).

Like Thailand and Argentina, the three polities on which we focus are all male-dominated. Parliamentary representation offers one sign of this gender disparity, particularly for Malaysia and Indonesia. As of 2019, 15.0 percent of members of the lower house of the national legislature in Malaysia were women, versus 21.9 percent in Indonesia, and 27.7 percent in the Philippines. (The world average in 2022 was 26.2 percent; the Asian average, 21.1 percent.)[8] Indonesia had a relatively large number of female candidates, at least in legislative elections, because the country enforces a 30 percent quota for women in parties' candidate lists: in the 2019 legislative election, just over 40 percent of national legislative candidates were women (Prihatini 2019; see also Aspinall et al. 2021). By contrast, in the Philippines, women comprised 19.4 percent of candidates in the 2016 national and local elections (Reyes 2019, 89); in Malaysia across both state and federal levels in 2013, only 8 percent were women (Sharifah Syahirah 2013, 5), and still only 10.8 percent in 2018 (tan et al. 2018, 282).

The brokerage structures we encountered during our fieldwork were likewise often highly gendered. In two of our countries, we have clear data suggesting candidates are more likely to rely on men than women to reach and mobilize voters. In the surveys of brokers we presented in Chapters 3 and 4, fully 87 percent of respondents in Indonesia and 80 percent in the Philippines were male. Muhtadi (2019, 172) likewise conducted a broker survey in four Indonesian provinces and found that 91 percent were men. Such findings suggest that in Indonesia and the Philippines – as in Thailand and Argentina – when candidates seek socially influential persons to contact voters on their behalf, they generally turn first to men. As we explain later, candidates often draw upon deeply entrenched views about the gendered nature of power at the community and household levels when explaining such choices. For example, Cruz and Tolentino (2019) used a survey of villagers in the Philippines to find women are less likely to be considered politically influential at the community level.

Unfortunately, we lack similar data on broker numbers for Malaysia, though our fieldwork observations suggest that women are prominent in party campaigning at the grassroots. That finding is unsurprising in light of the role of Malaysian parties as the source of brokers. Most Malaysian parties have separate, and often highly active, women's wings, carving out a niche for

---

[8] IPU Parline Global Data on National Parliaments," https://data.ipu.org/women-ranking?month=3&year=2022, and https://data.ipu.org/women-averages?month=3&year=2022, updated March 1, 2022 (accessed March 24, 2022).

women in mobilizing voters (even if this does not translate to many women standing as candidates) – a point to which we return later.

One potential line of inquiry concerns patterns of targeting of women versus men in vote-buying operations. These patterns might reflect either (or both) the gendered nature of clientelist networks or gendered assumptions about who exercises the greatest sway over voting decisions within the household (in fact, we encountered varied views from candidates and campaigners on such issues). In our surveys (see Appendix A), patterns are inconsistent, though they lean toward demonstrating somewhat higher targeting of men than women. In Malaysia, for instance – while vote-buying levels are very low overall, and social-desirability bias may yield gendered effects in who admits to having been targeted or swayed – men were about 50 percent more likely to report having been offered inducements than women in the 2008 general election (4.1 percent versus 2.8 percent of those sampled); in 2013, by contrast, these proportions were about equal (6.8 versus 6.7 percent). For the 2016 Sarawak state election (the only separately held state election in this period), the share of men acknowledging having been offered inducements was double that of women (4.6 versus 2.3 percent). In all three elections, over 80 percent of men and women said these offers did *not* influence their vote but that share was higher for men with regard to general elections in 2008 and 2013, and higher for women in the 2016 Sarawak state election. In Indonesia, we see similar shades of gendering, in the context of much greater receipt of – and openness to – gifts. In our survey immediately after the 2014 legislative election, men were only marginally more likely to report having been offered inducements than women (31.1 versus 27 percent). Of those receiving inducements, women were somewhat more likely than men to say that such inducements influenced their vote (45.3 percent versus 38.7 percent). Pulse Asia (2019b) finds that men were also slightly more likely than women to be offered a handout in the Philippines (23 versus 20 percent in 2016, and 26 versus 20 percent in 2019) and to accept that offer. However, inclination toward reciprocity – i.e. whether that payment actually influenced their vote – shows no clear pattern by gender.

A more fruitful area on which to focus, then, is on women as participants in the system, as brokers and as candidates. Starting with the latter: many female candidates we encountered had broken through barriers to participate in politics and shown considerable levels of ability in order to capture the attention of party leaders and raise the funds necessary to compete. Others had these positions by virtue of marriage to, or family connections with, powerful male politicians.[9] The increasing prevalence of dynastic and family-based politics in all three of our core countries (and its particular prominence and entrenchment

---

[9] For studies of female politicians that detail these and other barriers to female political participation in Indonesia, Malaysia, and the Philippines see, for instance, Derichs and Thompson (2013) (especially the chapters on these countries by Gerlach, Derichs, and Thompson, respectively); tan et al. (2018); Yeong (2018); Hillman (2017); Reyes (2019).

in the Philippines) is especially consequential for patterns of women's political participation. Dynastic politics, in which a single family entrenches itself in power in a particular locale over generations (e.g., Trajano et al. 2013; Mendoza et al. 2016), fosters a familial model of political campaigning. As part of this model women and men are essentially interchangeable as candidates, each representing the dynasty in turn – not least as successive scions are term-limited out of office. In the Philippines, for example, the local machine will typically mobilize in the same manner regardless of whether the family at its heart nominates a male or female candidate. In Indonesia, while dynastic politics is most visible in local executive elections, implementation of a mandatory quota for female candidates in legislative races means that parties sometimes nominate women "as stand-ins for their husbands" (Nugroho 2016, 157). The husband then acts as his wife's campaign coordinator and organizer or – especially if he is an incumbent regional politician himself – simply mobilizes his own political network to campaign for his wife (see also Kabullah and Fajri 2021; Wardani and Subekti 2021). Frequently, little is distinctive about such family-driven campaigns.

Yet candidates across these countries have strong incentives to engage women actively in campaigns as brokers and to target them as voters. Most obviously, in each country women form a large group – indeed, a slight majority – of potential voters, and may also vote at slightly higher rates. Thus, women would seem to constitute the ideal "minimal winning coalition." However, in patronage-based electoral systems, at least those that allocate seats on the basis of simple pluralities, women (or men, for that matter) would not appear to constitute an identity group ideally suited to electoral mobilization. Recall the assumption that identity comes to the fore in patronage politics inasmuch as it helps voters and politicians to determine who will – and therefore who will not – attain material rewards. Gender provides little assistance on this score because "the importance of families would encourage both men and women to share if their party wins" (Huber 2017, 40). Following this logic, gender-based allocation of patronage would end up potentially rewarding (almost) everyone in the society, defeating the purpose of using it as a framework for distribution.

But if we think of identity not as a set of rigid categories used for the distribution of excludable rewards but as a collection of formal and informal networks that help those categories cohere and that express and organize identity groups in social and political life – networks of affect – then it quickly becomes obvious that gender categories can be as convenient a vehicle as any other for distribution and, therefore, mobilization.

In fact, and despite the general picture of gender inequality in politics, each country also presents numerous associational avenues and informal connections through which candidates and parties can mobilize female voters, from women's religious-study groups in Indonesia, to women's self-help groups in the Philippines, to the women's wings of Malaysian parties. Accordingly, in the course of our fieldwork, we found ample evidence – despite a general pattern of male political dominance – of gendered campaign appeals and mobilizational efforts that targeted women, particularly, though not only, by female candidates. However, these efforts were generally inclusive rather than exclusive (again, more bridging than bonding). They were also less common, from what we observed, than integrated campaign efforts targeting women and men together.

Among our cases, Indonesia and Malaysia feature the most prominent gender-differentiated parallel structures but only in the former can that appeal be virtually exclusive. In Malaysia, women's wings of parties play a leading role in mobilizing women, especially outside urban areas. But their pitch centers more around two-way communications and the party-line than micro- or meso-level patronage, and no candidate can afford *only* to focus on women; outreach is simply often gender-segregated. In Indonesia, in contrast, candidates may opt to focus near-exclusively on women, with a campaign tailored to that purpose. It is not unusual to encounter candidates in Indonesian legislative elections who say they devote 70 or 80 percent of their campaign effort and resources to attracting female voters; one survey of 127 female candidates in the 2019 election found that 40 percent said that over 60 percent of their targeted voters were women (Aspinall et al. 2021). In large part, this strategy reflects the use of open-list PR: a candidate can win a seat by accumulating a relatively small proportion of the personal votes on offer.

Particularly important to this strategy in Indonesia is the prominence of women's associations. In line with the larger pattern of outreach we describe in Chapter 3, Indonesian candidates are likely to build links to female voters through established organizations. Especially important are neighborhood associations, notably the Pemberdayaan Kesejahteraan Keluarga (PKK, Family Welfare Movement); devotional groups that hold prayer meetings in homes or other venues; and large-scale women's organizations affiliated with major religious bodies, especially the NU-affiliated Fatayat and Muslimat organizations (Mahsun et al. 2021). Some candidates also target women's micro-enterprises, communal savings bodies, and other organizations. To reach women through such channels, candidates often recruit their leaders as brokers and tailor their campaign messages to them. They also frequently use gender-specific gifting when providing either individual or collective benefits: household items or articles of women's clothing – such as *jilbab* (headscarves) or *mukena* (prayer robes) – to individuals, cooking equipment for PKK groups or women's micro-enterprises, and so on.

Throughout our fieldwork, including in Indonesia, no candidates we encountered sought to mobilize *only* women (though some in Indonesia came close); they merely capitalized on what advantages they had, to work along separate (and often unequal) tracks. Two patterns were most prominent: either female candidates courted women especially assiduously – at least some female candidates in all our countries expected to be most popular among women – or they bifurcated their campaign structures to capitalize on gender-segregated opportunities for outreach (recall our Mindanao businesswoman politician at the beginning of this chapter). In 2014, we encountered a memorable example of the former pattern, directly motivated by Indonesia's quota for female candidates, in Palembang, South Sumatra. Partai Demokrat had recruited the founder of a local charity for orphans into its party list for the municipal council. Her low-budget (albeit still small-gift-oriented) campaign relied on family and friends as volunteers and supporters – in particular, what she dubbed her *tim nenek* (team of grandmothers). Her core messages centered around women and orphans; her in-person outreach was almost exclusively to women, for instance offering women snacks and colorful headscarves, together with guidance on how to fix the latter nicely.[10] The strategy this candidate had developed reflected the fact that women, like men, draw on their own networks in Indonesia, both to staff teams and to provide outreach opportunities (e.g., Nugroho 2016; Darwin 2017).

Grassroots party organization in Malaysia, in contrast, which typically features distinct women's and men's spaces, encourages gender-differentiated appeals even if strategists presume a family vote to be the norm (however declining in practice). Most Malaysian political parties have a women's wing (see Chapter 3), a practice with roots in the late colonial period, when women's organizations were among the groups that coalesced to form political parties; some also have separate young-women's wings. For instance, UMNO's women's wing, initially called Kaum Ibu (Women's Section) and now Wanita UMNO (UMNO Women), dates back to the party's founding (like UMNO itself, initially an amalgamation of local associations; Manderson 1977, 212–17); youth counterpart Puteri emerged in 2001. Having been actively involved in political parties since before independence,[11] Malaysian women still form a source of diligent door-to-door campaign machinery especially for rural-Malay-based UMNO and PAS, appealing to housewives while their husbands are off at work. This has been the case since the onset of elections, given parties' zeal to get out, and win, (Malay) women's votes (Manderson 1977, 220–23). As multiple candidates, both men and women, explained to us, local leaders of these women's wings have deep, up-to-date knowledge not just of who's who in the community but also of any local goings-on. Especially among the Muslim majority, moreover, women are not considered threatening

---

[10] Interview, March 21, 2014, Palembang.

[11] Women played active, visible roles in Malaysia's largely peaceful independence movement and in early politics – but as Manderson notes, turnover in Kaum Ibu's ranks, the limited available time and education most members had, and norms of subservience constrained the wing's ambitions. Women *did* assume both appointed and elected positions from early days of self-government, though almost immediately, Kaum Ibu found its members sidelined as UMNO selected nominees; its "ancillary status" became entrenched (Manderson 1977, 214–15, 218–19, 225–28; see also Khatijah 1995).

(in the way men are) when they enter a home to chat with the housewife; even if the housewife inclines toward another party, she will still usually listen politely.[12] Given available party channels, candidates funnel less outreach through nonparty women's organizations than in Indonesia; as in Indonesia, however, organizations such as PAS's Muslimat rely also on outreach through Muslim prayer and discussion groups.

All told, although women are less likely to stand for office in Malaysia than in Indonesia, they are heavily active in partisan politics. Many of those who do contest rise up through women's-wing ranks. However, since the party can pick only one candidate to stand in a given locality, that dual track may not advantage women: their party may opt to nominate a local male party leader instead of the local Wanita head. Despite being UMNO's largest wing, Wanita has supplied only 8 percent of the UMNO members in political office.[13] When they do contest, women may claim particular maternal legitimacy or stress their expertise in and attention to issues specific to women and children, posing challenges for women who also must appear professional and technocratic (Kloos 2020). Unlike Indonesian candidates, they cannot themselves train their gaze so exclusively on women; most of their vote is normally a party, not personal, vote, and the winning candidate requires a plurality of all votes in the constituency.

In the Philippines, we see less targeting of women *qua* women; female voters are simply integrated into, and their needs addressed through, the overarching local machine. That said, gendered appeals and women's networks *are* salient. Recall, for instance, the candidate for councilor we described at the start of this chapter, who styled her campaign message around defending families, especially against drugs – a problem, she argued, that the police could not crack but "we mothers" could.[14] However, given the relative interchangeability of men and women within family political dynasties, and often the mix of representatives of a dominant family on a given slate – perhaps one running for Congress, one for governor, and one for mayor, then switching places once term-limited out – clearly gender-differentiated electoral appeals could be counterproductive. And as we described in Chapter 3, candidates in the Philippines tend to rely less heavily on social networks than do their counterparts in Indonesia: the availability of comparatively stable, long-term local teams and collaborative campaigning reduce the need for candidates to mobilize personally salient identity-based or other networks on their behalf.

The key exception to this pattern in the Philippines is with party-list elections – contests among dozens of smaller parties for the 20 percent of reserved seats in the House of Representatives, reflecting the particularly strong

---

[12] Interviews with UMNO state legislator, January 3, 2015, Seberang Jaya; PAS parliamentary candidate, April 27, 2013, Pasir Mas; UMNO MP, April 24, 2013, Kemaman.

[13] Interview, UMNO state legislator, January 3, 2015, Seberang Jaya.

[14] Interview, May 2, 2016, Mindanao.

splintering effect of this element of the electoral system (see Chapter 2). Here, we do find a limited number of gender-based parties and specifically gendered appeals (along with parties for, and corresponding appeals to, teachers, LGBT voters, senior citizens, the fisheries sector, cooperatives, and other categories). Candidates may shift from party-list seats to contesting for constituency seats; in doing so, they might bring that identity-based or sectoral orientation with them. For instance, a councilor candidate in Davao City had previously represented the Gabriela Women's Party, which contests party-list elections as part of the broader left-wing Makabayan bloc of party-list organizations. Campaigning in 2016, she still listed her affiliation as Gabriela (even though the party was formed to contest seats in the national House of Representatives) but was now aligned with Duterte. Her campaign messages stressed issues such as domestic violence, but also broader matters, still reflecting Gabriela's overall left-wing bent, and the crowd she addressed the evening we met with her was not exclusively female (though it was mostly so).[15] But such a trajectory is clearly not the norm, nor does it tell us much about the gendered nature of patronage, given that Gabriela (as an exception to the Philippine rule) is not a patronage-oriented party.

Across our cases, where we did see efforts to build campaign teams focused on women, these were often accompanied by strongly gendered discourses that compared women's and men's attributes as brokers or voters. Especially in Indonesia, we encountered numerous candidates who argued that women tended to be more trustworthy and reliable as success-team members than men, less money-oriented, and less likely to cheat their candidates. Candidates repeatedly stated that women were more "loyal" and "faithful." By the same token, candidates often believed that, once female voters had received a gift, they were less likely than men to renege on a commitment to support a candidate. As one candidate in Aceh province in Indonesia put it: "The view here is that women are more loyal. If you give her a head scarf, she will not change her vote away from you."[16] A candidate standing for the NasDem Party in Indonesia's legislative elections in East Java in 2014 expressed a similar view. When asked how she built her campaign strategy, she explained that she was mobilizing via NU-affiliated women's organizations, then continued:

It's the women who are most effective. Men will talk money straight away. They ask for it outright. At one village I visited, they said outright: "If you don't bring money, then there's no votes." Also there are people in these areas – for example village heads or former village heads – who contact me directly and offer to get so and so many votes in their village, in exchange for money. They offer themselves to seek votes for me with money. But with women, the most they ask for is that if you get elected you will provide them material for their group – uniforms, a sound system, mats, plates, glasses, musical

---

[15] Field notes, May 1, 2016, Davao City. Though she was not elected, President Duterte later appointed her to a national government post.
[16] Interview, March 7, 2014, Bireuen.

instruments – things their organization needs. I will always say that I will help them with these sorts of things. That's important. These are real organizational needs. It's different to the men who will ask you straight out for money. And what do they want money for? To buy cigarettes![17]

That it was mainly in Indonesia that we saw such concerted attention to gender-specific micro- and meso-particularism perhaps partly reflects this faith in a higher rate-of-return when targeting women. It also, however, flows from the logic of segmented appeals in the context of open-list PR contests and the availability of many women in organized social networks, including state-sponsored mass organizations such as PKK, as well as the mass-based religious organizations.

Behind differing approaches to women as voters also lie differing assumptions of women's relative political autonomy at the household level. In both Indonesia and the Philippines, we encountered candidates and campaign workers who assumed a patriarchal organization of the family, and of society more generally, and therefore concentrated their persuasion and gifting on male voters. It is this logic that partly explains the male-dominated character of most brokerage structures, explained earlier. As one broker in the Central Visayas put it: "Here we usually try to convince the husband, then the wife follows."[18] A district legislative candidate for one of Indonesia's Islamic parties in Central Kalimantan explained that his success team was 100 percent male, although 60 percent of his target voters were women: in his region, women "always follow their husbands."[19] Such candidates and campaign workers in both Indonesia and the Philippines explained strategies premised upon a patriarchal household logic, in which the man of the house was either recruited as a broker or received a payment and then directed family members' votes – either for a single candidate or divvied up among those from whom he had accepted payments.

By no means all candidates subscribed to this perspective, however; many insisted that women were autonomous in their vote choices and that care need be taken in approaching them separately from their male relatives. In fact, in Malaysia, we were more likely to hear the reverse: that canvassers, frequently themselves women, target housewives and hope they will persuade their husbands and children.[20] We also found echoes of such assumptions in Indonesia: some candidates (mostly women, but also several men) felt women made better brokers because of the greater intensity of their interactions with

[17] Interview, March 6, 2014, Surabaya.   [18] Interview, May 4, 2016, Bohol.
[19] Interview, April 7, 2014, Kuala Kapuas.
[20] That Malay housewives are more likely to watch (at least until 2018, heavily pro-BN) state-run television, however, has historically made it harder for PAS and its women's wing, Muslimat, to make inroads with women. Prior to 2018, PAS could capture at least 40 percent of the Muslim male vote but only a maximum of about 30 percent of Muslim women (interview, former PAS MP, 4 August 2015, Shah Alam).

neighbors – and thus their knowledge of those voters' voting intentions and their ability to persuade them. Some Indonesian candidates even stated that it was preferable to use women as brokers because they could more accurately ascertain the voting intentions of their male household members and therefore avoid wasting cash payments. If a man directed his wife or daughter to vote for a candidate, the woman might give the impression of acceding but then vote her conscience, whereas a man would likely have no compunction in telling his wife he wanted to vote for someone else. Another broker in a focus group discussion in Central Java explained that men and women simply had different strengths as brokers, flowing from their different patterns of sociality: "Men like to drink coffee, they like to smoke, so they hang out a lot in various places: that's their advantage. But women's advantage is that they like to gossip."[21] A male candidate in the same province explained that his strategy was to rely more on women because "it's easier for women to go into [their neighbors'] houses, while borrowing a kitchen implement, or while gossiping."[22]

Overall, however, the fact that large majorities of brokers we encountered were men (recall the survey findings discussed earlier) should remind us of the gender inequality that continues to structure political life in each of these countries. When recruiting brokers, candidates look above all for individuals they believe can exercise social influence and authority in their communities; it is telling that the default position is so commonly to recruit men. Many of them did so without even thinking of themselves as running male-centered campaigns; their choices simply reflected unexpressed assumptions about the gendered nature of power and the reality of the many male-centered homosocial networks that constitute local sources of social and political authority. Again, we find that patronage politics tends to reflect and reinforce existing power inequalities, rather than undermining them.

In short, as with ethnicity and religion, gender matters for patronage distribution, but it mostly does so by providing gender-differentiated spaces and networks that help to scaffold mobilization efforts and define the sorts of gifts distributed. It is harder to discuss bridging and bonding effects in terms of gender, however, than for ethnicity and religion (not least since candidates often target women with the hopes they will also persuade the men in their lives, while others assume that the men will simply direct their wives). It is certainly easy to encounter female candidates – especially in Indonesia – who combine their targeting of women voters with a women's-empowerment and gender-equality agenda. But the fact that women are targeted separately from men more often reflects the availability and utility of gender-specific networks than an effort to deepen identity as women. Nor does it imply a zero-sum benefit only to women and not to men.

[21] FGD notes, August 21, 2014, Rembang.   [22] Interview, April 4, 2014, Rembang.

CLASS DISMISSED

Class divisions are central to the phenomena discussed in this book insofar as clientelist politics generally involves persons of higher social status and material wealth who, as political candidates, distribute benefits to poorer and lower-status individuals as voters, brokers, and supporters. Certainly, the comparative literature offers this understanding in suggesting that, in general, "scholars of clientelism treat and analyze the practice as an exchange between politicians and their poor clients" (Weitz-Shapiro 2014, 12). We delve more deeply into the extent to which these patterns hold across our cases in Chapter 8; for now, our key takeaway is that targeting the poor serves mostly to atomize voters. Patronage-wielding politicians neither address poor voters as a class, to be mobilized as such, nor seek to bond recipients around class-defined identity.

Throughout our field work, especially in Indonesia and the Philippines, we frequently met candidates who explained their targeting logic by highlighting the utility of cash payments and other gifts for poorer voters and noting that wealthier voters tended to be impervious to such inducements. But campaign workers' reluctance to target middle-class voters in Indonesia and the Philippines went beyond issues of the marginal value of payments. Several proposed that wealthier voters are more likely to condemn vote buying on moral grounds (issues to which we also return in Chapter 8; see also Nathan 2019). Others explained that it is more difficult to reach middle-class voters by way of campaign infrastructure, not only because such voters often live in gated communities, apartment buildings, or other types of dwellings that are difficult for brokers to access, but also because they tend to interact less with their neighbors and other citizens through social networks. Poor people are more accessible, either through religious and other organizations in which they participate or simply because they live cheek-by-jowl with brokers recruited from among their neighbors.

Given this background, it is not surprising that class-based targeting was all but ubiquitous across our cases, even if brokers did not exclusively target the poor. However, the critical distinction between this form of targeting and ethnic or even gendered appeals is that, in general, when candidates target lower-class voters, they do so in purely instrumental ways, without mobilizing or invoking a class identity. We might see these approaches as structuring genres of patronage more than structuring networks that function beyond elections. Put differently, we understand these strategies as working solely and instrumentally through (or implicitly forging, in the process of outreach) networks of benefit, not networks of affect. Indeed, by connecting brokers in poor communities – for example, the head of a fishing or farmers' cooperative, or a neighborhood broker in an urban slum – through chains of vertical dyads all the way up to the politician running for office (and beyond), clientelist brokerage structures undercut the potential for class-based mobilization. This form of politics orients clients upwards in the social structure precisely because it is based on "individual ties to a leader rather than on shared characteristics or horizontal ties among followers" (Scott 1972, 97). As a result, patronage politics has long been understood as inhibiting the development of class-based mobilization.

Many candidates we observed distributed patronage pitched to low-income or working-class population segments; material benefits derived from public sources ranged from subsidized fertilizer and fishing nets to low-cost homes and basic medical services, supplemented with privately provided club goods and individual gifts. However, when patronage politicians work with social organizations involving lower-class groups, they often choose brokers and groups that *already* exercise a controlling influence within the class hierarchy (such as co-opting as a broker a foreman at an oil-palm plantation) or that play a welfare or distributional rather than representational function – a workers' credit group, for example, rather than a labor union.

In Indonesia, one of the most common patterns is of candidates distributing livestock, seedlings, fertilizer, or equipment to farmers' cooperatives; boats and fishing equipment to fishers' cooperatives; and credit or equipment to micro-enterprises such as food-processing groups set up by groups of poor women. Cooperatives and micro-enterprises proliferate across Indonesia; often their primary function is to access grants and assistance provided through various government programs or by politicians at election times. Fishing communities offered an unsurprising target in the Philippines, too, wooed not just with boats but also with benefits such as piers for cleaning and storing fish and gear.[23] In Malaysia, Malay *padi* (rice) farmers have been a perennial core component of UMNO support. For instance, in largely rural Perlis, UMNO sustained its youth vote in 2013 in significant part by appealing with development projects, providing agricultural inputs through local networks to sons of padi farmers likely to retain family farms (Chiok 2014, 30). In short, the aim is opportunistic: to energize instrumental ties that reassure the group concerned that the candidate is aware of them and will not neglect them after the election, and provide them with club goods or individuals gifts in the meantime, while taking advantage of their organizational infrastructure as segments of a functional mobilization network.

However, it is important to note that, in the context of pervasive patronage politics, we also encountered what have been called (with reference to India) "post-clientelist initiatives" (Manor 2013), which fuse personalized and programmatic politics – in the process, leaving more space to articulate class-defined interests. These initiatives combine clientelist modes of networking and patronage deals with ground-up efforts at class-based politics and programmatic mobilization. (While the term is useful, in this context, our next chapter also offers a critique of its implied teleology.) The critical point here is

---

[23] Interview with campaign strategist, May 5, 2016, Siquijor.

that when organizations representing working-class interests – most notably, trade unions – have some degree of organizational heft independent of electoral politics, their leaders have the potential either to enter the electoral arena themselves or to bargain with elite politicians over the terms of their engagement. In the Philippines, for example, some leaders of moderate trade unions have been known to carve out promising political careers – and accumulate modest personal fortunes in the process.

Indonesia demonstrates this so-called post-clientelist landscape most clearly, hinting at increasing space for a politics not just premised on class divisions but potentially inclusive of class-based mobilization. There, labor unions have been experimenting with direct engagement in electoral politics through the post-Suharto period (Caraway et al. 2015; Caraway and Ford 2020). One of our research partners, Amalinda Savirani (2016), observed such an effort in Bekasi, outside Jakarta. There, labor unions organized a *"buruh go politics"* ("workers go [into] politics") campaign for the 2014 legislative elections. Building on experimental efforts in 2004 and 2009, the local metal-workers' union sought to have their own representatives stand for election, under different party banners. Their goal was to eschew "money politics" by neither paying parties to nominate their candidates nor seeking to buy votes. Instead, the union aimed to mobilize workers to vote *qua* workers for those candidates. Yet even these campaigns still needed to reach out to nonworkers; in doing so, they stressed programmatic policy goals but encountered many requests for cash gifts and club goods. As a result, these candidates fared well only among the heart of their industrial base (Savirani 2016); these industrial areas, moreover, constitute a tiny minority of districts across Indonesia.

In Indonesia, so-called political contracts (*kontrak politik*), which we touched upon in Chapter 5, involve a candidate striking a deal with a local community group to deliver all manner of benefits, from sports facilities to rubbish collection, should they be elected. These agreements often represent an intermediate form between the particularistic politics of patronage and the broad brush of programmatic politics. Through such arrangements, organizations, including ones with a socioeconomic-class basis, can both seek meso-particularistic club goods *and* push for programmatic goals. For instance, Savirani and Aspinall (2017) examine an urban-poor network that bargained with candidates in the 2017 Jakarta gubernatorial elections to secure political contracts that combined very specific promises about ending land expropriation and granting legal tenure with a range of much wider changes in the urban-planning framework.

Such political contracts are a prominent part of Indonesia's electoral landscape. Labor and peasant organizations, alongside all manner of community groups, villages, and neighborhoods, use them to wring concessions out of political candidates during elections, and to try to hold them to their commitments afterward. These contracts usually take the form of brief, pseudo-legal documents, signed by a politician and community representatives. They typically combine particularistic demands (such as the favorable resolution of a land conflict with a plantation company or recognition of squatters' rights to land they occupy in a specific neighborhood) and more programmatic ones (an increase in the minimum wage, or higher allocations for agricultural infrastructure). Such deal-making is by no means incompatible with patronage politics; indeed, groups may strike such deals with politicians who also engage in vote buying (Mahsun 2017), and the contract is often sweetened by both micro- and meso-particularistic deals. These initiatives suggest a twist on the phenomenon of poor voters' proactively requesting payments for their votes, as encountered in the Philippines vignette with which we opened this book (such requests occur elsewhere, as well: e.g., Lindberg 2010, 124–27; Nichter and Peress 2017).

In the Philippines, too, we find scattered indications of such "post-clientelist politics," in ways that tilt politics toward a more programmatic orientation – for instance, in Naga City. We return to these cases in Chapter 8. To some extent, the Philippines' party-list system has played a limited role in giving voice to trade-union and other lower-class interests. The system was intended to represent marginalized groups, but, in practice, has been plagued by an "incoherent accreditation process" that has sometimes favored "non-marginalized sectors" at the expense of "genuinely marginalized sectors" (Teehankee 2019). (At the local level, moreover, elite politicians have sometimes been able to translate control over their bailiwick into the election of a party-list representative.) Despite the obstacles, however, trade unionists affiliated with the left have organized several party-list parties (for instance, the Workers' Party and Anak Pawis, or toiling masses), and have also supported nonlabor-specific party-list parties such as the Gabriela Women's Party and the democratic-socialist Akbayan Citizens' Action Party (Amante 2019, 79). Members of the House of Representatives elected under the party-list system qualified for constituency development funds prior to the abolition of this type of pork barrel in 2013 (see Holmes 2019), but these modest dollops of patronage were not sufficient to pull them away from their role as small islands of relatively programmatic orientation within a sea of patronage-oriented politics.

A pattern of only scattered organized appeals directed at labor is also characteristic of Malaysia. The one exception is the small Parti Sosialis Malaysia (PSM), which *does* seek to fortify and mobilize around class identity but has never held more than one seat in Parliament; moreover, PSM's distinctly noncapitalist stance has prevented it from allying fully with a multiparty coalition, at the cost of mainstream political influence.[24] Rather, when Malaysian parties target workers or the poor, it is overwhelmingly via patronage appeals, to cement loyalty to and identification with the party and/or politician as benefactor – not to promote an empowering class identity.

---

[24] Interview, PSM activist, June 10, 2014, Kuala Lumpur.

Of course, there is a broader institutional and historical context for this overall weakness of class-based appeals. While trade unions have a more enduring history as politically engaged actors in the Philippines than in Malaysia or Indonesia, union density is in fact low by international standards in each country: in 2020, 8.8 percent in Malaysia, 8.7 percent in the Philippines, and 7.0 percent in Indonesia.[25] This weakness is in part a legacy of Cold War efforts to quash the organized political left (reinforced by subsequent pressure from American and other multinational corporations in search of low-cost, compliant workers). Such efforts were largely successful in Malaysia and Indonesia (in the latter case, bloodily so), somewhat less so in the Philippines.

The marginalization of the leftist tradition of horizontally organized class-based mobilization has generated a social landscape in which patronage politics readily takes root. It makes the mass of the poor relatively amenable – as individuals or as members of small communities – to particularistic appeals coming from above. By the same token, once patronage politics established itself as the dominant pattern, it became even more difficult for challengers to build horizontally organized programmatic alternatives from below. To succeed, such challenges would not only have to overcome daunting organizational obstacles, but they would also have to convince potential supporters that they have a realistic chance to win governmental power and redesign state policy. Patronage politicians do not face such heavy challenges: they can make use of whatever social networks are already available in their locale, and they do not need to win enough political power to remake policy. It is sufficient for them simply to gain a foothold in the state and access whatever slices of state resources they need to keep their immediate supporters happy.

CONCLUSION

Our review of the interaction of social identity and patronage shows that patronage politics in Southeast Asia tends, on the whole, to be socially conservative rather than transformational. In each of the polities we examine, it reproduces rather than challenges existing social structures, identities, and hierarchies. The reason is simple: in order to maximize their political influence, patronage politicians try to co-opt socially influential brokers and networks; it is generally more efficient to cooperate with influence-wielders within *already-formed* social structures and networks than to create clientelist networks from scratch, and more convenient to work along with rather than against the grain of dominant ideas about group ties, social power, and hierarchy. Patronage politics is, therefore, generally a politics for the strong, not the weak. Its practitioners rarely act as social innovators, even if they do on occasion take

---

[25] International Labour Organization, "Statistics on union membership," https://ilostat.ilo.org/topics/union-membership/, accessed July 30, 2020.

on prevailing authority structures – for example, by challenging an incumbent "warlord" or dynastic patron. It matters little to patronage politicians whether the brokers they work with are religious leaders, heads of women's cooperatives, or ethnic chiefs – what matters is the social influence that such figures *already* exercise.

At the same time, our discussion also shows that the complexity of Southeast Asian societies generates near-endless variation in patronage strategies. Politicians reach out to a bewildering variety of identity-based groups, and the extent to which appeals to those groups define a candidate's own political orientation also varies considerably. Candidates may try to mobilize cobbled-together sets of small or subdivided networks and groups, as when a politician in Sabah makes discrete appeals to varied ethnic and subethnic communities, or they may make a more coherent and narrowly targeted appeal, as when a politician in Java targets the bulk of her effort at women's affiliates of Nahdlatul Ulama. In the latter case, patronage may serve a bonding function, encouraging further cohesion and amplifying the group's claim to attention; in the former case, it may serve more to bridge community boundaries.

Overall, however, throughout our fieldwork, we were struck by the frequently opportunistic and even promiscuous nature of identity-based appeals. Even when identity-based mobilization and distribution come to the fore, they are rarely accompanied by a language of exclusivism. Across all three polities, candidates and parties respond to electoral incentives by hedging their identity strategies, making cross-cutting appeals, and forging inter-group alliances. Over the long term, the tendency of parties and candidates to appeal simultaneously to in-groups while also reaching out proactively across identity lines both reinforces existing identity categories and produces bridging effects. When candidates approach the gamut of identity-based groups as simply functional equivalents, over time, they undermine the value of, and hence suppress, assertive forms of identity-based mobilization. In other words, even as it valorizes and reinforces existing social identities and hierarchies, patronage politics also domesticates them.

8

Subnational Variation

Violence, Hierarchy, and Islands of Exception

In early 2013, as Malaysia's thirteenth general elections approached, our team visited Sabah and Sarawak in East Malaysia. We had just spent two weeks touring the states of the Malay peninsula and had become used to all the visible signs of party-based campaigning there: streets and highways festooned with national-party flags and symbols, and posters and banners touting national coalitions' programs and leaders. There was no mistaking the national-party affiliations of the individual politicians who also smiled out from posters – logos, color schemes, and outfits rendered most candidates the local face of the party. Suddenly in Sabah, we were transported into what seemed to be a different political world. The streets were now lined with posters and banners featuring images of individual candidates and bedecked with symbols of unfamiliar local parties. Our interviews, too, now contained many more stories about influential local leaders and their followings, rather than about national parties and their policies, as was common in West Malaysia. For those of us accustomed to the longstanding prevalence of candidate-based appeals in the Philippines, and the more recent prominence of such appeals in Indonesia, the environment suddenly seemed quite familiar. *Local* building blocks of politics were strikingly visible as the basis of electoral mobilization.

The incongruence went further, too. In peninsular Malaysia, we heard few stories of politicians providing cash payments to individual voters or late-breaking donations of infrastructure or other collective goods to communities – far more often parties merely proclaimed the specific public benefits (universities, hospitals, subsidized housing, and the like) that they would – if elected – channel back to the community. Now, in Sabah and Sarawak, our interviews were full of discussions of particularistic gifting and explanations of how it was organized.

Our contrasting experiences in these different parts of Malaysia bring home a core point: the level of intra-country variation in the patterns of patronage politics in Southeast Asia is nearly on par with the inter-country variation we have so far emphasized. The chapters above have focused on between-case variation: notably, the presence of relatively strong party machines in Malaysia, ad hoc teams in Indonesia, and local machines in the Philippines, as well as greater reliance on candidate-centered electoral clientelism, including micro-particularism, in Indonesia and the Philippines, versus more party-based patronage in Malaysia. But the within-case variation is almost as striking, as is its capacity to give rise to sometimes unexpected *similarities* across countries (such as the resemblance among East Malaysian, Philippine, and Indonesian patterns noted earlier).

Each of the countries we study demonstrates remarkable subnational variation in both the intensity of patronage politics and the forms it takes. In Indonesia, for example, micro-particularistic patronage in the form of distribution of cash to individual voters is so widespread in parts of rural Java as to be a normalized part of political life. But in Jakarta and several other big cities, it is much more rare. In the Philippines, we see notable "islands of exception" (Hicken, Hutchcroft, Weiss, and Aspinall 2019, 34–36) amid the general pattern of local patronage-oriented machine politics: at one extreme, Naga City has longstanding patterns of relatively programmatic politics; at the other extreme, patronage politics in Lanao del Sur province exhibits deeply entrenched, coercive bossism. In Malaysia, the expectations of urban voters in industrialized Selangor and Penang states differ dramatically from those of largely rural voters in, for instance, Pahang or Perlis: the former obdurately elected a strongly programmatic opposition coalition lacking access to federal funds in 2008 and 2013, whereas rural voters in the latter states were willing to tolerate increasingly daunting financial scandals to preserve their access to Barisan Nasional (BN) development funds and other collective and individual benefits.

What accounts for such differences? The paradigm for understanding such variation in most of the literature on clientelism derives from permutations on modernization theory, with a core thesis that clientelism is a product of economic underdevelopment (e.g., Scott 1972, 105–09). As discussed in Chapter 7, scholars have through the years provided voluminous evidence suggesting that poor voters tend to be much more susceptible to cash and other gifts than wealthier voters, having shorter time horizons and less confidence in (despite more personal need of) improved programmatic delivery as compared to those higher up the socioeconomic ladder (for instance, Dixit and Londregan 1996; Auyero 2000; Calvo and Murillo 2004; Weitz-Shapiro 2012; Jensen and Justesen 2014). Scholars presume an inverse relationship between levels of education and clientelism for similar reasons (Shin 2015), and between urbanization and clientelism, because living in cities erodes the rural social patterns of intimacy and reciprocity that facilitate clientelistic exchange (e.g., Anek 1996; Faisal 2015; but see Nathan 2019). What these explanations have in common is that they all broadly associate clientelism with underdevelopment and assume that economic modernization will eventually undermine it.

Our study of Southeast Asia provides modest but inconsistent support for this broad modernization paradigm, at least at a descriptive level. There is mixed evidence across and within our cases regarding whether politicians' patronage practices tend disproportionately to target poorer voters. And even where the poor tend to be targets, this pattern is far from absolute; nor is it the only explanation for the subnational variation we detect. We modify the modernization approach by bringing three additional factors into account.

First, it is not simply the *level* of economic development that is important but the degree of *concentration of control* over economic resources involved (here we build on Aspinall and Berenschot 2019, 203–48). When economic development occurs in a manner that produces local monopolies – for example, around mining, plantations, or some other resource-focused industry – it naturally tends to empower politically the economic elites who control the industry without concomitantly strengthening the mass of voters. A frequent result is forms of local bossism and elite political capture. This compounding of political power and material inequality makes reinforcement of patronage politics more likely, given the interest of those empowered in maintaining their political influence (and the access to mining licenses, contracts, or other resources that holding elective office facilitates) and the much greater marginal value a payment will have to those on the other end of the inequality spectrum. In sum, the material resources available to politicians, and the patterns of control that determine the use of those resources, constitute one key factor determining the nature of, and subnational variation in, patronage politics.

The development and relative stature of the local state is a second key factor. In regions where state institutions are relatively well-developed – especially where the state's central organization is effective and sufficiently autonomous that it can resist encroachment by local bosses and strongmen, and where its monopoly over coercion is relatively secure – politicians will have limited ability or impetus to reach beyond programmatic and patronage strategies toward coercion. Where the state is weak and local bossism is prevalent, programmatic politics is unlikely to be effective, because bureaucrats will lack capacity to deliver services effectively and be unable to resist politicians' meddling in their allocation. The dominance of patronage politics thus tends to be associated with state weakness. However, when the state is especially weak, patronage practices can shade into duress, such that powerful local bosses supplement, or even replace, handouts and club-goods strategies with intimidation, thuggery, and other forms of pressure on voters and their leaders. In sum, not just material resources but also *coercive resources* are critical.

A third and final mediating factor, building on observations in Chapter 5, is the relative *autonomy and hierarchy of local social networks and their leaders*: local clan chiefs, customary leaders, and the like. In places where these local leaders are sufficiently powerful to direct the political preferences of their subordinates without having to offer an immediate benefit in exchange, they are frequently incorporated into local political networks in ways that do not require them to share benefits directly with their clients. The community leaders' social influence can *substitute* for voter-targeted clientelistic exchange rather than being a conduit for it. The critical issue is the relative density of civil society and the extent to which local community members choose among networks or are tied to a single option, relying upon a single-stranded patron-client relationship (Hicken and Ravanilla 2021). Where their relationship with these leaders is more obligatory than voluntary, clients have little leverage to ensure patrons distribute the benefits of clientelistic exchange widely.

In sum, these three factors – economic concentration, state weakness, and powerful social leaders – give rise to different forms of *power concentration* that can affect local patterns of patronage politics. Their effects play out in different ways within our primary cases, reflecting differing background conditions. In Malaysia, the country with our highest level of state capacity and economic development, the relative economic underdevelopment, resource-based economies, state weakness, and strong social networks in peripheral areas, especially in East Malaysia, give rise to localized patterns of patronage politics that in some respects resemble the norm in Indonesia and the Philippines. Thus, in Sarawak and Sabah, we see comparatively high levels of micro-particularism, incorporation of social networks into local clientelistic arrangements, and fluid competition among local political bosses, though leavened by the constraints electoral authoritarianism places on contestation.

Regions marked by relative economic underdevelopment, natural-resource endowments, and/or state weakness in the Philippines and Indonesia, by contrast, give rise to patterns that deviate from these countries' norms not only, or even primarily, by being more intensely clientelistic, but also by incorporating a greater degree of coercion. The pattern is most stark in the Philippines: dominant political clans in Mindanao still rely heavily on the first two components of the Philippines' famous political triptych – guns, goons, and gold – even as politics in much of the rest of the country has come to lean ever more heavily on the third pillar. But in Indonesia, too, local politics draws in local toughs (termed *preman*) and other violent actors in varied modes across the archipelago; preman are especially influential where natural-resource industries predominate.

On the flip side of this equation are those regions where we see efforts to reduce the dominance of patronage politics. Such experiments are most advanced in regions with relatively developed and diversified local economies, robust state capacity, and both dense and relatively egalitarian local civil societies. In particular, across Malaysia, Indonesia, and the Philippines, large- and medium-sized economically diverse cities tend to be the engines of new forms of programmatic politics. This trend is most evident in Malaysia's urban centers – long the heartland of opposition to the old ruling coalition – where civil-society organizations have been most dense (Yeoh 2015). In Indonesia, too, performance-oriented and reforming local-government leaders have attracted considerable attention from citizens, media, and analysts alike over the last two decades of decentralization; most such leaders have been mayors of cities and towns, rather than *bupati* of rural districts (e.g., von Luebke 2009; Patunru et al. 2012; Tans 2012; Hatherell 2019). Of course, there is no simple one-to-one inverse relationship between urbanization and clientelism (Nathan 2019): the Philippines has urban machines throughout, including very prominently in Metro Manila. But in the Philippines, too, it is mostly in urban areas that we see experimentation with programmatic politics and hybridized forms of what Manor (2013) describes as "post-clientelist" politics.

We explore these subnational patterns through the remainder of this chapter. The first section briefly reviews evidence as to whether patronage tends to track patterns of economic resources. We find that in qualitative interviews, campaigns express a clear preference for targeting the poor, but evidence for a straightforward income effect is mixed in survey data. The second section examines the politics of patronage in peripheral regions. Finally, we look to islands of exception, or where there are efforts to make patronage a less central element of political contention.

POVERTY AND PATRONAGE

After Indonesia's 2014 general election, we encountered a candidate who had run for a seat in the Central Java provincial parliament. He explained that he had hit on an effective campaign method: sending letters to middle-class residents of his town condemning "money politics" and explaining its deleterious effects. More prosperous and better-educated people there, he said, were fed up with corrupt politicians who distributed cash at election times but then engaged in corruption after they were elected. These letters accorded with his vision to clean up politics in his region, and with the moral code he had learned through his association with Indonesia's large modernist Islamic organization, Muhammadiyah, of which he was a local leader. However, it turned out that he also sent about 10,000 envelopes containing small gifts of cash to residents of poor fishing villages along the coast near the same town. He explained that he did so because he felt sorry for his team members in these villages, some of whom were under such strong social pressure to distribute payments that they were prepared to spend their own money. As he summed up: "So though I distributed a letter calling on voters to reject money politics, in the end I was tempted to use money too!"[1]

This candidate's dilemma conforms with the findings of a large body of literature explaining that clientelist politics flourishes where voters are poor. Accumulated evidence suggests that clientelistic exchange is more common in poorer countries (though not exclusive to them) and that parties and candidates who use micro-particularistic strategies tend to target poorer and less-educated

---

[1] Interview, May 28, 2019, Rembang.

voters – as they find middle-class, higher-income, and better-educated voters less susceptible to such appeals (for one fascinating interpretation from Indonesia, see Pradhanawati et al. 2019). Scholars have presented a range of explanations. One of the most influential centers on the diminishing marginal utility of income: "poor people's utility of income is increased more than rich people's by a gift of any given monetary value; therefore, parties focus their largess on the poor" (Stokes et al. 2013, 161). Likewise, scholars have suggested that poor voters are more likely to value immediate benefits, however ephemeral, over the potentially greater but less certain long-term gains associated with programmatic politics (Kitschelt 2000; Kitschelt and Wilkinson 2013; Stokes et al. 2013). As Scott (1969, 1150) put it, "Poverty shortens a man's time horizon and maximizes the effectiveness of short-run material inducements" (see also Brusco et al. 2004; Calvo and Murillo 2004; Hilgers 2008, 137). Finally, others emphasize that poverty, and specifically vulnerability, drives the demand for patronage, as poor voters naturally seek material benefits as a way to mitigate the effects of economic shocks (Nichter 2018, Nathan 2019).

Overall, as we alluded to in the last chapter, our own qualitative findings cleave reasonably closely to these established patterns. In each country where we conducted research, we encountered numerous candidates and brokers who gave us their own versions of the marginal-utility or vulnerability explanations. Regarding the former, our informants would typically begin by comparing average vote-buying payments to the daily pay-rates of manual laborers or other low-income workers in the locale and end up explaining that while such a payment would be meaningful for a poor voter – particularly in the Philippines, where payments could amount to even a couple weeks' work (in Indonesia they rarely amounted to much more than a day's wage) – it would have little practical use for a wealthier person. A Gerindra candidate in Surabaya, for example, opined, "So many voters are poor, so they are transactional in their approach to the elections. For middle class people, 20,000 or 50,000 rupiah doesn't mean anything. But if you are a *becak* [trishaw] driver, that's a lot of money."[2] We also observed, and often heard candidates bemoan, the fact that poorer voters regularly turn to politicians for assistance, for everything from help with an unexpected medical bill, to food in the face of a job loss, or materials to repair a leaky roof. As the son of one candidate from Compostela Valley in the Philippines groused, "Once voters know you are running they take advantage. They come looking for medical assistance and financial help. You have to help everyone, even if it is just a little."[3]

Likewise, we encountered a number of politicians who, like the candidate from Central Java mentioned earlier, had class-differentiated campaign strategies, targeting poor voters in their constituencies with cash payments or other forms of patronage, while devising advertising, social media, or similar

---

[2] Interview, March 6, 2014.   [3] Interview, May 2, 2016.

image-building strategies to woo middle-class citizens. One candidate in Banjarmasin, the capital of Indonesia's South Kalimantan province, explained that while he organized community events like neighborhood rubbish cleanups in middle-class housing estates, he would "bomb" poor neighborhoods at the edge of town with cash: "You have to, they ask you for it straight out."[4] Or there was the senior broker in Sorsogon in the Philippines, who clarified:

> Now we don't differentiate between rich and poor voters, you give money to everybody. But there's no assurance if you give money to the educated. They may get the money, but there's no assurance they will vote for your candidate. They are independent minded. But if you give to the lower classes, there's a big chance they will toe the line.[5]

This broker went on to calculate how, in his fishing community, the cash payments a household received at election time could be equivalent to many days' work by the main breadwinner.

It is striking, however, that while many political actors reported a pro-poor bias in terms of who they targeted with handouts, our surveys did not always reveal a strong pattern. The national and local surveys we conducted in the Philippines did show a modest pro-poor bias when it comes to handouts, but class or income level was not a significant predictor of who was likely to be targeted with an offer of money in Indonesia (see also Muhtadi 2019, 97). In both countries, the distribution of cash gifts during elections has become so normalized that some middle-class residents receive such gifts as election day approaches. In peninsular Malaysia, electoral handouts are less common among any communities, but for those who do report receiving such offers, our survey data suggest slightly *higher* targeting of middle-income than poor voters, though minimal prevalence overall makes these data harder to assess.

We also find mixed evidence that class differences generate strong subnational patterns of variation in the intensity of clientelist patronage. Of course, within a particular city or rural area, there will generally be less patronage distribution in wealthy neighborhoods or housing estates than in poorer ones, but we are less certain that such differences aggregate across provinces or other large regions.[6] For the Philippines, survey evidence indicates that voters in rural areas are more likely to be targeted than voters in urban areas (PulseAsia 2019a). By contrast, Berenschot's expert survey in Indonesia, which used local experts' assessments to measure the intensity of clientelism across a range of measures in thirty-eight districts, showed gross regional domestic product and other socioeconomic indicators to be rather poor predictors of the intensity of clientelism (understood as a broad syndrome, involving personalized exchanges not merely between politicians and voters but also with other actors, such as

---

[4] Interview, January 26, 2014. [5] Interview, May 8, 2016.
[6] We must emphasize that we lack robust measures of inter-regional variation in patterns of money politics; the sample sizes in our national surveys are insufficiently large for confident assessments as to how regions differ.

bureaucrats and contractors). Instead, with the exception of individual-level vote buying, which did track closely with regional poverty levels, clientelism correlated more closely with the degree of concentration of control over economic resources (Berenschot 2018; Aspinall and Berenschot 2019, 228–48).

Our extensive qualitative research across our countries and the series of regional case studies our research partners produced also provide something of a mixed picture. In the Philippines, the prevalence of electoral handouts did not map neatly onto (generally poorer) rural areas and (generally more prosperous) towns and cities. Rather, all urban regions – even Manila's central business district of Makati – have large poor populations that machine politicians target (Calimbahin 2019). In Indonesia, poverty and vote buying seem generally associated, such that individualized vote buying is relatively rare in the (overall comparatively prosperous) capital city, Jakarta (Dewi et al. 2016). But this linkage is far from absolute: in some of the poorest parts of the country – most dramatically, in rural parts of Papua, in the far east – it is local community leaders, acting as brokers, who capture the lion's share of the resources politicians distribute. They pass relatively little on to voters (Nolan 2016). In Malaysia, retail clientelism tends to be most intense in the states of Sabah and Sarawak, where incomes and other development indicators are generally lower than in other parts of the country (see, for example, Puyok 2014). As we shall see, however, there are other explanations for this pattern, as well.

Our data allow us to probe some of the complexities in the link between poverty and patronage. As we explore the other dynamics at play, the next section turns to a deeper dive into several sub-national regions in which we find economic underdevelopment paired with higher-than-average levels of patronage.

PATRONAGE POLITICS IN PERIPHERAL AREAS

One of the striking findings of our research is how markedly patterns of patronage politics diverge from national patterns in relatively remote regions far from the national capital of each state. In these regions, the writ of the central state has historically been weak, plantations and natural-resource industries give rise to local economic monopolies amid generally widespread poverty and underdevelopment, and local clan or other community leaders dominate their communities. Such areas include, most obviously, Mindanao in the Philippines, the peripheral territories of Aceh and Papua in Indonesia, and the states of Sabah and Sarawak in East Malaysia; these are areas that Pepinsky (2017) calls "regions of exception," marked also by separatist movements or sentiments. But other remote, interior, and upland regions in each of these countries share such characteristics, to varying degrees.

Neither the histories, political economies, or institutional settings of Southeast Asia's peripheral and remote areas, nor the political patterns we observe there, are uniform. In these areas, local political leaders are able to mobilize differing mixes of coercive, social, and economic power, generating distinct patterns of patronage politics that are both more intense and generally far more firmly hierarchical and exclusionary than those prevalent in other parts of these countries. Mobilization regimes here often aim to shift blocs of votes, not single electors. In contrast to overall national patterns (but often notably comparable across peripheral zones), clientelist networks here leave less space for mediation by a bureaucratic state, since state capacity and reach are weak. They also leave residents little alternative but to affiliate with dominant networks, since resources tend to channel through the economic nodes their leaders represent or occupy. In these regions, too, local leaders are more likely to combine patronage carrots with coercive sticks, given the lesser penetration of the rule of law and the higher stakes that concentration of economic and political power entails.

The Philippines: Mindanao

We start with the southern Philippines, especially those areas of southwest Mindanao and the Sulu archipelago that are majority-Muslim and which, since the 1970s, have been sites of both secessionist Islamic insurgency and special regional government units set up under successive peace agreements – most recently as institutionally embodied in the Bangsamoro Autonomous Region in Muslim Mindanao, BARMM (see ICG 2019). These areas constitute a part of the Philippines where the reach of the central state has long been especially weak, such that "Manila's authority in the Muslim zones was and continues to be mediated through local power" (Abinales 2016, 48). This weakness has historical roots, dating to the late and conflictual manner by which the region was incorporated into the Philippine state, and the many compromises that Spanish and American colonial rulers, and then Filipino politicians, made to win over, and govern through, traditional leaders (*datus*) and other local authorities (Abinales 2000, 11–12, 132–33; McKenna 1998, 46–137). At the periphery of (and largely outside the control of) the Spanish colonial state, Muslim Mindanao was later ruled in very distinctive ways within the early American colonial state (Abinales 2000). After independence, Muslim elites found opportunities to integrate themselves into national political networks while populations within their bailiwicks remained impoverished. Even granting the general weakness of the historical process of state building in the Philippines, as discussed in Chapter 2, local bosses and clans in Mindanao are particularly powerful.

Compared with elsewhere in the Philippines, Muslim Mindanao also suffers chronic underdevelopment. Poverty rates are much higher, and other indicators of material well-being much lower, than in other parts of the country; indeed, some provinces of Muslim Mindanao have human development indices on par with sub-Saharan Africa (Monsod 2016, 209). The economy is comparatively undiversified, and where there are valuable natural resources, the profits are unevenly distributed (Tadem 2012). Internal-revenue transfers from the center to local governments are a particularly important and lucrative source of income for local elites who capture elected office. As one former mayor in Lanao del Sur explained to one of our research partners, "I know of no other business or sources of livelihood other than being mayor of my municipality and I am willing to sacrifice a lot and do anything to keep the position within my family" (Latiph 2019, 325). Other important sources of wealth in the region arise from a "shadow" economy involving such activities as illicit arms-trading, cattle-rustling, secondary land markets (as the influence of local strongmen over land use often trumps formal legal titles), cross-border trade between the Sulu archipelago and nearby Sabah in Malaysia, and sophisticated kidnap-for-ransom operations (Lara 2016).[7] Across all these activities, control of local-government office can provide a decisive advantage.

The material rewards of office being so great, and countervailing forces – political parties, civil-society organizations, private business, the middle class, organized labor, and the like – being so weak, local clan leaders in Mindanao fight tooth and nail to get into office. Once there, they sustain themselves through government revenues and enhanced control of the illicit economy. At the same time, local politicians are able to provide their national counterparts with critical swing blocs of votes during hotly contested national elections. They can mobilize clan loyalties, relying on subsidiary members of their families both to reach voters and to ensure they turn out to vote – sometimes producing entirely implausible margins for allies in national presidential and senatorial races. (In 2004, for example, widespread electoral fraud in Muslim Mindanao helped propel incumbent president Gloria Arroyo to resounding victory; Hutchcroft 2008.) Echoing American-era patterns of mediated state power, the influence local politicians can wield through such mechanisms raises their bargaining power vis-à-vis national officials. Epitomizing the distinction between weak states and strong societies, Muslim Mindanao's traditional elite and local strongmen enjoy social, political, and economic powers unparalleled elsewhere in the Philippines – even relative to other regions of the country with powerful local bosses.

In this context, patterns of patronage politics in Muslim Mindanao are extreme. During every election, media reports routinely describe widespread, blatant, and intensive vote buying, often with much higher payments than elsewhere in the Philippines (for example, Tomacruz 2019). But what really distinguishes politics in Mindanao is its unusually high level of coercion. Local political chiefs in this part of the Philippines often recruit virtual private armies and deploy them against rivals, particularly at election times. As our research

---

[7] The relative discretion that Philippine politicians enjoy in their dealings with the state may extend as well into a capacity to engage with relative impunity in illicit economic activities – particularly in weakly governed parts of Mindanao.

partner Acram Latiph (2019, 318–19) explains, "Candidates typically recruited goons from among the toughest and most notorious members of their own clan. Some of them were offenders or persons known for having brushes with the law, while others were former rebels (for example, from the MNLF [Moro National Liberation Front] or the MILF [Moro Islamic Liberation Front]) and former soldiers. ... A typical mayor in Lanao del Sur tends to have around thirty to fifty men to serve as a private army with high-caliber firearms." Candidates may use these goons not only to pressure voters to support them but also to disable rivals. All in all, this combination – concentrated economic control amid generalized conditions of poverty, state capture by local clans and their reliance on steeply hierarchical social networks, and coercive power – generates a situation of especially poor governance. As one leading scholar of Muslim Mindanao observes, "People hardly expect government to function. ... Instead, legitimacy is all about providing protection to your fellow clan members by trumping the firepower of your competitors, leaving people alone, and forgetting about taxes" (Lara 2009, np).[8]

However extreme electoral and other forms of political violence are in Mindanao, they reflect wider and historical patterns throughout the Philippines, as we sketched in Chapter 2 – rivaled in the region only by (less entrenched and less enduring) trends in Thailand (Anderson 1990; Prajak 2013). Relative to the other countries that we study, coercion in the Philippines is a more visible and quotidian, if arguably declining, ingredient of local politics. Throughout our research across the Philippines, informants recounted tales (very plausible but not verified as to specifics) of involvement of police, gangsters, and insurgents in electoral campaigns; candidates' shenanigans alongside such violent actors to intimidate voters or to frighten off or frustrate rivals; and the tight embrace between local politicians and the drug trade, gambling, and other parts of the black economy. To be sure, we do find electoral coercion and illegality also in Indonesia, but it is more widespread in the Philippines. What we see in Mindanao thus amplifies the more pathological aspects of political loyalty and mobilization elsewhere in the country.

In light of such phenomena, some scholars have argued for placing coercion, not clientelism, at the center of analysis of Philippines politics. In one especially influential analysis, Sidel (1999, 9) proposes that in the post-Marcos Philippines, the "descriptive and explanatory powers of patron-client relations appear extremely limited." He suggests that entrenchment of local oligarchs and "widespread electoral fraud, vote-buying, and violence" mean we achieve

---

[8] Nothing demonstrates election violence in Mindanao more starkly than the 2009 Maguindanao Massacre, in which militia forces of a leading political clan corralled and then killed fifty-eight persons on a lonely road off the main highway; the victims included both the female relatives of an electoral rival and thirty-two journalists who were accompanying them to try to ensure their safety (ICG 2009).

greater analytical leverage by viewing Philippines politics through the lens of "bossism," focusing on the role of "predatory power brokers who achieve monopolistic control over both coercive and economic resources within given territorial jurisdictions or bailiwicks" (Sidel 1999, 19). However useful this correction, as we explain shortly, we find Sidel's reframing overly stark.

Why is the Philippines such an outlier with regard to violence? Clearly socioeconomic development alone offers insufficient explanatory power, being unable to account, for example, for the difference between Indonesia and the Philippines. Rather, we turn to history. As detailed in Chapter 2, American colonials gave political power in the early twentieth century to a landed elite that had emerged in the late Spanish era. Prior to the development of robust and autonomous state institutions, powerful local dynasties assumed elective posts both in the provinces and in the national legislature. Thus emerged a national oligarchy, albeit one whose "economic base lay in hacienda agriculture" (Anderson 1988, 11). In order to secure and augment their landholdings and other property, dynasts built private militias and captured the organs of the local state. The fact that local police forces were, for much of the twentieth century, administratively subservient to mayors (still today, mayors play a role in the selection of local police chiefs) has meant that the police commonly serve as local politicians' enforcers (see Sidel 1999, 26). The relatively early introduction of elections during the colonial period, meanwhile, made electoral competition and coercive authority two sides of the coin of local political power. Dynasties mobilized both economic and coercive resources to dominate local elections, and, hence, the local state.

While recognizing the prominent role coercion plays in the Philippines, we differ from Sidel and others as we assert that patron-client and bossism frameworks should be viewed as complementary rather than as alternatives. Sidel's own account provides numerous examples of local politicians who distributed patronage to voters and supporters, and who built mutually beneficial relationships with higher-level political patrons (Hutchcroft 2003). Our interviews with political candidates and their operatives around the Philippines confirmed these patterns. Candidates and campaign organizers we met were often far from reticent about discussing their relationships with violent actors, but it was our strong impression that in most regions – even in the most clan-dominated corners – political candidates devote far more of their economic resources and attention to patronage-based strategies than to coercion.

History (and much of the literature) notwithstanding, our research partners overall "reported an electoral environment that was largely free of violence and intimidation" (Hicken, Hutchcroft, Weiss, and Aspinall 2019, 34–35). Our surveys, too, suggest that most voters do not feel that they are coerced into their vote choices – recall the vanishingly small number of respondents who reported fearing violence or intimidation if they failed to vote or voted "incorrectly" (see Table 4.6). While electoral coercion remains more widespread in the Philippines than in the other countries on which we focus, it is, on the whole, in decline. Reports of election-related deaths fell in 2010, 2013, 2016, and 2019 (Rappler 2013; Sauler 2016; Caliwan 2019b).[9]

When they did discuss violent actors and coercive tactics, our informants generally suggested they played a *supplemental* role in patronage-based strategies. For example, some politicians we interviewed talked of paying private goons, criminals, insurgents, former insurgents, or freelancing police and army forces to protect their vote-buying efforts. Such groups provided armed guards when politicians' operatives moved large consignments of cash from place to place. Politicians also sometimes laughingly boasted of how they used those same actors to frustrate their opponents' vote-buying efforts. Politicians can use the mere threat of coercion to gain substantial tactical advantage over their rivals. In one municipality in Sorsogon province, for example, we encountered an incumbent mayor who used the military to catch some of his rival's liders as they distributed cash to voters and confiscate the money. The organizer of his rival's campaign pointed out that the same man had used "the reds" (i.e., the local New People's Army insurgents) to do the same thing in the preceding election, but there had been a realignment this time: "Security wise, since they have the military, now we have the reds. We have our own guns, and we have the reds stationed at the different corners."[10]

More generally, to the extent that criminals and drug gangs are an important part of the local social ecology, candidates often draw them into campaign teams and integrate them into their electoral machinery. Doing so can have the added advantage of providing politicians with a credible threat with which to enforce clientelistic exchange with voters. Though this was not a widespread phenomenon even in the Philippines, it certainly was a feature in Mindanao where, in places like Lanao del Sur, "[s]uccessful vote buying depends on the ability of the giver of the money to punish those who do not keep their end of the bargain" (Latiph 2019, 318).

In short, the gap between Mindanao and the rest of the Philippines serves to demonstrate the continuing relevance of historical patterns, alongside the possibility for change. But it also illustrates the extent to which local political-economic and social-structural conditions may yield distinctive subnational mobilization regimes – in this case, one in which exclusive, single-stranded clientelist networks, concentrated and unequal wealth, and marginalization from the central state combine to foster and maintain far more significant levels

---

[9] Among the reasons for that decline were more focused police efforts against identified armed groups and bans on even licensed gun owners' carrying or transporting weapons for a six-month period spanning elections as of 2010, in the wake of 2009's Maguindanao Massacre. By 2019, the exercise resulted in over 6,000 arrests and confiscation of over 5,000 firearms and 50,000 other weapons (McIndoe 2010; Caliwan 2019a).

[10] Interview, May 8, 2016. Control over police appointments can also prove critical. The Duterte administration's replacement of the incumbent mayor's chosen police chief in Cebu City, for instance, seems to have disrupted vote-buying operations for the mayoral race in 2019; this contributed to the incumbent's defeat (Gera and Hutchcroft 2021).

of coercion (as a supplement to patronage strategies) than what are found elsewhere in the country.

Indonesia: Papua and Aceh

The Indonesian state exercises more of a monopoly over coercion than does its counterpart in the Philippines; as such, firearms have always been much less freely available in most parts of Indonesia than in the Philippines. For decades, the military was a pillar of Indonesia's authoritarian regime. Military commanders, working within a highly centralized institution, were responsible for maintaining political order at the local level and not beholden to local politicians. Even so, they filled the niche occupied by local strongmen in the Philippines, including in the illicit economy; military troops played a role that paralleled that of the strongmen's private militias and gangs. While there was a range of informal security groups and organizations of street toughs and gangsters (*preman*), these tended to operate under the informal supervision and control of state security forces (Aspinall and van Klinken 2011; Wilson 2015).

The state's monopoly on violence began to fray in the post-Suharto period. Numerous scholars have described the role played by preman, many of whom were organized into groups that affiliated with the military during the Suharto period, then shifted to freelance local protection and extortion rackets once that regime crumbled. Many hire themselves out as security for companies, where they can be useful for repressing protesting workers or pushing farmers off their land, and engage in the lower levels of the state patronage system – for example, bidding on local-government construction projects (see especially Wilson 2015). Such preman groups maintain subterranean connections with the police and military, but many also have turned to local politics. Some leaders have achieved electoral success in their own right (Ryter 2009), but the more typical pattern is that candidates recruit preman as success-team members, paying them for their support.

Overall, intimidation, let alone electoral violence, is rare – only 0.41 percent of voters we surveyed reported being aware of violence in their area, and only 1.57 percent were aware of intimidation. To a large degree, when political candidates draw preman into their campaigns, they treat them as they would members of any other social network: as a channel to voters, alongside the usual array of ethnic and religious organizations, sporting associations, neighborhood groups, and the like. As we suggested in Chapter 2, we trace the roots of this difference to the nature of the state: coercive capacity remains relatively centralized in Indonesia, rather than being dispersed among an array of private groups. Moreover, as Buehler (2009) has argued, the fact that the bureaucracy – rather than dueling local dynasties as in the Philippines – supplies a large portion of candidates for local political office limits the ferocity of political competition; even losing candidates often maintain connections in the state through which they can pursue their private interests should they lose. Dialing the heat down further are broadly inclusive patterns of patronage-sharing: losers typically have alternative ways to recover their expenditure, and truly wealthy Indonesian candidates rarely see themselves as engaged in winner-take-all contests that will determine their family's fate far into the future.[11] With less at stake, at least thus far, rival candidates have almost never killed each other in Indonesia, unlike in the Philippines or Thailand (Buehler 2009).

However, the significant variation we still do see within Indonesia is instructive. The general picture fits the pattern we sketched at the outset of this chapter: patronage politics tends to be more coercive and predatory in areas of relative state weakness and concentrated control over economic resources. We find these conditions especially in parts of the archipelago where mines and plantations produce rents that local political office-holders can capture. In provinces like South Kalimantan or South Sumatra, competition for local political office is dominated by coal, gold, palm oil, and similar magnates, or by bureaucrats who build close relationships with the private companies prominent in these sectors. Politics in such places tend to be unusually predatory, even by Indonesian standards, being frequently dominated by "mafia coalitions" (Tans 2012) that plunder the budgets of the local state, exchange resource licenses for payments and other favors from businesses, and manipulate the bureaucracy in an unusually vulgar manner. Concentration of control over economic resources undercuts countervailing sources of social power: when economic life in a particular district is heavily focused on natural-resource industries – or, for that matter, when the local bureaucracy is the engine of economic activity and main provider of middle-class jobs – local civil society and media lack autonomy and middle-class citizens, dependent as they are on a narrow economic elite for their prosperity, are reluctant to challenge power-holders (Aspinall and Berenschot 2019, 231–32).

Politics in such places can also be more coercive than in other parts of Indonesia. Though what one finds in these areas falls short of the private armies of the Philippines, it is still not uncommon to hear stories of rival candidates mobilizing teams of preman and engaging in cat-and-mouse games of trying to catch their opponents red-handed during vote-buying operations, or of thuggish success-team members backing their distribution of cash to voters with threats of punishment should they not deliver. Coal and palm-oil barons' local production processes already involve informal muscle – as they hire preman groups to suppress disruptive protests by local landowners, guard company property, and enforce labor discipline; this then enables them to mobilize much greater coercive capacity than that which is typically enjoyed by Indonesian politicians. Workers in mines or oil-palm plantations, meanwhile, often

---

[11] Dynastic politics *is* increasing in Indonesia, though it still lags far behind the Philippines, largely due to local families' generally more tenuous grip on power, given the continuing political dominance of the bureaucracy (Aspinall and As'ad 2016; Kenawas 2018).

constitute voter-blocs that can be mobilized on command, rather than through the patterns of persuasion and patronage-dispensation typical elsewhere in Indonesia. Finally, in many more remote parts of Indonesia, clan and customary chiefs exercise considerable authority in their communities, such that politicians can win elections by engaging their services – whether in exchange for private gifts or club goods – rather than by building more inclusive success teams and dispensing patronage more widely (Rohi 2016). In short, in such places, diverging from the nationally dominant mobilization regime, we see patterns of politics more reminiscent of the Philippines, albeit still less violent than what can commonly be observed in Mindanao.

It is in Indonesia's key "regions of exception," Aceh and Papua, where these dynamics play out to the fullest. Aceh is the site of a recently concluded insurgency, and in Papua insurgency continues. Both host some of Indonesia's most rent-rich resource industries – especially mining but also illegal logging and plantations. These political economies produce highly lucrative income streams for local politicians, security officials, national oligarchs, and foreign companies. The reach of the state is particularly weak in Papua, especially in the highlands, where airstrips rather than roads connect many settlements to district capitals and where absenteeism, corruption, and low capacity render even basic state functions such as healthcare and schools all but inoperable (Anderson 2015).

Politics play out in very different ways in these two provinces, however. Aceh was the site of a thirty-year insurgency, led during its final phase, between 1999 and 2005, by a relatively centralized guerrilla organization that mobilized a coherent sense of Acehnese identity (Aspinall 2009b). The inability of the central government to eradicate the insurgency completely (along with the Indian Ocean tsunami of December 2004, which badly affected the province) contributed to the government's willingness to negotiate a peace agreement that granted significant concessions. Unlike elsewhere in Indonesia, the Acehnese were granted the right to form local political parties that could contest for power within the territory. Former guerrilla commanders rushed to reinvent themselves as construction contractors, project brokers, mining operators, and party leaders; the party they established, Partai Aceh, achieved unusually strong results in local elections (Aspinall 2009a; Stange and Patock 2010; Barter 2011).

Partai Aceh became a provincial party-machine unrivaled in Indonesia. Beyond appealing to Acehnese identity, the former guerrillas also cemented their new dominance by mobilizing the coercive power embodied in their network of ex-combatants, which they used both to frighten off political and economic rivals and to intimidate voters. Electoral politics in the province have thus featured higher levels of violence than in other parts of Indonesia. However, over time, Aceh's politics have increasingly come to resemble broad Indonesian patterns. Corruption, factionalism, and other sources of popular disillusionment have driven a decline in the Partai Aceh vote and generated what one of our research partners described as "growing convergence between Partai Aceh and mainstream parties, with patronage politics becoming more influential than ideology, and Partai Aceh adapting to the techniques of patronage distribution" (Darwin 2016, 40; see also Sulaiman 2016).

Political patterns at the other end of the archipelago, in Papua, are much more fragmented; here we see a politics-of-the-periphery different from that found in Mindanao. Papua is the site of a low-level insurgency that has lasted far longer than that in Aceh. The national police and army continue to suppress resistance to the state and are deeply embedded in extractive industries. Papua's greater ethnic heterogeneity and less hospitable terrain, however, have fractured anti-Jakarta resistance and sapped its efficacy. Functioning state institutions barely penetrate large parts of the territory, especially in the remote interior. Instead, tribal or ethnic community chiefs (*kepala suku*) and clan leaders have emerged as key vote-brokers and mobilizers. Though electoral politics in Papua's urban centers do not differ markedly from those in other parts of the country (Ridwan 2016), politics in the province as a whole are highly corrupt. Suggested one analyst:

> Across the Papuan provinces, decentralization has turned many *bupatis* (district leaders) into feudal lords who often spend more time in Jayapura [the capital of Papua province] or Jakarta than in the areas they are supposed to govern. Occupying and distributing both civil servant positions and elected posts in local legislatures, as well as awarding contracts, are important parts of operating and perpetuating the pre-existing patronage system. Clans have therefore co-opted, rather than adapted to, electoral politics, using Indonesia's vacuous political parties as vehicles of competition. (Anderson 2015, 34)

At the same time, steeply hierarchical social organization – ethnic chiefs and Melanesian-style "big men" claim monopolistic authority to represent their communities – strongly favors brokered arrangements for the distribution of patronage. A local system of voting known as the *noken* system (named after traditional woven bags), in which citizens vote not as individuals but as village communities, immensely compounds this advantage. The result is a situation in which politicians can win elections simply by buying the loyalty of chiefs rather than voters:

> In the highlands, it is easy to determine whether brokers have delivered the blocs they promised simply by looking at the results. In many areas, there is no need for voters to turn up to polls – turnout was registered as being 100 per cent across the highlands, meaning all the votes were arranged beforehand and few people actually voted. The net effect of this system is thus to strengthen the influence of a narrow elite – the candidates and the brokers – at the expense of giving eligible voters a democratic voice. (Nolan 2016, 399)

This context yields a system in which plenty of money and other forms of patronage change hands at election time, but – more so than in most of Indonesia – much of it never makes it to voters. Ethnic community leaders instead expropriate these funds by selling their communities' votes wholesale, with outcomes determined in bargains struck among local election officials, brokers, and politicians in the lobbies of local hotels rather than through the ballot box (Nolan 2016, 411). In this context, it is not surprising, too, that electoral competition becomes imbued with traditional patterns of inter-clan warfare. Inter-group violence often erupts around elections and causes fatalities at levels that are "unprecedented elsewhere in Indonesia" (Anderson 2015, 34), including rare instances of murdered candidates.

In short, we see regional pockets quite out of sync with the ad hoc teams and micro-particularistic patronage so prevalent nationally in Indonesia. But the disparities fit the same general pattern we see in the Philippines: where concentration of resources, inequality, dependence, and sharply hierarchical and single-stranded clientelist networks prevail, the mobilization regime adapts and politics becomes more exclusionary and coercive.

Malaysia: Sabah and Sarawak

Politics in the East Malaysian states of Sabah and Sarawak presents yet another contrasting pattern. The coercion that features in Mindanao, Aceh, and Papua is almost completely absent, and party organization is stronger than in either the Philippines or Indonesia. Yet in other respects, as indicated at the start of this chapter, East Malaysian politics bears at least some resemblance to patterns in those two countries. Local political strongmen with party vehicles (rather than leaders elevated via parties), as well as their hired brokers, are more prominent in East Malaysia than in other parts of the country. Some of these political leaders come from politically prominent *towkay* (business-scion) families. Rent-seeking from logging, palm oil, and other natural-resource industries shapes the local political economy and electoral politics. Most importantly, for our purposes, distribution of club goods (irrigation schemes, bridges, road repairs, etc.), substantial household items (e.g., party-branded water tanks or zinc roofing material), and other forms of patronage are widespread at election times. Individualized vote buying remains less conspicuous than in the Philippines or Indonesia but is more common than elsewhere in Malaysia.

The relative absence of political violence in East Malaysia is striking in comparison to the peripheral regions of Indonesia and the Philippines but is part of a broader pattern in which violence has been notably absent from Malaysia's postindependence politics.[12] Even separatists in Sabah and Sarawak – not a large movement thus far – have pursued their goals almost entirely nonviolently, unlike the insurgencies in Mindanao, Papua, and Aceh. The largely peaceful nature of Malaysian politics is a by-product of the strength

---

[12] The few exceptions stand out for their rarity. Best known is the Malay–Chinese violence after the 1969 elections (see Chapter 2). A less well-known example is Sabah's 1986 "Silent Riot," which also came in the wake of an electoral upset (see https://thesilentriotdocumentary .wordpress.com/).

of the country's parties and long-time electoral authoritarian regime, as explained in Chapter 2. Unlike in Indonesia, where the military moved to the forefront of political life as parties began to falter in the 1950s, successive civilian governments in Malaysia have consistently maintained supremacy over the security apparatus. Indeed, preserving both military and police as over-whelmingly Malay forces helped maintain these institutions as vote-banks for the United Malays National Organisation (UMNO) for decades (albeit with the assistance of dubious postal-voting practices; see Noor'ain 2017). Unlike in the Philippines, where local political bosses and dynasts have sometimes used violence to give themselves an edge in the free-fight elections that determine local power, in Malaysia since the early postindependence period, the state (and by extension, federal) governments have been the gatekeepers of local political authority and security.

The path to power for ambitious politicians in Malaysia has always involved climbing the ranks of ruling-coalition parties. For mainstream parties, coercion has played a minimal part in that contest. (The exception is the far left: the Malayan Communist Party, which was banned in 1948, routed in the Emergency that followed, and never successfully revived.) Coercion has also rarely featured in parties' relations with voters. To maintain itself in power until 2018, the BN coalition relied on a range of sophisticated methods, including control of media, manipulation of electoral rules and constituency boundaries, and – on occasion – surgical use of repression against opponents. This included deployment of the notorious Internal Security Act (ISA), which was in 2012 replaced by the Security Offices (Special Measures) Act. Relying on brute force during elections to harass or intimidate citizens has thus been unnecessary and would have been counter-productive: the BN's legitimacy rested substan-tially on its claim that it governed with the consent of the people.

The relative strength of local parties has been another feature distinguishing politics in Sabah and Sarawak from politics in the other peripheral regions. In both states, at least until 2018, local versions of the ruling Barisan Nasional coalition had come to dominate state politics. This situation took time to evolve in Sabah, where for three decades after independence, the state was ruled by mutating coalitions, effectively a series of local parties representing religious and ethnic subcommunities and led by community elites, but less clearly organ-ized along stark communal lines than in peninsular Malaya. They aligned mostly, but not consistently, with the BN government at the federal level. This pattern changed in 1991, when UMNO moved into Sabah, joining forces with other local parties to form the BN Sabah. Its members came from the now-expansive Muslim Malay and Melanau communities (boosted since the 1970s by a state-led Islamization drive). UMNO's entry inaugurated a period of BN hegemony in which the state government integrated closely into the national ruling coalition – coinciding, too, with the growing demographic weight of Muslims in the state. That phase lasted until 2018, when UMNO Sabah ruptured and the splinter Parti Warisan Sabah (Sabah Heritage Party,

Warisan) formed the government in its stead, allying with the peninsular Pakatan Harapan coalition that ousted the BN (Faisal 2020). With the collapse of PH and rise of Perikatan Nasional at the federal level in early 2020, the Gabungan Bersatu Sabah (Sabah United Alliance, GBS), formed of (weak) opposition parties in still-Warisan-held Sabah, reunited with the BN in the new coalition. The key point is that, in Sabah, we see a more localized and fluctuating party landscape than in peninsular Malaysia.

The political pattern in Sarawak has been much more stable, with the state ruled by one family for much of the postindependence period (Chin 2015, 86). Melanau-Muslim Taib Mahmud served as chief minister from 1981 to 2014, ruling Sarawak almost as a personal fiefdom through the Parti Pesaka Bumiputera Bersatu (PBB, United Bumiputera Heritage Party), which he controlled (and which was essential to BN dominance as non-Malay peninsular voters deserted the coalition from 2008 on). PBB dominance outlasted Taib, but the party and its BN Sarawak allies exited the BN after the 2018 elections to form a state-specific Gabungan Parti Sarawak (Coalition of Sarawak Parties, GPS). GPS, like Sabah's GBS, subsequently allied with Perikatan Nasional in 2020.

Though East Malaysian parties and the coalitions they form have tended to be more fluid than in peninsular Malaysia, politics in these states has nevertheless centered around dominant parties in ways dissimilar from Indonesian and Philippine patterns. An important element of similarity, however, is in cash handouts and other forms of electoral patronage – consistently much more extensive in Sabah and Sarawak than in other parts of the Federation. Writing about the first decade of independent rule in both states, for example, Milne (1973, 902) reported that elections in Sabah and Sarawak involved "bidding for the votes of individuals" alongside "rewards for communities in the shape of community development projects." In particular, small-scale rural projects "were allocated largely with votes in view. Requests from particular communities were more likely to be granted if support was strong there for the government party." Decades on, patronage politics remained prevalent: in the 1995 general election, a Sarawak BN candidate distributed payments to voters of 50 ringgit, with an IOU note for another 100 ringgit if the candidate won; in the state election the following year, voters could collect 20 ringgit to vote for the BN candidate in one constituency; and for a by-election the next year, Sarawak BN feted sets of longhouses with food and alcohol to make voters feel obligated to reciprocate (Aeria 2005, 133–35). Writing of the 1999 Sabah state election, Case (1999, 13–14) noted that "Barisan officials were reported to have distributed water tanks, gas stoves, fishing nets, and the like in wavering districts, then monitored local 'responsiveness' by marshalling voters through a 'ten persons' *(kepala sepuluh)* system." The 2006 state election saw reports of supporters of a government candidate in one district who "were directed to go from village to village to give money to village headmen and community leaders so that they would support" the ruling party (Puyok 2006, 221). Another analyst noted of the same election that "state officials assist candidates and their agents in vote buying," especially "in rural areas, where elections provide a means of earning much needed revenue." Payments ranged from 20 to 200 ringgit per voter (Welsh 2006, 9).

Our own researchers in 2013 also found much evidence of micro-particularism (including such tactics as paying voters to display BN flags), alongside a great deal of meso-particularism. Again in Sabah in 2018, field researchers tracked efforts by both BN and challenger Warisan to buy votes, starting prior to the campaign, then picking up as polls approached (Weiss 2019b, 142, citing unpublished Merdeka Center data). Even so, distributing cash to ordinary voters is less widespread or frequent in Sabah and Sarawak, especially in urban and peri-urban areas, than in either the Philippines or Indonesia. The practice is also much more secretive: unlike in the other countries, we and our colleagues in East Malaysia were rarely able to conduct detailed interviews with vote-buying practitioners about their strategies and techniques, let alone witness operatives distribute payments or gifts. Instead, we mostly relied upon reports by politicians who spoke in the abstract about the practice (while sometimes hinting at personal knowledge and involvement) and by citizens and opposition politicians who related personal encounters with electoral handouts by others. Nevertheless, our own fieldwork findings and other reports make clear that East Malaysian patterns of patronage are distinct from those in the peninsula, where individual-level inducements, while not without precedent,[13] are relatively rare.

What might explain the greater salience of such forms of money politics in East Malaysia than elsewhere in the country? One explanation is the nature of local political economies and the material resources available to politicians. Both Sabah and Sarawak are frontier economies: from the 1960s through the 1990s they were sites of timber booms, characterized by "rent seizing" and unsustainable rates of deforestation (Ross 2001, 87–156). Because logging licenses and concessions are the domain of state, not federal, government, local politicians had tremendous capacity to enrich themselves by distributing such resources in exchange for kickbacks or assistance from timber barons. The funds they gained from such connections could be turned into patronage to build their parties, consolidate social support, and win elections. Politics in both states has thus long been known to be especially corrupt. Taib Mahmud, for example, presided over what has been labeled a "timber mafia" in Sarawak (Bruno Manser Fund 2012). Meanwhile, as deforestation depleted East Malaysia's tropical forests (and economic diversification proceeded slowly, at

---

[13] For instance, a judge nullified the 2018 result in Cameron Highlands, Pahang after finding evidence that agents of the BN candidate had given Orang Asli (indigenous) voters money to entice support (Bernama 2018). During the by-election to fill the seat, it was PH that drew flak for announcing new government-funded development projects in local villages; the agency head declared the party-branded signboards an "unintended mistake" (Malaysiakini 2019).

best), new primary products – especially palm-oil plantations – took their place, and have been equally lucrative for local politicians. As Cramb argues of the exceptionally rapid transformation of Sarawak's economy, "the dominant mode of oil palm expansion in Sarawak has been driven not primarily by technical or market imperatives but by the exercise of state power to maximise opportunities for surplus extraction and political patronage" (Cramb 2016, 192; see also Varkkey 2015).

This local political economy helps explain the ubiquity of patronage distribution around elections in Sabah and Sarawak, and the similarities with parts of Indonesia and the Philippines where we see comparably predatory interactions between local political and economic elites. In both Malaysian states, natural-resource rents simultaneously expanded the patronage resources available to politicians and increased their incentives to win in order to secure these prizes of political office. To be sure, the political architecture differs from that of our other cases, as elites still exercise power through parties. Thus, a distinguishing feature of "money politics" in Sabah and Sarawak has been the dominant role of ruling parties. But the practice of patronage politics on the ground – especially as ordinary citizens experience it during elections – strongly resembles what we see in our other country cases.

A second explanation for the greater prevalence of overt and individualized forms of patronage politics around elections in these states than in peninsular Malaysia – also connected to political economy – concerns the more steeply hierarchical nature of local social networks. As a result of both of the natural-resource industries that predominate in Sabah and Sarawak, and of the ethnically complex, still much more agrarian than urbanized character of these societies, local community leaders tend to exercise strong influence. This is especially the case among local indigenous groups such as the Iban, Dayak, and Kadazandusun, whose communities frequently live in longhouses that can house up to several dozen families. From early in the independence period, dominant parties in these states expanded by recruiting "hierarchical party officials, drawn from all the major ethnic groups," many of whom "were actually chiefs or headmen" (Milne 1973, 899). It is such local chiefs and headmen – many of whom are integrated into the structures of the local state, receiving civil service positions and salaries – who play key roles as brokers and gatekeepers, determining which parties even have access to longhouses and their residents.

Indeed, Sabah and Sarawak are the only parts of Malaysia where we see parties effectively buying blocs of votes, with the assistance of local-level brokers. As explained by one then-opposition legislator in Sarawak, rural voters are more likely to be swayed by payments than are urban voters – so, for instance, workers in this candidate's own oil-palm nursery told him that brokers came to take down their names as supporters, in exchange for 100 ringgit (USD24). Meanwhile, worried about declining returns and having recruited a set of wealthy tycoon candidates, the BN was upping their inducement for the

2016 state election, offering some voters 500 ringgit (USD120) in advance and another 500 ringgit if the BN won, even in a semi-urban area. According to this legislator, opposition parties generally had to write off places with a high "native" population share; deep-pocketed tycoon-politicians, money and machinery for campaign logistics, and preferential (or even exclusive) access to communities and longhouses gave the BN a near-unbeatable edge in Bumiputera constituencies. The opposition expected no more than 10–15 percent of the vote in these areas – even those residents who seemed to be inclined to their appeals lost interest when money turned the tide. When opposition parties such as the DAP did reach out there, they hired local brokers, to the consternation of their volunteers who came in from the peninsula to help and were not familiar with such practices. The parties felt they needed operatives who knew the local culture and communities. These brokers expected to be paid. As the legislator explained, you "simply have to expect" that these operatives may defect to a candidate who pays more, or simultaneously "work for the other team." Much as in Indonesia, a savvy candidate had to distinguish their loyal "A Team" and keep an eye on the rest (while nonetheless requiring their assistance). They had to be careful with information, too, in case brokers were spying for the competition.[14]

Again, our surveys show markedly low rates of vote buying nationwide in Malaysia, including in Sabah and Sarawak (a hardly credible 0.6 percent in East Malaysia said they had ever been offered a gift to induce them to vote a certain way). These low reported levels likely stem from a combination of lesser praxis than in Indonesia and the Philippines, social-desirability bias, and the normalization of certain types of gifts in East Malaysia, such that voters really do not see these as electoral inducements. Given the far more central role of enduring parties in Malaysia than in our other cases, such gifts are frequently less closely tied to elections themselves, which might help account for why they seem less obviously efforts at vote buying. Parties on all sides distribute party-branded household goods, club goods, and so forth on an ongoing basis, with particular zeal in East Malaysia; such efforts intensify during the campaign proper but are not confined to that period.

Overall, our own and others' qualitative research suggests decisively the higher prevalence of retail strategies in East Malaysia. These distinct patterns of patronage politics arise from the combination of a natural-resource-based and poorly diversified economy, a still largely rural and economically under-developed society, a more fragmented ethnic mix, and a political culture centered around political strongmen – especially community elites and tycoons. All told, these patterns on the Malaysian periphery look more like the Philippines and Indonesia than like the more structured competition on the peninsula.

[14] Interview, April 23, 2016.

ISLANDS OF EXCEPTION

A dramatic contrast to regions marked by coercive and exclusionary patterns of clientelistic politics are those islands of exception where political leaders and machines, with varying degrees of success, try to break the mold of patronage politics. It is here that we observe campaigns to clean up politics and appeals to voters by promising – and sometimes delivering – improved services rather than personalized benefits. These places are, in short, sites of programmatic politics, where distribution occurs according to public, formal, and actually applied criteria, rather than particularistic considerations (Stokes et al. 2013, 7). Though their leaders sometimes present such places as pioneers of new modes of politics in the countries concerned, these islands often coexist with rather than challenge dominant patterns of politics, presenting complex mixes of programmatic and patronage-oriented measures. They are, moreover, often subject to erosion, as the currents of traditional politics flowing around them often generate continual pressures to conform.

In each of our countries, we encounter local politicians who attempt to break out of the handouts-funded-by-corruption cycle and instead promise to clean up local government while putting more focus on programmatic appeals. In some places, these politicians have generated considerable popular enthusiasm as a result. One such reforming local leader in Indonesia, Joko Widodo (Jokowi), rocketed from being elected mayor of Solo, a mid-sized town in Java, in 2005 to winning the governorship of Jakarta in 2012 and the national presidency in 2014. In the Philippines, Leni Robredo, who arose from the country's best-known experiment in participatory local governance, was elected vice-president in 2016, but failed in her bid to be elected president in 2022.

What explains the emergence and distribution of such attempts to reduce the centrality of patronage politics, and what can we say about their transformative potential? We highlight four major elements: urban roots, a linkage to civil society, the importance of leadership, and the often tentative and incomplete nature of such efforts.

Our first point is relatively simple: as a general rule, islands of programmatic exception to the pattern of patronage-oriented politics are *urban*. Over the past two decades, most attempts to transform Southeast Asian local politics by weeding out corruption within government bureaucracies, reducing arbitrariness in the distribution of government benefits, and moving away from patronage delivery to election-time promises of programmatic policies – and the subsequent programmatic delivery of services – have occurred in towns and cities. Patterns differ, though, across the region. In Indonesia, a number of reforming urban leaders – including Jokowi but also his deputy and successor as Jakarta governor, Basuki Tjahaja Purnama (Ahok), as well as Tri Rismaharini (Risma, mayor of Surabaya, 2010–2020) and Ridwan Kamil (mayor of Bandung, 2013–2018) – have seized public and scholarly attention for their efforts to transform local governance in their cities: reducing project brokerage, cleaning up corruption, and improving government services and city amenities. In Surabaya, for example, by reforming the city's public procurement system to curb corruption and waste, Risma's city administration claims to have reduced the city's budget by 30 percent; she then redirected those savings toward improved government services and higher civil service salaries.[15] There was purportedly no vote buying in either of her election campaigns (the second of which she won with 86 percent of the vote), although the practice has been widespread in Surabaya's legislative elections.

In Malaysia, to the extent that opposition parties have modeled an alternative to the BN's patronage politics, they have done so primarily in the country's urban centers, notably Penang and the Klang Valley around Kuala Lumpur, though extending also to East Malaysian cities such as Kuching, Sarawak. Though ethnicity still provides the dominant frame for understanding Malaysia's politics, and observers frequently describe this more programmatic political mode as "Chinese," it makes more sense to see the rural–urban divide as setting the timbre of political change in the country. Indeed, during the 22-month Pakatan Harapan interregnum (2018–2020), it was mostly the coalition's more rural-based component parties – especially Parti Pribumi Bersatu Malaysia (Bersatu), an UMNO splinter party – that proved keenest to adopt new versions of the BN's old patronage-based strategies. Parties such as DAP and PKR, which draw more heavily on urban votes, remained more focused on new methods of building political support (Weiss 2020c, chaps. 5 and 7).

In the Philippines, experiments in programmatic politics are both more rare and more contingent than in Indonesia and Malaysia. Entrenched local machines dominate many urban centers in the Philippines, making patterns of vote buying and governmental corruption hard to break. Though it is possible to find reforming mayors and governors who engage in innovative programs to increase government revenues and improve services, it is much rarer that such politicians turn their backs on vote buying and machine politics altogether.

It is not surprising that the main islands of exception to patronage politics are found in urban areas, if we recall the arguments sketched earlier in this chapter. The same syndrome of factors – state capacity and penetration, the local political economy, and prevailing social networks and leadership – determine both where we find especially clientelistic and coercive *or* unusually programmatic political strategies. State agencies generally have greater reach and capacity in urban locations than in rural, especially remote, regions, making promises of improved government services more credible in cities. Urban areas generally house concentrations of relatively well-educated and wealthy citizens (for instance, Jakarta and Yogyakarta are consistently ranked

---

[15] Interview with Edi Cahyadi, head of the City Development Planning Agency, April 12, 2019, Surabaya.

first and second, respectively, for human development in Indonesia[16]); these citizens constitute at least a potential constituency for programmatic politics. Equally importantly, the development of industry, services, and other modern sectors widens the distribution of economic resources and reduces the relative economic power of local officials and their business backers, producing the converse of concentrated resource wealth that, we noted, facilitates coercive electoral mobilization. That same socioeconomic pattern increases the political salience of reliable public services to facilitate the requirements of urban life, from public transit for commuting, to water, sewage, and sanitation services adequate for high-density housing. The presence of diverse business and middle-class groups also strengthens sources of countervailing social power, producing more complex local civil societies – including NGOs, business associations, media, and other groups interested more in sustained policy advocacy and implementation than in securing short-term particularistic material benefits.

This brings us to our second observation: successful efforts to escape from patronage politics typically rely on either *direct or indirect linkages between politicians and civil-society groups* – linkages based not on patronage distribution but on participation in policy-making and implementation (Aspinall and Berenschot 2019, 220–24). The most prominent example of such a pattern occurs in the country where such efforts to exit patronage politics are the rarest: the Philippines. In Naga City, an otherwise typical regional center in the Bicol region, a reforming mayor, Jesse Robredo, introduced a new approach to city government after he was first elected in 1989 (Kawanaka 1998 and 2002; Borromeo-Bulao 2019; Scharff 2011). Though Robredo himself had relatively modest middle-class origins, he came to power in part through family connections (an uncle had been provincial governor). Once in office he instituted a new mode of participatory governance, drawing representatives of various people's organizations and nongovernmental organizations into a Naga City People's Council. He then empowered them to discuss and help determine town policies and budgets, including through representation in the city council. These organizations were thus able to promote the interests of their members, both by helping to design policies that benefitted the city as a whole – and to introduce new revenue measures to fund them – and by formulating and helping to implement a range of welfare-assistance, micro-finance, and similar programs that benefited poor residents. Members of this network of organizations then became a campaign organization at election time: "Team Naga." The machine Robredo established has been able to carry every election in the town since he first formulated the approach. It even endured beyond Robredo's death in 2012 (Borromeo-Bulao 2019).

---

[16] Badan Pusat Statistik, "Peringkat Indeks Pembangunan Manusia Menurut Provinsi, 2010-2018 (Metode Baru)," www.bps.go.id/dynamictable/2019/04/16/1615/peringkat-indeks-pembangu nan-manusia-menurut-provinsi-2010-2018-metode-baru-.html (accessed January 16, 2020).

While Robredo and his successors were especially assiduous in building connections with people's organizations, they were not alone in this practice: numerous other local politicians in the Philippines incorporate into their political machines groups representing the urban poor, pedicab drivers, market stallholders, and the like. Mostly, however, they simply use such groups as vehicles of distribution, in the process burnishing their popular appeal.[17] What made the Naga City model exceptional in the Philippines context was that, beyond using urban-poor organizations for distribution or appearances, Robredo gave them a seat at the table when it came to making decisions on the design of policies and allocation of resources. Yet the award-winning mayor was by no means exiting patronage politics. As Kawanaka (1998, 101–102, 4) explains, Robredo assiduously cultivated "networks with national power holders" able to "gain access to and monopoly over … state resources." His success came, ultimately, through combining "good governance" with "a strong political machine."

In Indonesia, consistent with the country's generally more fluid and transient local political alignments, such formalized relationships between civil-society organizations and local-government reformers are rare. Many reforming local politicians are former bureaucrats or other technocrats; relatively few have backgrounds in NGOs or similar groups. Even so, some effectively forge informal alliances with civil-society organizations, or lean on NGOs' support in their efforts to reform local government. It is, for example, perhaps not a coincidence that Jokowi first came to prominence in Solo, a city with a vibrant civil society. According to one account of his period as mayor, Solo's NGOs played "cardinal roles" in shaping Jokowi's agenda, including on budget transparency, popular participation in government, and the management of informal traders (Mas'udi 2016, 48). In Surabaya, a civil society-led movement in 2002 to oust authoritarian-era predatory elites from the city's government helped enable Risma's later attempts to construct a new model of governance; the movement "created a context conducive to the emergence of reform-minded political and bureaucratic leaders committed to popular demands" (Mustafa 2017, 90). Both Jokowi and Ahok used groups of volunteers to organize non-patronage-based election campaigns (Suaedy 2014). In fact, however, they and similar reforming politicians mostly relied on the media to appeal to voters directly, reaching over the heads of brokers in clientelist networks. Other more traditional politicians form what Tans (2012, 15) calls "mobilizing coalitions" that marshal NGOs, occupational groups, ethnic organizations, and the like behind their election campaigns; they often simply distribute patronage to these organizations, but sometimes also promise "policies that more broadly benefit

[17] For instance, seeking to reinvigorate his family's longstanding role in Cebu City's politics post-Marcos, mayoral candidate Tomas Osmeña spent a great deal of effort reaching out to the city's urban poor – even "sleeping in the city's impoverished communities" (interview, Francisco "Bimbo" Fernandez, Osmeña's executive assistant, Cebu City, May 11, 2019).

groups of supporters." Suggests Tans, "to the extent that those groups were previously excluded from receiving patronage, they place entirely new demands on the regime's resource base" (Tans 2012, 15; see also Savirani and Aspinall 2017). In short, such civil-society engagement in election campaigns often results in strategies that are, essentially, a mix of patronage and programmatic appeals.

Among our cases, it is in Malaysia, however, that civil society's reformist efforts are the most pronounced. Issue-oriented civil-society organizations have offered campaign and constituency-service volunteers over the years, particularly in urban areas, helping opposition parties chip away at the advantage enjoyed by the ruling coalition's party machines. Especially notable were the swarms of volunteers, some too young to vote, who in 2013 and 2018 fanned out as canvassers under the banner of the Bersih movement for electoral reform, touting issues of electoral probity and anticorruption broadly (Chan 2018). Civil-society organizations have also provided a wellspring of candidates for recent elections, including popular, principled, and often social-media-savvy activists (Weiss 2009, 754–56).

Perhaps most importantly, though, organizations and activists from civil society have helped over the course of decades to orient, promote, and defend reform agendas in Malaysia. Initiatives in civil society have accompanied and informed years of opposition-party innovation; civil-society activists have worked to define new policies, generate normative standards for governance, build bases for coalitions, and fashion mechanisms for accountability (Weiss 2006 and 2009; Liow 2009). Indeed, however symbiotic the ties between Malaysian civil-society activists and opposition political parties especially since 2008, middle-class, urban-based NGOs have pressed more aggressively and consistently than parties in support of such causes as the reinstatement of local-government elections, with the goal of institutionalizing participation and local democracy (Rodan 2014).

Third, *leadership clearly also matters to the emergence of islands of exception*. In the 1980s, there was little to differentiate Naga City's social structure and political history from those of scores of similar urban centers in the Philippines. What made Naga City distinctive was the presence of an innovative and charismatic leader in Jesse Robredo, who devised a creative approach to government. Christian von Luebke's (2009) analysis of local-government reform in Indonesia likewise emphasizes the role of leadership. And in Malaysia, leaders such as Anwar Ibrahim came to power on the back of civil-society organizations – in Anwar's case, particularly the extensive and well-organized Malaysian Islamic Youth Movement, ABIM. In the process, they helped to preserve access and influence for those organizations.

It is frequently mayors, rather than legislators, who emerge to drive reform in both the Philippines and Indonesia. This points to the critical role of institutions in structuring the opportunities available to reformers. Mayors in both countries (though especially the Philippines) have considerable authority and discretion over the use of government funds and the organization of the bureaucracy in their bailiwicks. Legislators typically have much less authority and, being required to act collectively, are much more likely to adapt to dominant patterns of resource allocation and political behavior. The resulting often highly personalized nature of local reform efforts in Indonesia and the Philippines – as opposed to their institutionalization through political parties in Malaysia – is one reason why reformers often find such efforts challenging to sustain (a point we return to later).

Though reforming leaders typically emerge in towns and cities, they are not unknown in rural areas. In such settings, they tend to find the structural context less conducive to reform, and therefore typically mix programmatic and clientelistic practices. Thus, Mas'udi and Kurniawan (2017) and Mahsun (2017) both describe the emergence of reformist *bupati,* or heads of rural districts, in Java. Influenced by the Jokowi model, these leaders came to power promising better delivery of health, education, and similar programs. They then won support for living up to these promises and, in at least one case, did so on the basis of collaboration with a network of local farmers' organizations. However, in neither of these locations (Kulon Progo in Yogyakarta and Batang in Central Java) were these politicians able to make a clean break from the politics of patronage, given that they governed in parts of Java where citizens were already deeply habituated to vote-buying practices. Thus, in one case, "the popular incumbent prepared a vote buying strategy, but he did not activate it" (Mas'udi and Kurniawan 2017, 451) because he realized his opponent was so weak that he would win anyway; in the other, the reforming candidate actually did distribute electoral handouts, albeit at a lower rate than his opponents. Members of the peasant organization that backed this candidate targeted modest payments to "poor voters, both farmers and workers, who were not members of the organization and who did not have a clear preference for any particular candidate" (Mahsun 2017, 480). The contrast with nearby Solo and Surabaya – the urban centers where Jokowi and Risma won without recourse to such distribution – is stark.

These observations about rural Java lead to a fourth point about efforts to reduce the centrality of patronage-based strategies in the countries we studied: overwhelmingly, such efforts have been *halting, contingent, incomplete, and hybridized.* Rather than break with patronage politics cleanly and completely, politicians more often mix elements of programmatic delivery and campaigning with clientelism: improving government services while also distributing personalized gifts, reducing patronage jobs in one government department while allowing them in another, ending morselization of one policy area – healthcare is a common example – while continuing it in others. As we alluded to in Chapter 7, our observations thus conform to what Manor conceptualizes as "post-clientelist initiatives" across the Global South, defined as "programmes and policies that are substantially or entirely protected from people who seek to siphon off resources for use as patronage" (Manor 2013, 243) but that "are almost always pursued *not instead of* clientelism but *in addition to* it, since it is politically risky to try to abandon clientelism" (Manor 2013, 244).

We reject, however, the implied teleology in the phrase "*post*-clientelism." Many politicians we encountered began with aspirations to practice performance- and policy-based politics but adapted to the realities of patronage once they became candidates or came to power. A particularly stark example: Malaysia's Pakatan Harapan coalition took office in 2018 substantially on the basis of programmatic appeals and promises to curb corruption. Less than a year later, in an unusually violation-laden by-election in Selangor state, PH became the primary culprit in election offenses ("exerting undue influence," distributing gifts or food, and employing violence and intimidation) (Fakhrull 2019). In fact, the ubiquity of hijacking programs through the morselization, facilitation, and credit-claiming we describe in Chapter 6 is a testament to the hybrid nature of much of the politics we observe in the region: patronage and programmatic politics fall on a continuum. Voters may support the same party or candidate either for reasons of performance or for the particularistic benefits they offer – or indeed for a combination of the two at the same time.

A related issue concerns the sustainability of programmatic innovations. In deeply patronage-oriented political contexts, islands of exception can be battered by currents that pull political actors back toward the dominant mode. Indonesia in particular supports a veritable cottage industry of scholarship pointing out how readily much-lauded local reformers adapt to the realities of patronage politics once in power, blending strategies to win re-election and govern, and drawing support from oligarchic actors as well as from the public (see for example Winters 2013, 13–15; Choi and Fukuoka 2015; Fukuoka and Djani 2015). In the Philippines, the politicians inheriting the Naga City model of alternative politics have seemingly begun to bend in the face of increasing political competition since Jesse Robredo's death in 2012. It appears that Team Naga has begun to distribute cash to at least some voters (Borromeo-Bulao 2019, 202), financed by funds obtained from contractors who are awarded construction projects in the city: donations amount to (a relatively modest) 5 percent of the projects' value.[18] In short, our islands of exception are subject to erosion; we should be cautious about viewing them as nodal points that mark shifts in trajectory.

CONCLUSION

Modernization theory gave social scientists of decades past confidence that development would render particularism and patronage mere relics of history. They were wrong. Despite decades of economic growth, rising levels of

---

[18] Anonymous interview, civil society advocates, Naga City, May 5, 2019.

urbanization, and the growth of middle classes in each of our three core countries, each remains firmly in the grip of patronage politics – albeit with distinctive national patterns that, as we have explained throughout this book, have more to do with past legacies of institutional development than comparative economic metrics.

This chapter has shown, however, that a focus on the subnational level – where we find real variation around national norms – can help us to tease out the ways in which patterns of development shape the form and intensity of patronage politics. We do see some, albeit mixed, evidence of a link between rising incomes, urbanization, and programmatic politics, but we also find both within- and cross-national variation in the strength of that relationship, as well as significant exceptions. Moreover, the mechanism at work is less economic development per se than state capacity and reach, the nature of the local resource base, and the character of social networks and leadership. In each of the countries on which we focus, we find both comparatively strong clientelistic and strong programmatic outposts, the former frequently on the geographic periphery and the latter more common in cities.

While the general pattern is clear, it is far from certain that the usually urban outposts of programmatic politics are harbingers of broader processes of political change. Dominant electoral mobilization regimes in each country exert strong pressures, and collective-action problems stymie politicians and citizens who seek to escape the cycle of patronage politics. It is at the subnational level that we can more clearly see the tensions among structural context, enlightened leadership, and entitled, empowered vested interests. Our final chapter considers prospects for political transformation and options for institutional reform that might coax politicians and parties toward a more heavily programmatic mix of strategies.

9

Conclusion

Patterns, Permutations, and Reform Prospects

We started to plan the research project that led to this book in mid-2012. The timeline was perfect: Malaysia's next election was then (we thought) imminent; it ended up being in 2013. Indonesia's next national election would be in 2014, Thailand's in 2015, then the Philippines' in 2016. Yet Thailand does not appear, except peripherally, in the preceding chapters. The reason captures a key caveat that limits our study: although the range of patronage politics we discuss in the book is important in all sorts of ways – for democratic buy-in (and, more fundamentally, the quality of democracy and democratic account-ability), for policy outcomes (and the relative salience of policy in political contestation), for partisan identity (and, even more importantly, the character of parties), and for political inclusion (and the depth and breadth of regime legitimacy), to name a few dimensions – it is only ever part of the story. Sometimes, other political processes and developments are more consequential.

In Thailand's case, the 2014 coup interrupted those planned-for elections; the generals managed a heavily manipulated electoral exercise in 2019, but, as we finalize this volume, substantive democracy is not yet in sight. Indeed, the years we have been researching and writing this volume have witnessed dizzying political summersaults across Southeast Asia. In the Philippine presidential elections of 2016, the authoritarian-populist Rodrigo Duterte charmed and blustered his way into office, after which he yanked down the democratic drapes to a soundtrack of belligerent attacks on journalists, social media manipulation, and gunshots directed at thousands of mainly urban poor citizens accused – without trial – of being drug users or dealers. (And in May 2022, as this book was going to press, authoritarian impulses in the Philippines became further entrenched. With Duterte term-limited out of office, Ferdinand Marcos, Jr., son of the former dictator, coasted easily into the presidency; Duterte's daughter Sara claimed an even wider margin for vice president.) In Malaysia, the elderly former authoritarian ruler Mahathir returned from retirement in May 2018, the winds of anti-corruption sentiment firmly at his back, to head a government of reform-oriented parties he once lambasted as charlatans and traitors – only to be outfoxed in a parliamentary coup less than two years later. And Indonesian politics became deeply polarized over issues related to different perspectives on the place of Islam in public life. Voters rejected an authoritarian-populist presidential candidate and former general, Prabowo Subianto, in 2014 and 2019; after his second defeat, his opponent, President Joko Widodo, invited him to join the cabinet, amidst a slow-moving democratic decline.

Events thus conspired to remind us that our framework does not explain everything about politics in the countries we have studied in this volume. The preceding chapters make plain our conviction, however, that patronage politics do matter greatly, in part precisely because they connect to many of the underlying sources of political weakness and grievance that continue to characterize democratic governance in Southeast Asia and, by extension, other parts of the world. As we explained in Chapter 1, while we focus here on a delimited set of countries, we expect the ideas we develop to travel widely. The three specific electoral mobilization regimes we describe are neither unique nor exhaustive. As we clarify later, with a preliminary extension of our comparative analysis to a broader set of cases, our objective in this book is to present a framework and method rather than a comprehensive typology. In this concluding chapter, we revisit our core questions, arguments, and contributions; review the sources of the patterns of patronage we identify; and speculate on where these practices may be going. This wrapping-up includes brief consideration of the implications of patronage politics for democratic rule, alongside an exploration of the reform options and prospects that arise from our analysis.

A RECAP: PATTERNS OF PATRONAGE POLITICS IN SOUTHEAST ASIA

We began this book, in Chapter 1, with a brief conceptual discussion that distinguishes patronage from clientelism and posits three major types of particularism based primarily on scale but also in terms of the degree of personalism they embody: micro, meso, and macro. This framework then led us into five core research questions, four related to how we conceptualize and identify patterns of patronage politics and a fifth that ties those threads together, suggesting an explanation of why we see the patterns we do. Our first two questions lay the foundation: what forms of patronage characterize electoral politics in Indonesia, the Philippines, and Malaysia, and what types of political networks are used to organize electoral competition and deliver patronage? Our third question bridges these two aspects, asking if certain types of patronage distribution tend to be associated with or map onto characteristic network forms. The fourth question delves into the effectiveness of this mode of politics: how do networks connect with voters and ensure that various forms of patronage boost the electoral success of the candidates who mobilize them? Having surveyed and assessed that descriptive and taxonomical terrain, our fifth and final question asks: how have these mobilization regimes emerged, and what explains the variations we find among them, both within and across countries?

Answering our first three questions yields the set of amalgams we term "electoral mobilization regimes" (see Table 3.1). This typology presents the gist of our first argument. The dominant mode in Malaysia is electoral mobilization through largely national-level parties, organized in encompassing coalitions. Candidates and politicians-in-office favor forms of macro-particularism as well as ethnic, geographic, or other community-level meso-particularism, throughout the electoral cycle (even if ticking upward at campaign times), alongside a healthy dose of programmatic goods and services. Far less common is micro-particularism, encompassing electoral handouts and other "retail" tactics. Why? The parties' capture of office over the long term – and from early in their nation-state's history – makes it relatively easy for them to focus on large-scale programmatic and patronage politics, thus rendering individual vote buying and similar practices unnecessary.

Parties are far weaker in the Philippines and Indonesia, but in the former we find local machines that are personalized and commonly family based. Like Malaysian parties, these machines are often enduring. They have ample access to state resources, through the country's extensive mechanisms of pork-barrel politics, which can be dispensed throughout the electoral cycle. Micro-particularism and collective meso-particularistic appeals are ubiquitous. Among our subtypes of macro approaches, morselization dominates; in effect, local politicians slice large programs into chunks that they hand out as political favors on a piecemeal basis, thus delivering maximum personalized value for money. Politicians with the right connections not only enjoy ready access to government resources, but they can also often bend government guidelines to their advantage.

In Indonesia, by contrast, though electoral rules ensure that national parties continue to play an important gatekeeping role, we find a preponderance of temporary networks: decades of disorganization of party life under authoritarian rule, combined with the much more recent adoption of candidate-centered electoral rules, mean that candidates mobilize personal teams for the campaign effort. After the polls, the teams commonly disband. The fact that many politicians lack consistent access to state resources means that they have little choice but to engage in micro-level distribution, backed up by meso-particularistic strategies; only a limited range of candidates can access the steady stream of state resources needed to make macro-particularistic strategies feasible. The tendency instead is to provide voters with a combination of personally bestowed individual gifts (micro-particularism) and club goods (meso-particularism), concentrated heavily around elections, and often financed with private resources. In sum, most Indonesian politicians lack not only the party-based largesse their Malaysian counterparts enjoy but also the extent of pork-barrel resources that flow downward in the Philippines amid a very weak party system and permeable state.

OUR CONTRIBUTIONS: RETHINKING THE WHAT, WHY, AND
WHENCE OF PATRONAGE POLITICS

Our approach contributes to the burgeoning literature on patronage politics, albeit with an approach quite distinct from prevailing contemporary work on the topic. First, we do not address only micro-level practices, the primary focus of the existing literature. Rather, we observe how varieties of patronage politics operate more broadly as coherent systems, in which certain institutional and network forms enable and coincide with particular patronage strategies. In other words, we extend beyond a focus on linkages between candidates and voters to a broader and more holistic concern with patronage linkages as they extend from the national government at the pinnacle of political systems to villages and urban wards at their base. Second, we probe the purposes patronage serves, concluding that much of the extant literature overestimates how contingent these distributions actually are; we find goals of brand building, credibility buying, and turf protection to be far more salient impetuses for patronage. Third, we step back from a primary focus merely on contemporary patterns, using a historical lens to examine the processes by which distinct varieties of patronage politics have emerged in each of our three settings. Fourth, we take seriously the social institutions embroiled in patronage politics, diverging from what is often a largely party-centered literature in our consideration not only of a wider range of networks but also of how the specific characteristics of social groups help to shape patronage patterns.

We summarize these contributions in turn.

Patronage in Context: Broadening the Analytical Lens

In our cross-national study, we were repeatedly struck by similarities both in the practices we observed across countries and in the language politicians used to describe those practices. Patronage politics is a concept that travels, not so much because the practice itself does so but because it evolves *in situ* in response to institutions, social settings, and political incentives that may on the surface seem quite comparable. On closer examination, however, we were able to dissect critical differences across the broad phenomenon of patronage politics. Through our development of the concept of electoral mobilization regimes, we conceive of patronage politics not merely as a set of discrete practices (vote buying, turnout buying, pork barrel, etc.) nor even as a homogenized syndrome of relationships ("clientelism") but as internally coherent and consistent systems of governance, with distinct clusterings of patronage forms and networks. By so doing, we advance an agenda for the comparative study of patronage politics (see also Berenschot and Aspinall 2020 and Stokes et al. 2013) that builds on but also goes beyond a focus on the microfoundations of clientelistic exchange that has been so central to much of the recent literature in this area.

Candidate Strategies of Patronage Distribution

With our delineation of electoral mobilization regimes as a foundation, we have proceeded to examine the strategic goals that motivate the distribution of patronage. For all the differences we trace across our three major cases, we note a common finding that runs counter to much of the conventional wisdom: we conclude that the element of reciprocity and contingency that features so heavily in literature on clientelism is frequently absent. Candidates and parties readily direct handouts to individuals and households, and meso-particularism to groups, in hopes that voters will reciprocate. They may even work to instill a sense of moral obligation in recipients and imply that resources are contingent on a voter's behavior. But we find that the conditions necessary to support the contingent distribution of patronage (i.e., the ability to monitor and punish individuals and/or groups if they fail to comply with a deal to deliver a vote or votes) are largely lacking in our cases. Campaigns do make some limited attempt to monitor their brokers, but devote very little effort to monitoring voters, either individually or collectively, and evince even less interest in punishing voters who defect. Instead, our work suggests that most of what we observe carries *no expectation of contingency* – neither from the perspective of voters who receive the funds nor even of the candidates who disburse them.

Rather, candidates distribute patronage to individuals and groups with different motivations. What may appear on the surface to be vote buying or turnout buying are efforts by candidates to boost their visibility (brand building), signal their viability (credibility buying), or prevent their supporters from defecting (turf protection). All this is undertaken in a noncontingent manner. Our analysis thus contributes to the growing study of clientelist-like strategies in the absence of clear contingency (Hicken and Nathan 2020). We hope these interventions might encourage sharper conceptualization within the literature, both to facilitate deeper and more incisive comparison and to interrogate commonly held assumptions – for instance, on the relative centrality of parties and expectations of contingency.

Explaining Patterns of Patronage Politics: States, Parties, and Electoral Systems

Another distinguishing element of our approach is a concern for not only analyzing contemporary patterns and dynamics but also understanding the origins of the patterns we find. Here, we advance a basically historical-institutional argument, reconnecting the study of patronage politics to political and institutional development from the late colonial era through to the emergence of postcolonial polities and the sometimes very tumultuous change experienced in the decades after independence (following Anderson 1983; Hutchcroft 2000; Kenny 2015).

As we place our study of patronage and clientelism in a broader historical and institutional context, we draw upon but also modify the insights of Martin Shefter (1994). The first key factor explaining the distinct origins of our array of electoral mobilization regimes is the long-term evolution of the state and of political parties. This includes examination of the origins of very distinct "constituencies for patronage" across our three major cases. A second and more proximate factor, albeit not without its own historical baggage, is the choice of electoral system. Third, we give close attention to the degree of discretion enjoyed by politicians in contemporary polities.

Distinct historical trajectories have shaped very distinct contemporary patterns of patronage politics in our three major cases. Under American colonial rule in the early twentieth century, the rapid expansion of electoral contestation in the Philippines undermined concomitant efforts to create a relatively insulated bureaucracy. This led, as Shefter would have anticipated, to the emergence of a strong constituency for patronage. This constituency remained intact into the postindependence period, and the combination of a perpetually permeable bureaucracy and inchoate political parties nurtured a mobilization regime rooted in local machines. These machines were created as the American colonial regime extended electoral contestation upward from towns to provinces to a national assembly, and they were sustained by ready access to and discretion over state-based patronage sources. After independence, local machines' ties to the two (largely indistinguishable) national parties commonly shifted with the prevailing political winds.

In Indonesia, the *beamtenstaat* developed by Dutch colonials in the early twentieth century disintegrated amid the tumult of Japanese occupation and the subsequent protracted war for independence. The period of parliamentary democracy in the 1950s was characterized by a highly fragmented form of patronage politics, with political parties effectively carving up much of state among themselves. The coherence of the bureaucracy was restored after the military assumed leadership of the state in the violent convulsion of the mid-1960s, but this led not to a "constituency for bureaucratic autonomy" but rather to the harnessing of the bureaucracy as the effective vehicle for the distribution of patronage. With the return of democratic elections, after the fall of Suharto's authoritarian government in 1998, candidates competed in an environment where the enduring strength of the bureaucracy limits politicians' access to discretionary resources for patronage. With limited access to state or party resources that could build and sustain local machines, Indonesian candidates instead rely on candidate-centered ad hoc teams in order to mobilize voters.

Finally, in Malaysia, the transition to independence led not to the *collapse* of the colonial beamtenstaat but rather to its *capture* by the well-organized United Malays National Organisation (UMNO) – intent on using its control over the state to consolidate its position. The bureaucracy became a rich source of patronage and an effective tool for UMNO and its partners in the dominant Barisan Nasional coalition.

The result, in a nutshell, has been strong local machines in the Philippines (with very substantial access to government resources split among myriad political actors), ad hoc machines in Indonesia (with politicians enjoying less access to government resources than their Philippine counterparts, albeit in similarly fragmented ways), and party-based patronage in Malaysia (where a single ruling coalition was able to monopolize access to government resources).

While this examination of political parties and bureaucracies is central to our explanatory framework, we also emphasize the impact of electoral systems as they have emerged and evolved across the three countries. In Indonesia and the Philippines, candidate-centric systems prevail, placing a premium on building personal bases of electoral support. Indonesia's shift to open-list proportional representation, between 2004 and 2014, led directly to the dramatic deepening of personalized patronage linking candidates and voters; thanks to strong regulations that perpetuate the role of national parties, however, the political system has been spared the fate that some commentators call "Philippinization." This phrase refers to the extreme weakness of national parties in the neighboring archipelago, where several elements of the electoral system strongly privilege candidates over parties – particularly in the absence of Indonesian-style regulation of parties. In sum, the choice of electoral systems has perpetuated the longstanding candidate-centric polity in the Philippines and led to a deepening of grassroots patronage in Indonesia. By contrast, in Malaysia, a single-member district plurality system provides some incentive to cultivate a personal vote, but absent the intra-party competition that characterizes many elections in the Philippines or Indonesia. Furthermore, in part given party control over nominations and most patronage distribution, party label carries much more weight for both voters and candidates.

While we devote substantial space to analyzing these cross-country patterns, we recognize that even distinctly national features of institutional and social history also may vary across regions or communities within a given country. In Chapter 8, we explored this within-country variation and identified how subnational differences correspond with, and sometimes supplement, our overall theoretical framework. Dissimilarities in the nature of state capacity, local economies, and the autonomy and hierarchy of social groups, we explained, produce subnational patterns of patronage politics that may tend to be more predatory and coercive in the peripheral regions of states. Thus, considerable subnational variation in attributes and tendencies complicates the conjunctures of networks and patronage types that we identify as dominant national modes. Moreover, as we stress in the foregoing chapters, we find the whole gamut of networks and of patronage types in each of our cases. Indeed, the subnational variation we identify is sometimes nearly as striking as the cross-national dominant patterns we trace – and we expect to see similar internal mutability in any other polity, as well.

Social Group Characteristics: A Further Determinant of Patronage Strategies

Our study also extends the frame prevalent in the literature by highlighting the ways in which broader social and institutional environments help shape the mix of strategies that candidates pursue – and, conversely, strategies pursued by those who are the beneficiaries of politicians' largesse. We show how the political-institutional environment – notably historically determined features of the state and party system, alongside electoral institutions – influences politicians' incentives and capacity to adopt micro-, meso-, or macro-particularistic strategies. But at various points in our analysis, we have also demonstrated how the characteristics of social groups affect the viability of contingency-focused patronage and the relative preference for targeting networks of affect (identity-based groups) versus networks of benefit (economically oriented and geographic groups) with meso-particularism. Finally, we have also explored how, at least in these cases, patronage distribution relies on and reinforces existing social networks and identities while also transcending those divisions.

The historical development and nature of social networks help shape how politicians organize their efforts and guide the sorts of patronage they deliver. Specifically, we focus on the relative autonomy, cohesion, and hierarchy of social groups as important variables. In terms of autonomy, Malaysia and Indonesia represent the two extremes (with the Philippines falling between the two). In Malaysia, most major social networks have attached themselves to political parties, facilitating meso- and macro-particularism targeted to well-defined groups of voters through party channels. By contrast, the more fragmented and autonomous social structure in Indonesia supports a plethora of social organizations that bargain with individual candidates (not parties) in order to secure club goods around elections. In the Philippines, relative to Indonesia, we observe less emphasis on group-targeted meso-particularism (club goods). There, we are more likely to see meso-particularistic pork-barrel projects benefiting geographic entities (congressional districts, municipalities, villages, etc.). As explained in Chapter 7, social groups in Indonesia, given their *relatively* higher levels of prominence, cohesion, and hierarchy, generally have greater electoral value than do social groupings in the Philippines, and their greater degree of autonomy from local machines and parties provides them with a greater degree of bargaining power to wrest patronage concessions from politicians. (As noted earlier, however, Philippine elected officials have access to quantities of discretionary resources that most of their counterparts in Indonesia can only dream of.)

In sum, our framework views patronage resources and the networks through which they flow as working in tandem; as representing a complex logic, but in which expectations of contingency or reciprocity are aspirational at best; as deeply rooted in historical and institutional factors; as reflecting not only top-down strategies, but also the shape and character of social groups and networks on the ground; and as being, hence, inherently difficult (albeit not, we believe, impossible) to curb. Before proceeding to the impact of patronage on democratic governance, and onward to an examination of options for reform, we broaden our comparative gaze beyond the three major cases on which we have focused thus far.

EXTENDING OUR COMPARATIVE ANALYSIS

In introducing our three major types of electoral mobilization regimes, we have emphasized that they are neither unique nor exhaustive. In other words, we are not claiming a one-of-a-kind stature for any of the key networks we have observed, whether Malaysia's party-based machines, the Philippines' well-established local machines, or Indonesia's ad hoc machines. Moreover, we expect to find similar patterns of micro-, meso-, and macro-particularism in settings throughout the world – patronage politics is prevalent in one form or another across the gamut of polities. Just as importantly, we are not claiming that the three types of electoral mobilization regimes examined in this study constitute the universe of such regimes throughout the world. We hope that our analysis will encourage other scholars to identify such regimes as they function in other settings.

In identifying additional cases that exhibit our three key types of electoral mobilization regimes, we focus in particular on our secondary cases; selected insights from comparative literature enable us to extend the range of cases even further. Of the three types of regimes described in this book, it is Malaysia's party-based regime that exhibits the largest number of analogs around the world, including, for instance, Japan, Mexico, and Turkey. Our secondary cases of Singapore or Timor-Leste also fit within this category: they rely on strong parties and lean toward aggregated rather than micro-level distributions.

The process of decolonization in Singapore loosely resembled Malaysia's: the British phased in local bureaucrats and elected politicians with progressively greater authority. Singapore's first two years of full independence were, in fact, as part of Malaysia, though differing racial patterns and vying personal ambitions in particular ended that experiment quickly, in 1965. In the process, however, the People's Action Party (PAP) consolidated its control. The dominant social cleavage structuring Singaporean political parties of the late 1950s through early 1960s was class. Class overlapped with ethnicity but incompletely and more at the level of sub-ethnic identification than the broad categories dominant in Malaysia. Chinese-educated ethnic-Chinese gravitated toward the PAP's most serious challenger, a splinter party called Barisan Sosialis (Socialist Front). Capitalizing on the same Cold War anti-leftist momentum that delegitimated class-based challengers in Malaysia (and indeed, in coordination with Malaya as the two polities moved toward merger), the PAP detained key Barisan politicians, hobbling this last real threat. The initially left-wing PAP then drifted progressively toward the political center, pursuing a developmentalist agenda that embraced both capitalist initiative and strong public support for housing, healthcare, and other needs (albeit eschewing terms such as "welfare"). Successive changes to electoral rules (for instance, shifting from fully single-member to mixed single-member and multimember constituencies), tight curbs on campaigns and civil liberties broadly, and attacks on opposition politicians (commonly through lawsuits that left them bankrupt and thus disqualified), combined with the simple fact of the PAP's occupation of the vast middle ground of politics, served to keep the PAP firmly emplaced. The PAP's successful pursuit of economic development and its frequent reminders to the population of Singapore's vulnerability amid larger (and heavily Muslim) neighbors reinforced its dominance.

As in Malaysia, state and party have fused to a substantial extent over time: the PAP claims credit as a party rather than on behalf of the state, for Singapore's progress and achievements (exaggerating the backwater status of the already-cosmopolitan colony upon the PAP's ascent to power). Although its politicians work assiduously to build personal ties with voters, they always stress their party label and the support received from their party machinery. Opposition parties have made headway in recent years largely by replicating that practice, albeit without benefit of significant party, let alone state, resources. The PAP uses its control of the state to limit the extent to which opposition parties can direct or claim credit for state funding even in the constituencies they hold. Moreover, to an extraordinary degree, parties control who stands for office and where. While independent candidates can and do contest (usually losing their very high deposits after securing trivial shares of the vote), joining a national party is the only viable path to office in contemporary Singapore (see Weiss 2020c for elaboration).

If a party-based regime characterizes politics in Southeast Asia's wealthiest country, Singapore, it also does so in one of the region's poorest: Timor-Leste. In this relatively new nation, parties are the key political actors. Their prominence is both a legacy of the country's independence struggle against Indonesia – with the sacrifices that struggle entailed generating lasting loyalties to pro-independence parties and leaders – and a product of the country's strongly party-focused electoral system (closed-list proportional representation with a single national constituency). Even as new patterns of patronage and corruption have taken hold, in part fueled by Timor-Leste's oil industry, relatively strong parties continue to mobilize around programmatic appeals and the charisma of their leaders.

In the course of fieldwork during Timor-Leste's national elections in 2017, we were surprised to encounter relatively low levels of micro-particularism, especially electoral handouts. Just over the border in Indonesian West Timor, an area with similar clans and ethnic patterns, political candidates adopt the usual Indonesian pattern of personalized success teams and delivery of cash and other gifts to individual voters. In Timor-Leste, we found very little evidence of retail clientelism: just 4 percent of respondents to a national exit survey conducted that year said they had received a payment for their vote, in contrast to about 30 percent in our comparable survey in Indonesia. Party cadres, or *militantes*, are instead the key actors in political mobilization. To the extent that patronage flows lubricate the political system, the key recipients are party leaders as well as community-level notables, such as former combatants, contractors, and village chiefs able to deliver a bloc vote (see Aspinall et al. 2018 for a detailed account of our findings). The contrast with Indonesia is instructive: both Indonesia and Timor-Leste made political transitions at around the same time, Indonesia toward democracy and Timor-Leste becoming independent, in the late 1990s and early 2000s. Both countries began these periods with at least the potential for relatively strong parties dominating the electoral and patronage landscape, but only Timor-Leste retained this system – with the country's party-centered electoral system serving as a centripetal counter-current to the extreme localism of the country's fragmented social structures.

As for local political machines broadly comparable to those we have described in the Philippines, Thailand is one obvious example. Such machines have certainly played important roles in the country, even if they have more recent origins than and are not nearly so well-entrenched as their Philippine counterparts. Whereas we can trace the phenomenon of local political machines in the Philippines to the expansion of elective posts early in the American colonial era, those in Thailand emerged only with the introduction of parliamentary democracy in the latter decades of the twentieth century. As Prajak Kongkirati (2013, 68–78) explains, local businesspersons were drawn to politics because of the value of connections with the national government – whether for special privileges (in the realms of natural resource extraction, construction, or businesses requiring special government permits) or for protection (related to drug trafficking, smuggling, illegal logging, prostitution, gambling, etc.). Because provincial entrepreneurs tended to pursue quite localized business opportunities, "[t]heir province forms their business 'enclave' or 'fiefdom' that they cannot afford to lose. ... In order to make a political impression nationally, provincial elites have to strive for a solid local political base" (Prajak 2013, 71–73). Local political families commonly put relatives in local offices, but the real prize – given both parliamentary structures and bureaucratic centralization – is to become a member of the national legislature. National-level dynamics could thus readily threaten the strength and endurance of local political machines; this vulnerability was apparent first in the quite successful "war" that populist Prime Minister Thaksin Shinawatra launched against provincial bosses in 2003 (see Prajak 2014, 395–401) and later in the wake of two military coups (in 2006 and 2014) that successively reduced the scope of electoral competition. In the Philippines, by contrast, many local political machines have seen the populist Duterte administration curb their influence (see Gera and Hutchcroft 2021), but there is little reason to doubt their ultimate staying power in the decades to come.

Third and finally, it is difficult to find exact cognates for Indonesia's regime of ad hoc teams coexisting with national parties. To be sure, in numerous polities, candidate-centered electoral systems generate intense competition among individual candidates, leading to the creation of personal teams and high levels of micro-particularism reminiscent of the Indonesian pattern. Relevant examples with which we are most familiar include the highly fragmented and personalized patterns of electioneering found in certain Pacific island states, such as Papua New Guinea and the Solomon Islands, where free-wheeling and highly clientelist forms of electoral competition revolve around politically influential individuals and bear more than a passing resemblance to the Indonesian pattern – albeit with a particularly heavy emphasis on clan, ethnic, and other forms of identity-based mobilization (see, for example, Kurer 2007; Wood 2014). Peru's political system, as Muñoz (2019) documents, also combines weak national parties with fluid patterns of political alignments and limited local machines at the subnational level. Candidates rely on elected community leaders, known as *dirigentes sociales,* to broker their relations with voters in a clientelistic political environment that leans heavily on one-off exchanges at election time rather than long-term relational clientelism. The highly fragmented political maps of such settings are, however, distinct from Indonesia's, where, as we have explained, electoral regulations continue to impart a ballast to political parties – at least as gatekeepers – that is frequently absent in other systems that combine candidate-focused electoral mobilization with high doses of micro- and meso-particularism.

It also seems likely that the Indonesian pattern is relatively rare because, in most cases, ad hoc and relatively temporary electoral teams tend to evolve gradually in the direction of more permanent local political machines. This shift happens as local politicians gradually colonize sources of state funding and use them to establish more permanent bases and clienteles. We even see elements of this pattern developing in Indonesia itself, as elected politicians struggle to wrest control over resources from local bureaucrats. As we discussed in Chapter 5, for instance, the increasing availability of "aspiration funds" allows members of subnational legislatures to build more permanent support bases among recipients of these resources. It is instructive that where we see the first hints of the emergence of local machines is around local executive offices, where incumbents enjoy relatively greater discretion over government resource allocation and where majoritarian electoral institutions do not involve intra-party competition. The rise of locally influential political dynasties likewise possibly presages the eventual emergence of more permanent local machines.

EFFECTS ON DEMOCRATIC GOVERNANCE

Throughout this study, we have focused on the mechanics, organization, and origins of the patterns of patronage politics we have observed across Southeast

Asia. Our primary goal has been to understand the inner logics of these systems, what makes them cohere, and their origins. Motivating that focus to a significant degree are the effects of these phenomena on democracy and governance. We thus come full circle by touching upon the consequences of the systems we have observed.

The comparative literature offers robust findings that patronage politics tends to produce bad outcomes for governance and democracy. As one of us has previously summarized, the "consensus in the literature is that clientelism has profound negative implications for the way in which democracy functions, citizen attitudes about the quality of their democracy, and the capacity of governments to produce needed public policies" (Hicken 2011, 302). Even though we did not focus on these implications while conducting our field research in Southeast Asia, along the way we found plenty of evidence to support all three propositions. Throughout the countries we studied, we encountered politicians intervening in programs that were supposed to direct government assistance to citizens who most needed it, or where it would promote the most beneficial developmental or welfare outcome. Politicians instead often intervened to direct funds to where they would instead deliver maximum political benefit. In the Philippines, even typhoon relief is allocated according to political criteria rather than going to the places of greatest need (Hicken et al. 2015); a similar logic has skewed local-level distribution of COVID-19 "social amelioration" subsidies (Gera 2020). Likewise in Indonesia, social assistance funds intended to help needy local groups are routinely allocated to clients of local district heads (Aspinall and Berenschot 2019, 163–75). And in Malaysia, opposition parties complained that their unequal opportunity to distribute, and to ensure their constituents received, state-funded aid packages during the COVID-19 pandemic (Ngu 2021) was par for the patronage course.

Even more perniciously, the politicians making such interventions frequently undermine bureaucratic capacity and independence: subverting policy-planning processes, sabotaging systems of accountability, and appointing cronies and supporters rather than professionals to key posts. In each country, patronage and clientelism have also gone hand-in-hand with corruption, most obviously in the Philippines and Indonesia, where incumbents plunder public coffers in order to fill war chests that can be used for vote-buying operations (or to repay the debts accrued in recent campaigns). As we alluded to in Chapter 6, in 2013, a pork-barrel scandal dating back to 2007–2009, during the presidency of Gloria Macapagal Arroyo, rocked the Philippines. A number of legislators were alleged to have channeled funds from the Priority Development Assistance Fund (PDAF) to spurious NGOs under their own control (many set up for the express purpose of serving as conduits of pork-barrel funds). These NGOs flagrantly violated guidelines for disbursement of funds, according to a report of the Commission on Audit, with one particularly notorious NGO receiving PHP10 billion (roughly USD210 million) in taxpayer funds (Holmes 2019,

297–301, 342–47). Another dramatic case came toward the end of our research in 2019, when Indonesia's Corruption Eradication Commission arrested Golkar politician Bowo Sidik Pangarso in connection with bribery in a procurement process, and paraded before the press 8 billion rupiah (about USD552,000) of his ill-gotten gains. The money consisted of 20,000 and 50,000 rupiah notes tucked into 400,000 envelopes and packed in 54 cardboard boxes – ready for his vote-buying operation in the legislative election that year (Hariyanto 2019). Malaysia also has ample corruption scandals, but the proceeds of the deals tend to be far more centralized or for the benefit of one or a few specific bad actors. Most famous is Malaysia's Najib Razak and his massive 1MDB scandal, as part of which USD700 million was diverted from a government investment fund to Najib's personal bank accounts, much of it to fund UMNO's 2013 election campaign (Wright and Brown 2015).

More broadly, patronage politics, as we explained in Chapter 7, tends to reinforce class inequality and strengthen the grip of wealthy actors on the political system: the dizzying sums political aspirants must invest in their campaigns often mean either that only rich candidates can win office, or that candidates must depend on wealthy business donors – support that must be repaid in office with favors and benefits. In this way, clientelism and patronage politics encourage elite capture of policy-making processes and entrench collusive relationships between political and business elites across Southeast Asia (You 2015). Put differently, engagement with patronage politics – whether directly, or indirectly through campaign contributions – is an important strategy of the oligarchic actors whose dominance has been so remarked upon in analyses of Southeast Asia (Gomez and Jomo 1997; Hutchcroft 1998; Robison and Hadiz 2004; Winters 2013).

Both politicians and ordinary citizens we encountered through our research frequently demonstrated that they recognize these effects of patronage politics, even if they saw no easy escape from them. Politicians, even while explaining their vote-buying operations and the vast investments these entailed, frequently shook their heads or shrugged their shoulders as they explained that they had no alternative but to compete in this way. They typically blamed voters and their incessant demands for patronage. Ordinary citizens, while often freely admitting that they expected their politicians to deliver largesse, even more often expressed disillusionment with official corruption and spoke in cynical terms about the very politicians from whom they expected benefits. Participants in broker and voter focus groups we ran in both the Philippines and Indonesia, for example, combined disarmingly straightforward explanations of how they expected their politicians to deliver cash to them in the lead-up to voting day with equally blunt messages about the effects of this practice. In focus groups in Central Java, many participants said that they knew the system of "money politics" encouraged, or even necessitated, their politicians to be corrupt. Some stated that politicians who distributed cash to voters rarely bothered to reappear in their villages between elections, feeling little need to pay attention to constituents once they had purchased their votes. Many participants explained that it made sense in such circumstances for ordinary people to make a little money for themselves at election time. As one low-level broker who worked for a candidate distributing cash to voters explained:

If we look at our experiences at the last election, it's really a cause of great concern for the future of democracy of this nation. It's not clear where we are taking our nation if the votes of the people can be bought. I really hope that what happened will not happen again in the future. . . . Representatives of the people? If it's like what happened last time, honest people will never be able to become representatives of the people. Not if they don't have money. That's the main point I got from my experience.[1]

Similar cynicism can be found among ordinary citizens in the Philippines, explains economist Emmanuel de Dios, where government is often viewed as "an abstraction, an alienated entity, whose only palpable dimension is the episodic patronage dispensed by bosses and politicians, which merely reinforces the poor's real condition of dependence" (de Dios and Hutchcroft 2002).

Such attitudes, in turn, contribute to repeated cycles of democratic setbacks experienced in Southeast Asia. Indeed, if disillusionment with "money politics" is present even among poor voters who receive patronage, it can be particularly severe among middle-class citizens who do not need such largesse. This tendency helps to explain the frequently ambivalent, if not downright hostile, attitudes to democratic government many middle-class Southeast Asians evince. In the Philippines, for example, it has long been observed that, as Schaffer (2005, 10) puts it, "Many in the middle and upper classes ... find elections to be a source of both frustration and anxiety. Election after election, politicians who they perceive to be inept, depraved, and/or corrupt are returned to power." Many middle-class and elite citizens locate the source of this problem in poor voters, whom they see as ignorantly and selfishly selling their vote to *trapos* (traditional politicians) at election times. From time to time, such disillusionment leads them toward authoritarian political positions, as when Rodrigo Duterte's persona as a tough leader who could clean up the country's dirty and ineffective politics helped propel him into office. Mark Thompson observes, for instance, that "Duterte's core supporters are from the middle class, not the poor," and his rise "has been driven by middle-class concerns about drugs and crime generally, as well as crumbling infrastructure, and continued corruption" (Thompson 2016, 58; see also Cruz 2016). In Thailand, too, we see broadly similar dynamics in frequent urban middle-class disdain for poor voters, which has itself contributed to the deep political conflicts that have rent that country's democratic politics in recent decades (see, for example, Connors 2003; Callahan 2005, 105; Glassman 2010).

---

[1] FGD notes, August 21, 2014, Rembang.

In Indonesia, the fragmented, personalistic, and collusive nature of the party and electoral system, as well as the identity-based cleavages that are a key determinant of voting behavior among middle-class and other voters, complicates the picture. When people criticize "money politics" in Indonesia, they relatively rarely target poor voters, more often attacking politicians. Even so, it is noteworthy that Prabowo Subianto tried to build his appeal on condemnation of money politics and elite corruption, and attained disproportionate support in his quest for the presidency among relatively urban, wealthy, and better-educated voters, especially in 2014 (Aspinall 2015).

Malaysia diverges from our other cases, insofar that the primary deleterious effect of patronage on democratic governance has been its buttressing of a decades-long system of electoral-authoritarian rule. Even so, in Malaysia, we find widespread recognition among citizens that vote buying is inappropriate and frustration among voters when politicians' rent-seeking grows *too* egregious, as in the case of the 1MDB scandal and a litany of progenitors. There is even open consternation within UMNO at the fact that it is for internal *party* elections that vote buying is most rampant: with increasingly high spoils attached to party office, vote buying has permeated UMNO elections, resisting efforts at reform (Transparency International 2010, 75–79; Funston 2016, 111–12). Frustration with patronage and its effects has contributed to support for political reform in Malaysia, particularly among the same sorts of urban middle-class voters inclined to push back in our other cases. But citizens tend to view meso-particularism as legitimate, and also see little wrong with macro-level strategies of credit-claiming and hijacked programs. Particularly important, the political economy is by now largely structured significantly around the same communal divisions as the long-dominant parties. As a result, the line between particularism and programmatic distribution can be very difficult to discern, as when dominant parties offer benefits that target the Bumiputera majority but do so in ways that parcel out benefits to particular groups or individuals – e.g., the phenomenon of privileged "UMNOputera," allied also with ethnic-Chinese business elites (Heng 1997, 289). The majority of voters thus have a vested material interest in maintaining the system as it is.

While we have emphasized in this study the self-sustaining nature of the systems of patronage politics we encounter in Southeast Asia – those in Malaysia and the Philippines have survived for many decades – we should not understate the role they play in undermining democratic legitimacy and, ultimately, stability. Even if the electoral mobilization regimes we have described do provide mechanisms for feedback and limited accountability among citizens, brokers, and politicians, the dominance of patronage nonetheless saps Southeast Asian governments' responsiveness and effectiveness and undermines citizens' trust in their politicians and political institutions. As such, patronage politics contributes in important ways to the periodic crises of democracy that run through these countries' modern histories.

PROSPECTS FOR SUBSTANTIVE REFORM

Thus far, we have put considerable emphasis on the staying power of patronage systems, with our framework helping both scholars and policy practitioners to understand varieties of patronage politics as they have emerged from specific and protracted historical-institutional contexts. The electoral mobilization regimes we have identified, moreover, operate as coherent and complex systems, stretching far beyond the short-term decision trees of candidates and voters to encompass a veritable forest of actors: executives, legislatures, and bureaucracies at both national and subnational levels; political-party operatives and leaders of societal organizations from the capital downward to the village level; local family-controlled machines comprising everyone from loyal relatives to needy hangers-on to trigger-happy goons; the hired talent who manages the activities of a *tim sukses* in the lead-up to election day and then ditches the campaign for greener pastures; and countless other personnel that vary from one context to another. Each of these coherent systems of patronage has been crafted by generations of political actors operating according to the constraints and incentives that distinct historical and institutional legacies bequeath. Reformers who want to set these polities on new paths will thus inevitably face formidable obstacles.

But change is not impossible; the systems we describe are not impervious to being altered through well-crafted reforms. While historical inheritances cannot be altered, critical junctures sometimes arise at which it is possible to reform the incentive structures within which political actors operate. Among possible reforms – including changes designed to decrease citizens' vulnerability, improve their access to public services, and decrease politicians' discretion over resource distribution – we highlight here the potential role of electoral-institutional reform. Electoral systems are an obvious target of reform, as they are central to shaping the incentives parties, candidates, and voters face; even more fundamentally, the choice of electoral system can play a critical role in determining whether a polity will be party-centric or candidate-centric. Why is this important? While patronage politics can exist under any system, party-centric rather than candidate-centric electoral systems tend to favor programmatic over particularistic interests and strategies, and to foster longer time horizons and greater party discipline (Hicken 2019). To the extent that patronage endures in a party-centric system, as in the case of Malaysia, personalized micro-particularism is less likely to predominate. Candidates may still cultivate a personal vote, on the premise that familiarity breeds loyalty (and assists politicians in understanding what specifically their constituents most need or value), but such a system also obliges them to stress what their *party* can deliver.

We have fairly good information, based on past experimentation and experience, as to what interventions actually change incentives or practices and in what directions. This is not to suggest that electoral-system reform is a magic bullet with no potential to trigger unintended consequences. The case of Malaysia reminds us that strong parties can coexist with high levels of patronage and low levels of democracy; at the same time, the longstanding dominance of Malaysia's patronage-oriented ruling party rested also on high levels of institutional manipulation, including the systematic use of malapportionment and gerrymandering. Across different contexts, and with goals that must be carefully attuned to specific contexts, institutional reform is one of the only levers available to reformers. It thus remains an appealing possibility, whether for nurturing programmatic parties in a candidate-centric system or for changing the stakes by building a more level playing field.

We also fully acknowledge that electoral-system reform must be viewed within a larger constellation of reform measures. One major realm, beyond the focus of this study, is reform of bureaucratic systems – including, for example, efforts to increase bureaucratic capacity; reduce politicization of appointment, transfer, and promotion processes; promote greater transparency in the provision of public goods; enhance the integrity of auditing procedures; and expand freedom-of-information statutes. Measures to limit politicians' discretionary control over state resources, provide transparent state subsidies to parties, and encourage open and more centralized party nomination procedures can complement such steps (see Hicken 2007; 2019a).

While it is beyond the scope of our analysis to provide a full picture of the potential and pitfalls of electoral-system reform, we briefly examine two cases: Japan's 1994 reform as a generally positive example of electoral-system redesign and Indonesia's more recent shift from open- to closed-list proportional representation as a generally negative example. Together, these two cases help to reinforce the point that relatively small changes in the institutional environment can have big impacts on political behavior – even to the point of challenging what may be viewed as deeply entrenched historical patterns.

Japan's pre-1994 electoral system, the single nontransferable vote (SNTV), ensured a high level of intra-party competition. As a result, candidates of the ruling Liberal Democratic Party (LDP) needed to differentiate themselves on the basis not of policies or party platform but rather on their ability to dispense patronage to their constituents. While the LDP carefully managed the system of intra-party competition at the national level (e.g., to ensure that legislators from the same constituency had distinct rather than overlapping policy specializations), LDP candidates had strong incentives to establish personal support organizations, or *kōenkai*, at the local level (Rosenbluth and Thies 2010, 56). Politicians could not count on attention to policies or substantive debates to raise their profile during campaigns; instead, they "maintained *kōenkai* by spending exorbitant amounts of time and money holding regular meetings with supporters, attending funerals and weddings, and organizing karaoke parties, golf tournaments, and bus trips to hot spring resorts" (Carlson 2007, 5). This micro-particularism did not extend to outright vote buying, given strictly enforced legal prohibitions on the practice,[2] but it was supplemented with huge quantities of meso-particularism targeted to constituencies as well as to such favored groups as farmers, small businesspersons, and the construction industry. "Unable to distinguish themselves on the basis of party label or ideology," Greg Noble (2010, 242–43) writes, "backbench politicians lobbied hard for opportunities to claim credit for bringing home the *tonkatsu* (pork)." The "centrifugal" impact of SNTV, with its high level of intra-party competition, nurtured within the LDP a set of rigid and "hierarchically organized factions," such that "each LDP candidate within a given district was backed by a different faction" (Rosenbluth and Thies 2010, 64–65).

Amid ongoing scandals involving leading LDP figures, including in 1988 and 1992, growing disenchantment with the political system brought mounting demands for reform – demands that soon converged on calls for electoral-system change (McElwain 2014, 97). The LDP's majority collapsed, in part due to defections, and, in the wake of the 1993 elections, the opposition took power – thus ending nearly four decades of LDP control over the government. A new electoral system was put in place the following year. Combining first-past-the-post with closed-list proportional representation in a mixed-member system, this reform led to major shifts in the character of Japanese politics. As Greg Noble (2010, 260) explains:

> The end of SNTV greatly decreased intraparty competition and reliance on delivery of pork barrel spending as a way for candidates to differentiate themselves. Party leaders gained more effective control over nominations. The role of factions declined, while party labels, ideology, and programmatic intentions grew more important, symbolized by the increasingly large role played by party manifestos.

Another important political reform supplemented electoral-system change: public financing of elections. This reform bolstered party leadership at the expense of factions. Three other major factors also helped erode particularism and spur a concomitant increase in programmatic spending: demographic change (an aging population, as well as shifts from rural areas to cities and suburbs, both of which increased concern for social welfare programs), a decline in partisan affiliation (with independents comprising more than half of the electorate by the mid-1990s), and administrative reforms in the early 2000s that streamlined the central bureaucracy and gave the prime minister and cabinet greater ability to control spending (Noble 2010, 257–64). Thus, electoral reform was a major driver, but not the only impetus, for a reduced role for patronage politics relative to programmatic appeals.[3]

---

[2] Rosenbluth and Thies (2010, 56) assert that the secret ballot made vote buying "impossible." On the contrary, we know from Philippine and Indonesian experience that vote buying can coexist quite easily with the secret ballot, even absent presumed contingency (as we discuss earlier).

[3] See Scheiner (2008) for a more critical assessment of the effects of these reforms on money politics in Japan.

Indonesia's experience with electoral-system reform between 2004 and 2014, already touched upon in Chapter 2, is primarily a story of the negative outcomes of an ill-considered shift from closed-list (party-centric) to open-list (candidate-centric) proportional representation. Though the change came about as a result of a court decision, the intent of those who supported the challenge to the existing system was at least partly democratic: they wanted to reduce the role of party brokers (amid popular disgust over reports of corruption in the construction of party lists) and to give voters greater voice in the choice of candidates on party lists. As we have explored in earlier chapters, the impact of the reform has been highly detrimental to democratic structures. Parties have become far less coherent, as intra-party competition puts a premium on the personal vote as opposed to programmatic appeals.

This change has led to an expansion and deepening of patronage politics; if the flow of money was formerly most apparent as political-party leaders gathered to choose and rank candidates, it can now be found at the grassroots level throughout the archipelago. This change, in turn, greatly increased the cost of electoral campaigns, with corrupt activities all too often a key source of finance. As one of us has concluded, the outcome was "a vicious cycle in which electoral patronage fuels corruption which in turns erodes the faith of Indonesian voters in their parties and elected representatives, making them ever more susceptible to patronage politics" (Aspinall 2019, 108; see also Aspinall 2014a). If in Japan one found a (relatively) virtuous cycle , in Indonesia, other reform achievements fell victim to this dynamic. A national legislature comprised largely of politicians with strong incentives to fund their individual campaigns through corruption, for example, became increasingly hostile to Indonesia's popular and effective Corruption Eradication Commission (Komisi Pemberantasan Korupsi, KPK). In 2019, these politicians passed amendments to the law governing the KPK that severely reduced the Commission's authority and autonomy (Butt 2019).

These two contrasting examples, of generally positive lessons from Japan and generally negative ones from Indonesia, highlight the capacity of electoral-system reform to shift incentives and change the way that politics is done – whether for better or for worse. Importantly, reforms do not operate in a vacuum. In a positive scenario, electoral-system reform may combine with other types of reform (as well as other factors, including demographic shifts) to weaken well-entrenched constituencies for patronage. Deeply entrenched historical inheritances, in other words, need not be destiny.

We must hasten to add, however, that the promulgation of electoral-system reform is very much the exception rather than the rule. There is a high degree of "stickiness" to most institutions, including electoral systems, with clear disincentives for politicians elected under a particular set of rules to want to shift to new arrangements. In addition, those who have historical experience with certain electoral systems – whether election officials, party bosses, candidates, or broader electorates – often lack the comparative vista even to be aware of the range of options that exist worldwide. In the analysis of one of our number (Hicken 2019b), drawing on lessons of reform experiences, three conditions must each be present for change to get underway. The first condition is *systematic failure*, which occurs "when the current electoral system fails to meet the normative expectations of the public." While this may be a necessary factor, it is not sufficient; indeed, some political systems may experience sustained systematic failure absent any push for reform. This leads to the second condition, a *catalytic event*, generally some sort of crisis through which key political actors "draw the connection between political and/or economic woes and the electoral system and thus generate demand for reform." In Japan, this came in the late 1980s and early 1990s, amid successive corruption scandals embroiling top LDP leaders. The third condition is a *specific calculus among incumbent politicians that reform is actually to their advantage*, whether because they view it as beneficial for their party ("outcome motivation") or because they expect support for reform to produce short-term electoral gains ("act motivation") (Hicken 2019b, 59–60).

In sum, the promulgation of electoral-system reform (or reform more generally) is not just willed into happening; rather, it becomes possible at particular historical junctures where these three conditions are present. Change is not easy, but nor is it impossible. While we emphasize the degree to which our electoral mobilization regimes have emerged over the *longue durée* of political history, as the result of specific historical-institutional factors, they can indeed be altered via reform. Our analysis suggests, too, that while redesign of electoral institutions offers one of the most promising avenues for reform, other context-specific changes may complement and amplify those benefits – especially reforms that encourage the emergence of a constituency for bureaucratic autonomy (such as the nurturing of more professional career pathways in the civil service, curbs on the capacity of politicians to exercise particularistic discretion over programmatic initiatives, or introduction of public funding for political parties).

We can now proceed to a brief discussion of what is *not* effective, focusing especially on well-meaning efforts to hector the electorate about the evils of vote buying. The exhortations common in voter-education drives – not to "waste your vote," or to "take the money and vote your conscience" – have not had significant impact where they have been tried, and, some evidence suggests, may make matters worse (Hicken et al. 2018). By understanding voters' propensity to sell their votes in simply transactional, instrumental terms, anti-vote-buying campaigns often display a strong class bias. In his analysis of contemporary Philippine elections, Frederic Schaffer (2008, 138, 143) explains that those running the campaigns are typically middle- and upper-class individuals who believe "that an important way to combat vote buying is to provide poor voters with a moral education to, in the words of one journalist, 'rescue' them 'from the bondage of ignorance.'" Many poor Filipinos, however, view voter-education materials as offensive – indeed, as "an attack on their dignity."

In fact, voters who accept handouts from candidates are generally not less knowledgeable than their crusading counterparts; they simply hold different preferences and face different incentives. In our view, it is far more promising to change underlying incentives and inducements than to discourage malfeasance through moral appeals alone (whether directed at voters or at candidates and other political actors). Thus, we emphasize the virtues of well-considered, well-crafted institutional reforms, including of electoral systems, difficult though these may be to bring to fruition.

THE GLOBAL CHALLENGE OF BUILDING BETTER AND MORE RESILIENT DEMOCRACIES

Over the course of this research, we joked that this book could well end up providing a how-to manual for the effective practice of patronage politics. That has certainly not been the goal, though we have learned a great deal along the way. Throughout the research process, we have been enriched by the opportunity for sustained, extensive immersion in diverse patronage systems, with our understandings enormously enhanced by the countless astute observations of our dedicated teams of research associates and by our interactions with them during our field research. The process has been immensely eye-opening and analytically alluring, while also providing us with many causes for concern about the impact of patronage politics on the quality of democracy. By diving into the nuts-and-bolts of electoral mobilization, we have been able not only to describe the character of the electoral mobilization regimes found in Southeast Asia but also to interrogate their origins. That immersion, too, has helped us to see where the extant literature has sometimes failed to account for the practices we encountered.

It is our hope now that other scholars will build on our work, defining the parameters and traits of additional electoral mobilization regimes, perhaps, or seeing what light our framework sheds on other cases that fall within our set of party-machine, local-machine, and ad hoc-team regime types. We trust that our analysis can offer valuable insights both to fellow scholars and to those who are intent on challenging diverse yet similarly entrenched practices of patronage politics through well-crafted reforms that are attuned to specific historical and institutional contexts. One of the most effective ways to combat global threats to democracy is for democrats throughout the world to exchange ideas on how to improve the quality of democratic structures. Ultimately, it is toward that goal that we have written this book.

Appendix A

Surveys

NATIONAL SURVEYS

We conducted a total of four national surveys of voters in Indonesia, Malaysia, and the Philippines in conjunction with national or regional elections. The surveys asked a variety of questions designed to elicit information about voters' personal characteristics, their political preferences and behaviors, and their experience with various types of clientelist politics – for example, offers of cash, goods, or other forms of individual-level assistance from candidates, parties, or their representatives, or delivery or promises of meso-particularistic goods and services. We also asked voters about their experience with violence or intimidation. For potentially sensitive items (e.g., questions about the distribution of cash or experiences with coercion), we employed list experiments in addition to asking direct questions of voters. The survey instruments are available on request.

All surveys were translated into local languages. Our survey partners in each country conducted them using enumerators they trained and employed. The surveys in the Philippines and Indonesia were face-to-face, while those in Malaysia were via telephone.

Indonesia

We conducted a national election survey in Indonesia in conjunction with the 2014 legislative election, held on April 9, 2014. Our partner for the survey was Indikator Politik Indonesia, a leading political survey firm affiliated with the Lembaga Survei Indonesia (LSI) (https://indikator.co.id/). The survey was carried out from April 20–26, roughly two weeks after the election. The sampling frame consisted of all Indonesian citizens who are eligible to vote. To create a nationally representative sample, Indikator selected respondents using a stratified multistage probability sample. In the first stage, they grouped the population by province and assigned each province a quota based on its number of voters. In the second stage, Indikator grouped the population by gender, to ensure a 50:50 distribution in the sample. Finally, they further stratified the sample to ensure that we included an equal number of urban and rural voters. Within each province, villages were randomly selected, with the number of villages sampled corresponding to the number of voters in the province. Indikator randomly selected ten voters per village (five women and five men), clustering them in five randomly selected *rukun tetangga* (RT, sub-neighborhoods). Within each RT, Indikator randomly selected two households then, also randomly, one respondent from the list of registered voters in each household, with a requirement of gender balance in each RT. The resulting sample consists of 1,210 respondents.

Table A1 reports the frequencies for key demographic variables.

Malaysia

We conducted two national surveys in Malaysia, one each in 2013 and 2015. Our partner for both was the Merdeka Center for Opinion Research, the leading political and social survey firm in Malaysia (https://merdeka.org/v2/).

Interviews for the 2013 survey were carried out in the week following the May 5 Malaysian general election, specifically, from May 9 to 12, 2013. Merdeka Center conducted the telephone survey using a national sampling frame they designed in consultation with the research team. To ensure a nationally representative sample, the sampling frame included all national parliamentary constituencies, with attention given to ensure the target sample for each state reflected the state-specific distribution of ethnic groups. The final sample consisted of 1,017 registered voters.

Merdeka Center carried out the 2016 national survey in the month following the May 7, 2016 Sarawak state elections. The survey was again conducted by phone, using a similar sampling frame, but with the addition of oversampling for Sarawak. The final survey sample consists of 1,110 registered voters, with ~30 percent from East Malaysia (Sabah and Sarawak).

Table A2 reports the frequencies for key demographic variables in both surveys.

Philippines

We conducted a single national survey in the Philippines in conjunction with the 2016 general election, held on May 9, 2016. We partnered with Pulse Asia Research, a leading survey research firm in the Philippines (www.pulseasia.ph/), and its affiliate, AccuPoll. The face-to-face survey was carried out roughly two weeks after the election. The sampling frame consisted of all Philippine citizens who are eligible to vote. Pulse Asia divided the country into four regions: the National Capital Region (NCR), Luzon (*sans* NCR), Visayas, and Mindanao, with a sample size of 300 respondents in each region.

To create a nationally representative sample, Pulse Asia selected respondents using a stratified multistage probability sample. In the case of Luzon, the Visayas, and Mindanao, they randomly selected fifteen cities/municipalities in each region, with probability proportional to population size (measured per number of households). Within each region, Pulse Asia randomly selected sixty *barangays* (villages and urban wards) from across the fifteen sampled cities, assigning each city/municipality a number of barangays roughly proportional to its population size, and making sure to include at least one barangay per city. (The sixty barangays in the NCR were divided among that region's seventeen jurisdictions.) In each sample barangay, Pulse Asia used interval sampling to draw five sample households, drawing a starting street corner at random. They then randomly chose a respondent in each selected household from among household members aged eighteen years and older, using a probability selection table. To ensure that half of the respondents were male and half were female, they pre-listed only male family members in the probability selection table for odd-numbered questionnaires and only female members for even-numbered questionnaires. The resulting sample consists of 1,200 voting-age respondents.

Table A3 reports the frequencies for key demographic variables.

TABLE A1. *Frequency table: Indonesia*

Variable	Category	Frequency (%)
Gender	Male	50.3
	Female	49.7
Ethnicity	Javanese	41
	Sundanese	14.9
	Buginese	3.3
	Batak	3.2
	Betawi	3.0
	Minang	2.7
	Malay	2.1
	Others	29.8
Age	16–30	19.9
	31–40	28.9
	41–50	25.6

(*continued*)

TABLE A1. (*continued*)

Variable	Category	Frequency (%)
	51–60	16.4
	>60	9.4
Province	NAD	1.8
	North Sumatra	5.2
	West Sumatra	2.0
	Riau	2.2
	Jambi	1.3
	South Sumatra	3.1
	Bengkulu	0.7
	Lampung	3.2
	Bangka-Belitung	0.5
	Riau Archipelago	0.7
	Jakarta	3.8
	West Java	17.5
	Central Java	14.6
	Yogyakarta	1.5
	East Java	16.4
	Banten	4.2
	Bali	1.6
	West Nusa Tenggara	1.9
	East Nusa Tenggara	1.7
	West Kalimantan	1.9
	Central Kalimantan	1.0
	South Kalimantan	1.5
	East Kalimantan	1.5
	North Sulawesi	1.0
	Central Sulawesi	1.0
	South Sulawesi	3.4
	Southeast Sulawesi	1.0
	Gorontalo	0.4
	West Sulawesi	0.5
	Maluku	0.6
	North Maluku	0.4
	Papua	1.7
	West Papua	0.4
Urban/Rural	Rural	50.2
	Urban	49.8
Religion	Islam	89.1
	Catholic/Protestant	8.4
	Other	2.4

TABLE A2. *Frequency table: Malaysia*

Variable	Category	2013 Frequency (%)	2016 Frequency (%)
Gender	Male	50.3	51.3
	Female	49.7	48.7
Ethnicity	Malay	50.3	40.8
	Chinese	30.0	32.0
	Indian	7.1	6.8
	Muslim Bumiputera	6.9	10.3
	Non-Muslim Bumiputera	6.6	10.2
Age	21–30	25.2	10.9
	31–40	24.5	38.1
	41–50	26.3	21.4
	51–60	16.4	18.2
	>60	7.7	11.4
Region	Northern	15.0	12.8
	Central	32.2	27.9
	Eastern (peninsular)	17.0	13.4
	Southern	19.4	16.2
	East Malaysia	16.5	29.6

TABLE A3. *Frequency table: Philippines*

Variable	Category	Frequency (%)
Gender	Male	50.0
	Female	50.0
Primary language spoken in home	Tagalog/Filipino	61.7
	Cebuano/Bisaya	26.0
	Ilocano/Iloko	2.3
	Bikol/Bicolano	1.9
	Ilonggo/Hiligaynon	1.8
	Pangasinense	1.3
	Waray	.9
	Others	4.1
Age	18–30	25.5
	31–40	22.2
	41–50	17.5
	51–60	19.1
	> 60	15.8

(*continued*)

TABLE A3. (*continued*)

Variable	Category	Frequency (%)
Region	NCR	35
	CAR	0.4
	Region 1	3.3
	Region 2	0.4
	Region 3	6.7
	Region 4A	20.0
	Region 4B	0.4
	Region 5	1.7
	Region 6	0.8
	Region 7	8.8
	Region 8	1.7
	Region 9	2.5
	Region 10	1.3
	Region 11	10.8
	Region 12	0.8
	CARAGA	1.3
	ARMM	1.3
	Negros Island Region	2.9
Urban/Rural	Rural	49.7
	Urban	50.2
Religion	Catholic	87.0
	"Born again" Protestant	3.6
	Iglesia ni Cristo	2.8
	Islam	1.5
	Other	5.1

LOCAL BROKER AND VOTER SURVEYS

Indonesia[1]

In connection with the 2014 election, we worked with our local research partners to collect broker and voter lists from candidates running for office in the Central Java III constituency (CJ3), a rural, rice-growing area, dotted with towns and industrial pockets, that is reasonably typical of constituencies in Indonesia. Our team was able to collect lists from eleven of the approximately 1,200 candidates running for office at the three legislative levels in CJ3. To the best of our knowledge, these candidates are, like CJ3 itself, fairly typical. We obtained these lists with the full knowledge and consent of the candidates,

---

[1] This discussion draws on Hicken et al. (2021).

within sixty days of the election. The full lists these candidates and their teams compiled varied in size from 3,000 names for a DPRD-K (Dewan Perwakilan Rakyat Daerah Kabupaten/Kota, district-level legislature) candidate to more than 300,000 names for a DPR candidate, reflecting the much greater number of voters in the latter constituency. In most cases, we were unable to collect complete lists because of limited resources and time constraints. (The largest list, on loose-leaf pages, filled a 2-meter by 3-meter storage cupboard.) Instead, we focused on specific administrative regions (usually subdistricts) within CJ3, collecting the relevant parts of each list. We are therefore able to compare candidates' voter lists with the vote they attained in a sample of villages, and to identify the brokers working for the candidates in those villages.

Although each campaign claimed that its voter lists were complete and accurate for the regions we targeted, we have limited ability to confirm whether this is true. We dropped one list that contained too much missing or incomplete data to be of practical use, leaving us with ten lists, eight from DPRD-K (district) candidates and one each from DPR (national) and DPRD-P (Dewan Perwakilan Rakyat Daerah Provinsi, provincial) candidates. We digitized the information we had for voters and brokers on each list. We assigned each broker and voter a unique code, then conducted all analyses on a dataset stripped of personal information, and containing 2,288 brokers and 94,437 voters. The number of brokers per candidate ranged from 11 to 509, as summarized in the Table A4.

We used our digitized list of brokers and voters as a sampling frame for a random-sample, face-to-face survey of the voters and brokers appearing on the lists. Working with a local survey firm, we surveyed 383 voters and 332 brokers three months after the April 9, 2014 election. We did not tell voters that they appeared on a voter list, nor that we would be surveying brokers. We told brokers that we had received their name from a given campaign, but not that we had received the voter list nor that we were also surveying voters.

TABLE A4. *Brokers by candidate*

Candidate number	Type of candidate	Number of brokers
1	DPRD-K	171
2	DPRD-K	46
3	DPRD-K	358
4	DPRD-K	56
5	DPRD-K	142
6	DPRD-K	150
7	DPRD-K	355
8	DPRD-K	490
9	DPRD-P	11
10	DPR	509

Philippines[2]

In the Philippines, in conjunction with the 2016 general election, we surveyed brokers and voters in two different municipalities (A and B) in Southern Luzon. Surveys in municipality B were administered in the same month as the May 11, 2016 election; those in municipality A followed three months later, in August. A local team of enumerators working with Innovations for Poverty Action administered the survey. They did so using iPads and an offline survey app (iSurvey).

To conduct these surveys, after the 2016 general elections, we obtained the broker lists for two candidates running for office in municipalities A and B: one a nonincumbent candidate for mayor (Candidate A), and the other a candidate for vice-mayor (Candidate B).[3] We worked with the candidates' campaign managers to draw up the full roster of brokers their campaigns employed throughout each municipality. The number of brokers per barangay varied depending on the size of the voting population, with the smallest barangays having only two brokers. Enumerators located respondents at their residential addresses and obtained their consent to participate in the study. Although some of these brokers also worked for other candidates running for other offices, they worked primarily for the aforementioned candidates. We were able to interview all but a handful of brokers in each campaign, for a total of 199 brokers for Candidate A and 270 for Candidate B.

For the voter surveys, we randomly selected target respondents from the Commission on Elections' (COMELEC) latest Certified Voters List (CVL). Stratifying randomization by barangay ensured that we drew a larger sample of respondents from larger barangays. The CVL lists the complete name, birthday, gender, and barangay of residence of all registered voters in each municipality. Enumerators located primary respondents at their residential addresses, invited them to participate in the research study using a recruitment script, and obtained their consent to participate in the study. When they could not interview a primary respondent due to their out-migration, refusal, or death, the enumerator instead sought out a randomly selected alternate respondent. Following this procedure, we generated a sample of 701 voter respondents in municipality A and 659 in municipality B.

[2] This discussion draws on Ravanilla et al. (2021).
[3] See Ravanilla et al. (2021) for more information about surveys connected to Candidate A's campaign.

Appendix B

Subnational Government and Electoral Systems

For readers seeking more detail on state structures and electoral systems in our three primary cases, this appendix provides a survey of the major tiers of government as well as the electoral systems used in national and subnational polls.

Indonesia

Indonesia has four tiers of subnational government, beginning with (currently) 34 provinces and extending downward to a second level that is bifurcated between (at time of writing) 416 largely rural districts (*kabupaten*) and 98 cities or municipalities (*kota*). It is this second level that benefited most dramatically from "big bang" decentralization measures introduced in 2001. While provincial governments were not entirely excluded, kabupaten and kota assumed major responsibilities in areas including health care, education, and land use; to facilitate devolution, more than two million national civil servants were transferred to the regions (Davidson 2018, 11). That decentralization devolved responsibilities not to the provinces but to the districts was a deliberate choice to bypass the provinces, some of which might otherwise consider themselves to be potentially viable independent states (Aspinall 2013, 129–34). The result was to increase dramatically the importance and stakes of local political contestation, amplifying the significance of local cleavages for electoral purposes and reducing the salience of macro-level cleavages, such as between Java and the Outer Islands.

Under kabupaten and kota is a third level comprised of around 7,000 subdistricts (*kecamatan*), below which is a fourth, grassroots tier composed of nearly 75,000 rural villages (*desa*) and roughly 8,500 urban wards (*kelurahan*) (Figure B1).

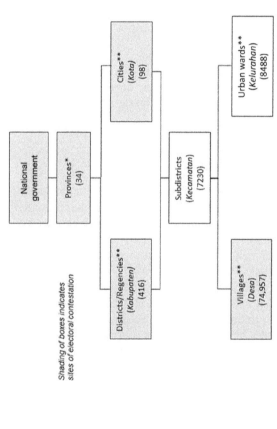

Shading of boxes indicates sites of electoral contestation

*Among the 34 provinces are five provinces with special status, below which lower tiers of government sometimes have distinct nomenclature. In *Jakarta*, the special capital region, an elected governor appoints one regent (*bupati*) as well as five mayors. In *Yogyakarta*, the executive post of governor is held by the sultan and is thus not elective. *Aceh*, which has special status as a result of the 2005 Helsinki Peace Agreement, has Islamic law and the right to form regional political parties; it is also provided with additional resources from the center. The final two special provinces, *Papua* and *West Papua*, have certain special governing arrangements amid a strong presence of central government security personnel; the provincial governments are also provided with additional resources from the center.

**Most *desa* (villages) are located in *kabupaten* (districts) and most *kelurahan* (urban wards) are in *kota* (cities), but there are also many *kelurahan* in *kabupaten*, as well as a smaller number of *desa* in *kota*.

Numbers of subnational units are as of 8 October 2019, as found in Regulation 72/2019 of the Minister of Home Affairs, at https://www.kemendagri.go.id/files/2020/PMDN%2072%20TH%202019+lampiran.pdf

FIGURE B1. Subnational structures in Indonesia

Voters in Indonesia elect both executives and legislators across some but not all tiers of subnational governance. This includes, most importantly, the top two levels: (a) provincial governors and provincial legislative councils (Dewan Perwakilan Rakyat Daerah Provinsi, or DPRD-P); and (b) *bupati* (regents) in rural districts and mayors in cities, along with their corresponding legislative councils (Dewan Perwakilan Rakyat Daerah Kabupaten/Kota, or DPRD-K). One major exception is the Jakarta Special Capital Region, where an elected governor appoints one bupati and five mayors. Another is Yogyakarta, where the gubernatorial post is not elective, but held by the sultan. The third level, the subdistrict, is headed by a civil servant appointed by the bupati or mayor. On the fourth tier, rural village heads (*kepala desa*) are elected but urban ward heads (*lurah*) are appointed by the bupati or mayor. This rural–urban distinction also extends to the legislative element of grassroots governance: the village council (Badan Perwakilan Desa), whose members are elected or chosen in village meetings, has no counterpart in urban wards.

Elections of provincial governors, bupati, and mayors are known as *pilkada* (from *pemilihan kepala daerah*, or elections of regional heads) and occur every five years. The polls are not held simultaneously with national presidential or legislative elections but are scheduled at different times (though they are gradually being synchronized across regions). Pilkada exercises are also not simultaneous with elections for local legislative assemblies (the DPRD-P and DPRD-K). The latter instead take place alongside the election of the national legislature (Dewan Perwakilan Rakyat, or DPR). In 2019, the election of legislative posts across these three levels coincided for the first time with the election of the president. These polls are an enormous logistical exercise, involving not only the election of 575 members of DPR but also all the legislators in the 34 DPRD-P and roughly 500 DPRD-K. On April 17, 2019, an estimated 154 million voters cast their ballots across about 810,000 polling places as more than 245,000 candidates from 16 political parties contested some 20,000 legislative seats (Arifianto 2019; Bland 2019).

Rules for pilkada have changed over time: since 2015, candidates are declared winners if they attain a plurality, unlike the two-round system used to elect the national executive (and the Jakarta governor). The direct election of regional heads, introduced in 2005, replaced a system in which they had been chosen by their respective DPRDs. Some national elites have opposed direct elections as not only too expensive but also inimical to social harmony. In 2014, opposition leader Prabowo Subianto pushed through a parliamentary measure that would have reinstated indirect elections in the regions; outgoing President Susilo Bambang Yudhoyono blocked this initiative (Aspinall 2019, 98).

As with the DPR, the electoral system used within multimember constituencies in the DPRDs had by 2014 shifted from closed-list to open-list proportional representation, with all the negative consequences emphasized in Chapters 2, 3, and 9. Sheer magnitude, however, yields clear differences in electoral dynamics in national as compared to regional legislative elections:

DPR constituencies may have more than three million voters while remote kabupaten constituencies may only have a few thousand.

The Philippines

The Philippines displays far less uniformity in its structures of subnational governance. The 1991 Local Government Code grafted *de jure* elements of decentralization onto a polity that has long been highly decentralized in *de facto* terms (Hutchcroft 2014a). Central-local relations were also the subject of much contention in the first three years of the Duterte administration, as the country debated a range of generally ill-defined proposals for a shift from a unitary to a federal system (Hutchcroft 2017).

The Philippines has eighty-one provinces, seventy-six of which sit as the first tier of subnational governance and five of which are under the Bangsamoro Autonomous Region in Muslim Mindanao (BARMM). Most of the Philippines has three levels of local governance, but even here we find exceptions (Figure B2). In general, the province is the top tier, followed by either cities or municipalities at the second tier. The seventy-six regular provinces sit under sixteen administrative regions, each of which has deconcentrated offices of national government agencies as well as a regional planning body (the Regional Development Council), commonly led by one of the region's governors. As these sixteen regions have no elective posts of their own (unlike the country's seventeenth region, BARMM), they are not treated as a tier of subnational governance.

The country has nearly 1,500 municipalities, all of which fall directly under the province. It also has 146 cities, 108 of which (as "component" cities) sit under the province but 37 of which (as "non-component" or "independent" cities) are actually a first-tier unit of governance sitting directly under the national government. (As explained later, one additional "independent" city sits directly under BARMM.) At the grassroots level of governance, situated under municipalities as well as under all categories of cities, are more than 42,000 *barangays* (villages or urban wards). These can generally be classified as the third tier of subnational governance, except when they fall under non-component cities – in which case they are the second tier.

Within BARMM are four tiers of subnational governance. The regional government constitutes the top level, followed by the five provinces as second-tier units, municipalities and component cities in the third tier, and barangays at the grassroots fourth tier. Once again, however, there is an exception to the rule: BARMM contains one "independent" city (Cotabato City) at the second tier of local governance (with its barangays thus constituting a third tier).

One commonality applies to the system as a whole: *all* levels of subnational governance involve elective posts. This roster of offices includes governors, vice-governors, and provincial boards across all 81 provinces; 146 city mayors,

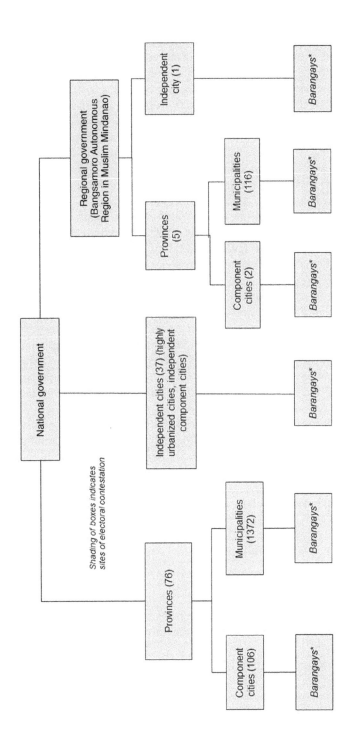

Barangay is usually translated as village but also includes entities better described as urban wards; there are a total of 42,046 *barangays* throughout the Philippines.

Numbers of subnational units are as of 31 December 2020, as found in the Philippine Standard Geographic Code, at http://202.90.134.34/classification/psoc/downloads/1_SUMWEBPROV-DEC2020-CODED-HUC_approved.pdf

FIGURE B2. Subnational structures in the Philippines

vice-mayors, and city councils; and nearly 1,500 municipal mayors, vice-mayors, and municipal councils. These local elections take place every three years, and coincide with elections for the national Senate and House; every six years, candidates for the country's president and vice-president are also on the ballot. In all, elections fill roughly 18,000 subnational posts, including 776 on provincial boards and 13,450 on city and municipal councils. These legislators, along with governors and vice-governors as well as city and municipal mayors and vice-mayors, are eligible to serve up to three 3-year terms. On a different electoral cycle are captains and councilors across the more than 42,000 barangays. The first election in the newly created BARMM is scheduled for 2025, after which polls are to continue on a three-year cycle.

Two key elements of the electoral system used at provincial, city, and municipal levels encourage candidate-centric rather than party-centric outcomes, as described for the national level in Chapter 2. First, as for president and vice-president at the national level, governors/vice-governors and mayors/vice-mayors are elected separately, so may emerge from different parties. Second, all provincial, city, and municipal legislators are elected via a multi-member plurality system. Party coherence is not only weak from national to subnational levels, but also from one election to the next. Across the first three elections of the twenty-first century, Ravanilla (2019, 177–78) explains, candidates from 202 parties ran for city or town mayor; winners came from precisely half that number of parties. In addition, the rampant turncoatism and split-ticket voting found at the national level are also endemic at the subnational level.

The prize of local electoral position has become all the more valuable since the passage of the 1991 Local Government Code, which provides substantial patronage resources through a generous revenue-sharing scheme that is the source of considerable political contestation (Hutchcroft 2012). Because these funds are not clearly tied to the Code's devolution of specific responsibilities to local government units, local politicians view the money as "their entitlement" and the responsibilities as "unfunded mandates" (Capuno 2017, 106). In some of the most impoverished parts of the country, this "internal revenue allotment" is one of the major sources of local largesse (Arguillas 2019).

Malaysia

The simplest and most straightforward structures of subnational governance are located in Malaysia, which – despite being our only federal case – also has by far the least extensive electoral contestation below the national level. This reflects the highly centralized nature of Malaysian federalism.

Comprised of eleven peninsular and two East Malaysian states – the latter with some of their own distinctive functions and structures – as well as three federal territories, Malaysia has only two subnational tiers, the lower one unelected (Figure B3). The thirteen states exercise strong control over the local

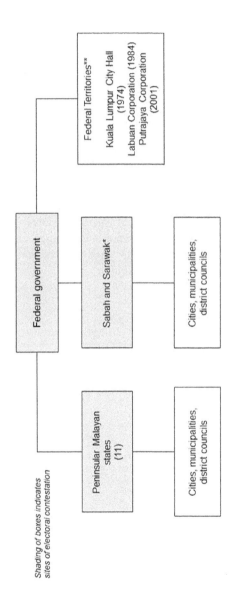

Shading of boxes indicates
sites of electoral contestation

```
                    Federal government
                    ┌──────────────────┐
        ┌───────────┤                  ├───────────┐
        │           └──────────────────┘           │
        │                     │                     │
┌───────────────┐   ┌──────────────────┐   ┌──────────────────────┐
│ Peninsular    │   │ Sabah and        │   │ Federal Territories** │
│ Malayan       │   │ Sarawak*         │   │                       │
│ states        │   │                  │   │ Kuala Lumpur City Hall│
│ (11)          │   │                  │   │         (1974)        │
└───────────────┘   └──────────────────┘   │ Labuan Corporation (1984)│
        │                     │             │ Putrajaya Corporation │
        │                     │             │         (2001)        │
┌───────────────┐   ┌──────────────────┐   └──────────────────────┘
│ Cities,       │   │ Cities,          │
│ municipalities,│  │ municipalities,  │
│ district      │   │ district councils│
│ councils      │   │                  │
└───────────────┘   └──────────────────┘
```

*Sabah and Sarawak have a distinct status relative to other states, with special provisions negotiated upon the creation of the federal state of Malaysia in 1963. This includes separate immigration controls, including on immigration from elsewhere in Malaysia. Their relationship to the federal state is the subject of ongoing discussion and contention.

**The three federal territories – capital Kuala Lumpur, administrative center Putrajaya, and the island of Labuan in East Malaysia – elect only federal legislators; administration is via a Federal Territories Ministry and local governments (an appointed city hall in Kuala Lumpur, and corporations in Putrajaya and Labuan).

FIGURE B3. Subnational structures in Malaysia

units that sit below them. Elections are held only for members of the federal and state parliaments; state governments then appoint local councils, village heads, etc. The electoral system used for federal and state elections is similarly uncomplicated: single-member district plurality. All elections are held simultaneously with the exception, at times, of a state government – usually Sabah and/or Sarawak, though recently also peninsular states – as well as episodic by-elections to fill vacancies. But not all districts enjoy the same political heft. Historically high levels of malapportionment and skew, including, for instance, "rural weightage" that favors *Bumiputera* (Malay and other indigenous) voters and gerrymandering that strategically "packs and cracks" opposition-leaning, usually urban constituencies, have given a decided edge to the Barisan Nasional coalition (Wong 2020; Weiss 2013, 1154–55).

As discussed in Chapter 3, Malaysian state governments appoint party loyalists as local councilors, under an also-appointed civil-servant mayor or president. In early postindependence years, towns and cities elected local councilors; the BN – which tended to fare poorly at this level, not least given the Chinese majority in many urban areas – then phased out local elections in the 1960s. Because the BN governed most states throughout its decades-long domination of the federal government, the absence of local electoral contests helped to streamline and solidify the ruling coalition's control over all tiers of government across much of the country. Even where non-BN parties controlled state legislatures, key resources flowed from the BN-held center.

Bibliography

Abinales, Patricio N. 2000. *Making Mindanao: Cotabato and Davao in the Formation of the Nation State.* Quezon City: Ateneo de Manila University Press.

2016. "War and Peace in Muslim Mindanao: Critiquing the Orthodoxy." In *Mindanao: The Long Journey to Peace and Prosperity*, edited by Paul D. Hutchcroft, 39–62. Mandaluyong City: Anvil.

Abueva, Jose Veloso. 1970. "The Philippines: Tradition and Change." *Asian Survey* 10 (1): 56–64.

Aeria, Andrew. 2005. "Sarawak: State Elections and Political Patronage." In *Elections and Democracy in Malaysia*, edited by Mavis Puthucheary and Norani Othman, 118–52. Bangi: Universiti Kebangsaan Malaysia Press.

Albertus, Michael, Alberto Diaz-Cayeros, Beatriz Magaloni, and Barry R. Weingast. 2016. "Authoritarian Survival and Poverty Traps: Land Reform in Mexico." *World Development* 77: 154–70.

Alesina, Alberto, Reza Baqir, and William Easterly. 1999. "Public Goods and Ethnic Divisions." *The Quarterly Journal of Economics* 114(1): 1243–84.

Alesina, Alberto, and Eliana La Ferrara. 2002. "Who Trusts Others?" *Journal of Public Economics* 85: 207–34.

Allen, Nathan W. 2015. "Clientelism and the Personal Vote in Indonesia." *Electoral Studies* 37: 73–85.

Amante, Maragtas S. V. 2019. "Philippines Unionism: Worker Voice, Representation, and Pluralism in Industrial Relations." In *New Labor Movements in Emerging Countries* [trans. from Japanese], edited by Hitoshi Ota, 63–103. Tokyo: IDE-JETRO.

Andaya, Barbara Watson, and Leonard Y. Andaya. 2001. *A History of Malaysia*, 2nd ed. Honolulu: University of Hawai'i Press.

Anderson, Benedict R. O'G. 1983. "Old State, New Society: Indonesia's New Order in Historical Perspective." *Journal of Asian Studies* 43(3): 477–96.

1988. "Cacique Democracy in the Philippines: Origins and Dreams." *New Left Review* I/169: 3–33.

1990. "Murder and Progress in Modern Siam." *New Left Review* I/181: 33–48.

Anderson, Bobby. 2015. *Papua's Insecurity: State Failure in Indonesia's Periphery.* Honolulu: East-West Center.

Anek Laothamatas. 1996. "A Tale of Two Democracies: Conflicting Perceptions of Elections and Democracy in Thailand." In *The Politics of Elections in Southeast Asia,* edited by R. H. Taylor, 201–33. Cambridge: Cambridge University Press.

Antlöv, Hans, Anna Wetterberg, and Leni Dharmawan. 2016. "Village Governance, Community Life, and the 2014 Village Law in Indonesia." *Bulletin of Indonesian Economic Studies* 52(2): 161–83.

Aquino, Tetchie D. 2019. "Compostela Valley Province: Machine, Logistics, and Solicitations." In *Electoral Dynamics in the Philippines: Money Politics, Patronage, and Clientelism at the Grassroots,* edited by Allen Hicken, Edward Aspinall, and Meredith Weiss, 297–308. Singapore: NUS Press.

Arguillas, Carolyn O. 2019. "Countdown: Justice for Ampatuan 58: The Poor Get Poorer, Ampatuans Get Richer as IRA Billions Pour In." Philippines Center for Investigative Journalism, December 8 [first published March 30, 2010]. https://pcij .org/article/3651/maguindanao-gets-poorer-as-ampatuans-get-richer.

Arifianto, Alexander R. 2019. "Indonesia's Election Leaves a Polarised Nation." *East Asia Forum,* May 1. www.eastasiaforum.org/2019/05/01/indonesias-election-leaves-a-polarised-nation/.

Aspinall, Edward. 2009a. "Combatants to Contractors: The Political Economy of Peace in Aceh." *Indonesia* 87: 1–34.

2009b. *Islam and Nation: Separatist Rebellion in Aceh, Indonesia.* Stanford: Stanford University Press.

2011. "Democratization and Ethnic Politics in Indonesia: Nine Theses." *Journal of East Asian Studies* 11(2): 289–319.

2013. "How Indonesia Survived: Comparative Perspectives on State Disintegration and Democratic Integration." In *Democracy and Islam in Indonesia,* edited by Mirjam Künkler and Alfred Stepan, 126–46. New York: Columbia University Press.

2014a. "Parliament and Patronage." *Journal of Democracy* 25(4): 96–110.

2014b. "When Brokers Betray: Clientelism, Social Networks, and Electoral Politics in Indonesia." *Critical Asian Studies* 46(4): 545–70.

2015. "Oligarchic Populism: Prabowo Subianto's Challenge to Indonesian Democracy." *Indonesia* 99(1): 1–28.

2019. "Lessons from a Neighbor: The Negative Consequences of Indonesia's Shift to the Open List." In *Strong Patronage, Weak Parties: The Case for Electoral Redesign in the Philippines,* edited by Paul D. Hutchcroft, 93–108. Mandaluyong City: Anvil.

Aspinall, Edward, and Allen Hicken. 2020. "Guns for Hire and Enduring Machines: Clientelism beyond Parties in Indonesia and the Philippines." *Democratization* 27(1): 137–56.

Aspinall, Edward, Allen Hicken, James Scambary, and Meredith L. Weiss. 2018. "Timor-Leste Votes: Parties and Patronage." *Journal of Democracy* 29(1): 153–67.

Aspinall, Edward, Amalinda Savirani, and Sally White. 2021. "Women's Political Representation in Indonesia: Who Wins and How?" *Journal of Current Southeast Asian Affairs* 40(1): 3–27.

Aspinall, Edward, and Gerry van Klinken, eds. 2011. *The State and Illegality in Indonesia.* Leiden: KITLV Press.

Aspinall, Edward, and Mada Sukmajati, eds. 2015. *Politik Uang di Indonesia: Patronase dan Klientelisme pada Pemilu Legislatif 2014* [Money Politics in Indonesia: Patronage and Clientelism in the 2014 Legislative Election]. Yogyakarta: Research Centre for Politics and Government, University of Gadjah Mada.

2016. *Electoral Dynamics in Indonesia: Money Politics, Patronage and Clientelism at the Grassroots.* Singapore: NUS Press.

Aspinall, Edward, and Marcus Mietzner. 2019. "Nondemocratic Pluralism in Indonesia." *Journal of Democracy* 30(4): 4–18.

Aspinall, Edward, and Muhammad Uhaib As'ad. 2015. "The Patronage Patchwork: Village Brokerage Networks and the Power of the State in an Indonesian Election." *Bijdragen tot de Taal-, Land- en Volkenkunde.* 171(2–3): 165–95.

2016. "Understanding Family Politics: Successes and Failures of Political Dynasties in Regional Indonesia." *South East Asia Research* 24(3): 420–35.

Aspinall, Edward, Noor Rohman, Ahmad Zainul Hamdi, Rubaidi, and Zusiana Elly Triantini. 2017. "Vote Buying in Indonesia: Candidate Strategies, Market Logic and Effectiveness." *Journal of East Asian Studies* 17(1): 1–27.

Aspinall, Edward, and Ward Berenschot. 2019. *Democracy for Sale: Elections, Clientelism, and the State in Indonesia.* Ithaca: Cornell University Press.

Auerbach, Adam Michael. 2016. "Clients and Communities: The Political Economy of Party Network Organization and Development in India's Urban Slums." *World Politics* 68(1): 111–48.

2019. *Demanding Development: The Politics of Public Goods Provision in India's Urban Slums.* Cambridge: Cambridge University Press.

Auerbach, Adam, and Tariq Thachil. 2018. "How Clients Select Brokers: Competition and Choice in India's Slums." *American Political Science Review* 112(4): 775–91.

2023. *Migrants and Machines: How Party Networks Form in Urban India.* Princeton: Princeton University Press.

Auyero, Javier. 2000. "The Logic of Clientelism in Argentina: An Ethnographic Account." *Latin American Research Review* 35(3): 55–81.

Baez, Javier E., Adriana Camacho, Emily Conover, and Román A. Zárate. 2012. "Conditional Cash Transfers, Political Participation, and Voting Behavior." IZA Discussion Paper Series. Bonn, Germany: IZA.

Barter, Shane J. 2011. "The Free Aceh Elections? The 2009 Legislative Contests in Aceh." *Indonesia* 91: 113–30.

Berenschot, Ward. 2014. "Political Fixers and India's Patronage Democracy." In *Patronage as Politics in South Asia,* edited by Anastasia Piliavsky, 196–217. Cambridge: Cambridge University Press.

2018. "The Political Economy of Clientelism: A Comparative Study of Indonesia's Patronage Democracy." *Comparative Political Studies* 51(2): 1563–593.

Berenschot, Ward, and Edward Aspinall. 2020. "How Clientelism Varies: Comparing Patronage Democracies." *Democratization.* 27(1): 1–19.

Bernama. 2018. "Election Court Nullifies BN's Victory in Cameron Highlands," Bernama, November 30. www.bernama.com/en/news.php?id=1670585.

2019. "PM Warns of Those Out to Topple Gov't for Fighting Corruption," *Bernama,* May 5. www.malaysiakini.com/news/474907.

2021. "UMNO Membership at 3.35 Million, Still Biggest Political Party – Sec-Gen," *Bernama*, March 28. www.bernama.com/en/news.php?id=1946322.

Birnir, Jóhanna Kristín. 2007. *Ethnicity and Electoral Politics*. New York: Cambridge University Press.

Bjarnegård, Elin. 2013. *Gender, Informal Institutions and Political Recruitment: Explaining Male Dominance in Parliamentary Representation*. Basingstoke: Palgrave Macmillan.

Bland, Ben. 2019. "Politics in Indonesia: Resilient Democracy, Defective Democracy." Lowy Institute, April 10. www.lowyinstitute.org/publications/politics-indonesia-resilient-elections-defective-democracy.

Borromeo-Bulao, Mary Joyce. 2019. "Naga City, Camarines Sur: An Alternative Mode of Politics under Strain." In *Electoral Dynamics in the Philippines: Money Politics, Patronage and Clientelism at the Grassroots*, edited by Allen Hicken, Edward Aspinall, and Meredith Weiss, 187–203. Singapore: NUS Press.

Brierley, Sarah. 2021. "Combining Patronage and Merit in Public Sector Recruitment." *Journal of Politics* 83(1): 182–197. https://doi.org/10.1086/708240.

2020. "Unprincipled Principals: Co-opted Bureaucrats and Corruption in Ghana." *American Journal of Political Science* 64(2): 209–22.

Brown, Colin. 2003. *A Short History of Indonesia: The Unlikely Nation?* Sydney: Allen & Unwin.

Bruno Manser Fund. 2012. *The Taib Timber Mafia: Facts and Figures on Politically Exposed Persons (PEPs) from Sarawak, Malaysia*. Basel: Bruno Manser Fund.

Brusco, Valeria, Marcelo Nazareno, and Susan C. Stokes. 2004. "Vote Buying in Argentina." *Latin American Research Review* 39(2): 66–88.

Buehler, Michael. 2009. "Suicide and Progress in Modern Nusantara." *Inside Indonesia* 97, www.insideindonesia.org/suicide-and-progress-in-modern-nusantara.

Butt, Simon. 2019. "Amendments spell disaster for the KPK." *Indonesia at Melbourne*. September 18. https://indonesiaatmelbourne.unimelb.edu.au/amendments-spell-disaster-for-the-kpk/.

Calimbahin, Cleo. 2019. "First District of Makati: Signs of an Electoral Backslide and Challenges to a Local Dynasty." In *Electoral Dynamics in the Philippines: Money Politics, Patronage and Clientelism at the Grassroots*, edited by Allen Hicken, Edward Aspinall, and Meredith Weiss, 134–50. Singapore: NUS Press.

Caliwan, Christopher Lloyd. 2019a. "Election Gun Ban Ends, 6.3K Violators Nabbed: PNP." *Philippine News Agency*, June 13. www.pna.gov.ph/articles/1072236.

2019b. "Election-related Violence Down by 60%: PNP." *Philippine News Agency*. www.pna.gov.ph/articles/1069778.

Callahan, William. 2005. "The Discourse of Vote Buying and Political Reform in Thailand." *Pacific Affairs* 78(1): 95–113.

Callahan, William A., and Duncan McCargo. 1996. "Vote-Buying in Thailand's Northeast: The July 1995 General Elections." *Asian Survey* 36(4): 376–92.

Calvo, Ernesto, and Maria Victoria Murillo. 2004. "Who Delivers? Partisan Clients in the Argentine Electoral Market." *American Journal of Political Science* 48(4): 742–57.

Canare, T. A., Mendoza, R. U., & Lopez, M. A. 2018. "An Empirical Analysis of Vote Buying among the Poor: Evidence from Elections in the Philippines." *South East Asia Research* 26(1): 58–84.

Capuno, Joseph J. 2017. "Tugs of War: Local Governments, National Government." Public Policy Journal (Center for Integrative and Development Studies, University of the Philippines) 16 and 17: 98–116.

Caraway, Teri L. and Michele Ford. 2020. *Labor and Politics in Indonesia.* Cambridge: Cambridge University Press.

Caraway, Teri L., Michele Ford, and Hari Nugroho. 2015. "Translating Membership into Power at the Ballot Box? Trade Union Candidates and Worker Voting Patterns in Indonesian National Elections." *Democratization* 22(7): 1296–316.

Carlson, Matthew. 2007. *Money Politics in Japan: New Rules, Old Practices.* Boulder: Lynne Reiner Press.

Case, William. 1999. "Politics Beyond Anwar: What's New?" *Asian Journal of Political Science* 7(1): 1–19.

Casiple, Ramon C. 2019. "The Political Party Development Bill: Strengthening Parties Toward the Goal of Strengthening Philippine Democracy." In *Strong Patronage, Weak Parties: The Case for Electoral Redesign in the Philippines*, edited by Paul D. Hutchcroft, 111–30. Mandaluyong City, Philippines: Anvil.

Central Intelligence Agency. n.d. *The World Factbook.* www.cia.gov/library/publica tions/the-world-factbook/.

Chan Tsu Chong. 2018. "Democratic Breakthrough in Malaysia – Political Opportunities and the Role of Bersih." *Journal of Current Southeast Asian Affairs* 37(3): 109–37.

Chandra, Kanchan. 2004. *Why Ethnic Parties Succeed: Patronage and Ethnic Head Counts in India.* Cambridge: Cambridge University Press.

Chauchard, Simon. 2018. "Electoral Handouts in Mumbai Elections: The Cost of Political Competition." *Asian Survey* 58(2): 341–64.

Chin, James. 2001. "Unequal Contest: Federal–State Relations under Mahathir." In *Mahathir's Administration: Performance and Crisis in Governance*, edited by Ho Khai Leong and James Chin, 28–61. Singapore: Times.

    2015. "Exporting the BN/UMNO Model: Politics in Sabah and Sarawak." In *Routledge Handbook of Contemporary Malaysia*, edited by Meredith L. Weiss, 83–92. New York: Routledge.

Chiok Phaik Fern. 2014. "Arau, Perlis: The Irresistible Charm of Warlords, Women and Rewards?" In *Electoral Dynamics in Malaysia: Findings from the Grassroots*, edited by Meredith L. Weiss, 17–33. Singapore: Institute of Southeast Asian Studies.

Choi, Ina, and Yuki Fukuoka. 2015. "Co-opting Good Governance Reform: The Rise of a Not-so-reformist Leader in Kebumen, Central Java." *Asian Journal of Political Science.* 23(1): 83–101.

Choong Pui Yee. 2014. "Kepong and Titiwangsa, Kuala Lumpur: Messages or Money?" In *Electoral Dynamics in Malaysia: Findings from the Grassroots*, edited by Meredith L. Weiss, 125–38. Singapore: Institute of Southeast Asian Studies.

Chua, Yvonne T., and Booma Cruz. 2004. "Pork Is a Political, Not a Developmental Tool." *Philippine Center for Investigative Journalism*, September 6. https://old.pcij .org/stories/pork-is-a-political-not-a-developmental-tool/.

Connors, Michael Kelly. 2003. *Democracy and National Identity in Thailand.* London: RoutledgeCurzon.

Coronel, Sheila S. 1998. *Pork and Other Perks: Corruption and Governance in the Philippines.* Pasig: Philippine Center for Investigative Journalism.

Corstange, Daniel. 2009. "Sensitive Questions, Truthful Answers? Modeling the List Experiment with LISTIT." *Political Analysis* 17(1): 45–63.

Costa, Robert, and Philip Rucker. 2020. "Trump Casts Himself as Pandemic Patron, Personalizing the Government's Spread of Cash and Supplies," *Washington Post*, April 10.

Cox, Gary W., and Mathew D. McCubbins. 2001. "The Institutional Determinants of Policy Outcomes." In *Presidents, Parliaments, and Policy*, edited by Stephan Haggard and Matthew D. McCubbins, 21–63. Cambridge: Cambridge University Press.

Cox, Gary W., and Michael F. Thies. 1998. "The Cost of Intraparty Competition: The Single, Nontransferable Vote and Money Politics in Japan." *Comparative Political Studies* 31(3): 267–91.

Cramb, Rob. 2016. "The Political Economy of Large-scale Oil Palm Development in Sarawak." In *The Oil Palm Complex: Smallholders, Agribusiness and the State in Indonesia and Malaysia*, edited by Rob Cramb and John F. McCarthy, 189–246. Singapore: NUS Press.

Cribb, Robert, and Colin Brown. 1995. *Modern Indonesia: A History Since 1945*. London: Longman.

Crouch, Harold. 1979. "Patrimonialism and Military Rule in Indonesia." *World Politics* 31(4): 571–87.

   1988. *The Army and Politics in Indonesia*. Rev. ed. Ithaca: Cornell University Press.

   1996. *Government and Society in Malaysia*. Ithaca: Cornell University Press.

Cruz, Cesi. 2019. "Social Networks and the Targeting of Vote Buying." *Comparative Political Studies* 52(3): 382–411.

Cruz, Cesi, and Charis Tolentino. "Gender, Social Recognition, and Political Influence". Working Paper, 2019.

Cruz, Cesi, and Christina J. Schneider. 2017. "Foreign Aid and Undeserved Credit Claiming." *American Journal of Political Science* 61(2): 396–408.

Cruz, R. G. 2016. "Why Duterte is Popular among Wealthy, Middle Class Voters." *ABS CBN*, May 1. https://news.abs-cbn.com/halalan2016/focus/04/30/16/why-duterte-is-popular-among-wealthy-middle-class-voters.

Cruz, Booma, and Yvonne T. Chua. 2004. "Legislators Feed on Pork." *Philippine Center for Investigative Journalism*, September 7. https://old.pcij.org/stories/legislators-feed-on-pork/.

Cullinane, Michael. 2003. *Ilustrado Politics: Filipino Elite Responses to American Rule, 1898–1908*. Quezon City: Ateneo de Manila University Press.

Daby, Mariela. 2020. "The Gender Gap in Political Clientelism: Problem-Solving Networks and the Division of Political Work in Argentina." *Comparative Political Studies* 54(2): 215–44.

Darwin, Rizkika Lhena. 2016. "Bireuen, Aceh: The Aftermath of Post-conflict Politics and the Decline of Partai Aceh." In *Electoral Dynamics in Indonesia*, edited by Edward Aspinall and Mada Sukmajati, 39–53. Singapore: NUS Press.

   2017. "The Power of Female Brokers: Local Elections in North Aceh." *Contemporary Southeast Asia* 39(3): 532–51.

Davidson, Jamie S. 2018. *Indonesia: Twenty Years of Democracy*. Cambridge: Cambridge University Press.

de Dios, Emmanuel S., and Paul D. Hutchcroft. 2002. "Philippine Political Economy: Examining Current Challenges in Historical Perspective." In Arsenio Balisacan and

Hal Hill, eds., *The Philippine Economy: Development, Policies, and Challenges*, 45–75. Quezon City: Ateneo de Manila University Press.

De La O, Ana L. 2012. "Do Conditional Cash Transfers Affect Electoral Behavior? Evidence from a Randomized Experiment in Mexico." *American Journal of Political Science* 57(1): 1–14.

Derichs, Claudia, and Mark R. Thompson. 2013. *Dynasties and Female Political Leaders in Asia: Gender, Power and Pedigree.* Berlin: LIT Verlag.

Dewi, Sita W., S. L. Harjanto, and Olivia D. Purba. 2016. "Central and South Jakarta: Social Welfare and Constituency Service in the Metropolis." In *Electoral Dynamics in Indonesia*, edited by Edward Aspinall and Mada Sukmajati, 167–83. Singapore: NUS Press.

Diaz-Cayeros, Alberto, Federico Estévez, and Beatriz Magaloni. 2016. *The Political Logic of Poverty Relief: Electoral Strategies and Social Policy in Mexico.* Cambridge: Cambridge University Press.

Dixit, Avinash, and John Londregan. 1996. "The Determinants of Success of Special Interests in Redistributive Politics." *The Journal of Politics* 58(4): 1132–55.

Dongoran, Hussein Abri. 2021. "Tsunami dari Juliari," *Tempo*, January 23. https://majalah.tempo.co/read/laporan-utama/162405/kegelisahan-anggota-komisi-viii-dpr-terseret-kasus-bansos.

Dunning, Thad, and Susan Stokes. 2007. "Persuasion vs. Mobilization." Paper presented at Conference on Elections and Distribution, October 25–26, Yale University.

Eifert, Benn, Edward Miguel, and Daniel N. Posner. 2010. "Political Competition and Ethnic Identification in Africa." *American Journal of Political Science* 54: 494–510.

Emmerson, Donald K. 1978. "The Bureaucracy in Political Context: Weakness in Strength." In *Political Power and Communications in Indonesia*, edited by Karl D. Jackson and Lucian W. Pye, 82–136. Berkeley: University of California Press.

Faisal S. Hazis. 2015. "Patronage, Power and Prowess: Barisan Nasional's Equilibrium Dominance in East Malaysia." *Kajian Malaysia: Journal of Malaysian Studies* 33(2): 1–24.

2020. "Elite Fragmentation and Party Splits: Explaining the Breakdown of UMNO in Malaysia's 14th General Election." In *Toward a New Malaysia? The 2018 Election and Its Aftermath*, edited by Meredith L. Weiss and Faisal S. Hazis, 41–60. Singapore: NUS Press.

Fealy, Greg. 2008. "Consuming Islam: Commodified Religion and Aspirational Pietism in Contemporary Indonesia." In *Expressing Islam: Religious Life and Politics in Indonesia*, edited by Greg Fealy and Sally White, 15–39. Singapore: Institute of Southeast Asian Studies.

Fealy, Greg, and Robin Bush. 2014. "The Political Decline of Traditional Ulama in Indonesia." *Asian Journal of Social Science* 42: 536–60.

Fearon, James D. 1999. "Why Ethnic Politics and 'Pork' Tend to Go Together." Paper presented at University of Chicago, May 21–23.

2003. "Ethnic and Cultural Diversity By Country." *Journal of Economic Growth* 8 (2): 195–222.

Feith, Herbert. 1962. *The Decline of Constitutional Democracy in Indonesia.* Ithaca: Cornell University Press.

Finan, Frederico, and Laura Schechter. 2012. "Vote-buying and Reciprocity." *Econometrica* 80(2): 863–81.

Fossati, Diego. 2019. "The Resurgence of Ideology in Indonesia: Political Islam, *Aliran* and Political Behaviour." *Journal of Current Southeast Asian Affairs.* 38(2): 119–48.

Fossati, Diego, Edward Aspinall, Burhanuddin Muhtadi, and Eve Warburton. 2020. "Ideological Representation in Clientelistic Democracies: The Indonesian Case." *Electoral Studies* 63: 1–12. https://doi.org/10.1016/j.electstud.2019.102111.

Fraser, Nancy. 2000. "Rethinking Recognition." *New Left Review* 3: 107–20.

Fried, Brian J. 2012. "Distributive Politics and Conditional Cash Transfers: The Case of Brazil's Bolsa Família." *World Development* 40(5): 1042–53.

Fukuoka, Yuki, and Luky Djani. 2015. "Revisiting the Rise of Jokowi: The Triumph of Reformasi or an Oligarchic Adaptation of Post-clientelist Initiatives?" *South East Asia Research* 24(2): 204–21.

Fukuyama, Francis. 1995. *Trust: The Social Virtues and the Creation of Prosperity.* New York: The Free Press.

Funston, John. 2016. "UMNO – From Hidup Melayu to Ketuanan Melayu." In *The End of UMNO? Essays on Malaysia's Dominant Party*, edited by Bridget Welsh (e-book). Petaling Jaya: SIRD.

Furnivall, J. S. 1956. *Colonial Policy and Practice: A Comparative Study of Burma and Netherlands India.* New York: NUS Press. Original edition, 1948.

Gallego, Jorge. 2015. "Self-enforcing Clientelism." *Journal of Theoretical Politics* 27: 401–27.

Gans-Morse, Jordan, Sebastian Mazzuca, and Simeon Nichter. 2014. "Varieties of Clientelism: Machine Politics During Elections." *American Journal of Political Science* 58(2): 415–32.

Geertz, Clifford. 1959. "The Javanese Village." In *Local, Ethnic, and National Loyalties in Village Indonesia*, edited by G. William Skinner, 34–51. New Haven: Yale University Press.

Gera, Weena. 2020. "Heightened Contradictions: Duterte and Local Autonomy in the Era of COVID-19." *New Mandala*, June 5. www.newmandala.org/heightened-contradictions-duterte-and-local-autonomy-in-the-era-of-covid-1/.

Gera, Weena, and Paul D. Hutchcroft. 2021. "Duterte's Tight Grip over Local Politicians: Can It Endure?" *New Mandala*, February 19. www.newmandala.org/wp-content/uploads/2021/02/Central-Local-Relations-under-Duterte.pdf.

Gottlieb, Jessica, and Horacio Larreguy. 2016. "An Informational Theory of Electoral Targeting: Evidence from Senegal." Working Paper, Harvard University/Texas A&M. http://cpd.berkeley.edu/wp-content/uploads/2016/01/GL_SenegalElectoralBehavior-1.pdf.

Glassman, Jim. 2010. "The Provinces Elect Governments, Bangkok Overthrows Them: Urbanity, Class and Post-democracy in Thailand." *Urban Studies* 47(6): 1301–23.

Golden, Miriam A. 2003. "Electoral Connections: The Effects of the Personal Vote on Political Patronage, Bureaucracy and Legislation in Postwar Italy." *British Journal of Political Science* 33(2): 189–212.

Golden, Miriam, and Brian Min. 2013. "Distributive Politics Around the World." *Annual Review of Political Science* 16: 73–99.

Golden, Miriam A., and Eric C. C. Chang. 2001. "Competitive Corruption: Factional Conflict and Political Malfeasance in Postwar Italian Christian Democracy." *World Politics* 53(4): 588–622.

Gomez, Edmund Terence. 2012. "Monetizing Politics: Financing Parties and Elections in Malaysia." *Modern Asian Studies* 46(5): 1370–97.

2014. "Malaysia's Political Economy: Ownership and Control of the Corporate Sector." In *Misplaced Democracy: Malaysian Politics and People*, edited by Sophie Lemière, 245–81. Petaling Jaya: SIRD.

Gomez, Edmund Terence, and K. S. Jomo. 1997. *Malaysia's Political Economy: Politics, Patronage and Profits*. Cambridge: Cambridge University Press.

Gonzalez-Ocantos, Ezequiel, Chad Kiewiet De Jonge, Carlos Meléndez, Javier Osorio, and David W. Nickerson. 2012. "Vote Buying and Social Desirability Bias: Experimental Evidence from Nicaragua." *American Journal of Political Science* 56(1): 202–17.

Gottlieb, Jessica, and Horacio A. Larreguy. 2016. "An Informational Theory of Electoral Targeting: Evidence from Senegal." Working paper. http://cpd.berkeley.edu/wp-content/uploads/2016/01/.GL_SenegalElectoralBehavior-1.pdf.

Greene, Kenneth F. 2021. "Campaign Effects and the Elusive Swing Voter in Modern Machine Politics." *Comparative Political Studies* 54(1): 77–109. https://doi.org/10.1177/0010414020919919.

Grimmer, Justin, Solomon Messing, and Sean J. Westwood. 2012. "How Words and Money Cultivate a Personal Vote: The Effect of Legislator Credit Claiming on Constituent Credit Allocation." *American Political Science Review* 106(4): 703–19.

Gurr, Ted Robert. 2000. *People Versus States: Minorities at Risk in the New Century*. Washington, DC: United States Institute of Peace.

Habyarimana, James, Macartan Humphreys, Daniel N. Posner, and Jeremy M. Weinstein. 2007. "Why Does Ethnic Diversity Undermine Public Goods Provision?" *American Political Science Review* 101(4): 709–25.

Hadiz, Vedi R. 2010. *Localising Power in Post-Authoritarian Indonesia: A Southeast Asia Perspective*. Stanford: Stanford University Press.

Hale, Henry. 2007. "Correlates of Clientelism: Political Economy, Politicized Ethnicity, and Post-Communist Transition." In *Patrons, Clients, and Policies: Patterns of Democratic Accountability and Political Competition*, edited by Herbert Kitschelt and Steven I. Wilkinson, 227–50. Cambridge: Cambridge University Press.

Hall, Anthony. 2012. "The Last Shall Be First: Political Dimensions of Conditional Cash Transfers in Brazil." *Journal of Policy Practice* 11(1–2): 25–41.

Hariyanto, Ibnu. 2019. "Kasus Bowo Sidik, KPK Geledah Ruang Kerja Mendag Enggartiasto Lukita." *Detik*, April 29. https://news.detik.com/berita/d-4529176/kasus-bowo-sidik-kpk-geledah-ruang-kerja-mendag-enggartiasto-lukita

Hatherell, Michael. 2019. *Political Representation in Indonesia: The Emergence of the Innovative Technocrats*. New York: Routledge.

Hendrawan, Adrianus, Aspinall, Edward, and Ward Berenschot. 2021. "Parties as Pay-off Seekers: Pre-Electoral Coalitions in a Patronage Democracy." *Electoral Studies*. 69: 1–10. https://doi.org/10.1016/j.electstud.2020.102238

Heng Pek Koon. 1996. "Chinese Responses to Malay Hegemony in Peninsular Malaysia 1957–96." *Tonan Ajia Kenkyu [Southeast Asian Studies]* 34(3): 32–55.

   1997. "The New Economic Policy and the Chinese Community in Peninsular Malaysia." *The Developing Economies* 35(3): 262–92.

Hicken, Allen D. 2007. "How Do Rules and Institutions Encourage Vote Buying?" In *Elections for Sale: The Causes and Consequences of Vote Buying*, edited by Frederic Charles Schaffer, 47–60. Boulder: Lynne Rienner Publishers.

   2009. *Building Party Systems in Developing Democracies*. New York: Cambridge University Press.

   2011. "Clientelism." *Annual Review of Political Science* 14(1): 289–310.

   2014. "Party and Party System Institutionalization in the Philippines." In *Party System Institutionalization in Asia: Democracies, Autocracies, and the Shadows of the Past*, edited by Allen Hicken and Erik Kuhonta, 307–27. Cambridge: Cambridge University Press.

2017. "The Political Party System." In *Routledge Handbook of the Contemporary Philippines*, edited by Mark R. Thompson and Eric Vincent C. Batalla, 38–54. London: Routledge.

2019a. "Why (and How) Electoral Systems Shape Development Outcomes." In *Strong Patronage, Weak Parties: The Case for Electoral System Redesign in the Philippines*, edited by Paul D. Hutchcroft, 27–40. Mandaluyong City, Philippines: Anvil.

2019b. "When Does Electoral System Reform Occur?" In *Strong Patronage, Weak Parties: The Case for Electoral System Redesign in the Philippines*, edited by Paul D. Hutchcroft, 59–95. Mandaluyong City, Philippines: Anvil.

Hicken, Allen, Edward Aspinall, and Meredith Weiss, eds. 2019. *Electoral Dynamics in the Philippines: Money Politics, Patronage, and Clientelism at the Grassroots*. Singapore: NUS Press.

Hicken, Allen, Edward Aspinall, Meredith Weiss, and Burhanuddin Muhtadi. 2022. "Buying Brokers: Electoral Handouts beyond Clientelism in a Weak-party State." *World Politics* 74(1): 77–120. DOI: 10.1017/S0043887121000216.

Hicken, Allen, James Atkinson, and Nico Ravanilla. 2015. "Pork and Typhoons: The Influence of Political Connections on Disaster Response in the Philippines." In *Building Inclusive Democracies in ASEAN*, edited by Ronald U. Mendoza, Julio C. Teehankee, Edsel L. Beja Jr., Antonio G. M. La Vina, and Maria Fe Villamejor-Mendoza, 74–101. Mandaluyong City, Philippines: Anvil.

Hicken, Allen, Paul Hutchcroft, Meredith Weiss, and Edward Aspinall. 2019. "Introduction: The Local Dynamics of the National Election in the Philippines." In *Electoral Dynamics in the Philippines: Money Politics, Patronage and Clientelism at the Grassroots*, edited by Allen Hicken, Edward Aspinall, and Meredith Weiss, 1–42. Singapore: NUS Press.

Hicken, Allen, Stephen Leider, Nico Ravanilla, and Dean Yang. 2018. "Temptation in Vote Selling: Evidence from a Field Experiment in the Philippines." *Journal of Development Economics* 131(March): 1–14.

Hicken, Allen, and Noah L. Nathan. 2020. "Clientelism's Red Herrings: Dead Ends and New Directions in the Study of Non-Programmatic Politics." *Annual Review of Political Science* 23: 277–294. DOI: 10.1146/annurev-polisci-050718-032657.

Hicken, Allen, and Nico Ravanilla. 2021. "Poverty, Social Networks, and Clientelism." Working paper.

Hilgers, Tina. 2008. "Causes and Consequences of Political Clientelism: Mexico's PRD in Comparative Perspective." *Latin American Politics and Society* 50(4): 123–53.

Hilley, John. 2001. *Malaysia: Mahathirism, Hegemony and the New Opposition*. New York: Zed.

Hillman, Ben. 2017. "Increasing Women's Parliamentary Representation in Asia and the Pacific: The Indonesian Experience." *Asia & the Pacific Policy Studies* 4(1): 38–49.

Ho Khai Leong. 1992. "The Malaysian Chinese Guilds and Associations as Organized Interests in Malaysian Politics." Working Paper #04, Department of Political Science, National University of Singapore.

Ho Yi Jian. 2014. "Gelang Patah, Johor: Did Lim Kit Siang Truly Win His Last Gamble?" In *Electoral Dynamics in Malaysia: Findings from the Grassroots*, edited by Meredith L. Weiss, 167–80. Singapore: Institute of Southeast Asian Studies.

Holland, Alisha C., and Brian Palmer-Rubin. 2015. "Beyond the Machine: Clientelist Brokers and Interest Organizations in Latin America." *Comparative Political Studies* 48(9): 1186–122.

Holmes, Ronald. 2019. "The Centrality of Pork Amidst Weak Institutions: Presidents and the Persistence of Particularism in Post-Marcos Philippines (1986–2016)." PhD dissertation, Australian National University.

Hooker, Virginia Matheson. 2004. "Reconfiguring Malay and Islam in Contemporary Malaysia." In *Contesting Malayness: Malay Identity across Boundaries*, edited by Timothy P. Barnard, 149–67. Singapore: Singapore University Press.

Horowitz, Donald L. 1986. *Ethnic Groups in Conflict*. Berkeley: University of California Press.

2014. "Ethnic Power Sharing: Three Big Problems." *Journal of Democracy* 25(2): 5–20.

2018. "Interethnic Vote Pooling, Institutional Frailty, and the Malaysian Elections of 2018." *International Journal of Constitutional Law Blog*. June 22. www.iconnectblog.com/2018/06/interethnic-vote-pooling-institutional-frailty-and-the-malaysian-elections-of-2018/.

Huber, John D. 2017. *Exclusion by Elections: Inequality, Ethnic Identity, and Democracy*. Cambridge: Cambridge University Press.

Hunter, Murray. 2019. "Malaysian Civil Service's Cancerous Culture," *Asia Sentinel*, October 23. www.asiasentinel.com/p/malaysian-civil-service-cancerous-culture.

Hutchcroft, Paul D. 1998. *Booty Capitalism: The Politics of Banking in the Philippines*. Ithaca: Cornell University Press.

2000. "Colonial Masters, National Politicos, and Provincial Lords: Central Authority and Local Autonomy in the American Philippines, 1900–1913." *Journal of Asian Studies* 59(2): 277–306.

2003. Review of *Capital, Coercion, and Crime* by John T. Sidel. *Pacific Review* 76(3): 505–07.

2008. "The Arroyo Imbroglio in the Philippines." *Journal of Democracy* 19(1): 141–55.

2012. "Re-Slicing the Pie of Patronage: The Politics of the Internal Revenue Allotment in the Philippines, 1991–2010." *Philippine Review of Economics* 49(1) (June): 109–34.

2014a. "Dreams of Redemption: Localist Strategies of Political Reform in the Philippines." In *Social Difference and Constitutionalism in Pan-Asia*, edited by Susan H. Williams, 75–108. New York: Cambridge University Press.

2014b. "Linking Capital and Countryside: Patronage and Clientelism in Japan, Thailand, and the Philippines." In *Political Clientelism, Social Policy, and the Quality of Democracy*, edited by Diego Abente Brun and Larry Diamond, 174–203. Baltimore: Johns Hopkins Press.

2017. "Federalism in Context: Laying the Foundations for a Problem-Driven Process of Political Reform." In *Debate on Federal Philippines: A Citizen's Handbook*, edited by Ronald U. Mendoza, 81–108. Quezon City: Ateneo de Manila University Press.

2019a. "Electoral System Redesign: An Opportunity for Effective Political Reform in the Philippines." In *Strong Patronage, Weak Parties: The Case for Electoral System Redesign in the Philippines*, edited by Paul D. Hutchcroft, 1–25. Mandaluyong City, Philippines: Anvil.

ed. 2019b. *Strong Patronage, Weak Parties: The Case for Electoral Redesign in the Philippines*. Mandaluyong City, Philippines: Anvil.

Hutchcroft, Paul D., and Joel Rocamora. 2012. "Patronage-Based Parties and the Democratic Deficit in the Philippines: Origins, Evolution, and the Imperatives of Reform." In *Routledge Handbook of Southeast Asian Politics*, edited by Richard Robison, 97–119. London: Routledge.

ICG. 2009. "The Philippines: After the Maguindanao Massacre." International Crisis Group, Briefing 98/Asia, December 21. www.crisisgroup.org/asia/south-east-asia/philippines/philippines-after-maguindanao-massacre.

   2019. "The Philippines: Militancy and the New Bangsamoro." International Crisis Group, Report 301/Asia, June 27. www.crisisgroup.org/asia/south-east-asia/philippines/301-philippines-militancy-and-new-bangsamoro.

Ichino, Nahomi, and Noah L. Nathan. 2013. "Crossing the Line: Local Ethnic Geography and Voting in Ghana." *American Political Science Review* 107(2): 344–61.

Iga, Tsukasa. 2017. "Political Economy of Affordable Housing in Malaysia." *Kyoto Review of Southeast Asia* 22. https://kyotoreview.org/yav/affordable-housing-imalaysia/.

Ismanto, Gandung, and Idris Thaha. 2016. "Banten: Islamic Parties, Networks and Patronage." In *Electoral Dynamics in Indonesia*, edited by Edward Aspinall and Mada Sukmajati, 137–54. Singapore: NUS Press.

Jensen, Peter Sandholt, and Mogens K. Justesen. 2014. "Poverty and Vote Buying: Survey-based Evidence from Africa." *Electoral Studies* 33: 220–32.

Jesudason, James V. 1999. "The Resilience of One-Party Dominance in Malaysia and Singapore" In *The Awkward Embrace: One-Party Domination and Democracy*, edited by Hermann Giliomee and Charles Simkins, 127–74. Amsterdam: Harwood Academic Publishers.

Johnson, Chalmers. 1986. "Tanaka Kakuei, Structural Corruption, and the Advent of Machine Politics in Japan." *The Journal of Japanese Studies* 12(1): 1–28.

Jomo, K. S., and E. T. Gomez. 2000. "The Malaysian Development Dilemma." In *Rents, Rentseeking and Economic Development: Theory and Evidence in Asia*, edited by Mushtaq H. Khan and K. S. Jomo, 274–303. New York: Cambridge University Press.

Kabullah, Muhammad Ichsan, and M. Nurul Fajri. 2021. "Neo-ibuism in Indonesian Politics: Election Campaigns of Wives of Regional Heads in West Sumatra in 2019." *Journal of Current Southeast Asian Affairs* 40(1): 136–55.

Kapur, Devesh, and Milan Vaishnav eds. 2018. *Costs of Democracy: Political Finance in India*. New Delhi: Oxford University Press.

Kawanaka, Takeshi. 1998. "The Robredo Style: Philippine Local Politics in Transition." *Kasarinlan: The Philippine Journal of Third World Studies*, 13(3): 5–36.

   2002. *Power in a Philippine City*. IDE Occasional Papers Series No. 38. Chiba: Institute of Developing Economies.

Kenawas, Yoes C. 2018. "Twenty Years After Suharto: Dynastic Politics and Signs of Subnational Authoritarianism." *Kyoto Review of Southeast* Asia 24. https://kyotoreview.org/issue-24/twenty-years-after-suharto-dynastic-politics-and-signs-of-subnational-authoritarianism/.

Kenny, Paul D. 2015. "The Origins of Patronage Politics: State Building, Centrifugalism, and Decolonization." *British Journal of Political Science* 45(1): 141–71.

Kenny, Paul D., Kirk Hawkins, and Saskia Ruth. 2016. "Populist Leaders Undermine Democracy in these 4 Ways. Would a President Trump?" *Washington Post*, August 18, 2016. www.washingtonpost.com/news/monkey-cage/wp/2016/08/18/populists-under mine-democracy-in-these-4-ways-would-president-trump/?utm_term=.af9da5bb3a5a.

Kerkvliet, Benedict J. 1977. *The Huk Rebellion: A Study of Peasant Revolt in the Philippines*. Berkeley: University of California Press.

Khatijah Sidek. 1995. *Memoir Khatijah Sidek: Puteri Kesateria Bangsa*. Bangi: Penerbit Universiti Kebangsaan Malaysia.

Kitschelt, Herbert. 2000. "Linkages between Citizens and Politicians in Democratic Polities." *Comparative Political Studies*. 33(6–7): 845–79.

2007. "The Demise of Clientelism in Affluent Capitalist Democracies." In *Patrons, Clients and Policies: Patterns of Democratic Accountability and Political Competition*, edited by Herbert Kitschelt and Steven I. Wilkinson, 298–321. Cambridge: Cambridge University Press.

Kitschelt, Herbert, and Daniel M. Kselman. 2013. "Economic Development, Democratic Experience, and Political Parties' Linkage Strategies." *Comparative Political Studies* 46(11): 1453–84.

Kitschelt, Herbert, and Steven I. Wilkinson. 2007. "Citizen–Politician Linkages: An Introduction." In *Patrons, Clients, and Policies: Patterns of Democratic Accountability and Political Competition*, edited by Herbert Kitschelt and Steven I. Wilkinson, 1–49. Cambridge: Cambridge University Press.

Kloos, David. 2020. "Personal Touch, Professional Style: Women in Malaysian Islamist Politics." In *Towards a New Malaysia: The 2018 Election and Its Aftermath*, edited by Meredith L. Weiss and Faisal S. Hazis, 171–93. Singapore: NUS Press.

Kramon, Eric. 2016. "Electoral Handouts as Information." *World Politics* 68(3): 454–98.

Kurer, Oskar. 2007. "Why do Papua New Guinean Voters Opt for Clientelism? Democracy and Governance in a Fragile State." *Pacific Economic Bulletin* 22(1): 39–53.

Labonne, Julien. 2013. "The Local Electoral Impacts of Conditional Cash Transfers: Evidence from a Field Experiment." *Journal of Development Economics* 104: 73–88.

Landé, Carl H. 1965. *Leaders, Factions, and Parties: The Structure of Philippine Politics*. New Haven: Southeast Asia Studies, Yale University.

1973. "Networks and Groups in Southeast Asia: Some Observations of the Group Theory of Politics." *American Political Science Review* 67(1): 103–27.

Lara, Francisco J., Jr. 2016. "The Shadow Economy and Strongman Rule in Mindanao." In *Mindanao: The Long Journey to Peace and Prosperity*, edited by Paul D. Hutchcroft, 243–72. Mandaluyong City, Philippines: Anvil.

Lara, Pancho. 2009. "The Ruthless Political Entrepreneurs of Muslim Mindanao." *Pime Philippines*, December 2. https://pimephilippines.wordpress.com/2009/12/02/the-ruthless-political-entrepreneurs-of-muslim-mindanao/.

Larreguy, Horacio, John Marshall, and Pablo Querubin. 2016. "Parties, Brokers, and Voter Mobilization: How Turnout Buying Depends upon the Party's Capacity to Monitor Brokers." *American Political Science Review* 110(1): 160–79.

Latiph, Acram. 2019. "Lanao del Sur: Gold, Goons, Guns, and Genealogy." In *Electoral Dynamics in the Philippines: Money Politics, Patronage, and Clientelism at the*

Grassroots, edited by Allen Hicken, Edward Aspinall and Meredith Weiss, 309–31. Singapore: NUS Press.

Lemarchand, René. 1972. "Political Clientelism and Ethnicity in Tropical Africa: Competing Solidarities in Nation-Building." *American Political Science Review* 66(1): 68–90.

Liddle, R. William. 1999. "Regime: The New Order." In *Indonesia Beyond Suharto: Polity, Economy, Society, Transition.* edited by Donald K. Emmerson, 39–70. Armonk: M.E. Sharpe.

Lindberg, Staffan I. 2010. "What Accountability Pressures Do MPs in Africa Face and How Do They Respond? Evidence From Ghana." *The Journal of Modern African Studies* 48(1): 117–42.

Linos, Elizabeth. 2013. "Do Conditional Cash Transfer Programs Shift Votes? Evidence from the Honduran PRAF." *Electoral Studies* 32: 864–74.

Liow, Joseph Chinyong. 2009. *Piety and Politics: Islamism in Contemporary Malaysia.* New York: Oxford University Press.

Lipset, Seymour M., and Stein Rokkan, 1967. "Cleavage Structures, Party Systems, and Voter Alignment." In *Party Systems and Voter Alignments: Cross-National Perspectives*, edited by Seymour M. Lipset and Stein Rokkan, 1–64. New York: Free Press.

Loh, Francis Kok Wah. 2005. "Strongmen and Federal Politics in Sabah." In *Elections and Democracy in Malaysia*, edited by Mavis Puthucheary and Norani Othman, 70–117. Bangi: Universiti Kebangsaan Malaysia Press.

Macalandag, Regina E. 2019. "First District of Bohol: Tradition, Innovation, and Women's Agency in Local Patronage Politics." In *Electoral Dynamics in the Philippines: Money Politics, Patronage, and Clientelism at the Grassroots*, edited by Allen Hicken, Edward Aspinall and Meredith Weiss, 242–58. Singapore: NUS Press

Magaloni, Beatriz. 2006. *Voting for Autocracy: Hegemonic Party Survival and Its Demise in Mexico.* Cambridge: Cambridge University Press.

Mahsun, Muhammad. 2016. "Palembang, South Sumatra: Aspiration Funds and Pork Barrel Politics." In *Electoral Dynamics in Indonesia*, edited by Edward Aspinall and Mada Sukmajati, 120–37. Singapore: NUS Press.

——— 2017. "Peasants and Politics: Achievements and Limits of Popular Agency in Batang, Central Java." *Contemporary Southeast Asia* 39(3): 470–90.

Mahsun, Muhammad, Misbah Zulfa Elizabeth, and Solkhah Mufrikhah. 2021. "Female Candidates, Islamic Women's Organizations, and Clientelism in the 2019 Indonesian Elections." *Journal of Current Southeast Asian Affairs* 40(1): 73–92.

Malaysiakini. 2015. "PM: More Money for BN MPs Next Year." Malaysiakini, August 16. www.malaysiakini.com/news/308789.

——— 2019. "Jakoa Head Apologizes for Project Signboards," Malaysiakini, January 25. www.malaysiakini.com/news/461747.

Malley, Michael. 1999. "Regime: The New Order." In *Indonesia Beyond Suharto: Polity, Economy, Society, Transition.* edited by Donald K. Emmerson, 71–105. Armonk, New York: M.E. Sharpe.

Manderson, Lenore. 1977. "The Shaping of the Kaum Ibu (Women's Section) of the United Malays National Organization." *Signs* 3(1): 210–28.

Mangada, Ladylyn Lim. 2019. "Leyte: Where Only the Wealthy and Powerful Survive." In *Electoral Dynamics in the Philippines: Money Politics, Patronage and Clientelism at the Grassroots*, edited by Allen Hicken, Edward Aspinall, and Meredith Weiss, 207–23. Singapore: NUS Press.

Manor, James. 2013. "Post-clientelist Initiatives." In *Democratization in the Global South: International Political Economy*, edited by Kristian Stokke and Olle Törnquist, 243–53. London: Palgrave Macmillan.

Mares, Isabela, and Lauren E. Young. 2018. "The Core Voter's Curse: Clientelistic Threats and Promises in Hungarian Elections." *Comparative Political Studies* 51 (11): 1441–71.

Mas'udi, Wawan. 2016. "Creating Legitimacy in Decentralized Indonesia: Joko 'Jokowi' Widodo's Path to Legitimacy in Solo, 2005–2012." PhD dissertation. University of Melbourne.

Mas'udi, Wawan, and Nanang Indra Kurniawan. 2017. "Programmatic Politics and Voter Preferences: The 2017 Election in Kulon Progo, Yogyakarta." *Contemporary Southeast Asia* 39(3): 449–69.

Mayhew, David R. 1974. *Congress: The Electoral Connection*. New Haven: Yale University Press.

McCoy, Alfred W. 1989. "Quezon's Commonwealth: The Emergence of Philippine Authoritarianism." In *Philippine Colonial Democracy*, edited by Ruby R. Paredes, 114–60. New Haven: Yale University Southeast Asia Studies.

1993. "'An Anarchy of Families': The Historiography of State and Family in the Philippines." In *An Anarchy of Families: State and Family in the Philippines*, edited by McCoy, 1–32. Madison: University of Wisconsin Center for Southeast Asian Studies.

McElwain, Kenneth Mori. 2014. "Party System Institutionalization in Japan." In *Party System Institutionalization in Asia*, edited by Allen Hicken and Erik Martinez Kuhonta, 74–107. Cambridge: Cambridge University Press.

McIndoe, Alastair. 2010. "Philippines Gun Ban Kicks Off Amid Campaign Violence." *Time*, January 13.

McKenna, Thomas M. 1998. *Muslim Rulers and Rebels: Everyday Politics and Armed Separatism in the Southern Philippines*. Berkeley: University of California Press.

Mendoza, Ronald U., Edsel L. Beja Jr., Victor S. Venida, and David B. Yap. 2016. "Political Dynasties and Poverty: Measurement and Evidence of Linkages in the Philippines." *Oxford Development Studies* 44(2): 189–201.

Mietzner, Marcus. 2009. *"Indonesia's 2009 Elections: Populism, Dynasties and the Consolidation of the Party System."* Sydney: Lowy Institute for International Policy.

2010. "Indonesia's Direct Elections: Empowering the Electorate or Entrenching the New Order Oligarchy?" In *Soeharto's New Order and Its Legacy: Essays in Honour of Harold Crouch*, edited by Edward Aspinall and Greg Fealy, 173–90. Canberra: ANU EPress.

2011. "Funding *Pilkada*: Illegal Campaign Financing in Indonesia's Local Elections." In *State and Illegality in Indonesia*, eds. Edward Aspinall and Gerry van Klinken, 123–38. Leiden: KITLV Press.

2013. *Money, Power, and Ideology: Political Parties in Post-Authoritarian Indonesia*. Singapore: NUS Press.

2020. "Indonesian Parties Revisited: Systematic Exclusivism, Electoral Personalisation and Declining Intra-Party Democracy." In *Democracy in Indonesia: From Stagnation to Regression?*, edited by Thomas Power and Eve Warburton, 191–209. Singapore: Institute of Southeast Asian Studies.

Milne, R. S. 1973. "Patrons, Clients and Ethnicity: The Case of Sarawak and Sabah in Malaysia." *Asian Survey* 13(10): 891–907.

Miranda, Armida R. 2019. "First District of Laguna: A Tale of Two Cities." In *Electoral Dynamics in the Philippines: Money Politics, Patronage, and Clientelism at the Grassroots*, edited by Allen Hicken, Edward Aspinall, and Meredith Weiss, 117–33. Singapore: NUS Press.

Mojares, Resil B. 1986. *The Man Who Would be President: Serging Osmeña and Philippine Politics*. Cebu: Maria Cacao Publishers.

Monsod, Toby C. 2016. "Human Development in the Autonomous Region in Muslim Mindanao: Trends, Traps, and Immediate Challenges." In *Mindanao: The Long Journey to Peace and Prosperity*, edited by Paul D. Hutchcroft, 199–241. Mandaluyong City, Philippines: Anvil.

Mubarakan, Munzalan. 2014. "Kisah lain caleg stress … blokir jalan dan bongkar atap pasar." *Simomot*, April 11, 2014. https://simomot.com/2014/04/11/ulah-caleg-gagal-dari-blokir-jalan-sampai-meminta-kembali-sumbangannya-weleh-weleehh/.

Muhajir, Ahmad. 2009. "Tuan Guru and Politics in South Kalimantan: Islam in the 2005 Gubernatorial Elections." MA thesis, Australian National University.

Muhtadi, Burhanuddin. 2018. "Buying Votes in Indonesia: Partisans, Personal Networks, and Winning Margins." PhD dissertation, Australian National University.

2019. *Vote Buying in Indonesia: The Mechanics of Electoral Bribery*. Singapore: Palgrave Macmillan.

Muñoz, Paula. 2019. *Buying Audiences: Clientelism and Electoral Campaigns when Parties Are Weak*. Cambridge: Cambridge University Press.

2014. "An Informational Theory of Campaign Clientelism: The Case of Peru." *Comparative Politics* 47(1): 79–98.

Mustafa, Mochamad. 2017. "Democratic Decentralisation and Good Governance: The Political Economy of Procurement Reform in Decentralised Indonesia." PhD dissertation, University of Adelaide.

N. Faizal Ghazali. 2017. "What's Wrong with PAS Logo on S'gor Gov't Aid Envelopes?" *Malaysiakini*, October 29. www.malaysiakini.com/news/399968.

N. Fakhrull Halim. 2019. "Harapan Biggest Culprit in Semenyih Polls Offences – Bersih," *Malaysiakini*, March 8. www.malaysiakini.com/news/467100.

Nagaraj, Shyamala, Tey Nai-Peng, Ng Chiu-Wan, Lee Kiong-Hock, and Jean Pala. 2015. "Counting Ethnicity in Malaysia: The Complexity of Measuring Diversity." In *Social Statistics and Ethnic Diversity: Cross-National Perspectives in Classifications and Identity Politics*, edited by Simon, Patrick, Victor Piché, and Amélie A. Gagnon, 143–73. New York: Springer.

Nathan, Noah L. 2016. "Local Ethnic Geography, Expectations of Favoritism, and Voting in Urban Ghana." *Comparative Political Studies* 49(14): 1896–929.

2019. *Electoral Politics and Africa's Urban Transition: Class and Ethnicity in Ghana*. New York: Cambridge University Press.

Ng Tien Eng. 2003. "The Contest for Chinese Votes: Politics of Negotiation or Politics of Pressure?" In *New Politics in Malaysia*, edited by Francis Loh Kok Wah and Johan Saravanamuttu, 87–106. Singapore: Institute of Southeast Asian Studies.

Ngu Ik Tien. 2021. "The Politics of Food Aid in Sarawak, Malaysia." *Contemporary Southeast Asia* 43(1): 83–89.

Nichter, Simeon. 2008. "Vote Buying or Turnout Buying? Machine Politics and the Secret Ballot." *American Political Science Review* 102(1): 19–31.

2018. *Votes for Survival: Relational Clientelism in Latin America*. Cambridge: Cambridge University Press.

Nichter, Simeon, and Michael Peress. 2017. "Request Fulfilling: When Citizens Demand Clientelist Benefits." *Comparative Political Studies* 50(8): 1086–117.

Noble, Gregory W. 2010. "The Decline of Particularism in Japanese Politics." *Journal of East Asian Studies* 10(2): 239–73.

Nolan, Cillian. 2016. "Papua's Central Highlands: The Noken System, Brokers and Fraud." In *Electoral Dynamics in Indonesia*, edited by Edward Aspinall and Mada Sukmajati, 398–415. Singapore: NUS Press.

Nolasco, Margie A. 2019. "Second District of Camarines Norte: Are Patronage Politics a Socio-Political Condition or Cultural Syndrome?" In *Electoral Dynamics in the Philippines: Money Politics, Patronage, and Clientelism at the Grassroots*, edited by Allen Hicken, Edward Aspinall, and Meredith Weiss, 81–96. Singapore: NUS Press.

Noor'ain Aini. 2017. "Stakan: Much Ado About Postal Votes?" In *Electoral Dynamics in Sarawak: Contesting Developmentalism and Rights*, edited by Meredith L. Weiss and Arnold Puyok, 43–65. Singapore: Institute of Southeast Asian Studies.

Novaes, Lucas M. 2018. "Disloyal Brokers and Weak Parties." *American Journal of Political Science* 62: 84–98.

Nugroho, Argoposo Cahyo. 2016. "Tangerang, Banten: Women Candidates in the Shadow of Men." In *Electoral Dynamics in Indonesia: Money Politics, Patronage, and Clientelism at the Grassroots*, edited by Edward Aspinall and Mada Sukmajati, 154–66. Singapore: NUS Press.

Ong, Elvin. 2015. "Complementary Institutions in Authoritarian Regimes: The Everyday Politics of Constituency Service in Singapore." *Journal of East Asian Studies* 15(3):361–90.

Pancho, Neil. 2019. "Compostela Valley Province: Machine, Logistics, and Solicitations." In *Electoral Dynamics in the Philippines: Money Politics, Patronage, and Clientelism at the Grassroots*, edited by Allen Hicken, Edward Aspinall, and Meredith Weiss, 281–96. Singapore: NUS Press.

Paskarina, Caroline. 2016. "Bandung, West Java: *Silaturahmi*, Personalist Networks and Patronage Politics." In *Electoral Dynamics in Indonesia*, edited by Edward Aspinall and Mada Sukmajati, 203–16. Singapore: NUS Press.

Patunru, Arianto A., Neil McCulloch, and Christian von Luebke. 2012. "A Tale of Two Cities: The Political Economy of Local Investment Climates in Indonesia." *Journal of Development Studies* 48(7): 799–816.

Penchan Charoensuthipan. 2019. "Vote-buying 'Rampant' Says Watchdog." *Bangkok Post*, March 25.

Pepinsky, Thomas B. 2007. "Malaysia: Turnover without Change." *Journal of Democracy*, 18(1): 113–27.

2017. "Regions of Exception." *Perspectives on Politics* 15(4): 1034–52.

Piattoni, Simona. 2001. "Clientelism in Historical and Comparative Perspective." In *Clientelism, Interests, and Democratic Representation: The European Experience in Historical and Comparative Perspective*, edited by Simona Piattoni, 1–30. Cambridge: Cambridge University Press.

Posner, Daniel N. 2005. *Institutions and Ethnic Politics in Africa*. Cambridge: Cambridge University Press.

Pradhanawati, Ari, George Towar Tawakkal, and Andrew D. Garner. 2019. "Voting their Conscience: Poverty, Education, Social Pressure and Vote Buying in Indonesia." *Journal of East Asian Studies* 19(1): 19–38.

Prajak Kongkirati. 2013. "Bosses, Bullets and Ballots: Electoral Violence and Democracy in Thailand, 1975–2011." PhD dissertation, Australian National University.

2014. "The Rise and Fall of Electoral Violence in Thailand: Changing Rules, Structures and Power Landscapes, 1997–2011." *Contemporary Southeast Asia* 36 (3): 386–416.

Prasad, Karolina. 2015. *Identity Politics and Elections in Malaysia and Indonesia Ethnic Engineering in Borneo.* Abingdon: Routledge.

Prihatini, Ella S. 2019. "Electoral (In)equity." *Inside Indonesia* 135. www.insideindonesia .org/electoral-in-equity.

Pulse Asia. 2019a. *Ulat ng Bayan* June 2019 survey.

2019b. "Report of voting buying in the Philippines over time." Internal report of historical survey results shared with authors.

Putnam, Robert. 1993. *Making Democracy Work: Civic Traditions in Modern Italy.* Princeton: Princeton University Press.

Puyok, Arnold. 2006. "Voting Pattern and Issues in the 2006 Sarawak State Assembly Election in the Ba' Kelalan Constituency." *Asian Journal of Political Science* 14(2): 212–28.

2014. "Kota Marudu and Keningau, Sabah: Personality, Patronage and Parochial Politics." In *Electoral Dynamics in Malaysia: Findings from the Grassroots,* edited by Meredith L. Weiss, 167–80. Singapore: Institute of Southeast Asian Studies.

Rappler. 2013. "46 Killed, 50 Wounded in Poll Violence." May 12. www.rappler.com/ nation/politics/elections-2013/28933-election-violence-fatalities-wounded.

Ravanilla, Nico. 2017. "Motives in Pork Distribution:Partisan Bias or Patronage?" Working Paper.

2019. "The Multi-Member Plurality System in the Philippines and Its Implications." In *Strong Patronage, Weak Parties: The Case for Electoral Redesign in the Philippines,* edited by Paul D. Hutchcroft, 169–87. Mandaluyong City, Philippines: Anvil.

Ravanilla, Nico, Dotan Haim, and Allen Hicken. 2021. "Brokers, Social Networks, Reciprocity, and Clientelism." *American Journal of Political Science* https://doi-org .proxy.lib.umich.edu/10.1111/ajps.12604.

Reyes, Socorro L. 2019. "Gender and the Electoral System: What Works for Women." In *Strong Patronage, Weak Parties: The Case for Electoral Redesign in the Philippines,* edited by Paul D. Hutchcroft, 72–86. Mandaluyong City, Philippines: Anvil.

Ridwan. 2016. "North Jayapura, Papua: Buying the Voters and Buying the Administrators." In *Electoral Dynamics in Indonesia,* edited by Edward Aspinall and Mada Sukmajati, 383–99. Singapore: NUS Press.

Robison, Richard, and Vedi R. Hadiz. 2004. *Reorganising Power in Indonesia: The Politics of Oligarchy in an Age of Markets.* London: Routledge.

Rocina, Jose Aims R. 2019. "Muntinlupa City: The Use of Monikers as a Manifestation of Programmatic Politics." In *Electoral Dynamics in the Philippines: Money Politics, Patronage, and Clientelism at the Grassroots,* edited by Allen Hicken, Edward Aspinall, and Meredith Weiss, 151–67. Singapore: NUS Press.

Rodan, Garry. 2014. "Civil Society Activism and Political Parties in Malaysia: Differences Over Local Representation." *Democratization* 21(5): 824–45.

Rohaniza Idris, and Veena Babulal. 2018. "Wanita Umno Starts Own Countdown to GE14." *New Straits Times.* March 15. www.nst.com.my/news/politics/2018/03/ 345549/wanita-umno-starts-own-countdown-ge14.

Rohi, Rudi. 2016. "East Nusa Tenggara: Patronage Politics, Clientelism and the Hijacking of Social Trust." In *Electoral Dynamics in Indonesia,* edited by Edward Aspinall and Mada Sukmajati, 363–82. Singapore: NUS Press.

Rohman, Noor. 2016. "Pati, Central Java: Targets, Techniques and Meanings of Vote Buying." In *Electoral Dynamics in Indonesia*, edited by Edward Aspinall and Mada Sukmajati, 233–48. Singapore: NUS Press.

Rosenbluth, Frances McCall, and Michael F. Thies. 2010. *Japan Transformed: Political Change and Economic Restructuring*. Princeton: Princeton University Press.

Ross, Michael L. 2001. *Timber Booms and Institutional Breakdown in Southeast Asia*. Cambridge: Cambridge University Press.

Rubaidi. 2016. "East Java: New Clientelism and the Fading of *Aliran* Politics." In *Electoral Dynamics in Indonesia: Money Politics, Patronage and Clientelism at the Grassroots*, edited by Edward Aspinall and Mada Sukmajati, 264–78. Singapore: NUS Press.

Rueda, Miguel R. 2015. "Buying Votes with Imperfect Local Knowledge and a Secret Ballot." *Journal of Theoretical Politics* 27(3): 428–56.

2017. "Small Aggregates, Big Manipulation: Vote Buying Enforcement and Collective Monitoring." *American Journal of Political Science* 61(1): 163–77.

Ryter, Loren. 2009. "Their Moment in the Sun: The New Indonesian Parliamentarians from the Old OKP." In *State of Authority: State in Society in Indonesia*, edited by Gerry van Klinken and Joshua Barker, 181–218. Ithaca: Cornell Southeast Asia Program Publications.

Samuels, David J. 1999. "Incentives to Cultivate a Party Vote in Candidate-Centric Electoral Systems: Evidence From Brazil." *Comparative Political Studies* 32(4): 487–518.

Sandberg, Johan, and Engel Tally. 2015. "Politicisation of Conditional Cash Transfers: The Case of Guatemala." *Development Policy Review* 33(4): 503–22.

Sarawak Report. 2020. "Making Political Capital Out of the Covid Crisis?" *Sarawak Report*, March 20. www.sarawakreport.org/2020/03/making-political-capital-out-of-the-covid-crisis/.

Sauler, Erika. 2016. "30 Killed, 22 Hurt in Election Violence – CHR." *Philippine Daily Inquirer*, May 12. http://newsinfo.inquirer.net/785237/30-killed-22-hurt-in-election-violence-chr.

Savirani, Amalinda. 2016. "Bekasi, West Java: From Patronage to Interest Group Politics?" In *Electoral Dynamics in Indonesia: Money Politics, Patronage, and Clientelism at the Grassroots*, edited by Edward Aspinall and Mada Sukmajati, 184–201. Singapore: NUS Press.

Savirani, Amalinda, and Edward Aspinall. 2017. "Adversarial Linkages: The Urban Poor and Electoral Politics in Jakarta." *Journal of Current Southeast Asian Affairs*. 36(3): 3–34.

Schaffer, Frederic. 2005. "Clean Elections and the Great Unwashed: Vote Buying and Voter Education in the Philippines." Paper No. 21. Princeton, NJ: School of Social Sciences, Institute for Advanced Study.

ed. 2007a. *Elections for Sale: The Causes and Consequences of Vote Buying*. Boulder: Lynne Rienner.

2007b. "Lessons Learned." In *Elections for Sale: The Causes and Consequences of Vote Buying*, edited by Frederic Charles Schaffer, 183–200, Boulder: Lynne Rienner.

2008. *The Hidden Costs of Clean Election Reform*. Ithaca: Cornell University Press.

Scharff, Michael. 2011. *Building Trust and Promoting Accountability: Jesse Robredo and Naga City, Philippines, 1988–1998*. Princeton: Innovations for Successful Societies.

Scheiner, Ethan. 2008. "Does Electoral System Reform Work? Electoral System Lessons from Reforms of the 1990s." *Annual Review of Political Science* 11: 161–81.

Scott, James C. 1969. "Corruption, Machine Politics, and Political Change." *American Political Science Review* 63(4): 1142–58.

1972. "Patron-Client Politics and Political Change in Southeast Asia." *American Political Science Review* 66(1): 91–113.

Shantz, Arthur Alan. 1972. "Political Parties: The Changing Foundations of Philippine Democracy." PhD dissertation, University of Michigan.

Sharifah Syahirah S. S. 2013. "Gender Roles in The 13th Malaysian General Election (GE13): Descriptive, Substantive & Surrogacy Representation Analysis." Paper presented at Seminar Media dan Pilihanraya Umum 2013, Kuala Lumpur, July 4.

Shefter, Martin. 1977. "Party and Patronage: Germany, England, and Italy." *Politics and Society* 7: 403–51.

1994. *Political Parties and the State: The American Historical Experience.* Princeton: Princeton University Press.

Shekhar, Vibhanshu. 2008. "Malay Majoritarianism and Marginalised Indians." *Economic and Political Weekly* 43(8): 22–25.

Sherlock, Stephen. 2010. "The Parliament in Indonesia's Decade of Democracy: People's Forum or Chamber of Cronies?" In *Problems of Democratisation in Indonesia: Elections, Institutions and Society*, edited by Edward Aspinall and Marcus Mietzner, 160–78. Singapore: Institute of Southeast Asian Studies.

Shin, Jae Hyeok. 2015. "Voter Demands for Patronage: Evidence from Indonesia." *Journal of East Asian Studies* 15(1): 127–51.

Sidel, John T. 1993. "Walking in the Shadow of the Big Man: Justiniano Montano and Failed Dynasty Building in Cavite, 1935–1972." In *An Anarchy of Families: State and Family in the Philippines*, edited by Alfred W. McCoy, 109–61. Madison: University of Wisconsin Center for Southeast Asian Studies.

1999. *Capital, Coercion, and Crime.* Stanford: Stanford University Press.

Sjahrir, Bambang Suharnoko, Krisztina Kis-Katos, and Günther G. Schulze. 2013. "Political Budget Cycles in Indonesia at the District Level." *Economics Letters* 120: 342–45.

Slater, Dan. 2004. "Indonesia's Accountability Trap: Party Cartels and Presidential Power After Democratic Transition." *Indonesia* 78: 61–92.

Smith, T. E. 1962. "The Local Authority Elections 1961 in the Federation of Malaya." *Journal of Commonwealth Political Studies* 1(2): 153–55.

Spater, Jeremy, and Erik Wibbels. 2018. "Social Density, Clientelism and Vote Banking." Unpublished manuscript. https://sites.duke.edu/spater/files/2019/08/Spater_Wibbels_Social_Density_Clientelism_4-15-19.pdf.

Sta. Romana, Michelle. 2019. "Fourth District of Laguna: A Tale of Two Parties." In *Electoral Dynamics in the Philippines: Money Politics, Patronage, and Clientelism at the Grassroots*, edited by Allen Hicken, Edward Aspinall, and Meredith Weiss, 97–116. Singapore: NUS Press.

Stange, Gunnar, and Roman Patock. 2010. "From Rebels to Rulers and Legislators: The Political Transformation of the Free Aceh Movement (GAM) in Indonesia." *Journal of Current Southeast Asian Affairs* 29(1): 95–120.

Stark, Jan. 2004. "Constructing an Islamic Model in Two Malaysian States: PAS Rule in Kelantan and Terengganu," *Sojourn* 19(1): 51–75.

Stokes, Susan. 2005. "Perverse Accountability: A Formal Model of Machine Politics With Evidence From Argentina." *American Political Science Review* 99(3): 315–25.

Stokes, Susan C., Thad Dunning, Marcelo Nazareno, and Valeria Brusco. 2013. *Brokers, Voters, and Clientelism: The Puzzle of Distributive Politics*. New York: Cambridge University Press.

Suaedy, Ahmad. 2014. "The Role of Volunteers and Political Participation in the 2012 Jakarta Gubernatorial Election." *Journal of Current Southeast Asian Affairs* 33(1): 111–38.

Sutherland, Heather. 1979. *The Making of a Bureaucratic Elite: The Colonial Transformation of the Javanese Priyayi*. Singapore: Heinemann Educational Books.

Sulaiman, Teuku Muhammad Jafar. 2016. "Bener Meriah, Aceh: Money Politics and Ethnicity in a New Electoral District." In *Electoral Dynamics in Indonesia: Money Politics, Patronage and Clientelism at the Grassroots*, edited by Edward Aspinall and Mada Sukmajati, 54–69. Singapore: NUS Press.

Swamy, Arun R. 2016. "Can Social Protection Weaken Clientelism? Considering Conditional Cash Transfers as Political Reform in the Philippines." *Journal of Current Southeast Asian Affairs* 35(1): 59–90.

Szwarcberg, Mariela. 2012. "Uncertainty, Political Clientelism, and Voter Turnout in Latin America: Why Parties Conduct Rallies in Argentina." *Comparative Politics* 45(1): 88–106.

Szwarcberg Daby, Mariela. 2016. "The Gender Gap in Clientelism: Outlines for a Research Agenda." Paper presented at the Annual Meeting of the American Political Science Association. Philadelphia, PA, September 1–4.

Tadem, Eduardo Climaco. 2012. "Development and Distress in Mindanao: A Political Economy Overview." *Asian Studies* (Philippines) 48(1&2): 19–34.

tan beng hui, Maznah Mohamad, and Cecilia Ng. 2018. "Still a Long Way to Go: GE14, Women and Political Representation." In *Regime Change in Malaysia*, edited by Francis Loh and Anil Netto, 282–93. Petaling Jaya: SIRD.

Tans, Ryan. 2012. *Mobilizing Resources, Building Coalitions: Local Power in Indonesia*. East-West Center Policy Studies No. 64, Honolulu.

Tawakkal, George Towar Ikbal, Ratnaningsih Damayanti, Tia Subekti, Faqih Alfian, and Andrew D. Garner. 2020. "Social Networks and Brokerage Behavior in Indonesian elections: Evidence from Central Java." *Asian Affairs: An American Review* 47(4): 227–244.

Teehankee, Julio C. 2012. "Clientelism and Party Politics in the Philippines." In *Party Politics in Southeast Asia: Clientelism and Electoral Competition in Indonesia, Thailand and the Philippines*, edited by Dirk Tomsa and Andreas Ufen, 186–214. New York: Routledge.

2019. "Untangling the Party List System." In *Strong Patronage, Weak Parties: The Case for Electoral Redesign in the Philippines*, edited by Paul D. Hutchcroft, 151–67. Mandaluyong City, Philippines: Anvil.

Teehankee, Julio C., and Cleo Anne A. Calimbahin, eds. 2022. *Patronage Democracy in the Philippines: Clans, Clients, and Competition in Local Elections*. Quezon City: Ateneo de Manila University Press.

Templeman, Kharis Ali. 2012. "The Origins and Decline of Dominant Party Systems: Taiwan's Transition in Comparative Perspective." PhD dissertation, University of Michigan.

Teo, Sue Ann. 2014. "Balik Pulau, Penang: Home Run for the Home Boys." In *Electoral Dynamics in Malaysia: Findings from the Grassroots*, edited by Meredith L. Weiss, 65–80. Singapore: Institute of Southeast Asian Studies.

Thompson, Mark R. 1995. *The Anti-Marcos Struggle: Personalistic Rule and Democratic Transition in the Philippines*. New Haven: Yale University Press.

2016. "Bloodied Democracy: Duterte and the Death of Liberal Reformism in the Philippines." *Journal of Current Southeast Asian Affairs* 35(3): 39–68.

2019. "The Rise of Illiberal Democracy in the Philippines: Duterte's Early Presidency." In *From Aquino II to Duterte (2010–2018): Change, Continuity – and Rupture,* edited by Imelda Deinla and Björn Dressel, 39–54. Singapore: Institute of Southeast Asian Studies.

Tomacruz, Sofia. 2019. "Threats, Vote-buying in Bangsamoro Region on Eve of Midterm Polls." *Rappler.* May 12. www.rappler.com/nation/politics/elections/2019/230383-bangsamoro-region-threats-vote-buying-2019Can-philippine-mid term-elections.

Tomsa, Dirk. 2008. *Party Politics and Democratization in Indonesia: Golkar in the Post-Suharto Era.* Abingdon: Routledge.

Tomsa, Dirk, and Andreas Ufen eds. 2013. *Party Politics in Southeast Asia: Clientelism and Electoral Competition in Indonesia, Thailand and the Philippines.* Abingdon: Routledge.

Tony Paridi Bagang. 2014. "Beaufort, Sabah. Whither Lajim's Popularity?" In *Electoral Dynamics in Malaysia: Findings from the Grassroots,* edited by Meredith L. Weiss, 223–33. Singapore: Institute of Southeast Asian Studies.

Trajano, Julius Cesar I., and Yoes C. Kenawas. 2013. "Indonesia and the Philippines: Political Dynasties in Democratic States." RSIS Commentaries, No. 18. Singapore: Nanyang Technological University.

Transparency International. 2010. *Reforming Political Financing in Malaysia.* Kuala Lumpur: Transparency International–Malaysia.

Tumandao, Donabel S. 2019. "Second District of Leyte: Money, Machinery, and Issues in Fighting Local Dynasties in the 2016 Election." In *Electoral Dynamics in the Philippines: Money Politics, Patronage, and Clientelism at the Grassroots,* edited by Allen Hicken, Edward Aspinall, and Meredith Weiss, 224–41. Singapore: NUS Press.

Ufen, Andreas. 2006. "Political Parties in Post-Suharto Indonesia: Between Politik Aliran and 'Philippinisation.'" Working Paper 37 (December). Hamburg: German Institute for Global and Area Studies.

2013. "Lipset and Rokkan in Southeast Asia: Indonesia in Comparative Perspective." In *Party Politics in Southeast Asia: Clientelism and Electoral Competition in Indonesia, Thailand and the Philippines,* edited by Dirk Tomsa and Andreas Ufen, 40–61. Abingdon: Routledge.

van Klinken, Gerry. 2007. *Communal Violence and Democratization in Indonesia: Small Town Wars.* New York: Routledge.

Van Zyl, Albert. 2010. "What Is Wrong with the Constituency Development Funds?" *IBP Budget Brief* 3(10). International Budget Partnership.

Varkkey, Helena. 2015. "Natural Resource Extraction and Political Dependency: Malaysia as a Rentier State." In *Routledge Handbook of Contemporary Malaysia,* edited by Meredith L. Weiss, 189–99. New York: Routledge.

Varshney, Ashutosh. 2002. *Ethnic Conflict and Civic Life: Hindus and Muslims in India.* New Haven: Yale University Press.

von Luebke, Christian. 2009. "The Political Economy of Local Governance: Findings from an Indonesian Field Study." *Bulletin of Indonesian Economic Studies* 45(2): 201–30.

Walker, Andrew. 2012. *Thailand's Political Peasants: Power in the Modern Rural Economy*. Madison: University of Wisconsin Press.

Wardani, Sri Budi Eko, and Valina Singka Subekti. 2021. "Political Dynasties and Women Candidates in Indonesia's 2019 Election." *Journal of Current Southeast Asian Affairs* 40(1): 28–49

Washida, Hidekuni. 2019. *Distributive Politics in Malaysia: Maintaining Authoritarian Party Dominance*. New York: Routledge.

Weiss, Meredith L. 2006. *Protest and Possibilities: Civil Society and Coalitions for Political Change in Malaysia*. Stanford: Stanford University Press.

2009. "Edging Toward a New Politics in Malaysia: Civil Society at the Gate?" *Asian Survey* 49(5): 741–58.

2013. "Malaysia's 13th General Elections." *Asian Survey* 53(6): 1135–58.

ed. 2014. *Electoral Dynamics in Malaysia: Findings from the Grassroots*. Singapore: Institute of Southeast Asian Studies.

2019a. "Duelling Networks: Relational Clientelism in Electoral-Authoritarian Malaysia." *Democratization* 27(1): 100–18.

2019b. "Money, Malfeasance, and a Malaysian Election." In *Missed Signs or Late Surge: Malaysia's 14th General Election and the Defeat of Barisan Nasional*, edited by Francis Hutchinson and Lee Hwok-Aun, 131–50. Singapore: Institute of Southeast Asian Studies.

2020a. "Legacies of the Cold War in Malaysia: Anything but Communism." *Journal of Contemporary Asia* 50(4): 511–29.

2020b. "The Road Ahead: How to Transform Malaysia's Regime." In *Toward a New Malaysia? The 2018 Election and Its Aftermath*, edited by Meredith L. Weiss and Faisal S. Hazis, 246–66. Singapore: NUS Press.

2020c. *The Roots of Resilience: Party Machines and Grassroots Politics in Southeast Asia*. Ithaca: Cornell University Press.

Weiss, Meredith L., Loke Hoe-Yeong, and Luenne Angela Choa. 2016. "The 2015 General Election and Singapore's Political Forecast: White Clouds, Blue Skies." *Asian Survey* 56(6): 859–78.

Weiss, Meredith L. and Arnold Puyok, eds. 2017. *Electoral Dynamics in Sarawak: Contesting Developmentalism and Rights*. Singapore: Institute of Southeast Asian Studies.

Weitz-Shapiro, Rebecca. 2009. "Choosing Clientelism: Political Competition, Poverty, and Social Welfare Policy in Argentina," SSRN Scholarly Paper (Rochester, NY: Social Science Research Network, 2009), 7, https://papers.ssrn.com/abstract=1450238.

2012. "What Wins Votes: Why Some Politicians Opt Out of Clientelism." *American Journal of Political Science* 56(3): 568–83.

2014. *Curbing Clientelism in Argentina: Politics, Poverty, and Social Policy*. New York: Cambridge University Press.

Welsh, Bridget. 2006. "Malaysia's Sarawak State Elections 2006: Understanding a Break in the BN Armor." Report prepared for the National Democratic Institute.

Widoyoko, J. Danang. 2010. "The Education Sector: The Fragmentation and Adaptability of Corruption." In *State and Illegality in Indonesia*, edited by Edward Aspinall and Gerry van Klinken, 165–88. Leiden: KITLV Press.

Wilkinson, Steven I. 2014. "Patronage Politics in Post-Independence India." In *Patronage as Politics in South Asia*, edited by Anastasia Piliavsky, 259–80. Cambridge: Cambridge University Press.

Wilson, Ian Douglas. 2015. *The Politics of Protection Rackets in Post-New Order Indonesia: Coercive Capital, Authority and Street Politics*. New York: Routledge.

Winters, Jeffrey. 2013. "Oligarchy and Democracy in Indonesia." *Indonesia* 96: 11–33.

Wong Chin Huat. 2020. "Reconsidering Malaysia's First-Past-the-Post Electoral System: Malpractices and Mismatch." In *Toward a New Malaysia? The 2018 Election and Its Aftermath*, edited by Meredith L. Weiss and Faisal S. Hazis, 211–45. Singapore: NUS Press.

Woo Kuan Heong. 2015. "Recruitment Practices in the Malaysian Public Sector: Innovations or Political Responses?" *Journal of Public Affairs Education* 21(2): 229–46.

Wood, Terence. 2014. "Ties that Unbind? Ethnic Identity, Social Rules and Electoral Politics in Solomon Islands." PhD dissertation, Australian National University.

Wright, Tom, and Ken Brown. 2015. "Malaysia's 1MDB Scandal: Political Intrigue, Billions Missing and International Scrutiny." *Wall Street Journal*, October 23.

Wurfel, David. 1988. *Filipino Politics: Development and Decay*. Ithaca: Cornell University Press.

Yeo Kim Wah. 1982. *The Politics of Decentralization: Colonial Controversy in Malaya, 1920–1929*. Kuala Lumpur: Oxford University Press.

Yeoh Seng Guan. 2015. "The Great Transformation: Urbanisation and Urbanism in Malaysia." In *Routledge Handbook of Contemporary Malaysia*, edited by Meredith L. Weiss, 249–59. New York: Routledge.

Yeoh, Tricia. 2012. *States of Reform: Governing Selangor and Penang*. Penang: Penang Institute.

Yeong Pey Jung. 2018. "How Women Matter: Gender Representation in Malaysia's 14th General Election." *The Round Table* 107(6): 771–86.

You, Jong-sung. 2015. *Democracy, Inequality and Corruption: Korea, Taiwan and the Philippines Compared*. Cambridge: Cambridge University Press.

Index

Milton Keynes UK
Ingram Content Group UK Ltd.
UKHW010153090424
440407UK00010B/126